THE MILWAUKEE ROAD

August Derleth, 1947

THE
MILWAUKEE ROAD

Its
First
Hundred
Years

By August Derleth

Foreword by H. Roger Grant

UNIVERSITY OF IOWA PRESS ⟨Ψ⟩ IOWA CITY

University of Iowa Press, Iowa City 52242
Copyright © 2002 by the University of Iowa Press
All rights reserved
Printed in the United States of America
Originally copyrighted in 1948 by August Derleth
and published in 1948 by Creative Age Press

Cover design by Felice E. Tebbe

http://www.uiowa.edu/~uipress

The publication of this book was generously supported by
the University of Iowa Foundation.

All Milwaukee Road photographs are from the Milwaukee Road Archives
of the Milwaukee Public Library. Other artwork from
the collection of H. Roger Grant.

Printed on acid-free paper

Library of Congress Cataloging-in-Publication Data
Derleth, August William, 1909–1971.
The Milwaukee Road: the first hundred years / by August Derleth;
foreword by H. Roger Grant.
        p.   cm.
Originally published in New York by Creative Age Press, 1948.
Includes bibliographical references and index.
ISBN 0-87745-801-4 (pbk.)
1. Chicago, Milwaukee, St. Paul, and Pacific Railroad Company—History.
2. Railroads—United States—History.   I. Title.

HE2791.C67 D47 2002
385'.06'577—dc21   2001052542

05 06 P 5 4

The smoothest roadbed I have ever known on
an American railroad is the velvet line
of the Milwaukee into Chicago.

John Gunther, *Inside U.S.A.*

Contents

Acknowledgments

W̲HILE preparing an edited version of the Iowa railroad writings by the late Frank P. Donovan, Jr., it struck me that the long out-of-print history of the Chicago, Milwaukee, St. Paul & Pacific Railroad, *The Milwaukee Road: Its First Hundred Years*, by the late August Derleth, should be readily available to those interested in this company and its extensive service territory. By the late 1990s this particular volume, when it could be found, was selling for more than $100 on the used book market. I soon discovered that the Milwaukee Road Historical Association was also interested in republication. I was able to work to this end with the able president of the MRHA, Bob Storozuk, who became the point man in this undertaking. Others, too, assisted, including April Derleth, Arthur D. Dubin, Don L. Hofsommer, Kay Price, Richard L. Saunders, Jr., and Jim Scribbins. Although the Derleth book is hardly perfect and is badly out of date, it remains the best overview of the Milwaukee Road. Perhaps this reprint will encourage a historian to write the complete story of this "fallen flag" carrier.

H. Roger Grant

Foreword

THE MILWAUKEE ROAD UNTIL 1948

In the late 1940s the Chicago-based Chicago, Milwaukee, St. Paul & Pacific Railroad Company (popularly called the Milwaukee Road) felt good about itself. Although this 10,684-mile company, with its approximately 40,000 employees, had encountered its share of rough times, especially during the Great Depression of the 1930s when it failed financially, war-time revenues and increasing business development fostered strong feelings of optimism among its executives, board members, and rank-and-file workers. Indeed, economic activities along the Milwaukee Road's twelve-state web of main and branch lines, which stretched from the limestone hills of southern Indiana to the mountainous forests of Washington, seemed to bode well for everyone's future.

A reflection of that corporate cheerfulness came in February 1948 with publication of a popular and well-crafted company history, *The Milwaukee Road: Its First Hundred Years*. The author was August Derleth (his last name is accented on the first syllable), whom the railroad proudly described as "the literary phenomenon of Sauk City, Wis." This special centennial book hardly came as a surprise. During the late 1940s and early 1950s various railroads, including the Illinois Central, Pennsylvania, and Rock Island, decided to spend some of the extra dollars on bolstering their image. After all, the old robber baron notion of an evil railroad persisted among the public, and the recent hard times hardly helped railroads' reputations. Railroads wished to convey the message that they were being well managed and were a smart investment. Some carriers spread the message of optimism through newspaper and radio advertisements, industrial films, brochures and similar outlets; others depended upon the Association of American Railroads, the industry's principal trade group. To create positive images, more than thirty companies participated in the Chicago Railroad Fairs of 1948 and 1949, which honored the arrival of the iron horse to the Windy City in the fall of 1848. Many railroads seized on other historical events, often a centennial, as the appropriate vehicle. Usually these were carriers that traced their origins to the late 1840s and early 1850s when the American railroad network began its first wave of major expansion. Perhaps, too, there had been an important achievement during that historic time period or something else in the past that seemed worthy of celebration.

The idea of a railroad-sponsored centennial celebration predates the post–World War II period. Industry personnel remembered the 1927 gala that the Baltimore & Ohio Railroad sponsored to commemorate its legitimate claim as "the pioneer railroad of the country." The company had thrown a year-long birthday party, highlighted by an elaborate banquet on the evening of February 28 in a premier Baltimore hotel. And a nearby Centenary Exhibition and Pageant between September 24 and October 16, popularly called the Fair of the Iron Horse, attracted more than 1.3 million visitors.

Corporate officials at the Milwaukee Road headquarters likely saw the possibilities for self-promotion. They realized that November 20, 1950, marked the 100th anniversary of the official opening of the Milwaukee & Mississippi Rail Road, the oldest segment of their system, twenty-one miles of primitive track between the Wisconsin municipalities of Milwaukee and Wauwatosa. This event was highlighted with a re-enactment of the line's first train excursion, using—as did the Erie and several other carriers—the stately American-standard (4-4-0) *William Mason*, owned by the Baltimore & Ohio Railroad. Also emphasized was the fact that the core company could trace its roots to a Wisconsin charter granted on February 11, 1847, to the Milwaukee & Waukesha Rail Road Company, allowing an ample window to ballyhoo the company's past, present, and future, although 1950 became the "official" centennial year.

The Milwaukee Road opted for a variety of promotional activities. In 1949 it released "A Railroad at Work," a twenty-minute promotional movie. "Millions of people whose lives are interwoven with the services" given by the Milwaukee Road was the recurring theme of the widely shown film. During 1950 Vice President and Western Counsel Larry H. Dugan spoke in Everett, Washington, as did Board Chairman Leo T. Crowley in Omaha, Nebraska. The Milwaukee Road's Mixed Choral Club of fifty voices, dressed in 1850-era garb, and the fifty-piece Hiawatha Band provided musical accompaniment upon return of the historic re-enactment excursion from Wauwatosa to the Milwaukee depot.

AUGUST DERLETH

The Milwaukee Road was fortunate to have had August Derleth write its corporate history. Some other railroads, however, were not so lucky. The Chicago & North Western Railway and the Delaware, Lackawanna & Western Railroad, for example, each hired the same two Chicago journalists, Robert Casey and W. A. S. Douglas, to pen their histories. At best the men produced third-rate studies, ones repeatedly criticized by professional historians and others knowledgeable about America's transportation past. Indeed, in the mid-1950s one talented freelance writer of railroad history, Frank P. Donovan, Jr., who wrote *Mileposts on the Prairie: The Story of the Minneapolis & St. Louis Railway*, said that Casey and Douglas, "with their very poor C&NW history book" had "cut off the market for just about all independent writers in the company history work." Clearly, though, Donovan did not have Derleth in mind.

Although August Derleth lacked training as a business historian, he was a skilled writer, an able researcher, and enormously knowledgeable about Wisconsin and the Upper Midwest, the historic heart of the Milwaukee Road. Born on February 24, 1909, in Sauk City, Wisconsin, August William Derleth received a solid education. He attended a parochial school and the public high school in his hometown before earning a BA degree in English from the University of Wisconsin in Madison. Derleth noted in a 1941 autobiographical sketch: "Began writing at thirteen, publishing at fifteen, have been publishing consistently since, often more than a hundred long and short titles yearly. Write poetry, essays, reviews, serious novels, short stories, novelettes, mystery novels, plays, biography, criticism." By the time of his death on July 4, 1971, this energetic author had written more than 150 books and seemingly countless short stories, both under his own name and the pen names Stephen Grendon, Kenyon Holmes, Tally Mason, Michael West, and Simon West. The range was impressive, including such sagas of the Wisconsin prairie as *Wind over Wisconsin* (New York: Grossett & Dunlap, 1938) and *Evening in Spring* (Sauk City, Wisconsin: Stanton & Lee, 1945), the popular "Judge Peck" mysteries, and numerous tales of fantasy, horror and the supernatural. As for these latter interests, in 1939 Derleth co-founded Arkham House to publish this genre of literature. "Arkham," in fact, is the name of a mythical community in New England that was home to many characters in the supernatural novels of H. P. (Howard Phillips) Lovecraft (1890–1937), whose works Derleth strove to keep before the public.

Some of Derleth's voluminous writings have remained remarkably popular. In the 1970s thousands of teenage boys particularly admired *The Trail of Cthulhu* (Sauk City, Wisconsin: Arkham House, 1962). The appeal of this work and others explains the creation in 1978 of the August Derleth Society, dedicated to the promotion of his work and preservation of his memory. This organization publishes *The August Derleth Society Newsletter* and maintains a web site.

An apparently driven person who died of a heart attack at age sixty-two, August Derleth was a "burly-chested blond," with an engaging personality. One acquaintance vividly recalled conversations with him at gatherings of the "Cliffdwellers," an intellectually oriented literary social club that met in the Chicago Loop. "Derleth possessed a wonderful sense of humor and was a real storyteller." Added this admirer, "He was so outgoing and such a person of talent you would always, always remember him."

As for Derleth's personal life, he married Sandra Winters in 1953, but six years later they divorced. Their marriage produced two children: a son, Walden William, and a daughter, April Rose. For much of his adult life, Derleth lived in an unusual, architecturally striking residence on the outskirts of Sauk City. It was constructed of native stone arranged so that its exterior formed a series of ledges "which are the happy nesting places of song birds in that beautiful countryside." Rather than a conventional shingle roof, the structure sported one of thatch, made from reeds imported from India, but according to his daughter, "The thatched roof proved unsuitable for Wisconsin winters . . . and was replaced by shingles after parts blew off."

Details of arrangements between August Derleth and the Milwaukee Road are not fully known. The company did not contact him to write the history but rather he took the initiative. Jim Scribbins, a former public relations officer of the Milwaukee Road, recalled, "August Derleth surprised everyone by showing up at the general office announcing he was going to do a history of the CMStP&P. The staff decided the company would fully cooperate." He added, "The Corporate History and the Chronological History, both at the rear of [the] Derleth [book] were developed over the years by the Road, and Derleth simply copied them word for word."

A more detailed commentary about the genius of the book came from the pen of a long-time employee of the Milwaukee Road's public relations department, A. G. Dupuis. As he wrote in 1970: "I think it was in about 1946 one day that the Leonine-headed bulk of August Derleth waddled into our office and announced that he had a commission from a publishing firm to do a historical account of the Milwaukee Road. This caused everyone to assume a rigid stance, which is a very appropriate corporate gesture, and quickly become uncommunicative; after all, who is this August Derleth, and what will he find if he begins stirring up history that may be better if not told? August sensed this, and he reared back and shook his bushy locks (and he had 'em, too) and I'll always remember his roaring speech to the delegation of little people with whom he was meeting: 'I am not a muckraker—neither am I an apologist for the corporate mistakes of the past. Now, if you cooperate with me and lend me your research facilities and cooperate with my effort, I will submit to you the material I prepare so you may have an opportunity to criticize it—or suggest alterations to accommodate the ends of accuracy—as you see accuracy.'" Concluded Dupuis, "I thoroughly enjoyed listening to that speech, and was delegated to help put material together for his book."

Unlike Casey and Douglas of North Western and Lackawanna fame, who were paid a flat fee by the railroad, Derleth and his publisher, the Creative Press in New York City, developed a mutually satisfying relationship with the Milwaukee Road. The public relations department furnished historical materials, including the subsequent book illustrations, and company representatives read proof. The railroad, however, made only a modest financial commitment to the project by purchasing some copies which it then distributed to "each public library and institution of higher learning in the principal communities" it served. Some employees also received complimentary copies. The Milwaukee Road helped with the book's promotion, with company representatives hosting special book-signing parties.

THE MILWAUKEE ROAD SINCE 1948

Were he to examine the Milwaukee Road half a century later, August Derleth would surely be shocked by the enormous changes that have transpired. As with most railroad entities that flourished in the immediate post–World War II years, the Milwaukee Road has entered the corporate graveyard. Bankruptcies, dismemberments, and mergers have radically altered the industry. Although hundreds of miles of the Milwaukee Road are still operating, some by shortline or regional carriers, large segments of its far-flung network of trackage have been abandoned, including extensive portions of the Puget Sound Extension. If the themes of the Derleth book were struggle, progress, and financial triumph, those of the Road itself since 1948 have been decline, retrenchment, and final demise.

During the 1950s signs of precipitous change were becoming evident. Even the strongest railroads began to face stiff intermodal competition, spawned in part by the National Defense Highway Act of 1956. This monumental piece of federal legislation, which did much to underwrite construction of more than 40,000 miles of high speed, divided highways, accelerated automobile usage and made it possible for trucking companies to eat away at lucrative, especially long-haul traffic that previously had moved on flanged wheels.

Although extra business generated by the Korean Conflict in the early 1950s and a robust national economy in the mid-1950s encouraged Milwaukee Road officials, events in the latter part of the decade brought apprehension. Both freight and passenger revenues were in decline due to the recession of the late 1950s and highway competition. Freight revenues dropped from $269.5 million in 1952 to $230 million in 1960 and passenger revenues slipped from $18.8 million to $15.1 million for the same period. Yet Milwaukee Road brass did not contemplate some catastrophic corporate failure. Since merger talks were in the air, triggered in part by several successful unions at the end of the 1950s, officials expressed interest in this emerging industry phenomenon, realizing that their company needed to be a player if the trans-Chicago railroad map were to be redrawn. They also knew that the substantial financial benefits realized from dieselization had largely run their course and new ways to save and generate money were needed.

Spearheaded by Ben Heineman, the imaginative and aggressive chair of the board of directors of the Milwaukee Road's historic archrival, the Chicago & North Western Railway, the two managements began serious merger negotiations in late 1960. Prospects looked promising. Said one participant, "In our opinion there are no two railroads in the country that in combination could bring greater benefits to all interested groups." But this phase of discussions ended when the Milwaukee Road fussed about the proposed formula for exchange of securities, which was somewhat ironic since five years earlier during the Paul Feucht administration, predecessor to the Heineman regime, the North Western had suspended similar, albeit preliminary, talks with the Milwaukee Road. Feucht and his associates feared they would come out second, even though a consulting firm had estimated an increase in net income for the combined roads of more than $40 million annually.

Still, the courtship continued. Since a partnership offered great potential, more meetings ensued and in September 1964 the two boards agreed to resume direct negotiations. Then in March, 1965, they approved a "definitive agreement" for merger. This unified property, the Chicago, Milwaukee & North Western Transportation Company, would issue securities that slightly favored investors in the North Western and would allow the Heineman road to name eight of the fifteen directors. Soon thereafter shareholders of both railroads endorsed the arrangement and in June 1966 the railroads filed their application for merger with the Interstate Commerce Commission. The process moved ahead with public hearings, and in July 1968 an ICC examiner sanctioned the proposal.

Yet the CM&NWTCo merger never came to fruition. When dissident Milwaukee Road stockholders accused their board of "selling out" to the North Western, the merger began to unravel. A larger concern among investors in the Milwaukee Road involved Northwest Industries, the holding company that by this time controlled the North Western. A sharp drop in earnings for Northwest Industries in 1969 and its failure to acquire several major non-railroad corporations bothered many. Troubled by the original stock-exchange ratio, the ICC ordered hearings to be opened. Ben Heineman, however, refused to renegotiate the exchange ratio and he surely shocked the Milwaukee Road board when he said that his railroad was for sale. But the Milwaukee Road was in no position financially to propose an acceptable offer for the North Western.

The 1960s held even more challenges for the Milwaukee Road. Although it was not on the brink of bankruptcy, earnings remained flat, actually dipping when adjusted for inflation. And costs for operations and maintenance increased. Indeed, the railroad's operating ratios, which show what proportion of operating revenues are consumed by operating expenses, rose from 74.97 percent in 1961 to 85.70 percent in 1969. Not surprisingly the property took on a run-down appearance: depots needed painting, branch lines became weed-covered, and pieces of rolling stock surpassed their normal life expectancy.

Yet there were bright spots. Competent and dedicated employees did their best to generate business, keep trains rolling, and develop the service territory. In 1967 the volume of piggyback shipments (trailers-on-flatcars) grew impressively, increasing that year by seventeen percent, while the industry average was less than four percent. The company greatly benefited from the expansion of its piggyback and container facilities system-wide, especially at its Bensenville (Chicago) yards.

The 1970s were not pleasant for the Milwaukee Road either. Although it extricated itself from the money-losing long distance passenger business in 1971 when the federal government created the National Railroad Passenger Corporation (Amtrak), overall savings were modest. In the early 1970s the railroad launched a holding company, Chicago Milwaukee Corporation (CMC), to enable diversification. This it did, acquiring such firms as Hi-Way Paving Company and Hanson Porcelain Company, but profits, even with the use of tax-loss carry forwards, were hardly spectacular. Unfortunately, the railroad started to hemorrhage red ink, mounting major deficits ranging from $8.6 million in 1972 to $11.4 million in 1975. Stag-flation in the wake of the Arab oil boycott of 1973 and 1974, excessive federal regulation, a decline in northern "smokestack" industries, and seemingly ever-increasing truck competition accounted for many of these financial woes.

The Milwaukee Road was hammered in other ways. As a consequence of the formation of Burlington Northern in 1970, the ICC allowed the Milwaukee Road to serve eleven new gateways in the West, including Billings, Montana, and Portland, Oregon. These promising opportunities led quickly to increased traffic on the Puget Sound Extension. Yet it did not take long before the Burlington Northern ("Big Nasty" in the minds of many Milwaukee Road employees) coerced some larger shippers into signing exclusive contracts, meaning that they would not patronize the Milwaukee Road. Moreover, the additional traffic on the Puget Sound Extension generated enough business to wear out an aging physical plant but hardly enough to rebuild it. "Slow orders" became ubiquitous and the frequent snail pace of freight trains increased labor costs and caused some customers to turn elsewhere. A disturbingly high number of derailments did not help either. Even pulling the plug in 1972 on the electric-powered operations on the Coast Division and two years later on the Rocky Mountain Division had little positive impact on the bottom line.

The Milwaukee Road could take little comfort in the fact that the railroad industry, especially in the East, had been experiencing some of its worst financial health since the Great Depression. By 1973 a number of railroads, including the Boston & Maine, Erie Lackawanna, and Lehigh Valley, had sought protection from creditors in bankruptcy court. But the greatest collapse of all had been the Penn Central Transportation Company. The highly touted merger in 1968 of the New York Central and Pennsylvania railroads failed within twenty-eight months. And the Midwest was not immune. Long-time competitor Chicago, Rock Island & Pacific ran out of money and on March 17, 1975, filed for protection under the federal bankruptcy act. The North Western, too, teetered on the financial brink. Indeed, the historic Granger Roads seemed doomed, with the notable exception of the Chicago, Burlington & Quincy, which in 1970 joined the Great Northern, Northern Pacific, and Spokane, Portland & Seattle to create Burlington Northern.

Unable to be a Burlington Northern, the Milwaukee Road became a Rock Island. On December 19, 1977, this beleaguered carrier filed a petition for voluntary reorganization under Section 77 of the Federal Bankruptcy Act with the U.S. District Court for the Northern Division of Illinois. Although a measure of relief spread through the Milwaukee Road family, the feeling prevailed that the North Western had become the "darling" Granger Road in the eyes of federal officials. A large infusion of government money, made possible by the 1976 Railroad Revitalization and Regulatory Reform Act (4R Act), did much to save the North Western. *If* comparable aid had been speedily given to the Milwaukee Road, its future *might* have been different.

Under bankruptcy statutes for railroads, the federal court needed to appoint a trustee for the Milwaukee Road, which it did on January 18, 1978. Stanley E. G. Hillman, long-time Chicago business executive and President of Illinois Central Industries, assumed command after his approval by the ICC. He was charged with formulating a plan of reorganization, one that would solve the company's financial problems. It might involve a "traditional" reorganization (reminiscent of the railroad's passage in 1945 out of its ten years in bankruptcy), merger with another carrier, or liquidation (the destiny of the Rock Island). But Hillman did not complete his duties, resigning on June 14, 1979, for health reasons. Shortly thereafter the court named his successor, Richard B. Ogilvie, a former governor of Illinois.

It would be Dick Ogilvie who would play a key role in the fate of the Milwaukee Road. A lawyer with important political connections, he proceeded to defend creditors and arguably the public interest as well. With court protection, the railroad deferred payment on certain invoices, claims, taxes, interest, and other obligations, allowing it to maintain service. It also used trustee certificates to finance rehabilitation of track and equipment. Even the federal government finally stepped in with aid, coming up with a $48.8-million package of loan guarantees in 1979.

Yet maintaining the Milwaukee Road as a 10,000-mile system seemed hopeless, even pointless. The property, according to one observer, had become a "transportation slum," particularly the Puget Sound Extension. On November 1, 1979, Ogilvie and the court embargoed the trackage west of Miles City, Montana. Only the swift congressional passage of the Milwaukee Road Restructuring Act, spearheaded by powerful Montana politicians, kept trains running to deep water. But this measure required that if service west of Miles City were to be preserved, shippers and localities had to form a sound financial plan by December 15, 1979. These efforts failed. At 11:50 P.M. on February 29, 1980, revenue service ceased west of Frenchtown, Montana (near Missoula). Ogilvie and the court, wishing to protect creditors by strengthening the railroad's core, also ended operations on most lines in South Dakota, on trackage north of Green Bay, Wisconsin, and on much of the route to Omaha, Nebraska, where not too many years earlier luxury *City* streamliners of the Union Pacific ran at breakneck speed. This was the largest rail line abandonment in American history, about 7,500 miles. What was now appropriately called Milwaukee II made the Milwaukee Road a mere shadow of its former self.

In the early 1980s the 3,269-mile Milwaukee Road, or Milwaukee II, still remained a company with valuable rail assets. Its double-track Chicago-Twin Cities line, path of Amtrak's *Empire Builder*, was one. Loans made available under the 4R Act had helped to upgrade this strategic trackage. The company's Chicago-Kansas City, Twin Cities-

Kansas City and Chicago-Louisville routes (the last nearly entirely operated on trackage rights made possible by an ICC ruling in the early 1970s) held potential. It also enjoyed access to lucrative traffic in greater Milwaukee and it possessed several good grain-gathering branches. Furthermore, reallocation and disposal of excess rail, locomotives, freight cars, and other materials, coupled with sales of unwanted trackage, which massive retrenchments produced, permitted management to strengthen the remaining network. And there were approximately 6,000 fewer employees than when the company entered bankruptcy in 1977.

There remained the conundrum of whether the truncated Milwaukee Road could survive as an independent regional railroad or whether it would need to join another carrier or carriers, either through merger or dismemberment. Although in a minority, some people within and outside the Milwaukee Road thought that the company could make it on its own; after all, several factors pointed in that direction. For one thing, partial deregulation of the railroad industry, which occurred in 1980 with passage of the Staggers Act, gave managers more options in rate-making and other aspects of their corporate affairs. Additional bright spots included elimination and restructuring of certain pressing debts and the fact that Chicago-area commuter operations became the responsibility of the Regional Transit Authority. Significantly, too, traffic spiked upwards in 1982, the result of an innovative voluntary coordination agreement (VCA) with the Grand Trunk Western Railroad (GTW). A representative of Grand Trunk said "We have established run-through trains, run-through locomotive power, expedited interchanges, pre-blocking arrangements and joint routes, rates and contracts, all stemming from the VCA."

If the Milwaukee Road were to disappear as an autonomous carrier, by 1982 the likely fate seemed to be amalgamation with the Grand Trunk Western, an affiliate of the Canadian National Railway (CN). The GTW concluded that the Milwaukee Road had much to offer. A railroad map of the Midwest revealed that the GTW, which linked Detroit and Port Huron, Michigan, with Chicago and Cincinnati via the Milwaukee Road, could connect with another CN affiliate, the Duluth,

Winnipeg and Pacific at Duluth, Minnesota (Milwaukee Road had trackage rights over the Burlington Northern between St. Paul and Duluth). With the merger, the GTW could reach the important gateways of Louisville and Kansas City and also increase its average line-haul mileage.

Steps were soon taken toward union. On May 24, 1982, the Grand Trunk Western and Dick Ogilvie announced the intent to transfer stock ownership in the Milwaukee Road to GTW parent Grand Trunk Corporation. The latter agreed to assume $250 million of Milwaukee Road debt and to allow Chicago Milwaukee Corporation, which owned ninety-six percent of Milwaukee Road stock, to retain the Milwaukee Land Company, a valuable non-rail asset. Both sides, too, liked an end-to-end merger.

Yet what the Grand Trunk Corporation considered to be "truly a marriage made in heaven" never happened. The earlier voluntary co-ordination agreement, which substantially bolstered earnings, made the Milwaukee Road appear to be a railroad prize. Even though Ogilvie recommended to the court that the Grand Trunk take charge, it and the ICC had to give their approval. At the last moment, the Chicago & North Western indicated that it wanted the Milwaukee Road, mostly to reduce competition in the Midwest. Even the Chicago Milwaukee Corporation, the Milwaukee Road's holding company, entered the picture, contending that the Milwaukee Road should remain independent. And to further muddy the waters, the Soo Line, a unit of Canadian Pacific, said that it too was interested. "The Soo officials assure me," remarked a railroad analyst, "that they are not going to sit back and let their traffic be eroded by a Milwaukee Road merger with either the C&NW or Grand Trunk."

Tensions increased. On February 7, 1984, the Soo Line entered the fray with a strong offer. It would pay $40 million in cash and would assume "all or most" of the Milwaukee Road debt. Soon the North Western proposed $60 million in cash and agreed to drop its plans to trim its competitor. By the time the contest moved to Washington, D.C., both the North Western and Soo Line had sweetened the pot. In early April the former raised its bid to more than $170 million in cash, cash equivalents and guaranteed stock, and the latter boosted its cash offering to $168.5 million.

The possibility of a victory for the Grand Trunk Corporation vanished. Its only hope was that the ICC would dismiss the rival application, but this regulatory body refused. Yet the ICC admitted that the voluntary coordination agreement between the Grand Trunk and the Milwaukee Road "is probably the most important reason for the Commission having a number of suitors for the Milwaukee before it today."

The battle between the North Western and Soo Line continued. On July 26, 1984, the ICC approved the Soo Line bid, but two of the four commissioners said they would not grant final approval unless the railroad agreed to renegotiate the traffic interchange agreement between the Milwaukee Road and the Grand Trunk. But that condition soon became moot when the Grand Trunk scrapped the arrangement. Still, the North Western remained in the picture. The Commission, which split on the North Western offer, returned the bid without action to the court. Finally, on September 10, the ICC gave "unqualified" support to the Soo Line position.

The North Western did not abandon its quest for the Milwaukee Road. On October 10, 1984, the deadline set by the court, the company improved its earlier offer by more than $200 million. The maneuvering persisted when the court reopened the bidding on October 29. It indicated that the Soo Line should have an opportunity to raise its offer, while saying that the North Western bid was final.

The Soo Line did not need to raise its offer. In December the ICC, by a four to three vote, backed the Soo Line proposal, worth an estimated $570 million. But the ICC also approved the North Western package, valued at approximately $785 million. It then returned *both* proposals to the court. On February 4, 1985, stunning news came from Chicago: the court preferred sale to the Soo Line. The North Western, Ogilvie, and the Chicago Milwaukee Corporation were shocked, and the North Western ended its quest.

The fate of the Milwaukee Road was sealed. At 11:58 P.M. on February 19, 1985, when the final legal papers were signed, the Chicago, Milwaukee, St. Paul & Pacific Railroad became a subsidiary of Soo Line

Corporation. Almost immediately the new owner obliterated nearly every vestige of the old Milwaukee Road's identity. Everything orange disappeared.

Nevertheless, the memory of the Milwaukee Road remains. Created in 1985, the Milwaukee Railroad Historical Association is the most conspicuous body that keeps alive the Milwaukee Road's past. Its more than three thousand members support a smart quarterly journal, the *Milwaukee Railroader*, hold annual meetings, and maintain a web site. And since the company's demise, it has inspired a raft of popular publications, including Stanley W. Johnson, *The Milwaukee Road Revised* (Moscow: University of Idaho Press, 1997); Steve McCarter, *Guide to the Milwaukee Road in Montana* (Helena: Montana Historical Society Press, 1992); Rick W. Mills, *The Milwaukee Road in Dakota* (Hermosa, South Dakota: Battle Creek Publishing Company, 1998); Jim Scribbins and Bob Hayden, *Milwaukee Road Remembered* (Waukesha, Wisconsin: Kalmbach Publishing Company, 1990), and Jim Scribbins, *Milwaukee Road in Its Hometown: In and around the City of Milwaukee* (Waukesha, Wisconsin: Kalmbach Publishing Company, 1998). Fascination with this "fallen flag" giant will likely continue for years.

H. Roger Grant

Acknowledgments
to the 1948 Edition

MANY SOURCES, references and people were consulted for the writing of this book. The sources were satisfactory, save that there were not enough of them to be consulted, and the references were satisfactory, by and large, only on occasion, though I was able to draw generously from Dr. Frederick Merk's excellent *Economic History of Wisconsin During the Civil War Decade.* In the main, however, scores of sources and references were consulted that never yielded a solitary reference to an event of such importance to the history of the terrain as the building of the Milwaukee Road. People were especially helpful, and I want to acknowledge particularly the tireless research of Miss Alice Conger; the co-operation of the Public Relations Department of The Chicago, Milwaukee, St. Paul and Pacific Railroad Company, headed by F. H. Johnson; F. J. Newell and A. G. Dupuis, Assistant Public Relations Officers; F. H. Allard, Assistant to Vice-President; M. L. Bluhm, General Solicitor; D. C. Curtis, Chief Purchasing Officer; J. C. Ellington, Industrial Commissioner; A. G. Hoppe, General Superintendent of Locomotive and Car Department; H. C. Munson, Assistant General Manager; H. Sengstacken, Assistant Passenger Traffic Manager; J. W. Severs, Vice President and Comptroller; H. S. Zane, Assistant Freight Traffic Manager; Marc Green, Editor of *The Milwaukee Magazine;* J. J. Roche, Chief Clerk, Vice President, and Comptroller; T. W. Burtness, Secretary of the Company; R. J. Marony, Vice President, New York; Paul S. Patterson, C. O. Salle, and J. M. Hazelton of the Accounting Department; and other Milwaukee Road personnel; the unsparing assistance of Dr. Benton Wilcox, Miss Betty Keown, and Miss Dorothy Allen of the Wisconsin Historical Society Library; Mrs. Esther Nelson of the periodicals division of that Library; Miss Alice Smith, Mrs. Ruth Yoke, and Mr. Ernest St. Aubin of the manuscripts division of that Library; and Miss Genevieve Winchester of the University of Wisconsin Library; as well as various helpful suggestions from A. O. Barton, A. C. Kalmbach, and the staff of the Kalmbach Publishing Company: Gustav Marx, Fred Spratler, Earl Broderick, Walter Bubbert, and C. P. Fox.

THE MILWAUKEE ROAD

I. Introduction

Not far out of Portage, I came to Dead Man's Cut on the
Milwaukee Road's line, and, nearby, a little place enclosed
by a white picket fence. I wheeled over to it and discovered there a lonely grave, over which towered two ancient
oaks, and I recognized it for the grave of a trackworker
killed during the building of the road in 1858. This isolated
grave was the subject of Alfred Burrett's poem, "The Grave
of a Section Hand":

> They laid him away on the brow of the hill,
>   Outside of the right-of-way,
> And the old boss whispered: "Peace, be still
>   Till the call on the Final Day."
> They had placed him where he had wished to lie
>   When his turn would come, he said;
> Where he'd list to the wires' mournful sigh,
>   To the foreman's "Joint ahead!"
>
> For many a year he had paced the beat;
>   He had pumped o'er every tie;
> And now from his narrow, last retreat,
>   He could feel the freights roll by;
> For from his rest, 'neath the willow's shade,
>   His spirit would guard the track;
> He would know when the engine struck the grade,
>   Hear the call, "Center back!"

The "willow" had somehow become oaks, but the grave
was unchanged, cared for still by the section crews of the
Milwaukee.

—STEPHEN GRENDON
Through Wisconsin on a Bicycle

At NO time since the invention of the locomotive and its adoption as a major means of transportation in the United States have trains diminished in the romantic esteem of the average American. As an integral part of the American landscape, the powerful locomotives, the cross-country streamliners, the long freights have had a tenacious hold on the imagination of old and young. There is no precise accounting for this appeal, since it is rooted in a thousand intangibles; but for many of us the fundamental concept of trains spanning the country is one of power hitherto unimaginable, one of the romance of far, unknown places. Doubtless psychiatrists might insist that the entire idea of locomotives and trains as passage to romantic places is rooted in a compulsion to flee from ourselves, or from the prosaic surroundings in which we find ourselves, but for every such explanation there are a half dozen others, and even the air age has not altered that basic image.

Only a short time ago, after I had begun the writing of this book, I was amused at the excitement of my four-year-old nephew, roused by the sound of the whistle of the locomotive on the single-track spur of the Milwaukee Road leading past my parents' home on the way from Mazomanie to the twin villages of Sauk City and Prairie du Sac, Wisconsin. Though he was at dinner, there was nothing for it but to take the child outside along the track, so that he might wave and be waved to by the amiable brakeman-conductor, Irvin Garner—"Ga'ner," he called him—as the train went by, just as in countless city neighborhoods, small towns, and country places innumerable engineers and brakemen and other personnel have waved at untold numbers of fascinated children watching with awe what must be, certainly, the most impressive sight yet to pass before their young eyes. Though it amused me, it was with that indefinable air of nostalgia which comes with the memory of past things—for so once was I, and so once were thousands of you.

For many years, in fact, I had no other conception of a train save that exciting vision of a locomotive followed by several freight and coal cars, an orange coach or two, and a caboose—the train up from Mazomanie, nine miles away, and back again, sometimes once a day,

2

sometimes twice, though in adolescence, for lack of anything else to do at night, a group of us used to drive to a neighboring town on a main track to watch "the night flyer" go through. In my childhood, which was in that halcyon time before extensive travel in cars, the train came twice a day, though, because of school, I could watch it come in only in the evening.

There is something fascinating almost beyond words in watching a train come in. I was aware of it without question when I was a child, and I was sharply conscious of it in later youth when I stood with other young fellows on the station platform to watch the through train go surging past, sometimes stopping briefly to discharge or take on a passenger or to drop mail; it was then a feeling of something immense, something from "outside" momentarily touching my own orbit, and I used to think of its passengers—most of them asleep at that late hour, some still clustered about tables in the smoker—as people passing in the night, so that somehow the night train came to symbolize for me the very mystery which is a fundamental of life. Even today I know an elderly gentleman of means and of far more than ordinary intelligence who makes a practice of going from one station to another in the city of Milwaukee to watch the trains come in. I do not know that that is as incredible as it sounds. There were such gentlemen in my childhood as well.

I remember one of them as clearly as if he were sitting at my side at this moment. He seemed old to me then, though he could not have been more than in his middle fifties—a short, bent man, with a straggling moustache and intense pale eyes. He always carried a corncob pipe between his toothless gums, and, as often as not, it was unlit. He never missed an evening of watching the train come into the station at Sauk City. On rainy nights he sat with the station agent, a sprightly and imaginative man named Porter, who was as likely as not to foster a practical joke of respectable dimensions, as on the occasion when, during World War I, seeing the phlegmatic and loyal tender of the Milwaukee Road bridge over the Wisconsin at Sauk City coming up the tracks for a little kerosene, he greeted him with a rapidly prepared telegram and in great excitement told him that the president had sent information that a German submarine was on its way up the Wisconsin to blow up the railroad bridge, which the tender must therefore guard with his life; as a result, the old man's lantern could be seen moving back and forth, over and across the bridge, all night long. But most of the time old Mike Weinzierl sat outside on the unloading platform, and sometimes, unfortunately for him, he sat on the long unloading plank, from which a group of mischievous boys habitually upset him by jumping without warning on the upper end, raised by the iron roller underneath.

But what I remember most about him is not his mere presence, not his antics when he took off in pursuit of the boys who teased him, not the fact that he emerged, moth-like, from his little house far out at the west edge of the village every evening for this ceremony of watching the train come in, but the way in which his entire face lit up at sight of the train coming around the bend from the canning factory and drawing into the station, a glow by no means accounted for by the reflection from the firebox. Indeed, his face underwent an astonishing transformation; his lackluster eyes shone, his listless pipe snapped to attention, and a naïvely pleased smile played about his lips, quite as if the routine of the train's arrival were a special arrangement of Providence for his benefit.

Nor was he the only watcher at the station in Sauk City. His kind could be found wherever trains passed; he could be multiplied by thousands throughout the country, and if every spur-line station had its watchers, how many of them were there who haunted the main line depots? He watched the train come in almost every evening of his life in his last twenty years—except Sunday, when there was no train; that must have been a dull day for him, surely. He missed perhaps only his last four or five days, when he was too ill to struggle down to the station; in the time between my first awareness of him and his death, all the station personnel and all the familiar faces changed several times, so that Mike alone represented the past. Next to the train's arrival and departure, he liked best to sit inside with the station master. Years later, when I myself sat there to talk with Fred Spratler, then the agent for Sauk City, I was keenly aware of what many others had been conscious of before me and many more will yet discover—that very definite and unmistakable atmosphere of a railroad station, particularly the small station: a compound of age, expectancy, and romance in the clicking telegraph key, the colorful travel folders, the typical "railroad" stove, all these factors combining to make up an aura to be found nowhere else on the American scene.

One of the station old-timers once attempted to put his fascination for trains into words. He said:

If that old locomotive could talk, it could recount comedy and pathos. Not only did it contribute to the growth of Sauk City, but it had its part in the drama of living there. It brought in the brides of the Sauk City lads; it carried away Sauk City brides. It brought home new-born babes; it carried away the dying and brought back caskets bearing the dead. Those who stood on the depot platform found in the locomotive whistle a response to their moods and emotions. The old depot platform was a scene of extreme happiness and sorrow.

Throughout America, men and women and children, the humble and the proud, the great and the unknown, old and young, watch the trains go by. Millions of eyes look to the trains of the widespread empire that is the Milwaukee Road. For every pair of eyes turned upon the familiar yellow-orange cars of the Milwaukee on the innumerable spurs of that great network of rails, there are scores who watch its famous through trains—the *Pioneer Limited*, the *Sioux*, and the *Hiawatha*—going to and fro between Chicago and the Twin Cities, Minneapolis and St. Paul; the *Olympian Hiawatha* and the *Columbian*, traveling between the home terminus and Seattle and Tacoma; the *Southwest Limited*, the night train between Chicago and Milwaukee and Kansas City; the famed fast mail, *Number 57*, between Chicago and the Twin Cities; the *Arrow* and the *Midwest Hiawatha*, between Chicago and Omaha; the *Copper Country Limited*, out of Chicago to the Michigan upper peninsula and back.

Day and night, the people of America turn to watch the trains flash past, impelled by an attraction that is almost a kind of primitive magic, as if for many of them the trains are things of beauty and wonder. And so they are—in themselves and as symbols of the wonder of man and his accomplishments. Many a lonely person has been cheered by the sight of the long trains of lighted cars going by in the dark of night; many a bed-ridden invalid has measured hours by the coming and going of the trains; many a tired laboring man or business executive looks upon the train as a gateway to escape from work which has become, however temporarily, drudgery. The magic of a train to a boy lingers in the heart of the man. And, just as trains going by draw the eyes, so do the whistles reach out; many a heart has lifted at the sound of the long wail, or the sharp challenge, or the pleasant music of the locomotive whistles giving voice over the sweet land that is America.

That the locomotive's whistle has captured the imagination of millions is not to be gainsaid; the whistle, too, is the voice of romance and flight. As thousands of faces are pressed to window panes to watch the train go by, even more thousands of ears are attuned to the whistling of locomotives which some eyes never see. Every night for years I have heard the whistle of the 11:05 passing down the Wisconsin River valley on the Milwaukee Road's first line to the Mississippi, soon a century old:

Past Mazomanie, Spring Green, past Lone Rock,
westward over night-bound earth, the 11:05
whistling lonelily, a thing alive,
hurtles with time around its faceless clock.

Westward down the river, over hills, through town
and hamlet sleeping now, westward the 11:05 cries down
the dark its lonely voice, whistles and cries
until its solitude fades, dies. . . .

A lonely sound—perhaps, for the lonely. Though the whistle sounds to
mark the approach to crossroads, to stations, and the leave-taking of
the towns, there is no question but that it communicates far more to
the isolated listener far from sight of the train's dark, coach-lit length
streaking through the night-held countryside. Only a short year ago,
the *Capital Times* of Madison, Wisconsin, marking the advent of the
Diesel's whistle, editorialized to the Milwaukee Road on the familiar
old whistle of the steam locomotive:

Time was when one could tell by the sound of the engine whistles
whether a train was due for the long pull on the West end, or was headed
for Watertown or Stoughton on the East. Those were the days of slower
and easier living when things weren't speeded up to a tempo that has
lost all resemblance to the good life as we knew it, say twenty or thirty
years ago. A part of this new and strange existence, at least insofar as the
railroad is concerned, is due to those "new-fangled" Diesels that go scoot-
ing down the rails at fifty or sixty per. When the engineer on these has
need of making some kind of a sound or warning, he presses a button
or something that brings forth the stentorian blast that denotes the Diesel
warning. Soon to go are those long, low, melodious, and mournful sounds
in the night that the steam engine issued to get a cow off the track, to
warn for a highway crossing, or sound a greeting to the man in the signal
tower. Something entrancing and significant will be lost to railroading when
they are gone.

The romance of a train is an enduring thing. I was conscious of it
years ago when I formed the habit of taking evening walks along the
railroad into the marshes south of Sauk City, primarily to watch the
seasons come and go, the embankment being high and dry enough
above the marshland all around to permit familiarity with the inhabitants of these lowland areas without the accompanying discomfort
of travel through the bottomland itself. I am no less aware of it today.
Many times I have had to stand offside while the evening train went
by, the same kind of train which in his day was watched by old Mike

and his brethren, and many times I have gone on watching the red
and green lights at the rear of the caboose dwindling down the track
before me. And one night I stopped along the track and tried to put
down something of the feeling for the evening train, something of
what must have been in old Mike's consciousness, something that
must be in the thoughts of many train-watchers:

> Under the new moon, the late train goes down
> from our town,
> goes fast, oh fast
>
> past the place where the old bo
> at his fire watches out of musing eyes,
> remembering how one time on the Santa Fé
> he caught them going faster, being nimble,
> being quick: a far time among the cactus,
> the yucca blooming, and the painted mountains.
>
> Fast past the lone
> returning angler, standing offside
> at the slough's dark edge,
> watching it go by, thinking of old Ryde
> tossed off the bridge into the river, where he died,
> by this same train, perhaps,
> the evening's last . . .
>
> Fast past Lenson's farm where as always now
> dogs bark, and she looks out
> and wishes she were going somewhere,
> anywhere away,
> anywhere . . .
>
> Under the moon the rails gleam like ribbons;
> telegraph wires hum as all day
> bees sang in apple bloom; the late train goes by
> with the brakie dreaming
> of home and wife and kids, soon reached;
> the engineer's eyes hard on the way
> ahead, out of Sac Prairie to another
> Sac Prairie and another . . .
>
> Under the new moon's yellow sickle,
> the rocking cars on the rickety, single-track line
> speak mutely of America,
> in worn printing on their walls: C. M. & St. P.,

Union Refrigerator, Chesapeake & Ohio,
Milwaukee Road, the New York Central Line,
the Santa Fé, the old U. P. . . .

fast, fast, going past
under the new moon's rind,
past the pulsing mid-spring's hyla choir,
past bo and angler and farmer's wife,
red eye, green
dwindling down the track
as sometime bo and angler and farmer's wife
dwindle and pass
and are gone into yesterday
fast, oh fast . . .

But even this country train is a far cry from the projects which
frightened the contemporaries of John Stevens more than a century
ago, when a road of seventy-odd miles left "small minds . . . paralyzed,"
while "even great ones only half grasped the idea," as A. D. Turnbull
reported in his biography of Stevens. Yet the spurs have always been
the feeders on many great systems. Quite often, on my travels down
and back along two or three miles of the Milwaukee Road tracks
leading into the Sac Prairie country, to the twin villages of Sauk City
and Prairie du Sac, I have observed extensive repairs in progress—not
just the brushing of a section crew or the replacement of ties, but
refills, riprapping, the almost complete reconstruction of bridges
which might have seemed sound enough to any untrained eye, so that
the question recurred frequently as to the justification of such maintenance expense.

Like many another region in the midwest, which is primarily the
domain of the Milwaukee Road, the Sac Prairie spur runs into predominantly agricultural country. What income sustains the spur? The
spur was established in 1881 at the behest of citizens living on the
prairie, men like Eugene Heller, the enterprising son of a founding
father of Sauk City, an intellectual revolutionary; he and his fellow
citizens organized the Mazomanie, Sauk City and Prairie du Sac Rail
Road Company, and looked forward with high vision to seeing the
twin villages rise to a position of importance on the railroad as once
they had been important on the great Fox–Wisconsin waterway. But
the hope that the Milwaukee Road would push through to Baraboo
and thus establish the twin villages on a through line did not mate-
rialize. For years, the spur was fed principally by agricultural products. Apart from a spurt of activity about 1908, when the Wisconsin

Power & Light Company constructed a power dam across the Wisconsin just north of Prairie du Sac, the spur was fed prior to 1941 by the needs and products of a canning company, a creamery, a granite works, several oil companies, one or two agricultural implements companies, a sawmill, a tractor works, a short-lived pickle factory, a small publishing house, a grain elevator, two lumber and coal companies, and stock shipping, initially by individual farmers and stock-buyers, now largely by a farmer's co-operative. The establishment in 1941 of the Badger Ordnance Company on the upper prairie country north of the twin villages greatly increased the movement of freight for the duration of the war and a short time thereafter, so that the familiar train of 6 to 10 cars with the caboose and locomotive—the coach had long since gone—suddenly became an almost incredible train of 30 to 50 and more cars rumbling into the prairie north of town and out again at all hours of the day and night, and sometimes, equally astonishing, there were three of these trains a day. But for years before the advent of the rise of motor-trucking service, less than carload lots for stores and small businesses contributed materially to the income of the spur, though such income was appreciably diminished with the upsurge of trucking services in the twenties; just as in the days before the building of the Milwaukee Road spur to the twin villages freight was hauled by horse-drawn express the 9 miles from Mazomanie, 50 years later it was brought in over highways from Madison, 24 miles away.

Consisting of not over 14 miles of track, counting all sidings, and not counting the short spur constructed temporarily to the site of the power dam in 1908, and the longer spur constructed—equally temporarily—into the Badger Ordnance Works in 1942, the Sauk City–Prairie du Sac branch, despite the vicissitudes of progress and competition, must have earned not only consistently enough to repay the cost of the line's extension from Mazomanie, but also an additional sum sufficient to cover the cost of service and maintenance. That not all such spurs have done so is manifest; competition and declining incomes have forced the abandonment of many a similar spur, many miles longer. Yet the Sauk City–Prairie du Sac spur continues to hold its own, despite all competition, and even so recently as the closing year of the Milwaukee Road's first century the company found it expedient to build a siding into an area of new construction for a large co-operative creamery in Sauk City.

In any small town, the train is "our train," however much it may be the physical property of the railroad company. The people of Sauk City and Prairie du Sac always had a proprietary interest in the local train, even to the extent of referring to it familiarly as the "peanut-roaster" or the "coffee-grinder." In Prairie du Sac it was known for years as "Uncle Jake's Teakettle," because the engineer, Jake Pugh of Mazomanie, was loved by all the young; and the doings of the train were made the concern of young and old alike. Whenever Uncle Jake's Teakettle ran off the tracks or failed to make a grade in the marshes, the news was duly relayed to absent sons and daughters. On the occasion, just before 1900, of the train's running through an open switch into the Wisconsin, Mrs. A. P. Cummings of Prairie du Sac devoted to the event more than a page of a letter to her daughter, Ella Cooper:

We have had quite an exciting time here. Last Monday Uncle Jake's Teakettle tipped over into the River. They came up in the afternoon to see that the road was all right; you know they always come as though their lives were at stake. They had only a caboose on, and never stopped at the depot. The men were working around, and for some reason had opened the switch. They shot on, and down the bank the engine went. Laid bottom side up. Uncle Jake was sent headlong into the River, and Whitney was thrown down the bank, but none was much hurt. They had to send for a wrecking train to come and get the engine out—a fine time for the loafing part of the community. . . . I hope it will learn them a lesson; they always come so fast. I came up one night when I thought it would swing off the track; no one could sit on the seat. Grampy said he wished Doody was here to go down and see how funny it did look with the wheels sticking up out of the water!

The trains of the Milwaukee Road are "our trains" pretty generally, not only in Wisconsin, but all along its tracks. It is a feeling that is strong in the Milwaukee's employees. One day in the spring of 1947, I stopped at the end of the east channel bridge across the Wisconsin to talk to Chris Martin of Prairie du Chien, foreman in charge of a crew snaking out and replacing 10-by-18-inch supporting timbers of the trestle at that end of the bridge, a crew which—a matter of justifiable pride to him—included two of his sons. He spoke proudly of "our road"; to celebrate the approach of his fortieth anniversary with the Milwaukee, he and his wife had traveled west the previous year to visit a son in Portland, Oregon. They had ridden "our road" almost all the way; there was just one stretch of track that they had had to take on another road. His face wrinkled up into a grimace when he talked to me about it, and a grimace was a noticeable thing on his normally pleasant features. "Think of it!" he cried. "They came through selling you pillows. Then, just after you got settled, they woke you up trying to sell you magazines, pop, sandwiches, and anything they could think of. And finally they set up a portable stove in one end of the coach and began to fry hamburgers! Think of that! That's something you'll never find on the Milwaukee! Not on *our* road!"

The feeling of ownership, of personal pride in possession, among the employees is accountable enough, since most of the men in the Milwaukee, from the bottom to the top, have been Milwaukee men a long time or have had the Milwaukee in the family for a long time, like Chris Martin and his sons, who represent many another father and son—and even grandfather, father, and son—on the Milwaukee. That people who are not employees feel a sense of possession is equally plain. Perhaps this is accounted for by the consistent friendliness of the Milwaukee Road's personnel, by that same courtesy which was disclosed to me by passengers who had traveled over every mile of the main line, as well as those who had traveled from spur to spur, as the reason for their conviction that no other system afforded the unfailing attention to its passengers that the Milwaukee Road did. All the way up and down the Wisconsin River valley where the tracks of the Milwaukee Road make their way, throughout all Wisconsin, the "our train" feeling persists. Perhaps it is no more prevalent than a similar feeling on the part of people living along other railroads, but certainly it is more consistent than any other I have encountered. Perhaps it is in part due to the fact that the Milwaukee Road is first and foremost a Wisconsin railroad, begun in Wisconsin, incorporated in Wisconsin, and for many years confined within the boundaries of Wisconsin.

Whatever the reason, the Milwaukee Road has an enviable reputation in this regard, and its reputation is no recent development. It began a long time ago, over a century ago, in fact, when a group of enterprising gentlemen in the growing, but still very young, city of Milwaukee determined that there must be a railroad from Milwaukee across the Territory of Wisconsin to the Mississippi. That was the first vision; others were to follow.

II. The Milwaukee and Mississippi

The old-timer was voluble, remembering the early days of the Milwaukee.

"Swamps and bogs, that's all there was," he said appreciatively. "Why, when we put in that line between New Lisbon and Star Lake—between Milwaukee and La Crosse, too, if it comes to that, and other places—we had to cross one swamp after another. Soft and tricky land, too. We couldn't place ordinary filling material, no sir, not unless we put in something to spread out the load over a larger bearing area. But we did it, and this is how we did it—we cut long trees, hauled 'em out on the ice, and put 'em down at right angles to the track, close together and on top of each other to make a kind of mat. Then we put earth, sand and gravel on top of that, and it got pressed down and down into the swamp until it hit a firm foundation. Then we put on more earth and sand and gravel, and then the ties and the rails.

"Now they tell me the Milwaukee dumped car bodies along a river bank out on the Kansas City Division and the Iowa and Dakota, wired 'em together to keep the flood waters down and hold the sand in to keep the bank the way it should be. But back in the fifties, we did it the hard way, we didn't have any car bodies to sink, we had to do it with trees—we had plenty of them."

—STEPHEN GRENDON
Through Wisconsin on a Bicycle

"OH, FOR a good road across the territory!" wrote the editor of the Grant County *Herald* early in 1843. "For want of it, the western part of Wisconsin Territory is actually going into decay!" The need was for almost any kind of road, be it of planks, a water route in the form of a canal, or, by some miracle, a railroad. Almost any type of road would have been better than that then prevalent and to prevail for some years to come, on one of which the editor of the Milwaukee *Sentinel and Gazette,* traveling across Wisconsin five years later, encountered a man with eight oxen hitched to a half-loaded wagon, and subsequently wrote: "The team seemed rather disproportionate to the load, but the man gave it as his experience that four yoke of cattle were not too many to hitch on to a buggy over such roads, and added that for his part, he didn't pretend to start out on any kind of business *with anything less than a breaking team!*"

The Territory of Wisconsin had hardly been created when its governor, Henry Dodge, a dashing, romantic fellow who had come into this eminence from the lead-mining country around Dodgeville and Mineral Point, appeared before the legislature assembled at Belmont and, stressing the need for internal improvements in Wisconsin, recommended the construction of a railroad commencing from a "suitable point" on the Mississippi River and terminating on Lake Michigan's shore—passing through the mining country en route, of course. The legislature responded with enthusiasm and sent a memorial to congress; $2,000 were appropriated for a survey, and an engineer was dispatched to survey the proposed route. But he, alas, turned out to be a lackadaisical fellow at heart; he went over but 20 miles of the projected course the railroad was to follow and turned in a report so adverse that it dampened the ardor of even the most enthusiastic adherents. That enthusiasm was still further dampened by the panic of 1837, by the slow growth of the Territory's population—by 1840 Wisconsin contained only 30,945 people—by arguments about waterways, plank roads, and other means of transportation, by the belligerence of the Jacksonian democrats toward railroads and the concomitant public sentiment which arose. But however much enthusiasm among the people lying outside of the Milwaukee region waned, their vociferousness in complaint did not.

In 1843 the farmers complained; there they were, occupying one of the finest agricultural sections of the Union, and they had no opportunity to dispose of more of their produce than they might sell or barter at home, what with the difficulties attending Mississippi River navigation and the all but impassable trails to the lake outlet to eastern markets. A decade earlier the lead-miners in southwestern Wisconsin had cried aloud for improved outlets to markets. Governor Dodge's support of a railroad derived from personal experience demonstrating the need. Shot and lead went either to St. Louis and New Orleans down the Mississippi, or to Chicago and New York by way of the Lake route and the Erie Canal. On the Mississippi and the Gulf route to New York, it cost the thrifty Cornish miners $1.56 to ship every 100 pounds of lead; the way of the lake and the canal was virtually impossible—*unless* there were a good road, preferably a railroad, when the total cost might come down to as low a figure as 75 cents!

Even as early as 1836, the territorial legislature had granted charters to two proposed railroads—the Belmont & Dubuque and the La Fontaine, neither of which came to anything, since the need was not manifest for the proposed routes. There was a need for a line from Milwaukee to the Mississippi, however, and B. H. Edgerton, a member of the Committee on Internal Improvements of the legislative council of the Territory of Michigan, of which Wisconsin was still a part at that time, proposed a memorial to congress on January 13, 1836, designed to calculate the "immense saving" that a railroad across the territory would mean to the lead-miners alone:

Persons shipping their lead by the way of the Erie Canal would be enabled to get the proceeds of their sales at least three months sooner than by the way of New Orleans. Valuing the lead at six cents per pound in New York, and deducting from the sum the amount of the transportation, a balance of $732,800 is left. The interest upon this amount, at seven per cent for three months lost time, will amount to $12,813, which, added to the balance in favor of the Erie Canal route, will amount to $123,413; add to this the saving of imports, and the amount will be nearly doubled.

The lead-miners were still at it half a dozen years later, when Moses Strong asked the territorial legislature to consider that the transportation of lead alone would pay 6 per cent on the investment in the proposed Milwaukee and Mississippi Rail Road. Strong came out of the heart of the lead-mining country, and failed to explain how an investment of $2,500,000—according to his figures—could build and equip a railroad from Lake Michigan to the Mississippi, even assuming that the entire shipping of lead could be readily diverted from the

Mississippi River and the Gulf route. In 1844 the *Sentinel and Gazette* still believed editorially that the transportation of lead would pay a "handsome interest" on a railroad investment.

But by 1846 the tariffs on the traffic between Milwaukee and the Mississippi amounted to $352,000, of which sum agricultural products accounted for more than half, or approximately $200,000, and lead less than one-seventh of the total. And the small weekly papers which had begun to sprout all over the occupied portion of the Wisconsin Territory, soon to achieve statehood, made vociferous complaint. "Large quantities of surplus produce have been left by our farmers to rot upon the ground the past season, for want of a good communication by which to find a market," cried the Grant County *Herald,* and went on to predict that if this sort of thing continued, the result would inevitably be "the gradual depopulation of the western part of the Territory."

Despite the imminence of statehood in 1848, the Territory of Wisconsin still had but two principal avenues of commerce, and, since the military road from Fort Crawford to Fort Howard was not too frequently in condition to bear anything but military traffic, it actually had only one—the great waterway up the Fox River from Lake Michigan at Green Bay and down the Wisconsin from Portage to Prairie du Chien. This waterway connected the Territory of Wisconsin through Mackinac on the north with the east, and through the Mississippi to New Orleans and the Gulf. Even this avenue of commerce was necessarily subject to weather, and it was principally useful to the fur-traders. But now, as the nineteenth century moved toward its latter half, the fur trade had declined, and, while the lead-diggings still flourished in southwestern Wisconsin, the pioneers on the land were turning more and more to agriculture and the products of agriculture. Northern Wisconsin was still largely a wilderness; some of the towns along the Fox and Wisconsin Rivers were already old towns, as towns were old in a new country, and so, too, were the towns of the lead-mining country, connected to one another by primitive stagecoach roads—Mineral Point, Dodgeville, Platteville, Linden, and Belmont vying for significance with Prairie du Chien, Oshkosh, Butte des Morts, Green Bay, De Pere, and Portage.

As long as the fur trade was dominant, the Fox–Wisconsin waterway did very well. Even the lead-diggings were served in large part by the Mississippi and the Wisconsin. But waterways were of commercial value only so long as their commerce arose along their shores and was not too far distant. Manifestly, the influx of pioneers—from the German countries in the 1840's, and, before that, from the east—

and the opening of the land to agriculture diminished the importance of waterways as commercial avenues. The first overland routes had been made by the roaming buffaloes, which had an unerring instinct for the best avenues of travel—the high ridges, the easy hill slopes; after them, the Indians followed the buffalo trails, making networks of narrow paths over the face of the land; and the pioneers followed the same trails on foot or on horse, or on a kind of snow sledge known as a "French train." These roads sufficed for the early stragglers into the middle west. After 1840, pioneers came into Wisconsin Territory like a tidal wave; they came up the Mississippi from New Orleans, they came overland to St. Louis or Chicago and up into Wisconsin, they came by water through the lakes, past Mackinac, to Green Bay or to Milwaukee—it was primarily to Milwaukee that the German people came seeking freedom in escape from their harassed and troubled native countries. And from Milwaukee they flowed out into the country, taking up land where it was to be had. Necessarily, the majority of available land was away from the avenues of commerce by water. The farmers had a legitimate basis for complaint.

Clearly, if any citizens of Wisconsin were to take the lead in bringing a railroad into being, it must be the citizens of Milwaukee, the Territory's largest settlement. Despite the fact that they were involved in the planning of plank roads as well as a grandiose scheme for a Rock River Canal, a committee of fifteen citizens was appointed in September, 1836, to petition the territorial legislature, at its coming session, to pass an act incorporating a company for the purpose of constructing a railroad from Milwaukee to the Mississippi, by way of Mineral Point. The committee included Samuel Brown, who presided at its meeting of September 17, Byron Kilbourn, who acted as its secretary, and such well-known men as Solomon Juneau, William P. Proudfit, S. D. Hollister, N. F. Hyer, H. Crocker, S. W. Dunbar, Horace Chase, William R. Longstreet, A. B. Morton, James H. Rogers, B. H. Edgerton, William N. Gardner, and Thomas Holmes. Though it was not until 1847 that the prospective company was chartered, it was at this meeting that there began an agitation and a dream which were to result in what became the Chicago, Milwaukee, St. Paul and Pacific Railroad Company.

None of these men, who represented Milwaukee business, was more colorful than Solomon Juneau; and none had his prestige. In 1818, when the only settlements in Wisconsin were at the terminals of the Fox–Wisconsin route—at Green Bay (then Fort Howard) and Prairie du Chien (then Fort Crawford)—Juneau came out of Canada and built himself a log cabin among the Indians along the lake shore at the site of Milwaukee. His full name was Laurent Solomon Juneau, though his first name was usually forgotten; he was a tall, barrel-chested French Canadian, very dark and swarthy.

Though he was not the first white man to settle in the Milwaukee region, he remained longer than any other, and to him has gone credit for the "founding" of Milwaukee. He came as a clerk to Jacques Vieau, then an agent for Astor's American Fur Company; he married Vieau's daughter, Josette, the niece of an Ottawa Indian chief, and soon established himself as an independent trader. None exceeded him in the trading of furs, since he customarily measured cloth from his nose down to his finger tips, so that for every yard the Indians gained a few extra inches, and although his speech may have been punctuated by colloquialisms in several languages, he used applied psychology in his dealings with the Indian who complained for any reason, habitually refusing to give him more than he had coming, yet managing to satisfy the Indian's pride by manhandling the complaining Indian sufficiently to justify instructing him to return to his people and tell them that he had "fought with Juneau." As a result, the Indians trusted him above all others, even to the extent of consulting him about the wisdom of scalping certain Yankees, whom they considered a tribe quite separate from the French Canadians.

For seventeen years, he was virtually the only resident white man in that section of the Territory, though he did not own the land on which he lived until the spring of 1835, when a land office at Green Bay brought into the market the land which was to become Milwaukee. Within a year, Juneau had built himself not only a new house, but also a large store and warehouse; moreover, he was doing a thriving business, not only as a trader, but also as a land agent. His wealth increased substantially during the winter of that initial boom, but his casualness about money was legendary. Alexander F. Pratt, a fellow businessman, wrote years later:

We often saw him in those days go into his store after business hours and take from the drawers the money that his clerks had received during the day for goods and lots, amounting often to $8,000 or $10,000, and put it loose in his hat; and upon one occasion we recollect of his hat being knocked off in a playful crowd, when some $10,000 flew in various directions. Money seemed to be of no earthly use to him. If a man called upon him to subscribe for either a public improvement or a charitable object, whatever was required he subscribed, without asking why or wherefore.

Juneau's honesty was likewise well known, and he had the unqualified respect of the Indians, who called him "Old Solomo," and of his fellow settlers, who, when the city of Milwaukee was incorporated in 1846, elected him its first mayor.

At the time of the first meeting in the interest of a railroad to serve Milwaukee, late in 1836, Milwaukee itself was in the midst of a boom of unparalleled proportions. While there had been only six occupied log houses early in 1835, by midyear the Green Bay *Intelligencer* was reporting the effect of the relinquishing of their claims to Milwaukee land by the Menominee and Potawatomi Indians in 1831 and 1833: "Squatters are taking possession of the country in that neighborhood in swarms. . . . A correspondent . . . says that quarter acre lots are selling at $500 and $600 each, and that by fall they will have one hundred buildings erected. There are already . . . 500 to 600 people living there . . . land speculators are circulating around there, and Milwaukee is all the rage." By 1836 another observer called Milwaukee "an unenclosed lunatic asylum." In all this, Juneau figured prominently; that section of the booming town where he lived was known as Juneautown, just as that section growing to prominence under the influence of the ambitious Byron Kilbourn was known, in rivalry, as Kilbourntown.

It was politic that Solomon Juneau be a part of any progressive movement; but it was seldom necessary to invite him to join such a movement; he no sooner heard of it than he came into it. As a trader of two decades' experience, Juneau knew better than anyone else how necessary were good roads, and he was therefore in the forefront of every movement to make Milwaukee more accessible to all parts of the Wisconsin Territory. In some cases, naturally, the Indian trails could be used, but this was not often, since the Indians traveled readily where wagons would not go, and the need was for wagon roads. Juneau and those businessmen who did not leave Milwaukee after the collapse of the initial boom set themselves to the task of establishing avenues of travel and trade. Though the agitation for railroads began in the early 1830's, most businessmen of Milwaukee were astute enough to realize that the railroads would not come until the Territory had been settled more widely, and that could not be accomplished, at least initially, without roads over which the immigrants might travel. So the plan for transportation moved readily from one level to another—from wagon roads to plank roads, from canals to railroads.

By 1840, there were five roads into Milwaukee, apart from the enduring Lake route. The Green Bay road led north; two roads led west to nearby Waukesha and Mequonago; another led south to Racine, and the Kilbourn road led southwest. In 1841 yet another road was opened northwest to Fond du Lac. But these roads were little more than makeshift wagon tracks, so that for many months of every year they were impassable because of snow, rain, or the rising of streams which washed out the poles and logs thrown across them in lieu of bridges. The enterprising citizens of Milwaukee constructed their first good road of plank in 1847, from their city to Watertown, at a cost of approximately $119,000. It was a toll road, and its success was so marked that a tremendous furore of agitation for more plank roads followed, with the result that another was built shortly thereafter to Janesville.

Yet the success of plank roads was a limited one, for the enterprising among the citizens of Milwaukee and the larger area around it did not think only in terms of their immediate counties or even of the Territory, but rather of all the vast, unpopulated lands west of the Mississippi; and it was therefore obvious that plank roads, however serviceable for a short distance, would never do for such commerce as these men envisioned. And by this time, also, serious doubts were arising as to the efficacy of the proposed canal to connect Milwaukee to the Rock River, and thence to the Mississippi, which the Rock River joined in Illinois not far south of the Illinois–Wisconsin boundary line.

The primary impetus toward the building of canals to further waterway traffic was, of course, the success of the Erie Canal, by way of which a great many pioneers had come into the Wisconsin territory, and a great many more were still coming. The initial agitation was for improvement of the Fox–Wisconsin waterway. The necessary portage between the Fox and Wisconsin Rivers at Fort Winnebago (Portage) had long been a source of irritation to the users of the waterway, and the irritation grew in direct proportion to the rise in population of the Territory, so that the construction of a canal to connect the two rivers was inevitable. Out of this immediate need, in turn, rose a movement to improve the entire route from Green Bay to Prairie du Chien. And this agitation stirred hope for a canal from Milwaukee to the Rock River, with ultimate improvement of the Rock River route only a matter of time.

Immigration to Wisconsin offered the key to the proposed waterway improvements, for the initial influx of immigrants had come by way of the Fox–Wisconsin route, both from the north and from the south; and secondarily, by the Lake route, though this route soon assumed primary importance, and Milwaukee rapidly became the leading city of the entire Territory. While the agitation for improvement of the Fox–Wisconsin waterway began in 1829, it was not until 1836 that plans were made for the Milwaukee and Rock River Canal. Byron Kilbourn, who was to emerge as one of the leading spirits behind the

Milwaukee & Mississippi Rail Road Company, took the lead also in the agitation for the proposed canal.

It was not by accident that Byron Kilbourn came to the fore in matters concerning the canal. Then in his early thirties, Kilbourn was the son of an Ohio congressman and the son-in-law of the inventor, John Fitch. He was very well educated, and had devoted a good deal of his time to surveying public lands in Wisconsin, as a result of which he came to make his home in Milwaukee in 1835. In addition to his surveying experience, he had been in charge as a civil engineer of the Lake Erie–Ohio River canal. He had come to Milwaukee with the manifest intention of making it into a great city, "the greatest city" in the midwest, he boasted. He had come from Green Bay, where he had been serving as surveyor, and he had decided that Milwaukee was destined to be the most important city of the midwest, if its citizens moved fast enough to keep ahead of Chicago. He was a proud, obstinate, sometimes arrogant man, certain that in all things he was right and all others were wrong. He came by his strong prejudices and dictatorial disposition quite naturally, since his ancestry had been distinguished for its proud men. He came to Milwaukee with one of the surveyors from the Miami Canal project, and with him made a rapid survey of the west side, a portion of which Kilbourn subsequently bought at Green Bay, thereby becoming a natural rival of Juneau, on the east side of the river, for, despite a brief time of actively promoting a city, Juneau did not at heart hope to see Milwaukee grow too large, whereas Kilbourn foresaw no boundaries to his dream.

Kilbourn interested himself energetically in the proposed canal, and he lost no time in setting before the Wisconsin territorial legislature, which was meeting for the first time that year in the provisional capital of Belmont, a petition, signed by many citizens, which revealed to that body some of the advantages of such a canal, and asked for passage of "an act incorporating a company for the purpose of constructing a *navigable canal*, from navigable water in the Milwaukee River, to navigable water in the Rock River," a procedure which resulted in the reporting of a bill "to incorporate the Milwaukee and Rock River Canal Company," which bill was tabled for the remainder of that session. Nothing daunted, Kilbourn and Increase A. Lapham, a distinguished civil engineer, later to become chief geologist of the state of Wisconsin, made a preliminary survey of the proposed project and an approximate estimate of its cost.

The agitation for the canal continued without cessation, despite some opposition from the adherents of the Fox–Wisconsin Improvement Company, who quite naturally felt that there was nothing to be gained from the establishment of a secondary route across Wisconsin, particularly since the Milwaukee–Rock River route would mean a much longer canal than that necessary for the Fox–Wisconsin portage. Nor was the legislative assembly particularly enthusiastic about the Milwaukee and Rock River Canal, though finally, early in January of 1838, following renewed petitions presented before the assembly meeting in Burlington, the company was incorporated, and the act of incorporation was approved by Governor Henry Dodge.

Having reached this basic goal, Kilbourn set himself to the task of achieving a greater—the granting of public lands to the canal company, of which he was now president. He lost no time; less than five weeks after passage of the Act of Incorporation, the directors of the new company adopted a memorial to congress asking for "A quantity of land equal to one half of five sections in width on each side of said canal, and reserving each alternate section to the United States, from one end of said canal to the other," a grant which the petitioners considered of such importance to progress that the congress would be impelled "to appropriate in aid of this work, an amount of land equal to that granted for similar projects elsewhere." The congress of the United States was somewhat more sympathetic than the legislative council of the Territory; in four months—that is, in June, 1837—a grant of 500,000 acres was made, a grant which turned out to be of far more importance to the Milwaukee & Mississippi Rail Road Company than to the Milwaukee and Rock River Canal Company, for, despite a few attempts at making a beginning of construction, the proposed canal came to nothing; the project was so slow in making headway that time and progress caught up to it and passed it. The canal began to assume less and less importance, particularly in view of the rising importance of the railroad as a mode of transportation, and, even before the granting in 1847 of a charter to the Milwaukee & Mississippi Rail Road Company—initially under the name of the Milwaukee & Waukesha Rail Road Company, to pass from Milwaukee to the village of Waukesha, formerly called Prairieville, twenty miles away—interest in the canal declined. The directors of the canal company began to move slowly but steadily behind the railroad—those who were not already a part of that company—and at the formal organization of the Milwaukee & Mississippi Rail Road Company in the spring of 1849, it came as no surprise to find as the first president of the new railroad the then mayor of Milwaukee, Byron Kilbourn. The amended charter permitted the extension of the proposed road to Madison, "and thence west to such point on the Mississippi, as the said com-

pany may determine." The authorized capital of the company was
$100,000, to be raised by subscription, in shares of $100 each.

Serving with Kilbourn as directors were few names familiar to legislators who had read the initial petition of 1836—J. H. Tweedy, Dr.
Weeks, Anson Eldred, James Kneeland, Alexander Mitchell, E. B.
Walcott, E. D. Clinton, and E. D. Holton. The directors were all enterprising men, with this difference: some of them were considerably
more enterprising and patient than others. These men faced the monumental task of carrying on the railroad; compared to the need for
financial resources, the initial hurdle of obtaining a charter, though it
had taken a decade to accomplish, was as child's play. By and large,
despite the boom, the citizens of Wisconsin were pioneers, whether
in an agricultural sense or in commerce; while every man had his
land and, often, his buildings, he had very little money to spare for
investments even so promising as a railroad.

Kilbourn and his group, however, were far more earnest about this
project than they had been about the Milwaukee and Rock River
Canal; moreover, there was a unity of purpose among them, and there
was very little dissension of the kind which had risen about the canal,
when there was ample reason to doubt the wisdom of building such a
canal against the rising tide of railroad transportation. Kilbourn, burning with ambition and vision, was especially anxious that railroads
should reach out from Milwaukee into the west, for he recognized that
Milwaukee's greatest potential rival was Chicago, and whichever first
established railroad communication with the west and northwest was
likely to become the major city. As early as 1835 he had written to
Senator Louis F. Linn of Missouri, pointing out that he had examined
the western shore of Lake Michigan, as well as the land in the interior
of Wisconsin; he knew that there were inhabitants and many more
coming, "And where there are inhabitants, there must be business; and
if business, it must be done somewhere . . . Green Bay, Milwaukee
and Chicago, each has its own appropriate country; and that naturally
united to Milwaukee by common interest is at least equal in extent
and fertility, and I hesitate not to add, will sustain a more dense
population than either of the others." But the key to fulfilment of
Kilbourn's dream lay not in plank roads, not in canals or other waterways, but in railroads. "If we build the first one and get to the Mississippi first, Chicago will not dare to approach our territory," he said
confidently. He gave graphic realization to his dream by preparing
a chart for his wall; there it hung from 1847 onward, and its ambi-
tiousness reflected Kilbourn's ambition, for the chart portrayed pro-

jected rail routes connecting Milwaukee to Dubuque, St. Louis, La
Crosse, St. Paul, and beyond.

The directors of the new company lost no time in soliciting subscriptions, and they did not scorn any kind of subscription; this meant, of
course, not only money—there was not much of that to be had—but
also goods, and this principle operated so well that when grading of
the proposed road was begun in the fall of 1849, the work was prosecuted for an entire year and paid for by orders drawn on subscribing
merchants, payable in goods—the harness-makers paid in harnesses
and repairs; the farmers paid in cattle, horses, beef, pork, oats, lumber,
timber, potatoes, and flour; the wagon-makers paid in carts and
wagons; and many people paid in labor, particularly as the line
reached out from Milwaukee; for which in turn all received stock.

The result was satisfactory, for nothing so encouraged promoters
and investors alike as the sight of the railroad grading on the initial
line to Waukesha, particularly since, though other railroad companies
had been chartered previous to the granting of a charter to the Milwaukee & Mississippi Rail Road Company, no other road had made
any kind of beginning. But here, in fact, was the grading for the rails;
here, the people saw plainly, was the beginning of a railroad beyond
any question, and nothing like it was to be seen anywhere else within
the boundaries of the infant state of Wisconsin!

Even so little a beginning was a triumph achieved with difficulty.
Out of the Jackson administration had come so many trumpetings
against "monster" corporations and "monopolies" that many people
were prejudiced against railroads. There were also bitter rivalries to
take into account; if legislators within Wisconsin were not prejudiced
by the Jacksonian attitude, they were a prey to divided loyalties, for
Milwaukee was not the only city seeking to become the eastern
terminus of a cross-state railroad. Even after outstripping Sheboygan
and Green Bay, the most eager rivals, Milwaukee still had to contend
with Racine and Kenosha, while at the western end Potosi and Cassville each maintained a better right to the western terminus than
Prairie du Chien. Each proposed site had its legislative adherent,
which made for delay upon delay, so that a charter which might have
been granted in 1837 was instead not granted for a decade after that
date. Moreover, there were special interests in Wisconsin which felt
their existence threatened by the "iron horse"; these were primarily stage
drivers and rural tavern-keepers, and these men gave vent to their
animosity not only by constant fighting with railroad laborers but also,
after the laying of rails had begun, by tearing up rails leading out of
Milwaukee toward Waukesha. The laying of rails, however, could

not begin without more money than had heretofore been available.

Unfortunately, the initial method of investing in the Milwaukee & Waukesha Rail Road Company was too primitive to procure the iron for the rails; this had to be bought, and it had to be paid for in money. By the spring of 1850, it became apparent that measures must be taken without delay for the raising of funds to the amount of approximately $250,000, which, it was estimated, would buy enough iron to reach from Milwaukee to Whitewater. The directors had to face two rather unpleasant facts; first, there was not that much ready money in the entire state; second, it was extremely unlikely that eastern banks would consider a railroad in Wisconsin adequate security for such a loan.

There was a good deal of discussion at the meeting, but it was not until one of its members made a somewhat unusual proposal that a direction was obtained. Mayor Joseph Goodrich, of Milton, rose and said, "See here; I can mortgage my farm for $3,000, and go east, where I came from, to get the money for it. Now, are there not one hundred men between Milwaukee and Rock River that can do the same? If so, here is your money." The idea was new enough to be startling, but, despite all the objections which were immediately made to it, it was adopted because no other idea was proposed; thus was born the plan of raising farm mortgages to aid in the construction of railroads. With the customary enterprise of the directors of the company, the required hundred men were found, and the needed money was covered in mortgages.

The plan for the mortgages was distinctly different and new. It operated in this fashion: farmers along the right of way were invited to purchase stock, and, lacking money with which to pay for it, they could give personal notes secured by mortgages on their farms, payable in 10 years, and bearing 8 per cent interest. The railroad stock was to pay a 10 per cent dividend, and the company planned to subtract interest due on mortgages from accruing dividends, permitting the 2 per cent difference in stock dividends to accumulate on the books until the time when the notes were paid. The plan called for sale of the mortgages as collateral security for its bonds, and it appealed to the settler, who felt that his stock would be worth far more than the price he had paid by the time his note came due, when he could either sell his railroad securities and cancel his mortgage, or keep the stock as an investment. The company's agents prosecuted this form of investment with vigor, and other railroad companies emulated the Milwaukee & Mississippi. While some of their agents were unscrupulous, men like Joseph Goodrich mortgaged his own farm for $10,000, and

E. D. Clinton, one of the directors, mortgaged his farm for $5,000. The plan was, in fact, so successful as a means of assuring investments that from the year of its inception to 1857, something like 6,000 Wisconsin farmers mortgaged their homesteads to the extent of approximately $4,750,000 to purchase railroad stock, though of this sum only $900,000 went to the Milwaukee & Mississippi Rail Road.

Negotiating the mortgages, however, was another thing; just as long as the directors of the company dealt with the people of Wisconsin, their dispatch and enterprise were speedily rewarded. But try as they might, they could find no market for mortgages, for mortgages as security were very uncommon in the 1850's, and in many parts of the country they were simply unheard of. The directors, however, discovered in the attempt to negotiate mortgages in order to raise money that bonds of the city of Milwaukee would be acceptable as security. Despite some debate pro and con in the press, the city responded with reasonable promptness, issuing bonds in the amount of $234,000, which were sold for cash at par, the money thus obtained being immediately invested in iron for the rails of the Milwaukee & Mississippi Rail Road Company. And with this purchase, the success of the new railroad seemed to be assured.

The railroad did not reach even this beginning without serious opposition. Not a few people looked upon the railroad as a rising monopoly, and the people of southwestern Wisconsin had had some experience with a monopoly when a few wealthy buyers in St. Louis effected a combine to keep down the price of lead. The argument waxed hot and long. Some of the newspapers of the day charged that the company was a monopoly; others, notably the Madison *Argus*, maintained that railroads were not detrimental to labor, tavern-keepers, country towns, the teaming interests, and the like, and held that corporations "are evil only when they are chartered to do that which ought never to be done by anybody, or that which should never have been made an exclusive privilege"; but that they were beneficial when they did that which it is desirable should be done, but which individuals either could not or would not try to do. This, maintained the *Argus*, was the nature of a railway corporation.

The energetic Byron Kilbourn, in his mayoral address of April 12, 1848, strove to allay the fears of his constituents about the railroads:

There is in the minds of many an unaccountable misapprehension as to the effect of railroads upon the prosperity of the country through which they pass, and the places at which they terminate. Some look upon them as a monopoly, for the sole benefit of those who build and control them.

Others admit that they are beneficial to the country, for the farming interests, but injurious to the business towns where they terminate. While others still claim that they contribute to the wealth of commercial points where they terminate, at the expense of the whole country, and especially to the destruction of inland villages. None of these views is correct. It may be laid down as a general maxim, that whatever facilitates and cheapens intercourse among men, in all their pursuits of business, must be to each and to all beneficial. It is beneficial to the producer, especially to the farmer and the miner, for the price of his commodity will be enhanced in value, to the same extent that the cost of transportation is diminished. To the consumer it is beneficial, for the commodities, which he is compelled to purchase from a foreign market, come to him charged with less expense, as facilities are increased and transportation reduced. These propositions . . . are so obvious that every reflecting mind will readily embrace them.

That every reflecting mind did not embrace them was evident in the newspapers. The directors of the Milwaukee & Mississippi, however, did not fail to accept the challenge of the writers of letters and editorials. E. D. Clinton, one of the directors, appealed directly to the monopoly-hating farmers in an open letter in the Milwaukee *Sentinel and Gazette* of June 8, 1849:

The interests of farmers have always been subject to a ruinous monopoly; which monopoly as used by the capitalists, has always been diametrically opposed to the ultimate success of the farmer. No one will for a moment contend that we have not had to contend with this monopoly; and yet the farmers of the country are those who hold the power to do away with this burden upon their energies. . . . The design of this railroad is ultimately to benefit the farmers of the country, in common with our commercial interests; and how is this to be effected? The farmer owning stock owns also a share in each depot on the line, and the person who has the charge of the depot is *his* agent. Now supposing, *your* agent in Milwaukee telegraphs to any agent on the line where your wheat is stored, that wheat buyers will give so much for a boat load of wheat; the cars will deposit that wheat in Milwaukee in six hours at the farthest, from the time the order was received. *Thus you will, by taking stock in this railroad, ruin this accursed monopoly,* and at the same time obtain the highest price for your wheat. . . . The railroad must be built, and it remains for you to say whether the stock-holders shall consist of enterprising farmers or eastern capitalists. If you refuse to take stock there is no alternative—eastern capital will step in *and we shall forever be cursed with monopolies.* . . . Let every farmer who has the interest of the farming community at heart step in ere it is too late.

Clinton's appeal may have been somewhat ingenuous, but it was not without effect, for the Milwaukee & Mississippi had no need to fear eastern capital for some time to come.

Lack of money and fear of monopoly were not the only difficulties to be overcome; there were also legislative hostility and the studied opposition of less successful rival companies. Each prospective railroad company had its champions in the legislature; the constituents of any county or district in which a railroad was being projected could naturally count upon the support of these champions for their own railroad, and their opposition to any other, without regard for merit or any other consideration whatsoever. They were also naturally on the alert for any suspected infraction of the law, and, even before the city of Milwaukee had assured the initial success of the new railroad by issuing bonds in its support, the issue of the Milwaukee & Mississippi was forcibly brought before the legislature.

There was in Wisconsin a school fund established by the sale of "school lands," a fund which the state constitution provided should be invested in the "most profitable manner." To the status of these lands under this school grant had been added, after the failure of the scheme for the Milwaukee and Rock River Canal, the 500,000 acres granted for the purpose of constructing the canal. These lands had not been added without a struggle. When it was first apparent that the canal project was not destined to be carried out, Byron Kilbourn, as president of the canal company, and as president-to-be of the Milwaukee & Mississippi, acted with the directors of the canal company to petition congress for a regrant of the canal lands to the directors of the new railroad company, urging that "as a mere Company," they had no desire to effect change, "but as citizens, the members of the Company wish to see public interest preserved, which we doubt not it would be in a most effective manner by the construction of a railroad."

The directors further urged congress to consider that the grant of land "was obtained through the sole agency of the Canal Company, without any aid or coöperation whatever on the part of the Territory— so that whatever interest the Territory may have in that grant, has been conferred upon it as a *gratuity* through the unaided exertions of the Canal Company. . . . Is there any better course to pursue," the petition went on to ask in regard to the land grant for the canal, "than so to use them as to secure the construction of a rail-road, binding together the great inland seas of our continent with the father of waters, with an iron band?" Surprisingly enough for a captious body, the press of the Territory seemed to be almost unanimously in favor of such a change, and even Governor Doty, in his annual message of December, 1841, looked with disfavor on the Rock River Canal project and recommended the building of "a rail or McAdamized" road between the lake and the Mississippi. The Milwaukee *Courier,* writing in support of the governor, reprinted a letter from an eastern paper, pointedly adding the letter's postscript: "Your territory must not think they can get the right kind of men to engage in building a Rail Road for them through so new a country without at least giving the canal lands out and out as a bonus. . . . They must not calculate to eat their bread and butter and keep it too."

The debate about the canal land grant was carried on from year to year, but in the convention of 1847–1848 it was proposed that the canal grant "shall constitute a perpetual fund, and the interest thereof, together with the five per cent of the net proceeds of the sales of public lands . . . shall be Annually appropriated to the construction and repair of roads and bridges in the several counties." In the face of this, Byron Kilbourn changed his tactics and demanded the fund for the support of public schools, contending that the system proposed by the amendment was wholly inadequate insofar as such large works as the proposed Milwaukee & Mississippi Rail Road were concerned. After the adoption of the amendment, it was augmented by a section specifying that "the State shall never contract any debt for works of internal improvement, or be a party in carrying on such works; but whenever grants of land or other property shall have been made to the State, especially dedicated by the grant to particular works of internal improvement, the State may carry on such particular works and shall devote the avails of such grants, and may pledge or appropriate the revenue derived from such works, in aid of their completion." This amended article was adopted by a vote of 50 to 15, and it was thought that by means of it the state would be able to further the construction of the Milwaukee & Mississippi Rail Road. Though subsequently some portions of the canal lands were allocated to the Milwaukee & Mississippi, opposition developed immediately—the nucleus of the public control against private ownership issue which was destined for a long history. The Madison *Argus* stated the case succinctly: "For a State to construct, control and manage a work of this kind, with profit to itself or advantage to the people, we believe to be entirely out of the question."

The failure of the attempt to obtain the canal lands for the railroads led subsequently to another, less devious attempt to obtain at least some benefit from those lands as well as the school lands. As early as March 3, 1849, the Madison *Argus,* ever the friend of the railroad, editorialized under the heading *Gold, Free Schools, and a Railroad* to the effect that the proceeds from the sale of school lands would be

far more than enough to "build and put into operation a railroad of
the first quality from Lake Michigan to the Mississippi River. . . .
In what way can the fund be better expended?" The *Argus* reasoned
that such an investment would not constitute an infringement of the
constitution, since it would be an investment so profitable as to compare favorably with the income New York had gained from the Erie
Canal. Nothing, in the opinion of the *Argus,* could possibly be so
profitable as the Milwaukee & Mississippi, and it was to the best
interests of the state of Wisconsin that the school fund be forthwith
invested in this railroad and so assure not only the expenses and repair
of the road, but also enough income to keep up all the schools and
libraries in Wisconsin besides. The *Argus* was doubtless carried away
by the enthusiasm of its editor, but whether this proposal was the
brain child of the *Argus* or whether it stemmed from the Milwaukee
citizens who were behind the new railroad is not on record.

It was not until almost a year later, in January, 1850, that the proposal was made again. This time it came out in a railroad convention
held in Madison, and it was proposed that "the school fund should be
loaned to the company on good security." In general, the newspapers
of southern Wisconsin came to the support of the plan, though not
without caution. The editor of the Milwaukee *Sentinel and Gazette*
wrote a long editorial in favor of the proposal, and other papers
reported meetings held in various parts of the state in favor of the
plan, though the Madison correspondent of the Prairie du Chien
Patriot bluntly charged that these "mass meetings" favoring the application for a loan from the school fund had been arranged by the railroad people. The *Patriot* itself, however, editorially supported the
plan, as did the Potosi *Republican* and many others. But opposition
was prompt from the north. The Fond du Lac *Journal,* in its issue of
February 1, 1850, editorialized:

School Fund.—That a desperate attempt will be made to swindle the
State out of the school fund is getting to be too plain a matter of fact to
be questioned; new-fangled projects of loaning it to railroad and other
corporations are being daily started, and each scheme, however extravagant it may be, finds its advocates. The Milwaukee & Mississippi R. R. Co.
coolly demand of the legislature a loan of only $100,000, preparatory to
making a larger haul. . . . The people of northern Wisconsin solemnly
protest against the laying of vandal and sacrilegious hands, by the incorporated companies, upon the school fund held sacred and set apart by
the laws of the State for the education of present and future generations.

The Sheboygan *Democrat* charged that "Byron Kilbourn, the projector of a canal that never was made, went up to the capitol with his picked men, made speeches, ate oysters, and drank beer" in an effort to lobby the proposal into law. This, however, was making somewhat free with Kilbourn and his fellow directors, for they simply addressed a memorial to the senate and the assembly, setting forth the importance of the railroad project, trying to make it clear that the "company presents no features of a monopoly," and urging that the legislature consider making the proposed loan, "which would benefit alike the interests of the school fund and of the State," and promising, finally, to produce data to show that the "nett income" of the railroad would be more than 14 per cent per annum. Sheboygan, moreover, was moved by personal reasons to oppose anything which might benefit the Milwaukee & Mississippi, not by the altruism of the editor of the *Democrat*, for Sheboygan, ever the rival of Milwaukee, had a burgeoning railroad hope of its own. A group of men from Sheboygan and Sheboygan Falls, led by Charles D. Cole, hoped to construct a railroad from Sheboygan to St. Paul, planning to push through Sheboygan and Calumet counties, through the Appleton country, and, beyond that, through the forests of northern Wisconsin; but every success of the Milwaukee & Mississippi diminished the chances of the Sheboygan plan.

The memorial was referred to a select committee, rather than to the standing committees on education and school lands, on the one hand, and on internal improvements and roads, bridges, and ferries, on the other; and this committee reported out the memorial with "strong solicitude for the complete success in the operation of the school fund," recommending its investment in the Milwaukee & Mississippi. But the opposition to it was too strong, and it was defeated by a vote of 41 to 21, whereupon the Sheboygan *Democrat* dispatched a parting shot at the directors: "We wish our friends of Milwaukee god-speed in every laudable enterprise for the growth and improvement of their town, but when they seek to clog up the fountain of learning and intelligence to increase their wealth and power, we can but congratulate them, and especially their children, in their failure."

Construction, meanwhile, went forward. Regardless of the difficulties, which were constant, regardless of the hostility of legislators and of the opposition, the Milwaukee & Mississippi—to use what was now once again its official title, its chartered title of the Milwaukee & Waukesha giving way in 1850 to the initial name—pushed steadily forward toward its first goal. The grading of the right of way was followed late in 1850 by the laying of the first rails, which were of the H-rail (commonly called T-rail) variety. The board of directors decided on a wide gauge of six feet—"the same as the New York and

Erie Rail Road Company"—because "for high speed, and for long
heavy trains with produce, and for general transportation, it is found
that such a Road. possesses many and decided advantages over the
ordinary road."

The Milwaukee *Sentinel* cheered the company. "Hurrah for the
Rail Road!" it cried on September 13. "The *first* rails of the Milwaukee
& Mississippi Rail Road were laid down yesterday, and the first Locomotive is of the largest size and best pattern, weighing some twenty
tons, and built in excellent style. It will whisk a train of passenger cars
from here to Waukesha next month, in ten minutes less time than Puck
required 'to put a girdle round about the earth,' which was 'in forty
minutes.'" This locomotive was built two years before by the Norris
Works of Philadelphia, and was called Old Number 1, later carrying
the names *Bob Ellis* and *Iowa*, and the number 71.

The *Sentinel* was naturally inclined to overestimate the speed with
which the tracks could be laid, overlooking the continuing opposition
of the special interests and their frequent assaults on the rail-laying
crews. But by November, five miles of track had been laid, and the
directors and other prominent citizens of Milwaukee were taken for
a ride on the first railroad in Wisconsin. Among the passengers was
Old Solomo, who expressed himself as astonished at the great changes
wrought by the locomotive; during the ride on the two uncovered
freight cars behind Wisconsin's first locomotive, traveling at 25 miles
an hour, he held forth at length and confessed that he had never
before even seen a locomotive, much less taken a ride on a train.

The young state's newspapers took official cognizance of the event.
The Madison *Argus* said forthrightly:

No State in the Union, and no country in the world has ever heard the
snorting of a locomotive at so early a period of its settlement. We once
thought, should we live to a good old age, we *might*, possibly, ride across
Wisconsin in a *stage coach*, but before we have begun to get old, the
locomotive is at our heels. No wonder the editors throw up their caps and
make a joyful noise. Had we been there, we would have thrown ours so
high that it never would have come down.

Even the Fond du Lac *Journal* grudgingly applauded:

We admire the spirit that the Milwaukeeans have shown in pushing
forward this important channel of communication with the interior of the
State. It shows what energy and self-reliance can accomplish. No city in
the west has done so much towards self-advancement. Look at her beauti-

fully graded streets—the unsightly hills, that a short time since environed her with hideous deformity, have contributed to fill her marshes and low lands—turning the frog ponds into a suitable habitation for men. . . . The Rail Road communication between the waters of Lake Michigan and the Mississippi will form a good channel of trade and travel—adding yearly its thousands to the population of the City, and its millions to her trade.

Early in 1851 the laying of the rails to Waukesha was completed, and the company had fulfilled the obligation fixed by the territorial legislature to "locate and construct a single or double track railroad between Milwaukee and Waukesha to transport, take and carry property and persons upon the same, by the power and force of steam, of animals, or of any mechanical and other power, or of any combination of them." On a memorable Tuesday, February 25, 1851, the first formal trip to Waukesha was undertaken. Naturally, the 20-mile road was opened with fanfare, and the company had printed an elaborate program to mark the occasion with suitable dignity and éclat:

MILWAUKEE & MISSISSIPPI RAIL ROAD

PROGRAMME

For the Occasion of opening the Rail Road to Waukesha on Tuesday, Feb. 25th, 1851.
The Cars will leave the Depot at Milwaukee at 10 o'clock A. M. precisely.
Fare for each Passenger out and returning $1.50.
All Passengers by the Train will receive a Dinner Ticket free of Charge.

HESS' BAND WILL ACCOMPANY THE TRAIN.

DINNER

Will be Served in the Company's new and spacious Car House, under the direction of the Committee of Arrangements at 1 o'clock P. M. Precisely.

AFTER THE REMOVAL OF THE CLOTH

Addresses will be made.

Among those who will address the Company, it is expected will be Judge Hubbell, Mayor Upham and Governor Tallmadge.
Ladies are expected to participate in the festivities of the Occasion.

THE RETURN TRAIN

Will leave Waukesha at 4 o'clock p. m. precisely.

Officers of the day: Byron Kilbourn, president; Joseph Turner, Waukesha; Rufus King, Milwaukee; Joseph Goodrich, Milton; Hans Crocker, Milwaukee; S. B. Grant, Milwaukee; Rufus Cheney, Whitewater, vice-presidents.

Committee of Arrangements: John P. Story, W. D. Bacon, Isaac Lane.

AN EVENING TRAIN

Will leave at 6 o'clock p. m. to take out those who desire to participate in the festivities of the evening. Fare for single gentlemen, the usual rates. For a gentleman and lady, out and back, two dollars.

E. D. Holton, Supt.

COMMITTEE ON ARRANGEMENTS

J. P. Story	W. D. Bacon
Isaac Lane	J. Smith
S. H. Barstow	William Smith
O. M. Hubbard	

The train was an exciting success. It was the first train to travel in Wisconsin, and all along its comparatively short route the people stood beside the line and cheered its passage. The dinner was everything it should have been, and the speeches foresaw a great future. The new road was "the first link in the great railway from Lake Michigan to the Mississippi"; its purpose was to "capture the towns with our iron horse and enrich our neighbors as well as ourselves," and the hope of the company was to "annex all towns." Moreover, President Kilbourn was ready within a fortright to announce that the railroad "is now being carried forward to Whitewater," with a new and improved "heavy iron rail" of appreciably more substantial construction than that used on the company's first twenty miles.

Enthusiasm for the first railroad in Wisconsin was widespread and infectious. On the morning of February 26, the Milwaukee *Sentinel and Gazette* echoed the sentiments of the wildly cheering spectators and participants:

Notwithstanding the unpromising look of the weather, and the superabundance of mud in the streets and roads, the Rail Road Depot was thronged, at the hour appointed for starting, and the accommodations provided by the Company tasked to the utmost to convey the passengers offering. About 250 of our citizens, including many ladies, took seats. . . . The Road, as far laid, is an excellent one; the cars neat and comfortable; the engines of ample power; the Depot and other Buildings at Waukesha, of the most substantial character, and everything, in short, connected with the enterprise giving the promise and offering the facilities for a large, increasing and prosperous business. So opens the first link of the iron chain which is to connect us with the Mississippi. May two years hence see it stretched across the State!

Satisfaction at the terminal end of the short new railroad was no less enthusiastically expressed. The Waukesha *Democrat* pontificated:

The opening of this road is the commencement of a new era in the history of Wisconsin, and the hastening of the "good time coming." The importance of such a road, connecting the greatest carrying highways upon the American continent, has long been acknowledged, and its feasibility is beginning to be tested. This is the beginning: but who can tell where and what will be the ending? By the eventual completion of this project, new markets will be opened in the interior; new incentives to the enterprise and energy of our people be produced; more activity in developing the agricultural and mineral resources of the country be occasioned; and a greater combination of the elements of State and national wealth be effected, than the most visionary ever dreamed would fall to our lot. A few years more, and the careful, prudent and economical prosecution of a proper system of internal improvements so favorably commenced, will startle the people by the magnitude of its results. The prosperity of the whole country bordering the line of the Milwaukee & Mississippi Rail Road and all those portions which by other improvements can be made tributary to it, will receive a new impetus, and an abundant wealth and full measure of happiness will be the reward.

The Milwaukee & Mississippi persevered. By April, the company posted notice of two daily trains to begin on the fourteenth. Trains would leave Milwaukee at 7:40 A. M. and 3:40 P. M., and would leave Waukesha at 10:00 A. M. and 6:00 P. M. "This," added the company, "will help in business transactions." Soon the company and its supporters had unsolicited assurance that the Milwaukee & Mississippi compared very favorably with the best of the eastern railroads; on May 5 the *Sentinel* and *Gazette* published a letter written at Waukesha by a traveler from New Hampshire:

Gentlemen: Having occasion to pass through your State, I rode over the Milwaukee & Mississippi Rail Road en route from your beautiful city to

this village, and I cannot forbear offering a word, through your paper, to
the public, in relation to the railroad, as I am inclined to opinion there is
a misapprehension abroad upon the subject. From what I had heard, I
expected to find the road rough and uneven, the cars inferior and uncom-
fortable, and the whole affair a very sorry imitation of what a well constructed, well conducted railroad ought to be.

But to my great surprise I found the road as smooth as the average
Eastern Trunk railroads. The car I rode in was spacious, plainly but well
finished, the upholstery done in modern and most approved manner. The
locomotive apparently new, in fine order, of large size, with four driving
wheels. Several stops were made upon the route, and from the perfect
ease with which the stops and starts were made, I would judge an excellent
engineer had charge of the engine. Upon one point I wish to speak particularly, that is—the quiet and unobtrusive manner in which the business of
the road is carried on. The courteous manner of the attendants would do
well to be patterned after by many older companies.

In fine, the morning was bright, quite a number of ladies were along,
and the ride was delightful; and as a traveler through your young and
beautiful State, I feel that I have been laid under obligation by the projectors and managers of the Milwaukee & Mississippi Rail Road, and would
recommend to all fellow travelers going West, instead of taking the dust
and sweat of the stagecoaches, or private carriages, to take the railroad.

However much the presence of the "number of ladies" may have
contributed to the New Hampshire traveler's enthusiasm, the success
of the Milwaukee & Mississippi seemed assured.

III. Expansion and Collapse

The engines in service in the sixties were all wood-burners, and to supply the wood necessary for fuel, wood yards were located at Pewaukee, Oconomowoc, Watertown, Columbus, Portage, Kilbourn, New Lisbon, Tomah, Sparta, and North La Crosse. The wood was cut in 4-foot lengths and was sawed in three pieces by a saw operated by a treadmill, on which horses furnished the power.

The right of way was practically all corded with timber, and fires were frequent and destructive. In 1866, 1700 cords of wood were burned two and a half miles east of LeRoy, now called Oakdale. At this fire the wood train and 40 laborers came to the assistance of the men fighting the flames, the wood ranks were separated and the ends of ranks covered with sand, furnishing protection against the flaming embers and intense heat, and saving the greater portion of the stock piles.

The engine hauling the wood train had a peculiar-sounding whistle, by which it was instantly recognized when heard in the distance, and in the event the whistle was sounded after the working hours, it was assumed to be a distress-signal, and trackmen immediately reported at their car houses ready for duty without waiting to be notified by special messenger, because when derailments occurred the task of re-railing the cars was largely a matter of physical strength, with the assistance of a system of leverage, in which the chains and tamarack poles were utilized in lifting and shifting the car trucks and bodies until the equipment was back on the rail.

—F. H. BUFFMIRE

THE Milwaukee & Mississippi, however, was destined for trouble.

The decade and a half between the inception of the plan for the road and the completion of the first section of the proposed line to the Mississippi was a period of rapid changes. The Territory of Wisconsin had become the state of Wisconsin in 1848, with a population of 305,391, of which 20,000 lived in Milwaukee. Fur-trading and lead-mining had irrevocably declined before the now overwhelming importance of wheat in the economic structure of the state. The once-dominant stream of immigrants from the east was matched by a steadily rising tide of Germans escaping the oppressions and the turmoil of Europe in the middle nineteenth century. And the state legislature was being besieged by newly formed companies urging that body to grant more railroad charters.

In the face of the rapid progress being made in the development of Wisconsin, it was imperative that the Milwaukee & Mississippi push its rails to the Mississippi with the greatest possible speed, and already the line was being laid toward Whitewater, with the immediate objective being the initial extension as far as Eagle, 34 miles from Milwaukee. The most pressing need, manifestly, was for more funds with which to push the construction of the road; it was estimated, on the basis of construction to Waukesha, that the first division of the road—from Milwaukee to Whitewater—would cost $607,160.81, or an average cost per mile of $12,163.22, an increase over the 1849 over-all estimate of slightly over $15,000. The road was chafing under such irritating difficulties as inexperienced and inefficient contractors, construction troubles, particularly over marshy soil, and the slowness of stock-holders in making their 5 per cent quarterly payments on stock held. Now, suddenly, early in 1851, the Milwaukee & Mississippi learned that its credit was being assailed—and this at a time when a mortgage of the line from Milwaukee to Waukesha was under consideration. The directors might have expected an assault on their credit, for they had refused to pay interest on bonds of the company which, they maintained, had been fraudulently obtained. President Kilbourn hastened to issue a statement to the papers making it clear that "The Company has promptly paid the interest on all their bonds which were *legitimately* sold."

Ironically enough, this first major trouble came not from outside, but from within the company's own ranks. The company, late in 1850, had given its treasurer, Walter P. Flanders, bonds and certain instructions which he was to deliver to the company's New York agent, Charles Crocker, for the purpose of negotiating the bonds and raising money for the company. Flanders had been proposed by E. D. Holton as the designated negotiator, but Holton's proposal did not have the support of either President Kilbourn or the board of directors; Flanders came into possession of the bonds, however, because he was in any case en route to New Hampshire, and there was no good reason for sending someone else to Crocker when Flanders was passing through New York. Flanders, however, disregarded his instructions, and, ignoring Crocker, himself entered into negotiation with a trio of New Yorkers, Messrs. Cryder, McKay, and Jaudon, for a loan of $100,000 on behalf of the company, with the company's real estate as security. He returned to Milwaukee and told a plausible story about knowing the applicants, whom he had met as friends through his wife's family. The company, thus lulled, was misled into approving the negotiation.

The transaction, however, was fraudulent because Messrs. Cryder, McKay, and Jaudon had misrepresented themselves, and, though Flanders returned with the $100,000 in cash, the trio of New Yorkers proceeded to misrepresent and sell the securities of the road to investors, including such well-known men as P. T. Barnum, when it had been understood and agreed that the trio would hold the securities against their loan. Flanders had been gulled, just as Kilbourn had feared he might be when he opposed Holton's proposal that Flanders negotiate the loan. Kilbourn explained later:

I objected, remarking that to do so would certainly be the means of getting him (Flanders) into difficulty; that he was quite too unsophisticated to be trusted with important interests in Wall Street, where he would have sharp men to deal with. Mr. Holton thought I under-rated Mr. Flanders, but yielded the point, and it was never again proposed. He was, therefore, not sent to New York for the purpose, nor with the authority to negotiate a loan, but, being on his way to New Hampshire, was sent by the way of New York simply for the purpose of delivering to Mr. Crocker, certain instructions . . . relative to negotiation, which the latter had in hand.

The extent of the fraud perpetrated upon Flanders with the help of Flanders' own desire to impress the company with his qualities as a negotiator was not fully apparent until the company found itself unable to pay interest on its obligations in April, 1851. The Milwaukee & Mississippi was immediately subjected to a storm of doubt and accusation, both within Wisconsin, where it came from rival companies, and in the east, where it rose from just such speculators as Messrs. Cryder, McKay, and Jaudon, who sought to gain by depressing the value of the company's securities, buying them back and then reselling, after re-establishment of the company's credit. Manifestly, the company's credit must be re-established before such manipulations could succeed, and to that end the securities obtained under false pretenses by Cryder, McKay, and Jaudon would have to be got back.

Kilbourn acted with his customary dispatch. He went east at once, where, as he reported to the board of directors later that year, "I soon learned that there were evil designing persons making themselves busy with our affairs, either for the purpose of discrediting us, so as to prevent our raising funds, and thus arresting operations, or for the purpose of coercing us into a settlement with the parties holding our securities, through those who had obtained them by fraud. Information . . . represented our Company as broken down." He succeeded in raising funds by a temporary loan from the Farmers and Merchants Bank of Hartford, and, appalled at the mass of calumny which was publicly uttered against the company, he persuaded a qualified representative of the business interests of Hartford to investigate the affairs of the company, its road, securities, and collateral. That representative, Stephen Spencer, came west at the behest of his associates and in June made the following report to Kilbourn and his company:

Agreeable to your request, I have visited Wisconsin, for the purpose of examining the Milwaukee & Mississippi Rail Road, and spent about ten days in the examination. I passed three times over the road, to the village of Waukesha, its present Western termination; being about 20½ miles from Milwaukee.

I consider the work well done, and the road in as good condition as any Eastern railroad I have seen, which has not been longer in operation than this; being laid with heavy T rail, and as far as I can judge, it has been built with strict economy.

From the village of Waukesha, I passed with two of your directors over the line of the road now under contract, to the village of Whitewater. From thence we proceeded leisurely on or near the line the road is to run, to Madison, the Capital of your State. We returned to Milwaukee in a more southerly direction, and passed a considerable number of the farms mortgaged to your Company.

From the fast increasing population, and capabilities of the country through which your road passes, I am of the opinion that you are fully justified in borrowing money to aid in its construction, at the rate of interest your bonds bear. So far as I have been able to examine the farms mortgaged by your Stockholders, and which you offer as collateral security for the bonds of your Company, I can say, that had I funds to invest, I should not hesitate to take your bonds.

I have had an introduction to all the directors of your Company, but with one exception. I believe them to be men of strict integrity and moral worth, and fully competent to manage the important trust committed to them. I arrived at this conclusion, not only from personal intercourse, but from enquiries of friends in Milwaukee, not Stockholders, and some of whom have long been known to me.

My opinion is, that when your road shall be completed to the valley of the Rock River, the business and income of the Road must be large.

This report went a long way to lull the suspicious eastern capitalists, but Kilbourn did not recover the bonds without considerably more trouble, and at some loss to the company. Undaunted by the suspicion of the New York capitalists, Kilbourn made direct application to Charles T. Cromwell, one of the holders of the disputed bonds, and the agent of the holder of most of the residue of the bonds, and proposed a settlement. Kilbourn was naturally anxious to avoid legal proceedings, since, as he put it in his report later, "If we . . . had even the fortune to succeed in such a suit on any grounds that promised success, that very result would have put an end to our obtaining further loans, as all capitalists would have been afraid to deal with us, lest we should take advantage of some technical defect which they could not discover"; but Cromwell temporized, once seemingly acquiescent, then again refusing to compromise in any way with Kilbourn, bringing about ruinous delays, so that in the end Kilbourn was after all forced to begin a suit against Cromwell and the other holders of the bonds. At this, however, Cromwell agreed to compromise, and surrendered the bonds. The company's loss was set at $14,518.44. What it suffered in prestige might have been much greater if, during the period of months while Cromwell delayed, the company had failed to pay the interest coming due in July; the company's payment of this obligation considerably mitigated the impression which Messrs. Cryder, McKay, and Jaudon had sought to foster in financial circles.

His ineptitude and incompetence revealed, Flanders charged that Kilbourn had in fact authorized him to take the course he did, and succeeded in creating such a furore that Kilbourn memorialized the directors with a long account of his difficulties in the Flanders fraud, and pointedly said, "In the different stages of this business, the difference between Flanders and myself was, chiefly, that, *without my aid*, he got the Company into the difficulty; and *without his aid*, I got them out of it."

The loss to the company was severe; Kilbourn did not exaggerate when he wrote:

This transaction . . . came very near ruining the Company entirely, and it was only by the most persevering efforts . . . that the difficulty was got over, and the credit of the Company resuscitated, in time to avert the calamity and save the Company from utter bankruptcy. The credit of the Company was completely prostrated, and its operations almost suspended; and it needed but little more to put on the finishing stroke, and to have ruined, not only the Company, as a corporation, but also every Stockholder who had given a mortgage to sustain the credit of the Company.

The resultant effect on the company's operations could be plainly seen at the end of that year, when the line had been extended only to Eagle, instead of to Whitewater, as had been confidently anticipated. It was not alone the Flanders fraud which had jeopardized the line; other factors were not far from disastrous in themselves. Sale of the company's real estate securities had not proceeded as readily as might have been supposed; this was very largely due to the cloud upon the credit of the Milwaukee & Mississippi, but also in part due to the financial disorder of the United States at the time, as well as to the accumulation of interest on unproductive capital and the increase of expenses attending the slow progress of the road, thus discouraging stockholders, who were, in any event, suffering because of the partial failure of two wheat crops in succession. The directors resolved to pledge the extension of the road to Madison to a third person, "of high character and responsibility, as trustee," for the payment of the bonds to be issued upon that portion of the road.

The directors admitted also, as 1852 approached, that their own members often mixed private interests with those of the company, and also occasionally misunderstood or misrepresented their duties. In the face of expenditures of $429,364.03 for 38.05 miles of track, and net earnings of $14,514.78, it was time that the directors altered previous policies both in regard to their own duties and the actual construction of the road. To that end, late in 1851, the company concluded a contract with Joseph and Selah Chamberlain, of Cleveland, for the section of the line from Eagle to the Rock River, a distance of 31.05 miles, the Chamberlains to finish the line between October 15, 1851, and November 1, 1852, under the direction of the company's engineer, at a stipulated remuneration of $12,000 per mile, payable in monthly estimates (reserving 10 per cent) "as the materials are delivered on the road and the work progresses—one-half to be paid in mortgage bonds, and the remainder in cash, monthly balances to draw 12% interest, until paid."

Even more important than construction difficulties, the seed of schism had been sown among the directors and the members of the company, opening the way to further dissension. Flanders' fraud was not in itself the basic reason for President Kilbourn's replacement. Though few of the men in the Milwaukee & Mississippi had the interests of that company more at heart than Kilbourn, and few worked as tirelessly as he, his energetic prosecution of the company's interests aroused the reasonable doubt of J. H. Tweedy, one of the directors. Kilbourn later accused Tweedy of acting because of an old grudge, but Tweedy had more than just a grudge with which to proceed against Kilbourn. He seized upon Flanders' fraud and, in addition, charged that Kilbourn, acting as the company's fiscal agent, issued to Jacob Bean, of Waukesha, $1,900,000 in stock in the company, receiving one mill on the dollar for it, an illegal issue; and, on the basis of these events, launched an attack which resulted in Kilbourn's removal from the presidency.

Kilbourn's defense, that he was "acting in the best interests of the Company," was considerably weakened by Bean's surrender of the stock. As a result of Kilbourn's removal, two boards of directors were elected in the subsequent election, and the faction supporting Kilbourn, which was in the majority, elected A. Finch, Jr., as president, while the Tweedy faction elected John Catlin. The two groups met at different places in Waukesha early in January, 1853, the Kilbourn party voting the disputed Bean stock as well. As a result of the election, there was a wild scramble for immediate control. According to the Milwaukee *Sentinel*,

. . . the Kilbourn party took the cars and the others started in sleighs for this city, to get possession of the books and other property of the Company. The sleighs got in a little ahead, and when the Kilbourn party entered the office, they found Dr. Weeks in possession of the books, which possession he managed to maintain for some time, while both parties indulged in severe and abusive threats. At length, Mr. Gridley came to the assistance of Dr. Weeks, who resigned his position—that of sitting on the books—and took the urn of the stove as a weapon of defence. This weapon was taken from him by the Kilbourn party, and one of the party succeeded in getting some of the books away as far as the bottom of the stairs, but here the Kilbourn party was met by the reserved force of their opponents, and by dint of some choking, it is said, were compelled to disgorge the plunder, which was safely secured by the others, leaving the latter in possession of the whole, which both sides seemed to think would be "nine points in the law." Dr. Weeks received considerable injury in the way of business, but nothing of a very serious nature. This is a frolic in high life. . . . We hope there will be no lives lost, and no blood spilt! We had thought that, by careful management, our Road might get along without *"accidents"*; but it seems "they will happen on the best of Rail Roads." But seriously, we think this muss is an unpardonable trifling with the best interests of the Road, as also with that of the traveling and business public.

The gentlemen engaged in the "muss" were of a similar opinion. It was Kilbourn who foresaw that this state of affairs would certainly ruin the company; he proposed that the two boards effect some kind of compromise. It lay within the power of either board—one being in possession of the books, and one of the road, fixtures, and property of the company—to ruin the company; and Tweedy and his faction left no doubt in the minds of Kilbourn and his that they meant either to run the road or ruin it. Faced with this alternative, Kilbourn and his board withdrew and left the road to be run by Tweedy's faction. This meant that Kilbourn, who had worked unsparingly for the company, and who had the best eastern connections in addition, was relegated to the position of a stockholder. He saw fit to review the succeeding report of the directors of the company in an open letter sent to the stockholders of the company.

The letter demonstrated again, as had his report on Flanders' fraud, that Kilbourn's education stood him in good stead. He warned ominously that the new board of directors lacked adequate wisdom to run the road, and pointedly added that "time will show us more fully" how they have administered the affairs of the company. His report included transcripts of minutes of earlier meetings, showing that Tweedy, in his attack on Kilbourn, had not kept to the facts on record. He stated bluntly that Tweedy and his supporters were guilty of "misdeeds and incapacity," and closed his long review with a paragraph to show that he bore towards Tweedy no

. . . feelings of hostility or hatred. . . . I do not wish even to convey the idea that he is a bad man at heart; but on the contrary, I know, and am free to admit, that he has many excellent traits; and were he in good health, believe he would be ashamed to do many things which he has done with apparent satisfaction, and even gusto. I think he is entitled to more commiseration than censure; and I am more disposed to pity, than to blame him. He is a person of peculiar organization and temperament, very excitable, and as I think, at times showing evident indications of lunacy. And, then, his frequent and tremendous bursts of passion on trivial occasions—his excited, unreasonable and extravagant manner of treating subjects, indicate a morbidly diseased state of the brain, and derangement which it would not be strange should grow on him to an alarming extent. Indeed, I should not be surprised if his unfortunate state of health should in a few years, or perhaps months, terminate in hopeless insanity.

Catlin, the new president, was in many ways the antithesis of Kilbourn. He was a Vermonter, just under 50 years of age. His forebears were merchants and farmers, though he himself, after an education at Newton Academy in Shoreham, Vermont, had taught briefly and then studied for a career in law. Three years after his admission to the bar in 1833, he came to Mineral Point to form a partnership with Moses M. Strong; 1836 was the year of Wisconsin's separate territorial status, and the growing Territory offered unlimited opportunities. As soon as the seat of the government had been removed from Belmont to Madison, Catlin became postmaster; this was scarcely a year after his arrival in the Territory, and, though he was removed on political grounds by President Harrison, he was soon reinstated by President Tyler.

He was not, however, to be limited to any one position; he was a persevering man, with no such vaunted ambitions as Kilbourn, but with the abilities to go with his perseverance. At the time that he served as postmaster, he was also clerk of the Wisconsin supreme court and, from 1838 to 1845, chief clerk of the house of representatives. Moreover, as soon as Dane County was organized, he was appointed district attorney, and for two years in the middle 1840's he was secretary to the Wisconsin Territory, by appointment of President Polk. At the time of his election to the presidency of the Milwaukee & Mississippi, he was Dane County judge. He had been interested in the Milwaukee & Mississippi for some time, and was convinced that its affairs were not being conducted in the best interests of the road or its investors, though he had made no injudicious criticisms, being a genial and affable man whose friendly, pleasant nature concealed a well-ordered mind. No sooner was he elevated to the presidency of the road than he began to urge that the banking law of the new state of Wisconsin include a provision making first mortgage bonds of railroads, to the amount of 50 per cent, the basis of banking under certain restrictions, pending which he meant to go to New York personally to negotiate for more money for the Milwaukee & Mississippi.

The physical property of the road, in the meantime, was steadily increasing, and the success of the Milwaukee & Mississippi—despite the fact that the projected goal for 1851 had not been reached—excited all the towns in the region through which the line was to run to the Mississippi. Even while Kilbourn was in New York jousting with

Cromwell and Barnum, the citizens of Madison were being spurred to greater activity and interest on behalf of the Milwaukee & Mississippi. Early in May the *Wisconsin Express* urged citizens to turn out and support the railroad:

It will be seen by a reference to another column, people are requested to meet at Well's Hall on Friday evening (at early candle light). It is high time the people of Madison were bestirring themselves in relation to subscriptions to the Milwaukee & Mississippi Rail Road. Why is it that such an apathy prevails among our citizens in regard to this great work? Is it because it is a fixed fact that the road is bound to go on without our assistance, and by the terms of the Charter must come to Madison? That the work is bound to go on is perhaps reduced to a certainty, but if our citizens expect *all* the benefits to our village that that work can bring, they will find when too late that they have been entirely too cool in regard to it. The country is wide awake. Farmers are subscribing liberally. They feel an interest in the early completion of this road and foresee some of the benefits that are to be derived from such a thoroughfare. The West, too, is all alive and putting forth truly commendable efforts. . . . Iowa anxiously waits to meet us at the western terminus and join hands. Westward Ho, To the West away!

Thereafter the *Express* ardently championed the Milwaukee & Mississippi, and its editor went out of his way to pass over "that part of the road, which is completed" so that he could assure his readers that it would "compare favorably with most eastern roads in its smoothness and firmness." Moreover, he pointed out from time to time, the Milwaukee & Mississippi was "doing a very fair business, and yielding . . . some seven per cent on its cost," and added, for the benefit of possible investors, "If this is the case, what may be expected from it when it shall have penetrated into the interior as far as the Capital? . . . Until it is completed, the vast resources of our State will remain, as it were, unknown—our wealth and importance are hidden, shut out from the world; but let this be done, and our riches will be developed, the tide of emigration to our State will be increased to a rapid rate, and Wisconsin will soon take its stand as one of the most important States in the Union." Doubtless the pleasure of the Waukesha *Democrat* was not lost on the *Express*, for the *Democrat* lost no opportunity to inform its readers: "It looks like business to see trains of lumber and goods rolling in, and we shall be much surprised if our village does not show an improved appearance in consequence before another year." "Let the people go to work in earnest," trumpeted the *Express*, "and 1852 will not close until the Iron Horse shall have found his way to the Capital of Wisconsin. Then will the glory of our young State have fairly commenced—and then shall we begin to live and prosper as we ought!"

But the Milwaukee & Mississippi was coming to Madison; there was no getting around that stipulation in the company's charter. Indeed, surveyors were at work on that part of the line between Whitewater and Madison in 1852, among them young Charles I. Linsley of Middlebury, Vermont, who came into the west with his eyes open, appreciatively enough, and wrote back east his impressions of that raw country. He found Chicago surprisingly "well laid out, with wide streets (planked), fine brick buildings & beautiful stores. It is built directly on a marsh & nothing to be seen on any side but a low wet prairie. But I should think it bid fair to be one of the largest of Western cities." He liked the surroundings of Whitewater even better: "I like the looks of this place very much. The country is quite hilly around here & more resembles N. England than the everlasting Prairie that we have come over. And the living is so cheap—butter 9¢ a lb., oats 13¢ per bushel!"

He proved to be a shrewd observer of men, as well. He had been in Whitewater but a few days when he wrote home:

Mr. Edgerton I saw a week ago today & have not seen him since. He told me to come on & take charge of the locating party from this place to Rock River & gave me an introduction to Mr. Shields, an assistant on construction who is stopping at this place. Well, I came on & made my appearance in the (apoligy for) Engineers Office which was over a store. Among the Paper bags & crockery leather flour &c a small low bench or table set near two small windows constituted the Engineers corner. Not a chair in the garret, but seats provided on raisin boxes &c if they hadn't been split into kindling wood. . . . I found Shields to be a very clever fellow, a Scotchman who came to this country at the time the road was commencing & has been on ever since. He commenced as chairman I believe & so along up. He is about 22 I should judge. He has charge of a division from this place east. As for the locating party I found a Mr. Little who was with me at Norwich & had been on here about a month running levels. He has been in the business about a year, is a clever fellow & a splendid mathematician. . . . They pay here—Rodmen, axemen, & all—$30.00 per month, making no distinction. They employ Irish & Scotch mostly & they are a lazy set to work.

I have thus given you a short discription of the engineering on the Road, but do not think it is worse than I expected to find it or that I am at all discontented. I only write it to show how much is lost by improper management & by not having a proper head. Mr. Edgerton appears to be a very fine man, of good education, & a well read man but no experience in building Rail Roads. He came on as a land surveyor at first & knew nothing about the true practical economy of Railroading. Conkey says that when he came

on here to lay track for them (that was done a year ago) he never saw
so green a set, not an engineer that ever saw any track laid & all were in
a fix & that is the way that he came to get the job so easily. He says he
was but two hours concluding the bargain. They never had an engineer
on here that had ever been on another railroad.

The observing surveyor, moreover, passed along the gossip which
flowed freely among the employees of the Milwaukee & Mississippi:
"It seems that the said Byron Kilbourne the former Presdt was a
scoundrel (to speak it plainly as it is said to me) & sunk a good deal
of money for the Company. He appointed himself Chief Engineer
& made a miserable location from Milwaukee to Waukesha, very
crooked & about four miles out of the way. Everybody appears to be
down on him, but Conkey says that Mr. *Holton* was always rather
friendly to him."

So well did Linsley look upon his position that he urged his brother
Dan "to take a look this way. The only thing in opposition would be
that the Company are rather poor. It is a hard scratch for the Engineers to get any money, I am told, but they say that the prospect of
the Company never was better, especially as they are rid of Kilbourn."

Nevertheless, Linsley had the typical prejudices of workmen from
the east:

I think that the country has been misrepresented in many ways. The climate I learn from unprejudiced people is very changeable if anything more
so than ours. They have a good deal of rain & snow. It is as cold as Vermont.
A good deal of the land is rolling but there are a great many marshes that
are low & wet & we shall have a plenty of them to go through. In regard to
fever & ague, I guess there is not much danger if we can keep out of the
wet land. It seems they have a good deal in some places, but scarcely any
unless in low land. The people here (unless they are from the East) are
the laziest set I ever saw, loaf around the taverns all day, drinking &
sleeping &c. At the Hotel where we board be it rain or shine the Bar room
is full of the worst kind of loafers & just so wherever I have been. People
seem to have an idea that the land is so rich they can live without doing
anything, & living is cheap, good board for $2.00 per week, clothing mostly
as cheap as with us if not quite.

The survey reached Milton, and still there was no sign of Edgerton.
In exasperation, Linsley wrote, "I commenced on my own responsibility
a preliminary survey to Rock River—eight miles—I commenced a new
line entirely different from any that had ever been run & think I have
about the thing." That was on March 28, 1852, the same day on which,
he reminded his family, he was "twenty-one years old." A week later,

he had not yet "seen a *sign* of Edgerton since the day I left Milwaukee
& no direction from him of any kind & I am almost swamped to know
what to do, but I *keep a doing.* . . . From Rock River to Madison is
28 miles & much of the way good land; the country also is said to be
somewhat settled with '*human people,*' but we should probably
camp out."

In less than a week, however, the perplexities of his job were
resolved when E. H. Brodhead accepted the office of chief engineer,
to begin May 1, though it was too late to shorten the line to Madison
some 12 miles; as Linsley put it, "all this deviation to hit some small
village or somebody's sawmill." Clearly, too, Linsley was much impressed with Brodhead, preferring him to Edgerton: "Brodhead is a
man apparently about 40 years of age, about 5 ft. 11 inches in hight,
well built, fine head,—small dark eyes, hair about as grey as Major
Hodges, & in short a man of very prepossessing appearance."

Small wonder that he preferred Vermont-born President Catlin to
Ohioan Kilbourn. For all his interest in Wisconsin, however, Linsley
hankered strongly after Vermont:

I find a good many Vermonters scattered through the country and they
are universally liked & considered the best population. They keep open
doors & never have taken a cent from us in pay for their hospitality. . . .
How I would like to step into our good cellar, get one good apple & steal
a piece of cheese. I miss these articles more than anything else. I have had
no cheese but once or twice & once only have I had the pleasure of eating
an apple. Apples are absolutely "*scarce*" here & are worth fifty cents a
dozen in Janesville. People here have very little fruit & but very few are
taking any pains to raise any, but they can if they choose raise good fruit.
As for cheese, they appear to be too lazy to make it or else they don't
know how, many know nothing about it.

An enlightening commentary indeed about the state which was to
become the foremost dairy state in the nation!

Toward Stoughtonville, he found "a hard country" with "no inhabitants scarcely but Norwegians, and they live in mud houses," but,
fortunately, Madison he found "a pretty place, the best I have seen in
the State. . . . There are a number of Vermonters here. I. T. Marston
and a Mr. Vilas both have fine places here." By the middle of July,
the survey to Madison was coming to an end, and the pecuniary
difficulties of the engineers promised to ease, for "Mr. Catlin has just
returned from New York & has sold $200,000 worth of the bonds at
96¾¢ & therefore they now have plenty of money."

President Catlin was not disposed to countenance any more delay than necessary. Even though the road had not yet reached Madison, he foresaw that it must reach the Mississippi as soon as possible. He sent the new chief engineer, E. H. Brodhead, out to report on the proposed extension of the line from Madison to the Mississippi.

Though several routes had been suggested, it was clear that the preferred one led from Madison into the Black Earth valley and down this to the valley of the Wisconsin, through which the railroad was to go to the Mississippi valley, and thence up to Prairie du Chien, one of the oldest settlements in the middle west. Prairie du Chien was the fixed terminus, not only because it opened most readily into Iowa and the west, but because Asa Whitney had some years before indicated that village as the point from which his projected railroad to the Pacific must take off. Besides, as Brodhead pointed out, "The northern portion of Iowa is settling rapidly, and will furnish a large business for a railroad. Minnesota is also settling, and is more accessible, as is all the Upper Mississippi country, to Prairie du Chien than any point below it. In fact, Prairie du Chien was settled as a trading post by the American Fur Company, on account of its ease of access to a large tract of country."

The proposed route to the Mississippi from Madison had other distinct advantages. Brodhead reported it correctly as "one uniform level plain on which the road can be constructed. I have never passed over the same extent of country anywhere . . . over which a road can be constructed as cheaply." Moreover, the route was singularly direct; portions of it could be laid in a straight line for twenty miles or more. Still further, it passed through good arable country. Brodhead made his observations carefully:

It is sufficient for me to know from actual observation . . . that the route passes through a highly productive country, diversified with the richest of level and rolling prairie land, and extensive "burr oak openings" withal, in the midst of plenty of timber for fuel and fencing, and well supplied with pure water, and with all in a healthy climate. The soil and climate admit of raising all the varieties of farming products which the Western States are celebrated for producing in great abundance.

The building of this road is to give a great stimulus to the farming interest of the State . . . every acre of land which comes within the influence of this road will be doubled and trebled in value as soon as it is completed. In the spring and fall, when the farmers would most prefer to haul their produce to market, as the navigation is then open, the roads are literally impassable except in the few cases where plank roads have been built. The soil is a deep black vegetable earth, which makes it so productive, but which renders it the worst kind of material for common road.

The route . . . also passes through extensive beds of lead ore [which] must furnish an article of considerable freight upon the railroad. . . . The . . . country must be supplied with pine lumber for building purposes. . . . I can see no reason why the supplies for this large population engaged in lumbering will not find its way over our road to the Wisconsin and then up that river, instead of . . . to Galena, then up the Mississipppi and the Wisconsin to the point where our road reaches the latter, 190 miles above Galena. . . . When I add that this road, being about 190 miles in length, connects on the west with the Mississippi River, which is navigable for 1,800 miles below, and with its tributaries for 800 miles above, the point where the road terminates, with 1,000 miles of lake navigation on the east, and that on each floats a commerce almost unequaled, it does seem to me that the question of the profitableness of the investment in the road is put beyond question.

The residents of the lead-mining country had hoped that the road would pass through their most prosperous cities; but, however much some officials of the road would have liked this to come about, it could not be disputed that the cost of passing through the hilly country around Mineral Point, Platteville, and Dodgeville would be excessive. Brodhead was adamant in his support of the easy Wisconsin River valley route, and the subsequent report of B. H. Edgerton, who undertook to examine the route through the lead-mining country, was conclusive. "The formation of the mineral region is not adapted to cheap railroad construction," he wrote. "A much greater amount of excavation and embankment will be necessary than in the eastern portion of the State, and it will in most cases be rock, costing six or seven times the price per yard that gravel or sand will cost. Grades and curves must be adopted that would also be objectionable, even on a road designed for local traffic."

Ex-President Kilbourn's apprehensions about mismanagement were not ill-founded, and he had some reason to be apprehensive. His review was released to the stockholders in January, 1853. In the intervening year the Southern Wisconsin Rail Road Company had been chartered to build, in the interests of the Milwaukee & Mississippi,* a line from Milton to Janesville, to be completed by 1853, and the LaCrosse and Milwaukee Rail Road Company had been chartered to construct a railroad between those towns, the projectors including Kilbourn and Moses Strong, and the president elected at the first meeting of the directors being Kilbourn.

* Under the presidency of John Catlin, the name of the company was officially changed May 24, 1853, from the Milwaukee & Mississippi Rail Road Company to the Milwaukee and Mississippi Rail Road Company, one of those minuscule alterations of tremendous importance to legal and technical minds.

In that year also the first locomotive was completed at Milwaukee under the direction of James Waters. It was the first locomotive to be built in the state and west of Cleveland, and was completed at the Menomonee foundry; subsequently, in 1853, it headed the first train into Stoughton. The Milwaukee shop had already proved a boon, so early in the career of the company. There a London-born carpenter, William H. McFarland, had built the company's first box car, and had risen to construction superintendent, though later, wishing to resign his construction work, he was persuaded to build a station between Madison and Stoughton on land bought by him, on the understanding that he was to become the agent there and the place was to be named after him; about this station the town of McFarland rapidly sprang up.

Kilbourn had kept a careful watch on the financial reports of the Milwaukee & Mississippi, and he was thus able to point out that the average cost per mile of the railroad was steadily rising. The average cost of the 62 miles from Milwaukee to Milton was "over $21,000 a mile. This average is higher, by some $4,000 per mile, including the cheap prairie line, than is the average cost of the road from Milwaukee to Eagle, including nearly all of the expensive work on the whole division. This difference, added to the line west of Eagle, would swell its cost to over $25,000 per mile." Having brought these facts into the open, Kilbourn bluntly asked, "Now how is it possible that such an expenditure could be made on this cheap portion of the line, unless it be through great mismanagement?"

The result of the mismanagement that Kilbourn foresaw was not, however, to be apparent for several years. Meanwhile, the road continued to expand and grow. Scarcely had the line to Janesville been completed by the Southern Wisconsin Rail Road Company (which was to become part of the Milwaukee and Mississippi in 1856), when the Madison and Prairie du Chien Rail Road Company, organized the previous year by Hercules Dousman, B. W. Brisbois, A. A. Bird, Simeon Mills, Elisha Burdick, and others, consolidated with the Milwaukee & Mississippi and built a road from Milton to Stoughton. The following year the Madison and Prairie du Chien Company, acting for the Milwaukee and Mississippi, extended the road from Stoughton to Madison, for the first time connecting the state capital with other major cities in southern Wisconsin.

The entry into Madison on May 23, 1854, was a gala occasion, indeed. The *Daily Argus and Democrat* went to press early enough so that it could call the program of the day to the attention of the citizens and its editors and employees could themselves be in attendance at the fete. Though some of the gentry from Milwaukee had already come to Madison the previous evening, the majority of them were scheduled to arrive at two o'clock, to be welcomed at the depot by Col. A. A. Bird, one of the oldest citizens of the capital. The procession, which would include "bands, the fire companies, the officers of the Road, the editorial corps, civic societies, the clergy, etc., with invited guests and strangers, would march to the Capitol Park, where a free collation will be served up under the direction of Mr. Stevens, the proprietor of the Capital Hotel, which will open the hilarities of the day." Having waited so long for the coming of the Milwaukee and Mississippi, Madison was determined to spare no effort. There would be an afternoon of speechmaking before the excursion train returned to Milwaukee late in the day, but those who stayed over would be "regaled with a supper at the Capital Hotel at 9 o'clock, which will be a festive occasion, and for which all the luxuries that the market and season afford, will be provided." Furthermore, there would be a ball at Fairchild's Hall, "for the benefit of those who wish 'to trip the light fantastic toe,'" and at midnight a supper would be provided for the dancers, after which the "exercises" would continue at the Hall, "as long as 'the beauty and the chivalry' see fit."

The train arrived punctually, the cynosure of thousands of eyes, for Madison was unexpectedly packed, particularly by farmers and their families, many of whom had never seen a locomotive. The train was of 32 cars, drawn by 2 locomotives. According to the *Argus and Democrat*, it "was about two-thirds as long as the bridge across the Lake, and was said to carry 1,800 or 2,000 people aboard." (This "bridge," which would have been accounted an extraordinary feat of engineering in 1854, was actually only partially a bridge, since its terminal end was hardly being completed when its beginning spans were being converted into an embankment, the shallow water of the lake being filled in, not without a great deal of trouble.) "Two fire companies, with their engines and a small piece of artillery were among the appurtenances. As the cars crossed the bridge and came up to the depot, the scene was a very gay one. The shore was lined with spectators; the parti-colored dresses of the firemen mingled with the sober black and grey of the 'privates,' the whistles shrieked, the cannon reported, the music burst forth, hats waved, and cheer after cheer went up from passengers and our townsmen. The cars stopped and the process of unloading commenced. A string of all ages, sexes, and characters wound its way up town, leaving a larger number still behind to take part in the ceremonies of the day." Col. Bird gave his welcoming speech with restraint and dignity, and the rest of the party proceeded up town.

Unfortunately, as the *Argus and Democrat* had to report on May 24, the people of Madison had been too conservative. They had prepared food enough for 650 people; there were over 2,000:

Those who were so fortunate as to arrive at the table first succeeded in satisfying their appetites [but] there was a great deal of grumbling about the scantiness of the supplies of provision. Our citizens contributed liberally to the expenses of the day, and an amount which it was supposed would be sufficient. If it was not, it was only because so many more were here than were expected. At any rate, it was quite as great a burden as they were able or disposed to bear for the benefit of Milwaukee and the Rail Road Company. It was a profitable day for the Rail Road, if for nobody else. Their receipts from passengers alone could not have been less than $2,500. With a contribution which they could well have made from this sum, there would have been enough to feed everybody and have made them comfortable. But we are not disposed to find fault. It was hardly anticipated that the occasion would result in anything but a failure, except so far as numbers were concerned, and nobody was disappointed. It is perhaps proper to say that there was but little disorder except the natural disorder of a great crowd. The expectation of the morning made way for the excitement of the afternoon, and that for the weariness and discontent of the evening. But few went to bed drunk, and none satisfied. At another celebration may we *not* be there!

The *Argus and Democrat,* after all its initial enthusiasm, carried on thereafter as if its editor had been one of those too late to reach the festive board. Not a month had passsed since that gala opening before it wanted to know in an editorial why the Milwaukee and Mississippi did not advertise. "We have visits almost every day from persons inquiring as to the time of the arrival of the trains at Madison and the departures thence. Our Madison papers are searched in vain for the desired information. . . . We believe that the trains start about daylight in the morning, and shortly after dinner in the afternoon, but not having seen a time-table, or had occasion to look one up, we cannot say precisely."

In July the editor scored the company's policy of "hauling off the train that ran from Milton to Janesville on the arrival of the western cars, and also the train that ran from Janesville to meet the cars coming west, giving us a direct connection with Janesville. Passengers going from here to Janesville by Rail Road will now be obliged to lie over at Milton about four hours, and the same coming from Janesville here. The change is made in order to force the travel to Milwaukee which formerly went by Beloit to Chicago. Such a Rail Road policy will hardly be endured when another road gets here." Within a week, the Milwaukee and Mississippi was again the target of attack, when the paper made an issue of a collision between two freight trains near Palmyra. "The collision was very violent, smashing up both locomotives badly, and two or three cars on each train. . . . The accident is attributed to the sheerest carelessness." The *Journal* joined the cry to such good effect that its editorials were reprinted by the *Argus and Democrat,* the editors of which concluded that the *Journal* had put the grievances succinctly when it editorialized on July 20, 1854: "It would seem to us to be wisdom on the part of the Milwaukee Directors, to so conduct their affairs as to give the greatest amount of satisfaction to this community, while theirs is the only road leading to this point."

These were but the beginning of the usual troubles of running a railroad. There is no evidence that the Milwaukee and Mississippi made any alteration of policy to answer its critics. However short a line it might have, it was now operating over a substantial portion of inhabited Wisconsin, and it was the most important of the railroads which had gone beyond the charter stage in Wisconsin. At the end of 1854 the company listed its equipment as 7 passenger cars (2 being constructed), 4 baggage cars, 201 covered freight cars, 50 uncovered freight cars, 40 gravel cars, 14 hand cars, and 22 locomotives, and announced that the company had "purchased and contracted for a right of way and depot grounds for the entire distance from Madison to Prairie du Chien."

Despite the company's "mismanagement," it seemed to prosper, although it continued to have its trivial troubles, such as certain trains which persisted in running off the track now and then. Chief Engineer and Superintendent Brodhead reduced their speed, explaining, "I have chosen to run the trains at a moderate speed, and at times to subject the passengers to delays rather than to hazard the risk of a collision between the regular trains, and those running at all times on construction account." And there were always "persons who from some unaccountable cause, on every Railroad, attempt to throw the passenger trains off the track, by placing obstructions upon it." However, by 1855, the company's special policemen "detected two of the ringleaders in the very act," and they, according to the report for that year, "are now in the Madison jail, awaiting their trial in April next," though presumably it was not necessary to proceed against them, their arrest alone perhaps serving to deter fellow miscreants.

The financial arrangements of the Milwaukee and Mississippi went ahead smoothly. In order to pay the Chamberlains for the construction of the road from Eagle to the Rock River, the company prepared $600,000 worth of bonds, bearing 8 per cent interest, payable semiannually, to be sold in New York "at the Banking House of Messrs. Duncan, Sherman, and Company," the trustee being George S. Coe, secretary of the Ohio Life and Trust Company; in May, 1853, the president, by a vote of the board, issued $650,000 worth of bonds, secured by a first mortgage on the Janesville branch, and on the road from the Rock River to the Wisconsin, a distance of approximately 64 miles. Again, in 1855, the Milwaukee and Mississippi offered for sale, through Messrs. Atwood & Company in Wall Street, $600,000 worth of first-mortgage bonds bearing 8 per cent. By May, 1855, the board had authorized the issuing of bonds totaling $2,500,000, half of which were to be set apart to be devoted to the construction and equipment of the road from Madison to Prairie du Chien, the trustee of the bondholders being Isaac Seymour, cashier of the Bank of North America. The fiscal report for 1854 listed a "floating debt" of $233,002.80.

During these years, the road crept slowly into western Wisconsin, from Madison to the valley of the Wisconsin, from Black Earth to Arena, and thence down river to Prairie du Chien; moreover, numerous smaller roads, including some companies which were actually at work for the Milwaukee and Mississippi, were extending their rails to various points throughout southern and eastern Wisconsin, looking to ultimate consolidation. The Milwaukee and Watertown, for instance, completed a section from Brookfield Junction, on the Milwaukee and Mississippi, to Watertown, though the employment of green hands resulted in at least one incident which became legend on the line, and subsequently on the Milwaukee and Mississippi, following consolidation; on one occasion, Michael O'Hara, a machinist and engineer, not quite convinced that the two-mile railroad bridge just east of Richards' Cut approaching Watertown would support the weight of a locomotive, started his locomotive,* then jumped off at the head of the bridge, letting the locomotive go on over alone to where the fireman waited to catch it on the far side.

Meanwhile, the LaCrosse Company also completed a line to Horicon; from the south, the Chicago and Northwestern entered Wisconsin from Chicago in 1855; and at last, with the opening of the Lake Shore Road to Chicago, Wisconsin had a rail connection with the east.

The report of the Milwaukee and Mississippi for 1855 was a proud one:

During the past year, two passenger trains have run each way daily over our road, with scarcely the loss of a single trip; we have also run not less than two, and for a considerable portion of the year, five freight trains each way daily. Wood trains have been moving constantly on the road, as well as construction trains. Only one slight collision took place between a wood and freight train, but without injury to any person. 146,185 passengers have

* The *Luther A. Cole*, formerly the Milwaukee, Watertown & Baraboo Valley Rail Road's Number 1, later the Milwaukee and Mississippi's *L. B. Rock*.

been transported over the road without the slightest injury to anyone, except a lady who had her shoulder injured by reason of the breaking of an axle, which threw the passenger car in which she was sitting at the time, off the track.

Indeed, the railroads appeared so prosperous that in April, 1854, the Wisconsin legislature took official cognizance of their prosperity by passing a law requiring the "several railroad and plank road companies now organized or hereafter organized in this State . . . to make out and return to the Treasurer of this State, a true and just statement of the gross earnings of their respective roads for the proceeding year, up to the first day of January . . . and to pay a sum equal to one per cent of the gross earnings of their respective roads."

There was more than one fly in the ointment, however. The defaulting of bonds by many smaller railroads, some of which had never turned a shovel on their proposed lines, coupled with frauds and scandals, brought about a situation which was bound to affect even the oldest and most firmly established companies. The Milwaukee and Mississippi found it necessary in 1854 to "adhere to moderate dividends," wisely "carrying forward to a reserve fund, for the purpose of renewal of the road, and for sinking its funded debt, rather than distribute the whole earnings, and leave the Company without the means of entrenching itself surely and strongly against any and all circumstances, which may chance to arise." The "circumstances" were hinted at in an inexplicably optimistic paragraph not far along in the same report:

The lesson taught this year has been a severe one, but its effects will be conservative and beneficial to the country. The long continued money stringency, the general prostration of railroad credit, and frauds in the overissue of stocks and bonds, will induce caution and give greater security to railroad property. There will be less to fear from competition. The good roads will be able to borrow money sparingly upon hard terms, and the bad will get no support except from their infatuated projectors. . . . The public cannot dispense with their use, and are interested to have them sustained. For these reasons we think the present revulsion in railroad credit will prove in the end beneficial to railroad property as well as to the country.

Such optimism, however, was ill-founded. The Milwaukee and Mississippi was but beginning an era of major trouble. This was due to no one circumstance alone, neither the mismanagement Byron Kilbourn suspected, nor the loss of public faith in railroads. Despite the fact that every sign pointed toward increasing difficulties, the Milwaukee and Mississippi persisted in expansion; it had set out to reach the

Mississippi, and it meant to reach that terminus. By the end of 1856, facing the panic of 1857, the company had gone so far as to make an arrangement with the Prairie du Chien and St. Paul Packet Company to furnish the railroad with two daily lines of steamers each way between Prairie du Chien and St. Paul, "to be in readiness at the opening of navigation in spring . . . to be new, of a large class, great speed, and more comfortably fitted up for passengers than any heretofore plied on the Upper Mississippi."

But 1856 was not ended without the execution to Isaac Seymour of a second mortgage upon the main line of the Milwaukee and Mississippi from Milwaukee to Prairie du Chien, at 10 per cent interest. The directors were, moreover, forced to admit in their report for that year (given in 1857) that the past year had been "one of great financial embarrassment," and that the cost per mile of the road had risen to approximately $29,000. And President Catlin, after several months spent in New York in an effort to raise more funds for the Milwaukee and Mississippi, wrote the treasurer of the road, Anson Eldred, in May, "There is no chance for railroads and will not be for ten years to come. I am only surprised that anybody should pay anything for the stock of any road. I am heartily sick of them." This was in May. By August, he had foreseen major trouble, for he wrote:

The Company must stop all further cash contracts. Will you see to this? We must try to get the road in operation to Prairie du Chien because there is no other way to get out as when through it will earn enough to pay off the floating debt, but if not through it will not earn any more than it is now doing. You must take such steps as you think necessary to meet the emergencies of the Company. I think the directors ought to be called together and the necessities of the Company laid before them. Money must be raised and it is impossible for me to raise it from the securities in time. Will you see to this? I have no notes of the Company to negotiate. You were to send me some. They should be drawn to your order as Treasurer and endorsed by you as Treasurer, say in odd sums—$4,800–$5,900–$9,600, etc., so that they will not appear to have been made paper. They may be drawn at three months, four months, five months, and six months. I could then let Bell & Company put his stamp on them or some other House and sell them through Robbins & Son. I don't see any other way to extend our indebtedness.

Catlin was not at all sanguine; perhaps he was aware of the impending panic of 1857, for in 1856 he declined to serve again as president of the Milwaukee and Mississippi.

He was replaced by the chief engineer, E. H. Brodhead. Having been active in the course of so much construction on the road since his arrival from New England in 1851, Brodhead was well known and equally well liked; his tall, large-framed, broad-shouldered figure was a familiar one. He was keen of eye and one of those firm-mouthed gentlemen who are commonly said to be self-willed and determined; certainly Brodhead was a self-reliant man and, though he was never hasty with his opinions, he spoke with authority when at last he did so. His dignity was such that he was respected by every man on the road, from director to construction worker. It was a somewhat exaggerated respect, in fact; for years a joke was bandied about among the construction crews, attesting to his importance in the eyes of the laborers. According to this story, two Irishmen, employed on the Milwaukee and Mississippi, began to quarrel and ended up with one choking the other. The two were parted, however, but, during the night, the one who had been choked, thinking things over, began to grow angry at the indignity he had endured. "Be gorra," he said, "I would not take that again from Pat!" This, however, seemed not strong enough for him; after a pause, he added, "Be dad, I'd not take it from the praist!" Still dissatisfied, after further cogitation, he exclaimed, "Be jakers, I'd not take it from the Pope of Rome." But he was not satisfied until he had expressed the ultimate in defiance with, "Be Jesus, I'd not take it from ould Brodhead himself!" after which his spirit was appeased and he could sleep.

Brodhead was a shrewd and unerring judge of men. Called upon to rebuke station agent Edward Barber for refusing to open his station at Milton on Sunday to accommodate local people, most of whom were Seventh Day Adventists and worshiped on Saturday, he supported him instead, making it plain that decisiveness of character in its employees was an asset to the Milwaukee and Mississippi, and, through Brodhead's commendation, Barber rose from Milton to station agent at Whitewater, Madison, and Prairie du Chien, as each station became a strategically important one on the growing line.

Brodhead served the road for a salary of $3,500 a year, with $1,000 additional to cover expenses, at which some of the directors protested vigorously against "making that New York fellow rich every year." The town of Brodhead, Wisconsin, was named after him; it had been laid out by him and five other men, who originally owned the town, in the spring of 1856, and it sprang into being the following year when the railroad reached there, populated largely by people from nearby Decatur, which had refused to make any donation to the railroad. Brodhead's term as president was not, however, to be of any great duration or significance; he came into control after a capable president had already decided that events were conspiring against the well-being of railroads.

Yet he made the attempt to take the reins, with his initial objective the completion of the line to Prairie du Chien, now in the last stages of construction down the valley of the Wisconsin, a line on which he left his mark in the platting and naming in 1855 of the village of Mazomanie, after an Indian chieftain whose name meant "he who walks with iron."

The rails pushed west from Madison to Black Earth, and beyond Black Earth to Mazomanie and Arena. Reaching the valley of the Wisconsin, the line passed the historic shot tower at the site of the lost town of Helena—lost because the regulars needed its buildings in the almost farcical war against Black Hawk and his Sac Indians over two decades before; it crossed the river near a little Welsh settlement where lived the forebears of Frank Lloyd Wright. Once on the level land on the west shore of the Wisconsin the railroad laborers erected shanties for a little settlement even while the land on which they built was being entered with the government. This land became the property of A. C. Daley, B. F. Edgerton, and A. G. Darwin, who presently platted a village there, which a widowed schoolteacher, Mrs. Thomas Williams, the first white woman to live at that place, asked permission of the United States land surveyors, who boarded with her, to name Spring Green, because north of her home, in the hollows facing south, the green came so much earlier in the spring than in the surrounding country. From the railroad shanties which were to become the nucleus of the village of Spring Green, the rails pushed steadily south past Lone Rock toward Boscobel and, finally, to Prairie du Chien, at the confluence of the Wisconsin and the Mississippi.

On April 15, 1857, the road to Prairie du Chien was opened, and the river towns near the confluence of the Wisconsin and Mississippi hailed with hurrahs the appearance of the locomotives of the Milwaukee and Mississippi on the shores of the great river. The *North Iowa Times* of McGregor, Iowa, foresaw a great future for northern Iowa:

Be it remembered that on Wednesday, April 15, 1857, at 5 o'clock in the evening, the cars of the Milwaukee and Mississippi Rail Road anchored on the banks of the great river. The shriek of the Lake Michigan locomotive was echoed by the bluffs and responded to by a shrill whistle of welcome from a Mississippi steamer just coming into port. Hundreds of persons were in attendance to witness the arrival of the first passenger train, and when the smoke of the engine became visible in the distance there was such an expression of anxiety as we have seen when a new and great actor is expected on the stage. As the train came in view, and the flags with which it was decorated were seen waving in the breeze, a shout of welcome broke forth from the gazers that told how many hopes of friendly reunions were awakened in the contemplation of an easy and speedy return to their eastern homes. One large banner carried on its silken folds the busy emblem of "Wisconsin, the Badger."

The train consisted of a locomotive, a baggage car, and three passenger cars; the locomotive was the *Prairie du Chien,* newly built at Jersey City, while the cars had been built in the company's shop in Milwaukee under the supervision of John Bailey. The cars impressed even older railroad hands as being handsome, sturdy, conveniently arranged, and well ventilated. A salute of 200 guns by the artillery company met the train at Prairie du Chien. The Milwaukee *Sentinel* signalized the event by announcing that the "iron horse, starting betimes from the shores of Lake Michigan, does at evening slake his thirst in the brimming Mississippi." To symbolize the new connection between the waters, an eight-gallon keg of Lake Michigan water was emptied into the Mississippi with all due ceremony.

The company's optimism in Brodhead's report that the extension of the McGregor, St. Peters and Missouri River Rail Road across Iowa would "increase the business of your road" did not fare well in the face of the mounting lack of faith in railroad companies which was a part of the panic of that year. Moreover, the Milwaukee and Mississippi had operating troubles which contributed to the general attitude. Superintendent William Jervis, reporting on the line to Prairie du Chien, set forth that the main line west of Boscobel was interrupted for a fortnight in May by "the unusual freshet in the Wisconsin River. This damaged embankments which had been put in in winter and not properly finished at the time. It occurred during the heavy spring business and resulted in our losing the bulk of the *through* spring business. Exaggerated reports of the damage had been circulated widely over the country, and although the trains were run, after the damage was repaired, with entire regularity, it was found impossible to counteract the influence of the interruption until the spring business was mainly over." Coincidentally enough, admitted Jervis, the increase in freight on the Upper Mississippi, though much larger than in any previous season, occurred "all in the earlier part of the season, at the time when we were not ready for it, or were suffering from the influence of the impression that our road was seriously damaged and even unsafe for passengers, so that in reality we have only had the benefit of through business about six months of the current year, when business of all kinds suffered from the general derangement, caused by the commercial crisis."

At the same time, alarm about accidents at crossings spurred the Wisconsin legislature to enact a law early in 1857 requiring all railroad companies to put up at highways where crossings occurred large signboards bearing the legend, LOOK OUT FOR THE CARS. Moreover, locomotives must ring bells before crossing any city streets, and trains must "go six miles an hour—no faster" within cities.

The company's plight was still further emphasized by the admission that, during the last quarter of 1856, salaries of agents and clerks, and wages of laborers, had all been reduced by "about twenty per cent." In its report for 1857, issued in 1858, the trend clearly continued, in the immediate conceding of the fact that the past year had been one of great depression, "operating with peculiar hardship upon railroads, and especially upon this Company, embarrassed as it has been with a floating debt of more than $600,000." The company went out of its way, too, to censure the state legislature because it had granted a charter to the Milwaukee and Watertown Rail Road in 1856, as a competing road, "after an expenditure had been made, by this Company, of nearly $5,000,000," and so helping to destroy credit in railroad securities in Wisconsin, a policy on the part of the legislature which was, to put it mildly, "destructive," particularly since that body refused to pass a general railroad law to protect competing lines in some measure. Such a policy, it seemed patent to the company, based on the assumption that competing roads would reduce the expenses of transportation, would serve only to frighten away foreign capital, and would in any case fail of its end except temporarily.

The plight of the Milwaukee and Mississippi was rapidly becoming public property, not so much because of its financial embarrassment, curiously enough, but because of public irritation in Wisconsin about what the public took to be "catering" to the Chicago traffic. The company in 1858 operated 234.41 miles of single track, with 28.28 miles of side track; it owned 43 locomotives, 31 first-class passenger cars, 2 second-class passenger cars, 13 baggage and post office cars, 411 covered freight cars, 107 platform freight cars, 40 gravel cars, 25 small ditching cars, and 37 hand cars. This equipment was sufficiently in evidence to keep up public confidence, but it did nothing to alleviate public irritation.

In mid-1858, the storm broke. On June 21, the Milwaukee *Free Democrat* angrily editorialized:

The mismanagement of this road is beyond human endurance. Milwaukee first breathed the breath of life into this road and has loaned its credit for over $530,000 to build it, and now that it is completed to the Mississippi, it is virtually a Chicago road, controlled by Chicago interests, and runs to Janesville half the time as a branch of the Chicago & St. Paul road, and passengers are dumped there and compelled to lie over for the Chicago train. The Milwaukee trains east and west that connect with the boats on the Mississippi from St. Paul, and the upper towns, stop at Janesville *five*

hours, while the Chicago trains go straight through. By this Chicago arrangement, passengers can start from Chicago some five or six hours later than from
Milwaukee, and reach Prairie du Chien at the same time, and passengers
from Prairie du Chien reach Chicago before the train leaves Janesville for
Milwaukee. The result is, nearly all the trade of Minnesota and Iowa, which
would naturally come to this city goes to Chicago, because it can go there
directly. And the citizens have the satisfaction of seeing the road, which
they have been mainly instrumental in getting built, act as a feeder to
Chicago. We venture to say that if a Chicago railroad had treated Chicago
as shabbily as this road is now treating Milwaukee, public meetings would
have been promptly called, to devise some remedy.

To this the *Sentinel* added a sarcastic note about a score of visiting
editors who "left by the afternoon train and arrived at Janesville at ten
o'clock. There they were kept *five* hours, by the delightful arrangement
of the trains on the Milwaukee and Mississippi Rail Road."

At the same time, the Madison papers cheered a legislative act that
made it a misdemeanor for members of a corporation to make or publish false statements in regard to the corporation, for the purpose of in-
ducing men to invest capital in it or to become members. "We invite
attention to the above clause," editorialized the *Daily State Journal,* "for
the reason that for the first time in legislation, it makes lying on the
part of a railroad officer a criminal offense. Heretofore railroad presidents have lied about their floating debt, etc., like pirates. This lying is
now a misdemeanour. Had this statute been in operation when E. H.
Brodhead issued his written statement about the amount of the floating
debt of the Milwaukee and Mississippi Rail Road, any stockholder who
felt himself aggrieved, or any one who subscribed to the second Mortgage Bonds, could prosecute him for what they deemed an incorrect
statement."

The newspapers of communities whose hopes for a railroad had been
dashed by the beginning of the Milwaukee & Mississippi were particularly unpleasant. The Sheboygan *Journal* pointed out that Milwaukee
and Mississippi stock was selling heavily in New York "at 45¢. This is
the railroad that a little over a year ago was vaunting a dividend of
19%. The shares have fallen about 30% within a few weeks." It went
on gleefully and with arrogant confidence to predict that "no railroad
terminating at Milwaukee will pay a dividend after two years."

The harassed officials were by this time impervious to such attacks;
they had far more serious matters to think about than these attacks, or,
for that matter, the determined feud which existed between the Milwaukee and Mississippi and the postmaster at Arena, which caused the
mail for Dodgeville, Mineral Point, Platteville, and other places between

Galena and Arena to be carried past Arena and left at Boscobel, certainly "a serious inconvenience to a large population," as the *State Journal* put it.

All along the right of way there was a noticeable decline in revenues. At McFarland, Station Agent McFarland recorded service charges which reflected those set down in the company's books from one terminus to another. For the week of June 20 to 27, 1857, for instance, McFarland's records showed a marked decline in the amount of merchandise received at his station:

June 20	J. W. Sharp	1 Box Mdse., 3 Cases Shoes	$ .92
24	J. Robson	5273 ft. Lumber & Loading	19.78
26	P. Johnson	2½ Doz. Forks, 2¼ Doz. Snaths, 1 Scales	.25
	A. Kurtz & Bro.	1 Bale Dry Goods, 1 Box Lustre, 1 Ball Rope, 1 Barrel Vinegar, 1 Box Tobacco, 1 Sack Coffee, 1 Box Saleratus	1.76
	J. W. Sharp	1 Hhd. Crockery, 1 Box Shoes	1.62

The total income was only $24.33. The corresponding week in 1858 was not a great deal better:

June 19	Wm. Hill	1 Cultivator	$ Free
21	W. McFarland	1 Reaper	4.62
22	E. Eighmy	65 Bbls. Salt	32.50
29	Geo. Fleming	1 Bundle C. Fish, 1 Bbl. Sugar	1.00

This showed a slight increase, thanks to Mr. Eighmy's 65 barrels of salt. Doubtless Mr. McFarland's receipts were typical.

Yet, in 1859, the officials of the company, intent upon giving the best possible service, moved to Prairie du Chien the *Lady Franklin,* a boat built to run either on water or on ice, and began to utilize it in ferry service across the Mississippi River to McGregor and north to Harper's Ferry. The *Lady Franklin* was a picturesque craft indeed; though it was small enough to be carried on a single flat car, and bore the name of the Prairie du Chien and St. Paul Railroad, it was for a time an integral part of the Milwaukee and Mississippi. But its use and the inauguration of other innovations could not stem the tide.

There was no discoverable note of optimism in the report issued in 1859, save a brief paragraph about the increasing local freight, which was admittedly "the only encouraging feature exhibited by the operations of the year." The rest of the report was an essay in profound pessimism; there had been no revival of business in the section of the country traveled by the road; the lumber traffic had declined, instead of rising, as anticipated; a steamer and a ferry had had to be purchased to secure the business of northern Iowa, marketed in McGregor. The directors had to admit that the plan for the funding of the floating debt had not been carried out, since "the creditors of the Company in the main refused to accept the third mortgage bonds, and the directors, in justice to those who had taken them, ceased their efforts in view of the declining business of the road, making it doubtful as to their ability to carry out the scheme."

Finally, for the stockholders, there came the most terrifying admission of all. "It is evident that without a vigorous effort, or an arrangement preventing competition, or a revival of business, the road cannot long be retained by the stockholders, and it is submitted to you whether it is not advisable, under the circumstances, to let the trustee of the sinking fund and second mortgage bonds enter into the possession, under an arrangement, or with the understanding that he shall forbear a foreclosure while there is a reasonable prospect that the net earnings will pay up all the mortgage interest now due, within the next two years." This was given out over the signature of President Catlin, who had in 1858 again consented to take the reins after Brodhead's brief incumbency. At the same time Superintendent Jervis admitted that competition had risen out of all expected proportion, that certain sections of the road needed repair badly, and that some portions needed a complete renewal. He pointed to increasing expenditures in the coming years, in addition to which the fencing laws, passed by the Wisconsin legislature and requiring that roads fence their rails away from farm stock, augmented the financial outlay of the company.

The inevitable, now plain even to the board of directors, could not long be held off. In 1860, the company defaulted on all mortgages made on the property, and on May 9, Isaac Seymour, trustee, was appointed receiver of the company, on foreclosure proceedings instituted by him. The claimed indebtedness of the company was close to $6,000,000, in addition to which capital stock in general issue and for farm mortgages amounted to $3,500,000 more. The cost of all the property owned by the Milwaukee and Mississippi was reported on December 31, 1859, to be $8,125,839.17.

On January 18, 1861, the property of the company was offered for sale; three days later the purchasers organized the Milwaukee and Prairie du Chien Railway Company at a purchase price of $7,500,000, payable in first preferred scrip stock with convertible bonds attached ($2,556,000), full paid first preferred stock ($1,095,400), full paid second preferred stock ($1,086,800), and full paid common stock ($2,761,800). The organization articles fixed the number of directors at nine, a majority of whom "shall be citizens or residents of New York"—a cutting blow at the citizens of Wisconsin, and the directors to be chosen by stockholders, each share entitled to one vote, but the directors to elect the officers. From the organization, L. H. Meyer emerged as president, and, thus reorganized, the railroad prepared to carry on its business despite the now trying competition being offered by lines reaching into Wisconsin from Chicago.

The Milwaukee and Prairie du Chien Railway Company had approximately six years to exist before it underwent a metamorphosis which was destined to give it a stability it had never had. It was not a coincidence that its ultimate stabilization came about at the hands of one of the most capable men who had sat among the early directors of the Milwaukee and Mississippi. That man was Alexander Mitchell.

IV. Alexander Mitchell Takes Control

I remember that tea was then $2.00 a pound. That was in 1872 or thereabouts. A price like that was pretty high and Col. W. H. Hamilton never allowed a chest of tea to remain in a way car over night, for fear someone would steal it. On several different occasions he got up in the middle of the night in violent wind and rain-storms to set the brakes on every box car in the yard, so that they would not run out on the main track. Col. Hamilton was very conscientious; he probably worried more about the business of the Milwaukee than he did about himself or his own affairs. The only thing about him—he was a "paper-mill operator," and he wouldn't discard the mill no matter how often I told him I could read by sound; so I had to use the contrivance for some time.

—C. J. CAWLEY

ALEXANDER MITCHELL was perhaps the ablest of all the men who had any part in the formation of the great network of rails which was to grow from the Milwaukee & Mississippi. He was resourceful, intelligent, canny, and in personal integrity had few peers. By the time that he emerged in a controlling position, he was already in some respects a legendary figure. Moreover, he had had ample experience with trouble of all kinds to qualify him for the dominant position in the greater Milwaukee and St. Paul Railway Company to come.

Mitchell had arrived in Milwaukee in 1839. He announced his presence in that village of slightly more than a thousand people in the Milwaukee *Advertiser* of June 15 of that year with a reminder that all insurance stockholders must make a payment of $10 on each of their shares on August 1 at the company's Milwaukee office. Two months later, the *Sentinel* carried a somewhat more expanded announcement:

> Insurance.—The Wisconsin Marine and Fire Insurance Company have commenced business in Milwaukee, and are ready to enter into contracts of insurance at low rates of premium. The Company will also receive money on deposit, and transact other moneyed operations in which by their charter they are allowed to engage.
>
> Alex. Mitchell,
> Secretary.

This company was, in fact, a bank. It was not called a bank because banks were in such bad odor at the time that they were universally distrusted, by legislators as well as the people. This distrust, however, and the disastrous experiences that many had had with the rag money of worthless institutions, did not in any way do away with the need for banks. Some kind of circulating medium had to come into being, quite apart from the common tickets then in circulation, marked "Good for a drink," "Good for a pound of tea," and the like; and it was George Smith, a Scottish farmer, who, with a group of banking friends, formed in Chicago an "insurance company," the charter of which, while specifically denying banking privileges in general, did permit some banking privileges in detail.

68

Smith's certificates of deposit, engraved by the Boston Bank Note Company, with promise of payment on demand, were put forth as banks put out notes, but, unlike many contemporary banks, Smith invariably redeemed his issues whenever and wherever they were presented for payment. His success in Illinois turned his attention to Wisconsin, where he approached a Milwaukee friend, Daniel Wells, and prevailed upon him to get for him "a charter with franchises as like a bank as you can, but call it what you will." Wells' insurance bill allowed Smith's company, in addition, "to insure on ship and shore," to receive money on deposit, to give certificates, to loan on the same terms as individuals, and to employ its surplus capital in moneyed operations, "provided nothing herein contained shall give banking privileges."

This charter was passed by the territorial legislature and approved by the governor late in February; by May, $101,300 had been subscribed, and a salary of $1,100 was voted to the secretary of the new-born company. To serve as that secretary, Smith had ready in Chicago a fellow Scotsman he had imported from the farming country northwest of Aberdeen, a young man of some banking experience, following his brief native schooling, and also some legal training. Though he was not yet 22, a fresh-looking young man with mild blue eyes and ruddy cheeks, Alexander Mitchell came to Milwaukee, and thereafter steadily and consistently demonstrated the shrewd judgment of George Smith, who left everything to Mitchell's own decision and did not need to check or advise the reticent, taciturn, firm-chinned young man in whom he had such well-placed confidence.

The insurance business was not intended to be anything more than a front for the banking activities of the establishment, though some insurance policies were issued. Mitchell pursued the business of banking assiduously, and with meticulous care. The citizens of Milwaukee tended to doubt that anyone who looked so young could possibly have enough experience to succeed; moreover, the spruceness of Mitchell's long-tailed dress coat and Scotch plaid pantaloons excited a good deal of laughter, and the fact that he lodged in his office and kept it clean himself also made of him an object of sport. Mitchell had no time to take notice of doubts about himself; he had little time for society, and he maintained his business with scrupulous exactitude. Before he loaned or accepted money, he knew everything that could be known about the applicant or depositor; he kept himself fully informed not only about the businesses of his fellow citizens, but also about such aspects of their private lives as might be presumed to affect their business dealings. In this he was aided by Daniel Wells, who knew Milwaukee and Wisconsin of that day as well as anyone. In a very short time, those sharp gentry who had thought Mitchell might prove an easy mark to fleece had learned to leave him strictly alone.

The immediate business of the firm was the buying of farms for in-coming settlers who did not have the money to pay the prices demanded in advance by the government, and then signing a contract to deed the farms to the settlers at the end of four years, or sooner, if settlers paid down an advance upon the government price. This was a service which won Mitchell and his establishment untold numbers of friends. The secondary business in which Mitchell engaged was the issuing of cer-tificates of deposit. Within ten years of the opening of his office, Mitchell had in circulation certificates amounting to $1,000,000, prom-ising payment on demand, and serving as legal tender far more reliably than any bank notes put forth except those of the Chemical Bank of New York, certainly more so than the bank notes in common circula-tion, so readily repudiated in the midwestern states and territories of that time, when specie often had to do duty in as many as ten banks, being rushed from bank to bank just in advance of the inspector's arrival, and thus, in time, contributing to the collapse of banking. Mitchell's methods were astonishingly scrupulous; time and again his certificates were questioned; on one occasion $100 worth of them were collected from doubtful holders in La Porte, Indiana, and sent by mes-senger to Smith's Chicago office for redemption, and, on being re-deemed promptly, dollar for dollar, increased faith in the establish-ment of which Mitchell conducted the Wisconsin branch.

Mitchell's success was so outstanding that, within 14 years of the time when he began working at less than $100 a month, Mitchell had bought out George Smith and was the complete master of the entire business. He had to contend not only with the doubts of many people, which subsided as his record of immediate redemption of his certificates grew longer and longer, but also with the envy of imitators, who could not achieve his success, and the suspicion of the legislature. Repeated panics were fomented against his establishment, even before Mitchell had bought Smith out. On the day after Thanksgiving, 1849, Chicago and De-troit bankers combined to crush Mitchell by presenting a large amount of certificates for redemption at the same time that their paid agents circulated in Milwaukee with tales of the collapse of Smith's bank, the source of Mitchell's money; but Smith's swift riders had reached Chi-cago and money had begun to flow to Milwaukee before Mitchell had exhausted the specie on hand, so that by nightfall money had begun to come back into his bank, and the raid had failed. Such incidents served only to renew and strengthen public confidence.

Mitchell managed also to maintain his establishment against legislative charges of illegality. Strictly speaking, Mitchell's banking activities may very well have been contrary to the intention of Wisconsin territorial law; but the law in question was a negative one, not.a law recognizing the need for an institution like Mitchell's and putting it under strict regulation—though no law could have regulated it with any greater strictness than Mitchell himself did. Yet year after year every legislature attempted to put his affairs into the hands of a receiver, several times vacating his charter, but with such unsureness that no steps were actually ever taken against Mitchell, and always contrary to the will of the people. The hilarious stupidity of the distrustful legislature was nowhere better illustrated than in the fact that, while it drew up acts declaring Mitchell's certificates to be of no legal value and imposing a five-dollar fine for every one taken in or paid out, the expenses of the same territorial government were being paid by Mitchell's establishment out of money borrowed against the always late payments of the United States. As a crowning irony, when later the bonds of the state of Wisconsin had fallen into disrepute, it was Mitchell who saved them by the simple expedient of recommending to the state government that insurance companies should be obliged to add Wisconsin bonds to their securities; the ensuing competition for them among the companies brought them back up to par and secured the sinking credit of Wisconsin banks. Mitchell's business did not openly become a bank until the Wisconsin act of 1852 authorized banking once more.

Meanwhile, Mitchell had from the beginning of the agitation for railroads shown a strong interest. He was content to sit back and watch developments for some time, though he was part of the directorate of the Milwaukee & Mississippi from 1849 to 1855, and once again in 1858, when, presumably well aware of the fact that the company was tottering, he did not elect to serve again. As a financier, Mitchell's primary interest lay in preserving as much of the control of the railroads as possible in Wisconsin; he looked upon Asa Whitney's project of making Wisconsin the emporium of the greater west, which was to include all the Pacific domains even beyond China, as far too visionary for immediate consideration. He was only amused by the attempts to influence the territorial legislature on any such grounds, though supporters of Whitney's project, who saw the Milwaukee & Mississippi as a link in that project, were vociferous in their petitions to the legislature, aided and abetted by memorials from surrounding states and from eastern states as well. Nevertheless, Mitchell well knew that Whitney's agitation, which ranged from the Royal Geographical Society of London to the territorial areas of the old northwest, and included even Robert Stephenson, the inventor of the locomotive, could not but aid the con-

struction of railroads throughout Wisconsin, and, though he knew that
the project Whitney cradled was impractical for the time being, he did
not speak out against it.

The practical-minded Mitchell tended to look to first things first. He
saw the products of Wisconsin mines and farms going to waste or selling at a loss; he envisioned the same thing happening to Wisconsin lumber, as that industry developed beyond the stage when the rivers served
it, and he was one of the first advocates of a railroad to Superior, through
the heart of the Wisconsin forests. Interest in the Milwaukee & Mississippi was not enough to contain his own enthusiasm, however; he did
not see the Milwaukee & Mississippi in itself as the necessary railroad;
he saw only the importance of extending rail connections as widely as
possible throughout Wisconsin, and then beyond its borders.

Mitchell, however, did not come actively to the fore in the consolidation and control of railroads in Wisconsin until 1863, when, on May 5,
the Milwaukee and St. Paul Railway Company was organized under his
aegis. However, Mitchell had been so active in the background that it
is no exaggeration to say that he had a greater personal investment in
railroads in Wisconsin than any other man. Moreover, he had had from
the beginning a quiet conviction that the spawning of small, separate
roads could not go on, that some unification must come. As a financier,
Mitchell well knew that only a strongly unified system built around
the original Milwaukee & Mississippi line could begin to compete with
railroads outside the state. Not only did he have a financial interest in
almost every line, but he was in some unobtrusive way connected with
almost every one, beginning with the old Milwaukee and Waukesha.
He was one of the first commissioners of the Milwaukee and Watertown, chartered in 1851, he served for a time as a director of the
La Crosse and Milwaukee, and in a similar capacity he served lesser
roads. In almost every road with which he was connected, however
remotely, he dispensed wise counsel, which was not always heeded.

Mitchell's canniness served him in good stead. He was a shrewd and
capable judge of men. He knew very well that Kilbourn, for instance,
was impulsive and impatient, as well as ambitious, and, for all his knowledge, could not be depended upon to act with the greatest caution and
wisdom; he was also aware that Moses M. Strong, first president of the
La Crosse and Milwaukee, was motivated in all his acts connected with
railroading by the personal discomfort he experienced jogging over the
primitive roads of the day to and from his home in Mineral Point. He
could observe the carelessness with which Strong committed himself to
every suggestion. When H. Croswell of Ripon wrote to Strong suggesting that a railroad might well be practical to connect Mineral Point

with the Baraboo Valley, to connect with the La Crosse in the north, and the Illinois Central in the south, Strong replied in such terms that Croswell could not doubt but that the rails were coming straight up from Mineral Point without delay; when Christian Obrecht wrote from Sauk City to inquire about the chance of a railroad from Mineral Point to Sauk City, despite the proximity of the Milwaukee and Mississippi tracks nine miles away at Mazomanie, Strong assured him that he was "interesting" himself "in it all I can," and saying that only pending legislation in Madison was needed to amend the charter and so bring this about, to which end he had already asked Senator Quimby of Obrecht's home county to introduce a bill. All these promises came to nothing, and Strong was even then well past the peak of his popularity in legislative and railroad circles, just as Kilbourn was, for Kilbourn had become so involved in scandal that his retirement from railroading was an urgent necessity.

Unlike these and other gentlemen, Mitchell exercised the greatest caution at all times. He seldom committed himself to anything on paper; the correspondence of Strong, Kilbourn, and others is filled with terse notes from Mitchell in this vein: "I have been unable to induce the Directors . . . to do anything about your application. When you come over here I will talk the matter over with you." Quite manifestly it was the design of Alexander Mitchell to take no responsibility for the actions of people who, though seeking his advice, did not accept it consistently enough to help themselves; in this he used the kind of common sense which too many of the promoters lacked, and it was this common sense which enabled him to deal with the collapse of railroading in Wisconsin touched off by the panic of 1857.

Yet, to anyone with less vision and self-confidence, the time of Mitchell's emergence as a powerful force in railroading would have seemed anything but propitious, for the railroads were never in worse odor. This was due in Wisconsin to two factors that were in turn the direct result of early Wisconsin legislation, which included a prohibition against state aid of any kind for any internal improvement. The factors were such as to arouse the maximum opposition to further railroad enterprises on the part of both the people and the legislature, for both bodies were vitally concerned. Of the two, the more important was the aftermath of the Milwaukee and Waukesha's unique farm mortgage plan.

The collapse of the Milwaukee and Mississippi, and the simultaneous collapse of other lesser roads, brought about a similar collapse of the farm mortgage system, and laid the farmers open to foreclosure. Since the railroad companies had sold the mortgages given to eastern interests at something less than face value in order to obtain ready cash, the foreclosure could justifiably be looked upon as a profitable investment. Farmers all over Wisconsin had taken part in the railroad mortgages, and the actual fact of foreclosure enraged them; all their one-time enthusiasm turned into a bitter conviction that they had been swindled, and they swiftly organized, even to the extent of publishing a newspaper, the Hartford *Home League*, which late in 1860 charged the railroads with seven specific illegalities by means of which the farmers had been swindled. According to the *League*,

They took stock of the farmers upon the express condition that the roads should be laid in certain localities, and after the stock was thus obtained, the right of way was altered to suit the private speculations of the directors. They made out false reports and false statements in order to show the road to be in a better condition than it really was, and to induce the farmers from such statements to mortgage their farms for stock. They issued large amounts of bogus and fictitious stock in order to overshadow the Farm Mortgage interest, and perpetuate themselves in office. They sold the capital stock of the Company at a ruinous discount in order to raise money with which to pay semi-annual dividends that they had declared, falsely representing that the money thus paid out was the legitimate earnings of the road over and above expenses. They colluded with each other and made contracts with themselves for the building and operating of the road at the most extravagant prices. They bought up large tracts of real estate, and then altered the line of the road so as to accommodate their own land and enhance the value of their own property. They continued to take Farm Mortgages when they knew that their corporations were bankrupt.

In these circumstances, the farmers insisted, the eastern investors were little more than accessories to the swindle.

The *Home League's* attack on the railroads, particularly the Milwaukee and Mississippi, aroused considerable bitterness, particularly because the vociferous secretary of the *League* was one Deacon Justus Carpenter, who loudly trumpeted that "not one of these mortgages now outstanding was obtained by other than false and fraudulent representations." Deacon Carpenter, however, had himself been one of the most active supporters of the farm mortgage plan, and had urged farmers to mortgage their farms and invest the money in the Milwaukee and Mississippi. Carpenter's attack particularly irritated the Milwaukee and Mississippi, and the company made an official reply:

It is worthy of notice, that Deacon Carpenter not only regarded the enterprise in a pecuniary light, but he got it associated with the millenium [referring to Carpenter's early support of the railroad]. In some way or other it was to hasten the introduction, or facilitate the approach, or constitute one of the chief glories of that blissful era. But we have no evidence that the Road has yet ushered in the millenium. . . . Now that the Deacon has got the road, he is rather anxious than otherwise to defer the millenium until he has got rid of paying his mortgage, and had sufficient time to slander and abuse some of us who were the earliest and most useful friends he had in the State. If in some of his serenest hours he could be induced to remember a pecuniary obligation to one of us, of many years standing, for obtaining for him a discharge from his debts under the bankrupt law, and could be induced at the same time to cancel said obligation, we should thereafter tolerate his abuse with remarkable composure. We expected the Deacon would favor "repudiation," for it is a habit of long standing with him. We know of no one more devoted to that principle, and would respectfully recommend him as a candidate for higher honors in the *League*. He would also wear the "livery of Heaven" in serving the mortgagors, and without doubt "repudiate" the purchase money of that article.

The company pointed out further that

Messrs. Finch, Brodhead, and Eldred, neither secured any mortgages, nor made any efforts to obtain any, and Mr. Holton is responsible for the means adopted in securing but a few of the vast number that now perplex the State. Let the farmers consider who these men are, against whom the *League* brings this terrible charge of falsehood and fraud. The most active agents in projecting and enforcing the farm mortgage scheme, are now the leading members in honor and influence in the *League*. If, in obtaining the mortgages, they deceived and betrayed the farmers, will they be less likely to deceive and betray them now? . . . It is alleged that in order to obtain mortgages from the farmers, the Directors executed mortgages upon their own property, which they released as soon as the farmers were thoroughly entrapped.

The company also issued a list of the mortgages outstanding against the directors, revealing that Crocker, Clinton, and Tweedy each had $5,000 outstanding, while Walker and Kneeland had $10,000, and, altogether, the directors of the Milwaukee and Mississippi had invested through mortgages no less than $54,500.

But the hapless farmers were far more ready to be whipped up into a fever of indignation against railroads than to listen to any argument in support of the railroad's position. The newspapers advised caution. The *League's* charges against the directors of the Milwaukee and Mississippi did not impress the Madison *State Journal*, which editorialized at length: "While we would not sustain the Shylocks who fatten upon the blood taken from the heart of honest industry, we would not counsel resistance to legal claims, however inequitable, until all reasonable means of compromise and relief have been exhausted. . . . The address in our judgment savors rather too much of personal bitterness and malevolence to commend it to the favor of the Company or the sympathies of the people."

M. H. Carpenter, an attorney for the state, proposed a remedy—one of many, most of them hysterical—when he called for the repeal of all the railroad charters in Wisconsin. He would have had the state "resume the franchises and property of the corporations; form new companies in which the stock should be held in proportion to the means really invested in the building of the roads, and thus fully protect all the just rights of all parties." The *League* managed to foresee every angle in its approach to the problem; in a paragraph about dealing with the legislature, it offered the proper course for dealing with an elected official who did not "do right"—his constituents must, "on his return from the trust he has violated, greet him with a halter and hang him on the highest tree in his district!"

The furore became so great that the state government, particularly the legislature and the governor, had no alternative, as politicians, but to fall into line. In his annual message of 1861, Governor Alexander W. Randall charged that "The railroad mortgages were conceived in fraud, executed in fraud, and sold or transferred in fraud," a charge which could hardly be substantiated in fact, but which was mild compared to what was to follow in the determination of the legislators to satisfy the yearning of their constituents for vengeance upon all those who, as they maintained, had "swindled" them. The farmers were already banding together to thwart foreclosure sales; they attended sales en masse, intimidated undesirable bidders, and, in some cases, kept bidders away by violence. This form of pressure was brought also against men who were candidates for any office. "No man in the vicinity," said a writer in the *League*, "has any right for an office of trust, profit, or honor, in the gift of the people, unless he is known to be 'sound on the goose,' and any attorney who dares to receive their mortgages for collection, has a poor show for anything better than to be 'hanging around loose' somewhere in some out of the way locality where solitude is the chief attraction."

The farmers realized that only by legislation could their homesteads be saved, and to that end they dedicated themselves. The legislators were not at all averse to legislating to save the farmers. Immediately after they came together, after the disaster of 1857, they enacted a law providing that if the mortgagor could prove to the satisfaction of a court or a jury that he had been induced to sign by fraudulent representations of the railroad company's agent, the action of foreclosure should be discharged, and costs assessed against the plaintiff. If the railroads had still owned the mortgages, this law might have been valid; in most cases, however, the eastern purchaser represented a party not covered by the law, which could not—even though it attempted to do so—apply to such purchasers. The result was, of course, twofold; while the law was on the books and en route to the Wisconsin supreme court, it constituted a delaying action during which no proceedings could take place lest their legality be challenged; in 1860, the supreme court, with no alternative, declared the law invalid.

The tactic, however, was not abandoned. Promptly in 1861, the legislature passed the farm mortgage stay law, with twenty-seven separate sections, which included the unconstitutional law of 1858, designed primarily to so handicap and tax those taking action to foreclose railroad farm mortgages as to discourage any such action from the start, and to make impossible the successful prosecution of any such suit. As a result, the east began to look upon Wisconsin as a hotbed of radicalism, and its legislature was charged with deliberately aiding the state's citizens to repudiate their just debts, though the same cry rose in protest from the commercial centers of Wisconsin. The legislature's action aroused such rancor that it was seriously proposed in the east that petitions be circulated to urge the legislature of New York state to empower aggrieved citizens of New York to seize the property of Wisconsin citizens within the jurisdiction of the state of New York in satisfaction of the mortgages, should the proposed legislation be enacted into law. Law it became, nevertheless, and once again Governor Randall approved and signed it, and once again, in the following year, in the case of Oatman vs. Bond, the Wisconsin supreme court dismissed the law as invalid.

The legislature's next act, after adopting a statute authorizing railroad corporations to reimburse the makers of mortgages in certain fixed proportions—an authorization none of the corporations felt inclined to act upon—was to pass a law to compel the Milwaukee and St. Paul to retire mortgages given to the La Crosse and Milwaukee and the Milwaukee and Horicon, two lines which the Milwaukee and St. Paul had taken over, by forcing the company to pay an annual 12 per cent of its gross earnings into a state sinking fund, until such time as the company had accumulated in this manner enough money to lift the mortgages. Failure to comply would result in receivership. This law was too much for even the governor of Wisconsin, and no attempt to enforce it was ever made. Succeeding legislation, modeled upon the legislation of 1858, followed a course now rapidly becoming a pattern: from heated enactment straight through slow court procedure to invalidation by the Wisconsin supreme court, every legislature from 1858 to 1863 passing one or more such laws, numbering fourteen in all, in the hope of relieving the railroad farm mortgagors.

While these laws were invariably declared unconstitutional, and while they fixed Wisconsin in the eyes of the financial circles of the east as a very bad risk, they did serve, paradoxically, to alleviate the difficulties of the mortgagor, for, because of the laws, so many eastern mortgage holders, fearing to gamble with costs of prosecution to foreclose, came to some compromise with the mortgagors. No matter how much the farmers were enraged at the actions of the supreme court, the court had no alternative but to declare the mortgage legislation unconstitutional under the constitutional provision prohibiting the state legislature from passing laws which impaired the obligation of an existing contract; despite the fact that eight out of the ten circuit courts in Wisconsin disagreed with the position of the supreme court, the high tribunal was correct, and subsequent attempts to purge the court were of no avail, and though the last attempt, in 1863, in the contest between Judge Dixon and M. M. Cothren, was almost successful, the farmers had to face the fact that a reckoning must at last be made.

There were still malcontents; it was too much to expect the embattled farmers simply to give up. More homesteads were saved by intimidation of lawyers and agents at foreclosure sales and by ostracism or rough treatment of purchasers of mortgaged farms. The state league of mortgagors sent a long address to the Milwaukee and Mississippi, not only reciting the history of the mortgagors, but indicating that greater violence might be the only solution. "Will you *force* us from our homes?" the league demanded. "When you resort to force, this promise we will keep, though it should be the last:—*We will meet that force in kind.* In doing this, we shall not stop to reckon how much we can bleed and live. With our lives only, will we render up our firesides."

The roads had also to contend with violence to railroad property. The angered farmers and their adherents developed an all-consuming hatred for anything pertaining to the railroad; they placed obstructions on the tracks, damaged trestles, displaced rails, destroyed bridges, cut telegraph poles, and even went so far as to fire depot buildings. Track torn up on the Milwaukee and St. Paul Railway, coupled with other outrages, made it necessary for a time for the company to abandon its night passenger service between Milwaukee and St. Paul. In the midst of this violence, the Milwaukee and Mississippi underwent its sale on January 18, 1861, to L. H. Myers, on behalf of the trustees, creditors, and assenting bondholders, for $2,165,400. And within the week thereafter, the road fought its first major snowstorm, which blocked traffic so effectively that trains leaving Milwaukee took hours to reach Waukesha, and got no farther. Amusingly, a snowbound train out of Madison carried legislators and lobbyists en route to Washington, D. C., so that the *State Journal* had a note of humor with which to leaven the anger of the farm mortgagors in an article about the train which "had on board not only Judge Howe and Messrs. Sloan and Hanchett, but a large force of lobby members, a majority of whom are earnest applicants for official positions under Mr. Lincoln's administration, and 'sharp-set' for endorsements from our Senators or members of Congress. What a night those unfortunate members of Congress must have passed, stuck in a snowdrift and all retreat from the aforesaid applicants cut off!"

The farmers, aided by hamstringing legislation, however illegal it was, could afford to bide their time. This policy served them well, for, as time passed, the majority of the farmers managed to come to some kind of settlement, favorable on the whole, with the eastern mortgage holders, the average basis of cancellation being approximately 50 per cent of face value.

The railroad companies, suffering too because of the panic of 1857 and its aftermath, did not sit idly by during all this agitation. The Milwaukee and Mississippi made particularly gratifying settlements at the time of its reorganization in 1861 as the Milwaukee and Prairie du Chien Company, when stock held by its mortgagors was exchanged at a ratio of two shares of new stock for three of the old. In the summer of 1862, the Milwaukee and Prairie du Chien entered into an agreement with a committee of mortgagors to retire all its farm encumbrances, and on extremely liberal terms satisfied $500,000 worth of mortgages. The result of this action was highly beneficial to the Milwaukee and Prairie du Chien; approximately 750 farmers escaped foreclosure along its line because of the settlement made by the company, and this, in the light of considerably less satisfactory settlements by other roads, heightened public appreciation of the road and considerably alleviated the adverse impression made by its collapse only a short time before.

The railroad farm mortgage situation was destined to drag on in one form or another for two decades, but the peak of the agitation was in the Civil War years, at a time when the railroads were performing many wartime services, particularly in the carrying of soldiers, who were transported at the same rate as for any government service. To bring about the realization of his dream of keeping for Milwaukee its own back country, and not permitting it to go to Chicago railroads, Alexander Mitchell had to struggle grimly against the antirailroad sentiment which was rife throughout Wisconsin, and particularly in the very areas through which the roads were laid. Nor was this the only major difficulty Mitchell had to face; with acquisition of the La Crosse and Milwaukee in 1863, the Milwaukee and St. Paul inherited also its land-grant troubles and the dubious distinction of ownership of a scandal of such proportions that for decades after its exposure the people of Wisconsin harbored a profound distrust of every kind of corporative business.

It inherited also a feud already famous in the annals of central Wisconsin, one which was to end in the establishment of the most famed vacation spot in the state within a few miles of a ghost town. The La Crosse and Milwaukee, moving north from Portage in 1852, crept slowly toward Newport and the crossing of the Wisconsin at that point, where it was hoped that the road would "take a portion of the immense lumber trade of the north, and be thus directly connected with all northern Wisconsin." However, the Newporters, confident that the La Crosse and Milwaukee must come by way of Newport, persuaded themselves that they might get rich by holding their land at a fantastically high price. What they did not know was that engineers of the road had already looked favorably toward an alternate route not far away which would enable the road to save on the construction of a bridge at a place where the river passed between rock walls in a comparatively narrow gorge, which a bridge only 310 feet long could span, rising 80 feet above the water, sufficiently high to allow for a double wagon-way beneath the track. Aware of this possibility, certain of the Newporters, irate at those of their fellow citizens who were holding their land for high prices, removed to the proposed site of the alternate crossing and founded Kilbourn City, a mile or so away. The railroad was not the only consideration; the location of a dam across the Wisconsin was also in doubt, but this, too, was shifted to the site of Kilbourn City, though, as Josiah Bailey later explained in a public statement published in the *Wisconsin Mirror*, of Kilbourn City, even after the land for the dam had been selected, Garret Vliet, who had led the exodus from Newport, suggested that $1,000 only be paid down for the land, and the balance in 90 days, thus allowing the Newporters to come to their senses and sell their land reasonably, in which case the $1,000 would be forfeited. But the Newporters, serenely confident that the dam and railroad must be built at Newport, refused until too late; the directors of the La Crosse and Milwaukee fixed upon Kilbourn City as the site for the crossing, and the *Mirror* proudly announced on July 1, 1856, that the road had been "permanently located at Kilbourn City . . . beyond all possibility of a disturbance hereafter." This was a body blow to Newport, and the *Mirror* added insult to injury when it referred to Kilbourn City as a separate city, quite different from Newport, which, it took pains to point out to its exchanges, was but "a small village a mile and a half below Kilbourn City." By the end of 1857 the first train crossed the bridge at Kilbourn, and the travelers on it had opportunity to see the wild beauty of the famous Dells of the Wisconsin; while down the river, within shouting distance, Newport was languishing and fading into the ghost town it was destined to become, abandoned and forgotten.

The land-grant scandal, like the railroad farm mortgage problem, rose from the constitutional prohibition against state aid in any kind of internal improvements apart from those promulgated by the state itself. Congress, however, had bestowed upon Wisconsin an area equivalent to one-tenth the total land area of the state for the purpose of encouraging railroad projects. The initial grant provided for one northeastern and one northwestern railroad, and there was an immediate contest for possession of these land grants among the various railroad companies chartered. In October, 1856, the northwestern grant was conferred upon the La Crosse and Milwaukee, while the northeastern grant was conferred upon the Wisconsin and Lake Superior Railroad, agent of an association later to become the Chicago and Northwestern.

It was soon learned, however, that the first act granting the La Crosse Company these lands had been vetoed by Governor Coles Bashford; that, subsequent to this veto, Byron Kilbourn, president of the La Crosse Company, paid a visit to the governor and spent some time in Madison; that a second act was then passed substantially the same as the first, which the governor signed. Two more revelations were quick to follow. Ex-Governor Barstow was president of the St. Croix and Superior Railroad Company, chartered in 1853, which had an agreement with the La Crosse Company that it share the La Crosse Company's grant, an arrangement which was consummated in January, 1857, when $1,000,000 of unsecured bonds of the La Crosse Company were issued and delivered to the St. Croix Company in satisfaction of any claim it might have to the line of the road. The second revelation was even more startling: unsecured bonds of the La Crosse Company were put on sale by unauthorized persons who were not known either to be in the business of buying and selling securities or to be investors in railroad securities.

Two years after the 1856 grant, Governor Alexander W. Randall instituted an investigation into the grant to the La Crosse and Milwaukee Company, and this investigation revealed that Byron Kilbourn's visit to the capital had been an extremely lucrative one for the state government, for Kilbourn had managed to effect a bribe of such proportions that, in effect, he had bought up the entire state government, exclusive of the supreme court. No less than $842,000 of the La Crosse Company bonds had been distributed by the enterprising Kilbourn, whose point of view had clearly undergone some alteration since his experiences with the Milwaukee & Mississippi. Of the total amount of the bonds, $50,000 had gone to the governor, $335,000 to state assemblymen, $175,000 to state senators, $16,000 to clerks, and $246,000 to various persons in and near the capital and presumably of some influence. Specifically, 13 senators and 59 assemblymen received stocks and bonds in amounts up to $25,000 each, none lower than $5,000; Governor Bashford, in addition to his $50,000, had virtually blackmailed the La Crosse and Milwaukee Company out of $15,000 more by refusing to certify the first 20 miles constructed under the grant until the company had cashed bonds to that amount at par value. In addition to the governor, assemblymen, senators, clerks, and other influential persons, Editor Rufus King of the Milwaukee *Sentinel* received $10,000 in bonds, while Editor Moritz Schoeffler of the *Wisconsin Banner* and Editor S. D. Carpenter of the *Wisconsin Patriot* received $5,000 each in bonds.

Though Madison, as early as the 1850's, had become a mecca for lobbyists, where they spent most of their time entertaining legislators in a house at the corner of Monona Avenue and West Doty Street facetiously called "Monk's Hall"—though the public called the rendezvous the house of "the Forty Thieves"—it remained for Byron Kilbourn and the lobbyists for the La Crosse and Milwaukee Railroad Company to teach the lobbyists the meaning of real corruption. Kilbourn's overweening ambition, coupled with his impatience, contributed to his downfall; his associate was the one-time legislator and speaker of the Wisconsin House, Moses M. Strong. Together, they managed to obtain the land they wanted and to prevent an investigation for some years.

But the investigation instigated by Governor Randall went forward, nevertheless, and uncovered as unsavory a scandal as Wisconsin ever experienced. The report which was subsequently published went out of print almost overnight, because many persons named in it got hold of it and destroyed copies by the score. The report was issued on May 13, 1858, and was as notable for the extent of the corruption revealed as it was for the narratives of the few legislators who had not yielded to temptation. Senator C. Latham Sholes of Kenosha, later an inventor of the typewriter, refused to consider the offer of Kilbourn and his associates; so did Senator Amassa Cobb of Mineral Point, who said he had been approached by an agent of Kilbourn's and explained, "I asked him what was the amount of the capital stock of the company. He replied, $10,000,000. I told him to say to Byron Kilbourn that if he would multiply the capital stock by the number of leaves in Capitol park and give me the amount of money, and then have himself, Moses Strong, and Alex Mitchell blacked and give me a clear title to them as servants for life, I would take the matter under consideration."

Other legislators were not so staunch, however. The methods used were in themselves not unique. "The bribery or the buying up of a great majority of the legislature is discovered in the background as a tame fact," according to the report, "while the ingenuity displayed in the attempt to veil the transaction beyond the possibility of deception is so supremely unique as to extort attention. The actors seem not to have been mindful of the fact that no lid was ever large enough to completely cover up itself." Kilbourn laid the groundwork for the corruption of the legislature by making it known that, if his company received the land grant, all legislators who supported that end would be "liberally rewarded":

Before leaving Madison . . . Mr. Kilbourn had two lists made out, in which were placed the amounts which each member and others were to have, except some of the directors of the La Crosse Company, who were afterwards added by order of the executive committee. These lists were numbered in regular order from one to the numerical end. The first had the name of the person set opposite the number, which in the second list would represent the person. The first was the magic key with which to unlock the "mysterious chest." That, before a person putting up the bonds, was a sure guide, giving the exact number of the bonds of $1,000 each which he should enclose in a "package" for some person named thereon. This work done, and the key destroyed, the memory of man in a few years was not likely to retain who was represented by the figures 1, 5, 10 or 50 with that certainty which would warrant the finding of a verdict against anyone. To avoid the use of this list as evidence, Mr. Kilbourn destroyed it, as he says in his answer to the ninth interrogatory.

Kilbourn, however, cheerfully admitted the bribery of Governor Bashford: "I deemed it necessary to propitiate the governor's feelings with reference to future operations of the company. I subsequently placed in the hands of Governor Bashford the bonds of the company to the amount of $50,000, and at a later period I exchanged with him $15,000 in money at par, of which $10,000 was in January, 1857, as I think, and $5,000 in March or April following." Moses Strong, however, did not have such a good memory; asked about the delivery of the "package" containing the bonds, he answered the investigators:

I cannot and do not pretend to any perfect recollection of the names of the persons to whom I delivered the "package." I preserved no memo-

randum of the matter and have nothing with which to refresh my recollection. It has been the habit of my life to make and preserve written
memoranda of all events or circumstances that I desired to remember. I
had no desire to remember anything about the delivery of the "package."
My office for a day or two was thronged with members of the legislature
and others, who I suppose came to receive their "package." I got rid of
them as soon as possible. I was acting as a ministerial officer of the company
and delivered to the different members of the legislature, whose names were
written upon them, and to others, the several packages in my possession.
It would be invidious to mention the few, whose names accident enables me
to recollect, and having already stated that I delivered all which were left
at my office, I desire to be excused from making any more personal answer
to this interrogatory. I delivered the "package" in person and took no
voucher or receipt from any person.

The scandal burst out of the borders of Wisconsin into newspapers
throughout the nation, and the indignation of Wisconsin citizens rose
to fever pitch. Ex-Governor Coles Bashford, caught in the middle of
the scandal, hastily moved, bag and baggage, to Tucson, in Arizona
Territory. Byron Kilbourn tried in vain to stem the rising tide of anger
by issuing a statement contradicting the findings of the report; all was
to no avail, and Kilbourn's ingenious "explanation" of the whole affair
was as ridiculous as it was farfetched.

What no one turned up was the extent of the influence of Russell
Sage on Kilbourn's actions. Sage, an upstate New Yorker, had had his
fingers in many a highly questionable pie previously; he was a bond-
holder looming large in the background of the La Crosse and Milwaukee, and in effect a controlling owner who turned out to be the
owner also of a $2,000,000 third mortgage on the eastern division of
the La Crosse and Milwaukee, or that portion of the road extending
from Milwaukee to Portage, a mortgage for which not more than
$280,000 had been paid in money, according to a subsequent review
of the case by the United States supreme court. And it was Russell
Sage, by what the court called "a fraudulent arrangement," designed
to mulct stockholders and creditors, whose third mortgage was given
precedence over the first and second mortgages. Out of Sage's foreclosure of the eastern division grew the Milwaukee and Minnesota
Railroad Company, and Sage's fraudulent activities were to plague the
Milwaukee Road for years.

The La Crosse Company, however, was not only corrupt; the charge
of "mismanagement" hurled at the Milwaukee & Mississippi by Byron
Kilbourn had come home to roost; corruption and bad management
doomed the company from its beginnings. After distributing so large

an amount of bonds and achieving its goal, the company neglected to secure the grant by fulfilling the requirements imposed by it, so that when the company's directors in 1858 asked the governor to certify to the completion of twenty miles of its road, Governor Randall proceeded swiftly against the company. He flatly refused to make any such certification, and, moreover, blocked the patenting of 230,400 acres in the general land office at Washington, though Governor Bashford had previously certified this acreage. Though the La Crosse and Milwaukee Company repeatedly appealed to Governor Randall and succeeding governors to reconsider the action, the executive office refused. In this most of the newspapers of Wisconsin upheld the governor. The Madison *Argus and Democrat* never ceased to cry out in anger not only against the La Crosse and Milwaukee Company, but also against the investigation. The investigators, asserted the editor (one who had not been bribed) "proved what everybody knew long ago, but have done nothing about it. They wasted public funds—about $30,000—to prove people rascals, proved it, and left the rascals just where they found them." This was principally because no actionable evidence could be adduced, but also, as the Milwaukee Road's able general attorney, John W. Cary, pointed out later, because "no provision was made for payment of bonds given to the legislators, when the company reorganized." They were "*permanent* investments."

This was the situation when the La Crosse and Milwaukee Rail Road was sold to William H. White and William W. Pratt, April 25, 1863. These gentlemen immediately filed with the secretary of state articles of association as the Milwaukee and St. Paul Railroad Company, and Alexander Mitchell (who had withdrawn from the La Crosse and Milwaukee before the scandal, so that linking of his name with it in any way was purely presumptive) once again loomed behind the new road, playing a part in his carefully conceived plan of persuading creditors of failing lines to merge their interests under his leadership to enable him to foreclose, consolidate, and construct a unified railway system in Wisconsin.

Understandably, public feeling against railroad companies ran very high, but, because of its settlement with the farm mortgagors, the Milwaukee and Prairie du Chien Company, including the Milwaukee and Mississippi, which no longer existed as a separate company, had many more friends than most railroads then operating in Wisconsin. Moreover, the Milwaukee and Prairie du Chien was clearly emerging as the foremost and biggest of the state's railroad companies, despite the fact that the company had hardly been reorganized to include the Milwaukee and Mississippi when the 1 per cent tax on gross earnings was raised to 3 per cent, so that, by 1863, the road paid $51,029.71 in taxes to the state of Wisconsin. Earnings, however, steadily increased; from $414,740.81, reported in 1862, net earnings rose the following year to $453,510.35—this despite the expansion of the company and the increase of its property, such as a large grain elevator at Prairie du Chien, which was built, with track laid to it, by late 1862, and a fortuitous arrangement with the McGregor Western Railway in Iowa, which furthered the connections of the Milwaukee and Prairie du Chien.

The railroad also had powerful supporters, among them the pioneer fur-buyer, Hercules L. Dousman, of Prairie du Chien, a director of the road, "who, aside from many, I might say, almost daily valuable and gratuitous services to the Company," wrote President L. H. Meyer in the reports for 1863, "with a full knowledge of its necessities for land at Prairie du Chien, has by exchange, acquired a piece of land of the first importance to us, and donated it to the Company. This service is the more valuable, as we could not, by purchase, acquire the desired property. On this piece of land it is intended to erect the station building, provided no arrangement can be made with others to build a hotel thereon and give the Company necessary accommodations in it."

Furthermore, the directors of the company were somewhat more capable than the earlier merchants who had gone into railroading with little knowledge of procedure and even less judgment, however much they accomplished for railroads in the middle west; they were no longer so ready to extend their lines and to expand if conditions did not warrant it. "The increased prices for labor and all materials used for renewals," according to General Manager J. C. Spencer in the same report of 1863, "with the increased taxation and reduced earnings for the first eight months of the year, caused less to be done in renewal of track than was intended, or the road needed, until the certainty of a fair crop, insuring good earnings, demonstrated our ability to do more." This policy paid well; in the report for 1864, taxes paid amounted to $72,229.88, net earnings to over $500,000. And the company reported that the total number of miles run stood in 1864 at 938,183, as against 795,527 in 1861. The company's dividend, declared on January 22 of that year, was in cash, amounting to $155,060.

The goal of the line was fixed in President Meyer's 1864 report:

To work our line as economically and make it as productive as possible, there is but one sound course to be pursued, and that is, by securing feeders or extensions West to ensure a more regular and evenly distributed business—a business that will keep our rolling stock reasonably employed all the year round, with time to make timely repairs, instead of having too much of it idle for a long period and then to be so pressed with business that for a while not even necessary repairs can be made.

The agreement with the McGregor Western Company was a step in this direction; by 1864, that railroad was open for 23 miles from North McGregor. In 1865 the Milwaukee and Prairie du Chien obtained a lease of the McGregor Western Railway with an option to purchase, and at the same time surveyed the Mississippi to determine that a bridge "is entirely practicable"—and necessary, since "the business of the McGregor road is already too large for the detentions and uncertainty of the present mode of transfer"; since the "present mode" was by steamship, it could be done reasonably well enough, however expensively, in the season, but could not be done at all in winter, so that freight accumulated on the Iowa shore, waiting for the opening of the Mississippi River in the spring, a fact which would "throw the trade to competing roads in Iowa or Minnesota, should they . . . secure a bridge before we do." In that year, 1865, the company declared two cash dividends, amounting together to almost $1,000,000.

In 1866 a significant change took place in the Milwaukee and Prairie du Chien. Alexander Mitchell was elected to the presidency of the road, and S. S. Merrill became the general manager in place of J. C. Spencer, thus bringing both the Milwaukee and St. Paul and the Milwaukee and Prairie du Chien under the same management. The two roads had in the previous year exchanged agreements, particularly a running arrangement by which the Milwaukee and Prairie du Chien agreed to stock and divide earnings with the Milwaukee and St. Paul, mile per mile, allowing 50 per cent to each for operating expenses. At the end of that year, when the roads could fairly assess the advantages of their agreement, they "became satisfied that it was for the interest of both roads as well as that of the public, that a closer connection should be formed between the two Companies." Negotiations to that end were begun immediately in 1866, resulting in transfer of the majority of the Prairie du Chien stock to the trustees of the Milwaukee and St. Paul in exchange for stock in the latter road, subsequent to which the elevation of Mitchell to the presidency took place. Thus the two roads, which had the same starting point in Milwaukee, each having a western terminus at the Mississippi less than 100 miles apart, now also shared a common administration, and the board of directors foresaw that the immense freight business of the two roads could be more conveniently and economically managed, with grain elevators owned by the roads available to both lines, and "many expensive and useless agencies, commissions and drawbacks will be discontinued, and we are enabled, without sacrifice, to serve the public with more liberality, cheapness and efficiency."

The absorption of the Milwaukee and Prairie du Chien, however much it may have seemed a mutually advantageous business arrangement as presented in the reports of the Milwaukee and St. Paul, was something a little more than that; it was a consummation brought about by a series of moves as carefully planned and made as those of a chess game, though the Milwaukee and St. Paul, paradoxically enough, was not the moving agent. The Milwaukee and St. Paul had, in fact, made two previous offers to consolidate lines or to pool earnings. The first of these had been made in the summer of 1863, when the Milwaukee and St. Paul was emerging from a period of court receivership, and when the railroad scene was undergoing noteworthy changes, with the Chicago and Milwaukee and others consolidating under Alexander Mitchell, the Chicago and Northwestern taking over the Kenosha, Rockford and Rock Island, and hungrily eying the Racine and Mississippi Road. Newspapers carried rumors of an impending consolidation between the two lines, and for a time even hinted that the Chicago and Northwestern and the Milwaukee and St. Paul, together with the Milwaukee and Prairie du Chien, might consolidate; the result of all this was not only that the stock of the Milwaukee and Prairie du Chien took a sharp rise in the market, but also that the people of Wisconsin began to express fear of monopolistic control of rail transportation and brought about pressure on the legislature to stand firmly against consolidation. Partly as a result of public feeling against monopolies, partly because the terms offered by the Milwaukee and St. Paul did not seem favorable enough, the Milwaukee and Prairie du Chien declined to pool earnings or consolidate.

The second offer was made two years later, when the Milwaukee and St. Paul, hard pressed by a series of misfortunes (the diminution of freight traffic owing to the failure of the wheat crop, then Wisconsin's primary grain crop, and the lessening of passenger traffic as an aftermath of the Civil War) made an offer of outright sale. This, too, was rejected, very largely because the Prairie du Chien could not see the way clear to buy, and because some of the directors of that company suspected that, though such a sale might be consummated, the ultimate result might be quite the reverse—instead of owning the Milwaukee and St. Paul, the Prairie du Chien might find itself owned by that road. The third was the proposal for a system of prorating earnings in 1866; this was agreed to and was in tentative operation when the acts in the drama that was to bring about the absorption of the Milwaukee and Prairie du Chien began to take place.

The drama started in New York, with speculation in the common stock of the Milwaukee and Prairie du Chien, and the bringing about of what was known as the "Prairie Dog Corner" on the New York Stock Exchange—"prairie dog" being, of course, the English for the French "Prairie du Chien." Several men, in no way connected with either the Milwaukee and St. Paul or the Milwaukee and Prairie du Chien, were engaged in this transaction under the leadership of the brokerage firm of Henry Stimson & Company. They had been preparing for this speculation for some time, and had bought up at generally prevailing low prices all 29,880 shares of the common stock of the Milwaukee and Prairie du Chien then available in New York, a block of shares representing a majority. Having accomplished this quiet purchase, they loaned many of these shares to friends who were not informed of their plans, and scattered other shares in Wall Street, subject to short call. Early in November, 1865, the speculators acted; without warning, they notified all borrowers to return their loans, and all shares which had been sold short were called in. The result was sensational, for brokers who were not prepared to deliver poured into the Exchange to buy stocks so that they might fulfil the speculators' demands, and there found Milwaukee and Prairie du Chien common stock to be had only at incredibly high prices, stocks selling for $64.50 less than a fortnight before now being held at $230. Messrs. Henry Stimson & Company and their associates had the distinction of earning the accolade of the New York *Times*, which called the operation "the sharpest and beyond all precedent the most sudden corner known to the forty years' history of the New York Stock Exchange."

The speculators, however, were not aware of a somewhat unusual provision of the Milwaukee and Prairie du Chien charter which denied common stockholders the right to vote for directors of the company, and they found themselves in the unique position of owning a majority interest in a distant railroad without an accompanying control of the administration of that road. They were not long balked, however; in the spring of 1866, a Madison lawyer, engaged by them, was in attendance at the session of the Wisconsin legislature to secure an amendment to the company's charter to permit the common stockholders to vote. How this was to be accomplished was left to the lawyer; his fee of $5,000 had been set. By late March, the Stimson measure was openly introduced in the Wisconsin senate; on the preceding day, however, the shrewd lawyer had succeeded in introducing into the assem-

bly another bill which was designed to accomplish the same end far
more indirectly.

The Milwaukee and Prairie du Chien Company's representatives in
the legislature discovered the senate measure at once, and discovered
also the forces behind it; and, when the company threatened to flood
the market with new issues of common stock, which would effectively
ruin the Stimson holdings as well as dispossess the group of potential
control should their bill find its way through into law, the Stimson
group brought about a withdrawal of the senate measure. The company and its legislative representatives relaxed, believing that they
had forestalled and ended the attempt of Henry Stimson & Company
to wrest control of the Milwaukee and Prairie du Chien from its board
of directors. Unaware of the retention of the Madison lawyer to represent the Stimson interests, the company did not establish the connection between the assembly bill, which, according to the lawyer who
had succeeded in introducing it, was intended to apply to a corrupt
petroleum mining company, but actually covered the Milwaukee and
Prairie du Chien and similar companies as well. The legislature was
at this time considering half a hundred measures relative to regulation
of petroleum companies; as the lawyer had foreseen, the measure introduced at his instigation was not carefully scrutinized; moreover, the
legislature was moving toward adjournment and acted in haste—the
supposed "petroleum" measure was passed by assembly and senate
as one of two dozen similar and related measures, and signed by Governor Lucius Fairchild—a momentous pen stroke, since by it Henry
Stimson & Company and their associates came into control of the Milwaukee and Prairie du Chien Railway, and forthwith that group
brought the drama to a close by selling its holdings—and thus the railroad—to the Milwaukee and St. Paul.

The Wall Street speculators profited handsomely by their venture,
receiving in exchange for their Milwaukee and Prairie du Chien holdings an equal number of Milwaukee and St. Paul preferred shares and
25 per cent more of common; it was, manifestly, this block of shares
which made a majority, so that at the election of directors in June of
that year, 1866, Alexander Mitchell and his associates were elected to
full control of both the Milwaukee and St. Paul and the Milwaukee
and Prairie du Chien, which were soon to be known only by the name
of the former company. The late directors of the Milwaukee and
Prairie du Chien fought briefly to retain possession of their road, but
to no avail; discouragement overtook them late in 1867, and they sold
out their interests to their rivals, though not before instituting suit to

enjoin the extension of that road by way of Janesville and Monroe to Dubuque, causing the projected extension to be abandoned.

The new management immediately set about making an examination of the condition of the Milwaukee and Prairie du Chien, the astute Mitchell and his equally capable general manager, Merrill, being determined that nothing was to be accepted at face value. They found several aspects of the property and the company's agreements not to their liking. For one thing, the road itself was not in as good condition as they had expected it to be, and a study of the ravages of flood waters the previous April in the valley of the Wisconsin indicated that portions of the track there would need to be raised as much as two feet for an aggregate distance of ten miles. A contract with John Lawler of Prairie du Chien, made by the McGregor Western in 1863, and supposedly assumed by the late directors of the Milwaukee and Prairie du Chien, particularly excited their disapproval; it seemed to the new directors that the contract was improvident. Small wonder that the transportation of freight from the McGregor terminus into Wisconsin was not as profitable as it should have been, when Lawler was to receive, according to the contract, $6 per car of livestock, not more than $8 on all fully loaded cars in which there was no change of bulk, and other charges similarly scaled, together with an agreement granting all transfer business exclusively to Lawler and his assigns for 15 years, making no reservation to terminate or to qualify it in any way in case the company should decide ultimately to construct a bridge across the Mississippi.

The acquisition of the Milwaukee and Prairie du Chien gave the Milwaukee and St. Paul control also of the McGregor Western Railway, placing in the hands of the company the entire line from Milwaukee to Minneapolis and St. Paul, by way of Prairie du Chien and McGregor. Exclusive of the line on the west bank of the Mississippi, the combined Milwaukee and St. Paul and Milwaukee and Prairie du Chien now, in 1867, had 820 miles of track and listed net earnings at $2,017,922.77. Of property, it owned the largest amount of any railroad or combination of railroads in the middle west at that time; in addition to its road, it had 125 locomotives, 60 first-class and 8 second-class passenger cars, 6 sleeping cars, 48 baggage, mail, and express cars, 398 flat cars, and 1,850 box and freight cars, together with 80 acres of land with buildings thereon in the city of Milwaukee. While no dividend was declared in 1867, the company requiring all net earnings to pay for new buildings and equipment, the line on the Minnesota division was extended 85 miles from Crescoe, Iowa, to Owatonna, Minnesota, and the entire line west of the Mississippi, including both the Mc-

Gregor Western and the Minnesota Central, was purchased at a cost to
the new company of slightly over $9,000,000.

The Milwaukee and St. Paul had no difficulty in obtaining legislation approving the consolidation of the lines, since by this time the
recalcitrant legislators in Madison were beginning to have grave doubts
about the advisability of unrestricted competition in ventures which
employed so much of the public's capital. Moreover, after a litigation
of several years, following the taking over of the old La Crosse and
Milwaukee Company, the Milwaukee and St. Paul finally won a decision in the United States supreme court, granting the company the
eastern division of the La Crosse and Milwaukee, ownership of which
had been in dispute.

It was manifest by this time that the greatest rival of Milwaukee for
the traffic and freight of the area west of the Great Lakes was Chicago,
specifically the Chicago and Northwestern, which, like the Milwaukee
and St. Paul, had grown and been consolidated as a result of the panic
of 1857. The consolidation of the Milwaukee and St. Paul was a blow
to the Chicago and Northwestern, which ran from Green Bay by way
of Watertown and Janesville to Chicago, a route which intersected
both the La Crosse and Milwaukee and the Milwaukee and Prairie du
Chien lines west of Milwaukee. This break in connection enabled the
Chicago and Northwestern to find it possible and desirable to play the
La Crosse and the Prairie du Chien against each other and thus compel both roads to send their freight and passenger traffic largely by
way of the Chicago and Northwestern from these junctions. Now,
however, the connection with the Chicago and Northwestern was made
from Milwaukee by the Milwaukee and St. Paul.

It is not too much to say that the consolidation of the Milwaukee
and St. Paul was very largely the work of Alexander Mitchell. After
two decades as a banker—whether openly or *sub rosa*—Mitchell foresaw the fate of the many small railroad companies which had obtained
charters and begun building in Wisconsin, and when, after the collapse
of 1857, most of these companies were almost hopelessly bankrupt,
Mitchell moved with his associates to begin consolidation. He began
with the Chicago and Milwaukee Railroad, of which he was president,
and he moved simultaneously toward rapprochement with both the
Milwaukee and Prairie du Chien and the La Crosse and Milwaukee,
which, bankrupt in 1859, was sold in 1863 and reorganized as the
Milwaukee and St. Paul Railway Company, which, after reuniting the
eastern and western divisions of the old La Crosse and Milwaukee,
added three other bankrupt lines—the Milwaukee and Western, the
Milwaukee and Horicon, and the Ripon and Wolf River; and, by 1867,

with the absorption of the Milwaukee and Prairie du Chien, the Milwaukee and St. Paul had no major rival other than the Chicago and Northwestern.

Though Mitchell well knew that the most important direction in which the road should expand must be westward into Iowa, Minnesota, Nebraska, and the Dakota country, there was still further consolidation to be done in Wisconsin. There were several small roads, not yet affiliated with any larger, and of these at least one, the Racine and Mississippi, was being sought by the Chicago and Northwestern, which was integrating as swiftly as the Milwaukee and St. Paul, extending up into Wisconsin through the valleys of the Rock and Fox Rivers toward Green Bay, running north and south, as against the Milwaukee and St. Paul's predominant east-west directions. There was also the West Wisconsin Railway, which was constructing a line from Tomah to Hudson at the Minnesota boundary of Wisconsin, close to the Twin Cities. In addition to these, there were still annoying problems left by the La Crosse and Milwaukee Road.

The most important of the La Crosse and Milwaukee problems was, clearly, the situation brought about by the bribery of the legislature and the events which followed subsequent to the discovery of Byron Kilbourn's act. The Milwaukee and St. Paul found itself in the unenviable position of having paid for lands in such a way that it could neither repudiate payment nor, because of Governor Randall's forthright action before the general land office in Washington, take possession of the land. The Milwaukee and St. Paul was, in fact, entitled to a portion of the lands in question because of the construction of 61 miles of road from Portage to Tomah, except for a technicality based on the failure of Byron Kilbourn's board to qualify the grant. Mitchell made several appeals to Governor Randall, asking some alleviation of the punishment inflicted upon the La Crosse and Milwaukee, and now borne by the Milwaukee and St. Paul. Popular sentiment was strongly against any modification of the governor's decision—the people still smarted under the conviction that they and not the companies were the victims of scandalous goings on and they were determined that monopolies should not rise to plague them—and, finally, in 1868, the company agreed to abide by an act of congress conferring a large part of the land in question upon the Wisconsin Railroad Farm Mortgage Land Company; it was ultimately sold for the benefit of Wisconsin's railroad farm mortgagors. The remainder of the disputed La Crosse and Milwaukee grant, covering some of Wisconsin's most valuable timber lands, was distributed among three lesser railroads in the northern part of the state. However much of a loss this represented for the

Milwaukee and St. Paul, the company was well rid of the protracted litigation which the action begun by the La Crosse and Milwaukee years before entailed.

The West Wisconsin Railway presented no great problem, once it was faced. Mitchell and his associates had no trouble in obtaining a lease of the line in 1868. The Racine and Mississippi proved somewhat more obdurate, so Mitchell set about with dispatch to buy control. He bought up such shares as he could find, and then discovered that a large block of stock in the Racine and Mississippi was held, presumably out of his reach, in the City Bank of Glasgow, in his native Scotland! Nothing daunted, the resourceful Mitchell combined business with pleasure, and in the winter of 1868–1869, while on a visit to the city of his birth, he bought the stock from the bank. Thus he had a controlling interest in the Racine and Mississippi, which was brought under the domination of the Milwaukee and St. Paul; and by the end of 1869, the Milwaukee and St. Paul controlled every through route in Wisconsin from the lake shore to the Mississippi, finally fulfilling the dream of the directors of the old Milwaukee & Mississippi. Moreover, the keen rivalry between the Milwaukee and St. Paul and the Chicago and Northwestern had been abated to such an extent that not only had directors of the two companies been elected to each other's boards, but by the end of 1869, the quiet, determined Scottish boy who, 30 years before, had come into Milwaukee as a clerk in an insurance company office was president of both the Milwaukee and St. Paul and the Chicago and Northwestern, controlling 2,300 miles of railroad lines, representing perhaps the greatest concentration of railroad mileage then in existence. Indeed, the sole competition—if such it could be called—was offered within Wisconsin by two companies, controlling between them less than 100 miles of track. The Chicago *Post* saluted Mitchell:

History repeats itself. The tears of Alexander the Great, because he had no more worlds to conquer, are familiar to every school-boy, and here we have another Alexander, surnamed Mitchell, who, starting out with the Milwaukee and St. Paul railroad, first gobbled the old Milwaukee and La Crosse, then the Prairie du Chien, then half a dozen small railroads in Wisconsin, Iowa, and Minnesota, then the Western Union, and now, *eheu iam satis!* the Northwestern, with all its branches, spurs, divisions, and ramifications! As there are still other lines to gobble, however, we suppose the weeping will not commence until such little sidetracks as the Union Pacific, New York Central, etc., are added to the inventory.

Mitchell could afford to smile.

Despite all the antimonopoly sentiment of his time, he had performed a signal service for the people of the middle west. He had made a comprehensive and through-route system out of fragmentary, bankrupt lines; he offered conveniences and economies of management which had not been dreamed of before; he ended the local jealousies of the little railroads.* More important, he opened the way for the Milwaukee and St. Paul to become, not a regional network alone, but a continental system, flung across the west to the Pacific.

* Manifestly, it was not a coincidence that, just as Alexander Mitchell pioneered in railroading, so his famed grandson, Captain Billy Mitchell, pioneered in air travel.

V. The Road Fights Regulation

When General Manager S. S. Merrill was on a train, he invariably told the conductor, "Pay no attention to me. I want the same treatment as other passengers." Near Libertyville Junction (now Rondout), during the construction of the Libertyville branch, a large number of cross ties were piled. Mr. Merrill took a short walk to inspect these ties during the station stop of the train. Its work done, off went the train. About a mile east of Libertyville, the conductor on his round found he had lost the Manager. He gave a stop signal to the engineer, Al Fuller (who always had to be shown), and said, "Al, we'd better back up to Libertyville." "What for?" asked Al. "To get the Old Man." "Where is he?" asked Al. "I think at Libertyville," said the conductor.

After overcoming Al's remonstrance, the conductor had his way, and the train backed up. The curious passengers pushed their heads out of the windows, looking for the reason of the reversed movement. The reason was soon in sight, looking like a thundercloud on the station platform. The Old Man made a big noise, greatly to the delectation of the passengers and the consternation of the crew. Only the presence of ladies in the chair car prevented Mr. Merrill's forceful comments "on a conductor who didn't know better than to leave me." He said, however, that "it's the last time I'll ever be left." That, however, was in error; years later he was left at Lakefield, on the Southern Minnesota. That time the train went thirty miles before the Old Man was missed!

—The Milwaukee Magazine

THE decade of the 1870's was an historic one, challenging every resource of even so astute a leadership as that of Alexander Mitchell and S. S. Merrill, for in mid-decade state governments made the first attempt to regulate the freight and passenger rates of railroads. The Milwaukee Road could hardly have had more capable leadership than that of Mitchell and Merrill, who were to control the road for almost two more decades, until Mitchell's death in 1887. Indeed, the period of Mitchell's aegis might well be looked upon as the golden age of the Milwaukee Road, for his influence was tremendously effective, his business methods were sound, he had alert and intelligent vision, and he had the knowledge of every facet of the road necessary to best further its interests. Though he tended toward a conservative outlook, Mitchell never lacked in boldness, and did not hesitate to make use of anything new which appeared to him of possible benefit to the road.

Long before his death, Mitchell's sturdy, stocky figure, with its fresh-colored face framed in whiskers, was a familiar one not only in the middle west, but in every part of the nation in which there was any concern at all for railroading. Always immaculate in dress and courteous in deportment, whether he was assisting a lady from a carriage or defying the sovereign power of the state of Wisconsin, Mitchell rose to eminence not so much through wealth in itself as because of his canny judgment. Merrill was in many ways complementary—a tall, angular man, careless in dress, nervous and impulsive in his movements, he was markedly aggressive, as opposed to the deliberate calculation and strategy of Mitchell. In a portrait of Mitchell and Merrill—"The Railroad Giants of the Northwest"—the Boston *Herald* in 1882 opined, "One spurs constantly, the other holds a constant check; and each in his accomplished work reaps larger success because of the office work of the other."

The 1870's were ushered in by the fulfillment of a long-standing wish of Mitchell's—the construction of a line from Milwaukee to Chicago, in place of the entry into Chicago over the tracks of another line. Mitchell had argued for a connection to Chicago over a decade before, even as he had fought for early entry into the timberlands of northern Wisconsin, and with equal lack of success. In 1871, the Wisconsin Union Railroad Company obtained a permit to build from Milwaukee south to the state line; in 1872 the Chicago, Milwaukee and St. Paul Railway Company of Illinois was organized for the purpose of building from Chicago north to the state line. Construction was carried forward at once, and in the spring of 1873, after these two roads were transferred January 1, 1873, to the Milwaukee and St. Paul Railway Company, the line between Milwaukee and Chicago was put into operation, while at the other end of its line the road was opened to Minneapolis, via Calmar, Iowa, Austin and Owatonna, Minnesota; between St. Paul and La Crescent, the company established a car ferry of two barges and a steamboat named *Alexander Mitchell,* which served the company until a line was later built from La Crosse to St. Paul.

When the line was built into St. Paul, service to Minneapolis was provided via a circuitous route, which involved crossing one bridge over the Mississippi River from St. Paul to Mendota, and then over the Minnesota River from Mendota to Minneapolis. The direct ten miles between St. Paul and Minneapolis, which involved again the crossing of the Mississippi, was called the "Short Line," and it is still referred to as that by old railroad men on the road and in the Twin Cities. The Short Line provided the only interurban service between St. Paul and Minneapolis, with passenger trains being operated every half hour and making frequent stops along the route. The trains did a land-office business not only in the regular traffic, but also because convivial citizens of one city, who considered it unwise to spend an evening of play in the home town, would board the train to seek entertainment in the other city, so that St. Paulites encountered a great many St. Paulites in Minneapolis, and Minneapolitans encountered a great many Minneapolitans in St. Paul, all having a good time uninhibited by the fear of discovery by any acquaintances except those bent on the same goal. The conductor on that run, Charles Langdon, in later reminiscences, told how a Minneapolis newspaper editor, who was a well-known total abstainer in Minneapolis, customarily went over to St. Paul for an evening. At the time of departure of the last train for Minneapolis, the editor would lurk in the shadows of one of the station pillars until the conductor's go-ahead signal, then run out to the rear car of the train and deposit himself upon the top step of the open-vestibule car then in service, always managing to drop from his perch as the train slowed down to stop in Minneapolis, well shielded from the sight of any fellow citizens who might have been inside the car.

The new Short Line had hardly begun operations before the panic of 1873 struck the country. H. H. Porter went to New York without delay, but there was nothing to be done to stem the mushrooming panic, even though President Grant himself met with Commodore Vanderbilt and others in New York in an effort to devise some plan of relief. Though the immediate upsurge of panic was over in two months, the return to normal conditions was delayed for more than four years. It was during this time that the railroads in Wisconsin had to make their most historic struggle against government regulation.

The decade of decision which the 1870's became was one in which, asserted the late Senator Robert M. La Follette years later, the railroads began "to dominate politics for the first time in this country; they began indeed to corrupt all the States of the Middle West." For the leaders of the Milwaukee Road, it was a decade in which the railroads had to choose between domination by politicians or self-government. The issue came to the fore in 1874, but the lines of battle had been drawn years before. Despite previous attempts to legislate control of the railroads, the Wisconsin legislature had not yet successfully sought to impose any strictures on freight and passenger rates; the company had always fixed its own rates without interference. Now, however, the legislature of the state of Wisconsin passed an act fixing arbitrary rates for freight transported in Wisconsin, and limited the passenger rates of the Milwaukee Road to 3 cents per mile.

Though there was no precedent in Wisconsin for this legislation, it had not come into being without considerable support. The law in question became known as the Potter Law, because R. L. D. Potter, Wisconsin state senator from Waushara County, introduced the bill in the legislature. But the measure had grown directly out of animosity for the railroads, much of it ill-considered and baseless, because it sprang out of the long-standing anger and frustration which had been the result of the farm mortgage foreclosures of over a decade before. The farmers of the state of Wisconsin had long memories, yet the fact that the Milwaukee Road had been far less a party to farm mortgage foreclosures than had most other roads meant nothing to them; the farm mortgage foreclosures had simply aroused bitterness against and distrust of railroads, and the relationship of any one road to the foreclosures carried little weight.

Despite all the remedial methods followed by the railroad companies, 3,785 farm mortgages valued at over $4,000,000 were foreclosed, leaving most of the farmers concerned bankrupt. These and sympathetic fellow farmers had organized into a society called the Grange, which included women as well as men. The idea of the

Grange had had its inception in the brain of Oliver Hudson Kelly, a government clerk in Washington. Kelly had been impressed by the conviction of the farmers in the nation that, having furnished a large share of the funds for railroad construction, they had a right to more of the advantages of railroad service. He had not failed to notice the losses sustained by investing farmers as a result of receiverships and reorganizations, and, after a trip through the south, where he was impressed by the lack of any kind of unity among farmers—a lack which contributed to a stagnant state of conservatism—Kelly interested W. M. Ireland, another clerk in the Post Office Department, and William Saunders of the Agricultural Bureau. These three "founders" added others, and immediately began an agitation for the organization of the Patrons of Husbandry, as the Grange was first called, but it was not until August, 1868, when Col. D. A. Robertson of St. Paul was enlisted in the movement, that the first permanent Grange was organized. By 1873 the Grange was reorganized on a permanent basis, with control actually in the hands of farmers. The Grangers made it clear that they were champions of the dispossessed farmers, and agitated constantly for "punishment" of railroads and for restrictive legislation, finally making a study of railroad rates and concluding that regulation ought to be imposed by the people who had given the companies their charters.

The Granger agitation stirred others to study the situation, so that even in 1866 the Milwaukee *Sentinel* was editorializing:

The proposition will hardly be disputed that a railroad company should have the right to maintain such charges upon its business as will pay a net profit upon capital prudently and economically invested, corresponding to the average net profit on capital otherwise employed. The public is not bound to pay this net profit on the whole nominal cost of the road, if one half, or any other proportion of the capital has been squandered or stolen by the managers. The company cannot justly demand the usual net profit on capital for stock diluted in this or any other way, but only on the cash cost of the road, economically and faithfully constructed.

The *Sentinel*, as well as the Grangers and other reformers, had several facts in mind. The Milwaukee and Horicon Rail Road had been purchased in 1863 by Russell Sage, Washington Hunt, and others, under foreclosure, for $670,000; but a short time thereafter it was consolidated with the Milwaukee and St. Paul on a stock-and-bond basis at a value of $1,050,000. Similarly, the Northwestern Road in 1864 credited the Galena & Chicago Union Railroad with $12,000,000 on consolidation, though the total stock issues of that road had amounted to but half that figure. Most of the consolidations of this period were effected in this manner, and the answer to questions about such inflation, which was generally that the stock of the parent company had been so diluted previously as to make this inflation necessary, was held not acceptable.

The constitutionality of such regulation quickly became an issue, even before legislation had actually been passed. The railroads maintained that no governing body apart from their own had any right to fix transportation charges; to this the reformers replied that the railroads were quasi-public industries, and the fact that the companies accepted land grants and exercised the rights of eminent domain was evidence that they themselves so understood their status. Furthermore, retorted the reformers, no legal or moral violation of the original charters was embodied in the proposed legislation to regulate rates. The companies held, also, that regulation would not only restrict and handicap Wisconsin railroads and thus ultimately ruin them by making it impossible for them to compete with roads in neighboring states, but also that such regulation would frighten railroad capital from the state. It was this argument which aroused northern Wisconsin, then still anxious for railroads, to cry out against legislators urging regulation, branding them "popularity-seeking demagogues riding a dishonest political hobbyhorse." The Eau Claire *Free Press* on June 13, 1867, editorialized against the regulators: "These tariff agitators know full well the disastrous consequences that would follow the success of such a bill, in the way of discouragement to railroad enterprise, thus subjecting the [north]western portion of the State for years to the inconvenience of stage coach travel and transportation of freight by wagon."

The legislature of the state of Wisconsin, however, made several attempts before the passage of the Potter Law to regulate the railroads. The initial attempt was made in 1860 in the introduction of a bill to establish railroad charges. Similar attempts were subsequently made, but all were easily defeated. In the session of 1864, Assembly Bill Number 298, a rate regulation measure, was prompted by memorials and representations from all sides. "More petitions on this subject found their way to the capitol in 1864 than had been presented on any other subject for years," wrote the historian, Frederick Merk, in his *Economic History of Wisconsin During the Civil War Decade*. The press, especially of southern Wisconsin, hailed the measure as one which was "universally demanded by the people."

The bill, however, quite justifiably alarmed the railroads, for it contained severe restrictions. For instance, it divided freight into sixteen classes, setting forth the articles to be included in each class, and the rate of charges to be fixed. It set first-class passenger rates at not more than 3 cents per mile, and second-class at not more than 2 cents per mile, while state officers, judges, and members of the legislature were to be carried without charge—the legislators, even in the heat of public pressure, not forgetting to look out for themselves. After some further regulations, the bill provided that any corporation deliberately violating the law must forfeit its charter immediately. As a result of their alarm, the railroad companies brought out the ablest lobbyists at their command and succeeded in having the dangerous bill amended to such a watered-down stage that it could hardly be considered an act of regulation at all, for, when finally passed, it contained only two provisions—one prohibiting railroad agents from carrying produce or lumber over roads with which they had any official connections; the other permitting companies to refuse to carry wood during their busiest seasons—a reduction to ridiculous status of the once alarming bill.

The legislature, however, had only begun to attempt legislation. No less than thirteen similar bills came before the legislature in 1865, eight in 1866, seven in 1867; at every session to follow, similar measures were introduced—some of them carefully thought out, but the majority simple, unworkable measures designed only to fix rigid schedules of charges and service. Fortunately for the principles of industrial progress represented by the railroads, none of these measures ever became law. The bitterness of railroad critics and reformers about the railroad companies' lobbyists was but one side of the picture ("A wet rag about a washerwoman's thumb is not more pliable than some of our Wisconsin solons are in the hands of these shrewd and skillful lobbymen," according to the Janesville *Gazette*, January 5, 1866); the companies had one very sound argument against such legislation which could not be gainsaid, and that was the contention that the legislators were not qualified to enact such laws, since they did not possess any adequate basis of information from which to work upon such regulatory legislation. In many cases even the railroad company officials themselves were none too sure about the principles of rate-fixing, electing to fix all noncompetitive charges on the basis of approximately what they could get for such services. The legislators had neither the special knowledge nor the training necessary to effect regulatory legislation which would not in fact impose an insurmountable burden on the roads themselves. In final analysis, it was this fundamental fact which brought about the defeat even of the Potter Law, which was the result of somewhat more careful preparation.

The Potter measure was passed in the legislative session of 1874, and was promptly signed into law by Governor W. D. Taylor, who had achieved office largely through the support of the now powerful Granger organization. Ex-Governor Cadwallader Washburn had been a consistent advocate of railroad legislation, but Governor Taylor had made it clear in his very first message that his position in favor of such legislation was even stronger than his predecessor's. Moreover, attempts at legislative control had been given a noteworthy impetus by an injudicious decision on the part of some railroad officials to raise rates on agricultural products in the fall of 1873, a year in which the harvest was abundant. This raise was arbitrarily ordered in the face of a long-standing roster of complaints about high rates.

Ironically enough, the Potter Law was passed as a direct result of the activities of the lobbyists for the railroad companies. The assembly of the state of Wisconsin had passed a measure prohibiting any rates higher than those in force during the first week in January, 1872, without special permission from a railroad commission which was to be established. The measure was innocuous enough, but the lobbyists decided that it must not pass the senate; so, reasoning that, if so harmless a measure had passed the assembly by a vote of 69 to 14, a really severe regulatory measure would not pass, they brought forward the rate-fixing measure of Senator Potter, which called for rates far lower than those then charged on Wisconsin railroads. The Potter measure passed the senate by a vote of 20 to 7, but was laid aside in the assembly, just as the lobbyists had expected. Unfortunately, the lobbyists had failed to count upon the fact that the Grangers in the legislature could hardly dare face their constituents without some kind of measure, and, much to the surprise of the railroad lobbyists, the Potter measure was passed by both houses and signed into law.

The elaborate Potter Law grew directly out of all the Granger complaints against the railroads and embodied a great many controversial provisions. The initial section of the law divided all railroads in Wisconsin into three classes—A and B, which were specified, and class C, which included all the rest, particularly those lines which were new and less important. In the second section, the law fixed the maximum passenger rates at 3, 3½, and 4 cents a mile in classes A, B, and C, respectively. The third section provided for the classification of freight into four general and seven specified classes—class D, for instance, constituted grain in carloads; class G, lumber in carloads; class H, livestock in carloads—and so forth. The fourth section fixed graduated maximum rates for the transportation of freight in the seven special classes on the A and B roads, and the fifth provided that maximum charges for freight should be the rates in force June 1, 1873. The final sections of the law provided for the establishment of a railroad commission of three members, who should have the power to reclassify all freights except those in classes D, E, G, and H, and to reduce rates still further on any road in any class if a majority of the commission held that it could be done without injury to the road.

The law appeared to the railroad companies to be a violation of the terms of their charter under which the roads were constructed, for the charter granted to companies the right in express terms to fix their own rates for freight and passengers. President Mitchell, acting for the Milwaukee Road, and President Keep of the Northwestern—Mitchell having vacated the presidency of the Northwestern Road not long after achieving it, deciding that it was not fitting that companies which were essentially rivals should be headed by the same man—sought the opinion of their legal counsel, and, being advised by them that the legislation seemed to be "in conflict with the constitution of the United States and not binding upon the several companies" involved, decided to defy the law. Mitchell thereupon immediately wrote to Governor Taylor of Wisconsin in unmistakable terms. "Being fully conscious that the enforcement of this law will ruin the property of the Company and feeling assured of the correctness of the opinions of the eminent counsel who have examined the question, the directors feel compelled to disregard the provisions of the law so far as it fixes a tariff of rates for the company until the courts have finally passed upon the question of its validity." The Milwaukee Road and the Northwestern made no attempt to revise their tariffs to conform to the Potter Law, and settled back to wait upon the outcome of legal action.

Mitchell's letter, which was promptly made public, was considered as a direct challenge to the state government, and Governor Taylor lost no time in answering the challenge by a vigorous proclamation in which he called upon "all railroad corporations, their officers and agents, peaceably to submit to the law, for since the Executive is charged with the responsibility of seeing that the laws are faithfully executed, all the functions of his office will be exercised to that end; and for this purpose he invokes the aid and co-operation of all good citizens." Taylor followed this proclamation with an open address to the people three weeks later, enjoining citizens to pay no higher charges than the law allowed, and to report all "extortions" to the district attorney. At the same time he called upon all officers to enforce the Potter Law within their jurisdiction, and promised executive aid in any circumstances requiring it.

The enemies of the railroads, who ticked off Mitchell's letter as an act of incredible brazenness, might well have reflected that the company could have evaded and conspired against the law much more deviously and perhaps more effectively than by this forthright defiance which was made in the sincere belief that such regulation endangered the very existence of the railroad. The subsequent conduct of the railroads was in accordance with established legal procedure. Having given notice that they would contest the legislation, the railroads brought the issue into the United States circuit court for the western district of Wisconsin when the bondholders of the Chicago and Northwestern Railway began an action to enjoin the adoption or enforcement of the rates prescribed in the law of 1874; in this action, the Chicago and Northwestern was joined by the Milwaukee Road. The district court, however, after hearing the motion for an injunction, ruled in favor of the defendants, who were the railroad commissioners and Attorney General A. Scott Sloan of the state of Wisconsin, denying the injunction and dismissing the bills. An appeal from these decrees was immediately carried to the United States supreme court.

Meanwhile, the attorney general of Wisconsin, in an effort to force compliance with the Potter Law even before the United States supreme court could hand down a decision, asked the supreme court of Wisconsin for an injunction to restrain the Milwaukee Road from charging higher rates than those established in the law of 1874. The case was argued for eight days before that court, and on September 15, 1874, Chief Justice Edward G. Ryan delivered an historic decision granting the injunction. The press of southern Wisconsin hailed the decision as "the most important ever delivered by the Supreme Court." The decision was lengthy and thoughtful; it required three and a half hours to read. Its salient portions were as follows:

The Legislature is under a moral obligation not to reduce the tolls of railroads below a fair and adequate remuneration. But their power over the franchise is absolute. But the power to alter or repeal cannot affect the property of corporations other than the franchise. Such right of property is inviolable. . . . Chapter 273 of 1874 [the Potter Law], so far as its provisions are before the Court in these cases, is a valid amendment of the special charters of the defendants, granted by the State. . . . There is a judicial discretion to withhold injunction and mandamus in aid of private remedies. But there is no such discretion at the suit of the State in matters *publici juris*. In such cases writs go peremptorily *ex debito justiciae*. The court has no discretion to withhold either of the writs in cases of positive violation of positive law to positive public injury. . . . It would have been a mockery of justice to have left corporations counting their capital by millions . . . subject only to the common law remedies sufficient for the common carriers who carried passengers and goods by a weekly wagon. Common law remedies are impotent against the great railway companies. . . . Every person suffering their oppresssion by a disregard of corporate duty may have his injunction. . . . The motions of the Attorney General must be granted; and the writs issue as to all the roads . . . built under the territorial charter of 1847, 1848.

The Wisconsin press was articulate. In reviewing the history of the litigation, the Janesville *Gazette* scored the railroads:

Their action up to the present time has been in the nature of a rebellion against the people, with the additional feature of extortion. In view of that fact, it would be unjust in the last degree to consider any suggestion for the relief of the offenders until complete submission has been made. If the people had behaved toward the companies with a tithe of the injustice which the community has endured from the monopolies referred to, the whole world would have rung with what would have been called a crime against capital; and whilst we have no revengeful feelings to gratify, we must not be oblivious of the deference which is due to the principle of common honesty and observance of law which has been flagrantly and continuously outraged.

The Milwaukee *Sentinel* and other papers termed Judge Ryan's an "historic decision," which indeed it was, since it was soon established as a judicial principle nationally as well as in many other state courts. The *Sentinel*, however, gave some indication of a division of opinion when it quoted a group known as the Boscobel Reformers as announcing, "The Legislature has bravely exercised the right and duty of protecting the people from extortion and unjust discriminations by chartered monopolies, *a right never to be surrendered*," and the Milwaukee Reformers, a group of similar nature though on another side of the fence, as saying, "Every interest of the State demands *the immediate repeal of the infamous Potter Law*." To these quotations the *Sentinel* sagely added: "These little differences, you know, can be settled after the election." The *Sentinel's* words were prophetic.

The railroads had until October 1, a fortnight, in which to arrange their rates to conform to the Potter Law. To this injunction, of course, all the railroads paid heed, pending final hearing of the case before the Unites States supreme court, to which body the Milwaukee Road planned to appeal again from the expected enjoining decree, which John W. Cary, the road's counsel, urged the Wisconsin supreme court to hand down as quickly as possible after the decision of September 15. But the United States supreme court, in its decision of April 13, 1875, upheld the Potter Law by supporting the decision of the Wisconsin supreme court, and the railroads were thus faced with the necessity of taking other means of avoiding the real and imagined dangers of the Potter Law and of such similar legislation as had been passed by the state legislatures of Iowa and Minnesota.

The most evident means of circumventing the Potter Law and such other acts of regulation as had been passed was, of course, to bring political pressure both by lobbying and by the support of candidates for public office who were pledged to repeal the oppressive legislation. In their subsequent campaign to effect the repeal of the Potter Law and similar laws in other states, the railroads were repeatedly accused of corrupt practices. There exists in fact no evidence of corruption of any kind. True, the railroads supported candidates who were less likely to enact regulatory laws, but there was nothing corrupt in this; it was but the exercise of a constitutional privilege. An agreement said to exist (compare the *Industrial Age,* January 17, 1874) between officials of the Milwaukee Road and Republican party leaders in Wisconsin calling for the killing of railroad legislation or the amending-to-death of such measures doubtless led to the association of the Republican party with "corporate interests," an association which was to become more pronounced in later decades. But even this did not constitute corruption, and no evidence of outright bribery was ever adduced, despite the shrill cries of reformers that the system of free passes for legislators was a kind of bribery—a charge to which the Milwaukee *Sentinel,* by no means on the side of the railroads, retorted, "We are not among those who believe that Wisconsin legislators are so cheap that a pass will buy them. If that were so, would it not be questionable whether such cheap trash was worth purchasing at all?"

The railroads set out to educate the public by illustrating the injustice worked by the regulatory laws. The degree of their success was not at once evident, for the legislative session of 1875 in Wisconsin did little to relieve the railroads in that state, though an amendatory act was passed, if not the one asked by the Milwaukee Road's representatives. However, the act did serve to increase slightly some rates established in the session of 1874, though it also decreased others. President Mitchell, in his report to the directors, said that the amendatory act gave no "material relief." In Minnesota, on the other hand, the restricting legislation was repealed, leaving the roads to fix their own rates as before; and the Iowa law, which had not been as definitive as Wisconsin's Potter Law, was not held to be oppressive enough to fight actively, excepting in its limitation of 3 cents per passenger mile.

The charge of heinous practices by the railroads was loudly trumpeted throughout Wisconsin, thus further adding to the animosity which had lain sullenly in the minds of many people. The Milwaukee *Sentinel,* as early as a week after Justice Ryan's decision in September, 1874, asserted flatly that orders had been issued that John A. Hinsey, detective of the Milwaukee Road, must be nominated for sheriff of Milwaukee County; John W. Cary, the company's attorney, must be nominated for state senator, and that "no man must be nominated for any office on the

Democratic, alias 'Reform' ticket, that is not known to be sound on two points; i.e., Mitchell for U. S. Senator, and the repeal of the Potter Law." The *Sentinel* went on to scourge Mitchell, saying:

Mitchell, the $15,000,000 capitalist, President of the St. Paul Railway Company, President of a bank, an insurance company, and several other corporations, is to be the Democratic, the "Reform," the Anti-Monopoly candidate. The old times are to be realized: "Reform" is to be led by Mr. Mitchell, who is redolent with memories of corruption bonds and stump-tail currency; the Potter Law is to be enforced by the Reformers, through Mitchell, the President of the railway company and the author of the revolutionary proclamation defying the authority of the State to regulate railway management; corporations are to be curbed by the greatest corporator in the State; the Potter Law is to be repealed in the interest of the Reform party of Wisconsin; devils are to be cast out through Beelzebub, the chief of devils.

Mitchell, being the president of the largest railroad company in Wisconsin, seemed fair game for the newspapers. One after another, the papers reported that their "correspondent is informed that Alexander Mitchell, J. P. C. Cottrill, Judge Mallory, Samuel Howard and others held a secret meeting this week, at which $15,000 was pledged for the defeat of Senator Carpenter and election of Judge Mallory to Congress." The indignant denial of the story was greeted with, "We understand this denial rests upon very technical grounds; that is, the sum was $25,000 instead of $15,000." The *Sentinel* summarized the attitude of the papers toward the railroads' entry into politics, as noted by the *News:*

In districts where the railroad interest is strongest, the Democrats are advised to run an anti-Potter Law man; but where the farmers have the power, then a Potter Law man is not to be put in nomination. In this way the *News* hopes that, by utter abandonment of all consistency, all principle, all honesty, a succotash Legislature may be elected, which will agree in nothing save in their opposition to the Republican party, and in a disposition to elect Hon. Alexander Mitchell to the Senate.

The newspapers of the day were somewhat less than fair, manifestly, for the personal attack on Mitchell was completely unwarranted, whatever may have been the justified sentiments in regard to candidates for public office supported by the corporate interests. As a matter of fact, the reduction in rates demanded by the Potter Law did not actually work such a hardship on the railroads as was at first contemplated. The framers of the law had not prepared it out of any genuinely informed knowledge of how a railroad company must be run; they had taken the lowest rates then in force, and arbitrarily reduced them 25 per cent. The alarmed Mitchell had declared that the reduction of 25 per cent meant a reduction of equal proportion in the gross earnings of the Milwaukee Road. When at last the commissioners appointed under the Potter Law released a study of the subject, their mathematical conclusions were that the Potter Law entailed a reduction of less than 5 per cent on the gross earnings of freight traffic, and less than 14 per cent on passenger traffic, assuming that the amount of business did not materially decrease. The company's passenger rates per mile for 1875 amounted to $.0390, as against $.0359 in 1872, for instance; while the average price per ton per mile received for freight was $.0210 in 1875 as against $.0243 in 1872—in neither case a very substantial reduction. The company's total revenue on freight in 1876 amounted to $5,384,230.46, as against $4,566,991.24 in 1872, while the passenger revenue amounted to $1,899,058.54, against $1,775,714.84 in the respective years.

The defiance of the railroad stirred old enmities, but the cries of alarm aroused the legislators. Senator Moses Strong was particularly indignant over President Mitchell's assertion that the railroads would be forced to operate at a loss under the Potter Law, and spoke at length in defense of the legislative action, particularly scoring the railroads for inflated values:

In regard to the suggestion of Mr. Mitchell, that if the Legislature should "repeal our charter, they can go no further. They cannot touch our property without indemnifying us for it," and so forth: the constitution settles this matter. If private property is taken for public use, "just compensation therefor" must be made. This does not necessarily mean $38,000 per mile, or any other arbitrary sum which the President or other officer of the Company may fix upon it, but only such just compensation as shall be determined in conformity with some just rule to be prescribed by the superior power of the State. The existing mortgage liens upon the Road exceed $21,000 per mile; and a "just compensation" for the equality of redemption which is all the stock-holders could claim, would not exceed $4,000 per mile, or less than $250,000, and it would be better for the people to pay that sum, and have the road run in their interest, than to pay annually, in extortions, more than a fourth that sum, and have the road run "for the benefit of the stock-holders."

Moses Strong's attack on the railroads and his support of railroad legislation were very largely personal attacks on Mitchell and the Milwaukee Road, and Strong went to some lengths to give vent to his spleen. "Every person who knows anything of the cost of railroad construction in Wisconsin, knows that the reported cost of this railroad is greatly exaggerated, and that a very large proportion of reported capital stock represents nothing but *water*," he cried. He harked back to 1867 to say, "A charge was publicly made in the State Senate, in 1867, by General A. W. Starks, then a Senator from Sauk County, that Alexander Mitchell had promised, for the purpose of obtaining some desired legislation, that the Milwaukee and St. Paul Company, would extend their road from Portage City to Baraboo, and without the slightest pretense of apology, had never made an attempt to redeem the solemn promise." Coming from Strong, who had himself made more wild promises of railroad extensions than any other official of any other railroad in Wisconsin, this was evidence of how far he could go to show his spite. The suspicion was well-founded that Strong was not nearly so angry at railroads as he was at Mitchell because the canny Mitchell had withdrawn support from Kilbourn and Strong in the La Crosse and Milwaukee venture.

If Mitchell was aware of Strong's attack, he gave no sign. In any case, Mitchell, following a long-established custom, made no statements, issued no announcements to the press of any personal nature, and bided his own time. Moreover, he was at the moment engaged not alone in battling against the Potter Law, but in fighting eastern control of the Milwaukee Road, a fight which came into the open early in May, 1875, when Mitchell issued to the stock and bondholders the following circular: "We invite you to sign and return the enclosed authority to vote for you at the annual meeting of the stockholders of this Company, to be held at Milwaukee on the 12th of June next. . . . Among other contemplated reforms, it is intended that the office in New York shall be used exclusively for the business of this Company, and be under management that will have no interest in the stock market inconsistent with that of the shareholders." The day after the circular was sent out, the newspapers had decoded it, and the *Sentinel* said flatly, "This is a struggle to decide whether New York or Milwaukee shall control the future of the Road . . . and whether the policy of the Company shall be dictated by Russell Sage and his friends, as representing the interests of New York, or by Mitchell and his friends, as representing the interests of Milwaukee, and the Northwest."

Russell Sage had been vice-president of the Milwaukee ever since the reorganization, but it had become manifest to Mitchell that Sage saw the Milwaukee through New York eyes and the stock exchange, which, to Mitchell, meant an impending battle for control. Mitchell thereupon moved with his customary deliberation and with more dispatch than usual to acquire absolute voting control, and, inexorably, Sage was "bounced," as the papers had it, and Julius Wadsworth succeeded to the vice-presidency. Though the acquisitive and unscrupulous Sage subsequently attempted to keep his hold in the Milwaukee by legal action, his suit was finally dismissed in mid-1879 on grounds of limitations. Sage's immediate ouster was Mitchell's only pressing concern; having succeeded in this, he could once more give his undivided attention to defeating the provisions of the Potter Law.

The railroad companies persuaded many people, despite animosity, that the restrictive laws were not only injurious and unjust to the companies, but that they brought about disadvantages to the traveling and shipping public. After the decision handed down by Chief Justice Ryan, President Mitchell, in informing the governor that the Milwaukee Road would conform to the provisions of the Potter Law, said again that the law would prevent any further development of railroads in Wisconsin, and that the company faced the alternative of either cutting down service or transacting business at a loss. At the same time he indicated that the company would elect the latter alternative in the hope of ultimate repeal of the laws in question. The primary opposition to the campaign of the railroads was carried on by the Grangers, but these predominantly agricultural people were not in a position to withstand all the support the railroads could command. Eastern papers looked toward Wisconsin with alarm; the influential *Nation* advised capitalists not to invest in the state, and other papers expressed similar views. Within the state itself, a growing concern was expressed by newspapers. The Evansville *Review* wrote typically that "since the establishment of the Potter law, not a spadeful of earth has been raised towards the construction of a single line of road."

By 1876, enough sentiment had been aroused against the Potter Law and subsequent regulatory measures to foreshadow their emasculation. The new Republican majority in both houses of the legislature was headed by a Republican governor, Harrison Ludington of Milwaukee, who, in his initial message to the legislature, spoke of the plight of the railroads and urged that the Potter Law be repealed. Despite the opposition of the Grangers, the Vance Bill, introduced by supporters and champions of the railroads, was passed and became law March 1, 1876; this law effectively scuttled the principle of effective control of rates and ended the Granger legislation against railroads. The Vance Law provided for a single commissioner with the power only to supervise, specifically repealed the restrictive legislation of 1874, and limited the freight rates to those in force on the Milwaukee Road in mid-June, 1872, rates the railroads had no wish to exceed. With the appointment of Dana C. Lamb as railroad commissioner, the fight against regulation by the state was won for some years to come.

The aftermath, however, was unfortunate. While the Granger activity against railroads continued, the railroads held up the Potter Law and similar legislation as horrible examples, and, whenever any new danger loomed, these horrible examples were dragged out anew, despite the fact that it was never shown that regulatory laws were responsible for a decrease in new line mileage in Wisconsin; this was, presumably, incapable of proof. But the horrible examples served a purpose all too well; years later, President A. B. Stickney of the Great Western Railway admitted that the Granger laws "served the purpose of a 'bloody shirt' to conceal incompetence in railway management for twenty years at least."

The Milwaukee Road, however, had no need to wave this bloody shirt. The year 1874 was an historic one for more reason than that afforded by the Potter Law, for it was a year of change and expansion. In February of that year, the name of the Milwaukee and St. Paul was officially changed to the Chicago, Milwaukee and St. Paul Railway Company. In that year also, Gustavus Swift introduced refrigerator cars, and within a year the Milwaukee Road began to haul butter and eggs in them. The Wisconsin Valley Railroad Company, incorporated three years before, built from Grand Rapids to Wausau, and the Milwaukee and Northern Railway built to Fort Howard, while the Chicago and Pacific, soon to be absorbed by the Milwaukee Road, was well along on a road to Byron. In 1874, the company laid 13,513 tons of steel and iron rails, a decrease of only 3,000 tons from the preceding year, and by the end of that year it had a total of 1,399 miles of road, costing $53,273,494, or $38,080 per mile, while the value of its supplies and materials was over $700,000. It had run 4,699,871 miles, and its net earnings for 1874 were $3,081,900.73. Moreover, earnings rose in both 1875 and 1876, and the company continued a modest program of expansion.

As a part of that program, the problem of spanning the Mississippi to further the road's westward push loomed increasingly large. The Milwaukee Road's arrangement with John Lawler at the Prairie du Chien–McGregor crossing had never been entirely satisfactory, and now, with increasing traffic to westward, the Lawler arrangement of towing four cars on a barge between two steamboats was too slow, and a pile bridge to the channel did not materially help, since river traffic had likewise increased. It was evident that some new arrangement would have to be made within the conditions of the Lawler franchise.

In Lawler's employment at this time was a Bavarian shipbuilder, Michael Spettel, who had come into Lawler's service through the

offices of Edward H. Brodhead, chief engineer of the old Milwaukee &
Mississippi. In common with others among Lawler's employees, Spettel had observed the difficulties manifest in the treacherous transfer
from pile bridge to barge in the crossing of the Mississippi. Many carloads of wheat, farm implements, and lumber rocked off the barge
bridge into the river, so that Lawler not only repeatedly lost the toll
charge, but also had to reimburse the company for cargo and cars.
Added to that were damages to his property and often painful delays
in service, both by train and steamboat. Lawler had, in fact, hired
Spettel on Brodhead's recommendation for his understanding of the
science of buoyance and the knowledge he had of timbering water-
craft. The chief difficulty with the barge-bridge arrangement occurred

Spettel's design for the pontoon bridge.

in mounting and leaving the ends of the barges, the heavy locomotives
sinking one end and tilting the other. Spettel's answer to the problem
was a pontoon bridge, a model of which he designed and whittled out
with a penknife.

Spettel eliminated low- and high-water approaches and dry-dock-
ing; his model permitted calking to be done without interference with
train movements and delays; buoyancy was taken care of 20 feet from
the ends of the pontoon, with aprons carrying rails forming part of the
pontoon track, the outer ends of which rested on the pile approaches,
thus reducing submersion to only 18 inches even under the crossing
of the heaviest trains on the line. General Humphrey, chief of engineers of the U. S. Army, examined Spettel's specifications and reported
the pontoon bridge "exceptionally free from obstruction as to navigation; it conforms to existing laws regulating the bridging of the
Mississippi River, and affords excellent facilities for steamers and rafts
to pass through the draw openings."

The pontoon bridge, which was an engineering feat of rare genius, was, however, patented not by Spettel but by John D. Lawler, who, as Spettel's employer, followed a common precedent in taking credit as an employer for work done by an employee. The injustice thus done the inventor, Spettel, subsequently precipitated a long-standing controversy, which was begun by Spettel's discharge—and that of all his adherents—in 1887, and which was carried on by the respective heirs. The pontoon bridge was the property of Lawler beyond question, since he financed its construction, though it was the invention of Michael Spettel, in whose name the patent should have been taken out. There is no evidence that Lawler notified Spettel of his intention to patent the bridge when he took the whittled model to Washington and entered it August 11, 1874. Since, however, the pontoon began operation in April of that year, there exists no explanation of why Spettel himself had not arranged for a patent prior to Lawler's action, save perhaps the fact that the relations between Spettel and Lawler had always been cordial until it became known that Lawler had appropriated the patent for his own, after which Lawler made a concerted effort to justify his course, evidently with some initial success, for Spettel continued to work for Lawler until 1887.

During the two decades in which the pontoon bridge was the property of the Lawler interests, almost a million railroad cars passed over it at a charge of a dollar per car; but not long after Lawler's death, in 1891, the Chicago, Milwaukee and St. Paul took over the bridge, which is still in operation on the road.

The company effected a third crossing of the Mississippi with the construction of an iron bridge at La Crosse in 1876, by means of which, according to the directors' proud report, "we are enabled to bring the whole of the river division into full use in conducting the business of the Company."

The company expanded in other ways, despite all the difficulties caused by Granger legislation in Wisconsin and in adjoining states. By the end of 1876, the Milwaukee Road owned five elevators in Milwaukee, capable of storing 3,000,000 bushels of wheat, and it valued its wharfs and grounds in that city, exclusive of buildings, at $2,000,000. Moreover, it owned all the sleeping cars then in use on its lines, and that year paid a tax of almost $300,000, despite a reduction in the average price per ton per mile of freight carried of from $.0210 in 1875 to $.0204 in 1876. Nevertheless, the Granger legislation was not the only thorn in the side of the road, for it had constantly to deal with lesser annoyances. In 1876, for instance, the wheat crop in the midwest failed more completely than in any year since initial construction of railroads; in that year the company hauled only 6,824,108 bushels of wheat, or slightly over half the amount hauled the preceding year. However, as Alexander Mitchell pointed out, "The value of such a property [the Milwaukee Road] cannot be permanently affected by the exceptional failure of a single crop."

In 1876, the Milwaukee abandoned the practice of naming locomotives. This custom had reached its height in the early seventies, but not long after the consolidation, when the number of engines rose to 200, the company thought it wise to stop naming them. Previously, engines had been named for a variety of reasons—in honor of some old-time employee, after a director or officer of the company, for a town along the right of way, in tribute to well-known military or other leaders, and generally "to perpetuate the honor cast upon those who were deemed worthy of having locomotives named for them," according to Charles Lapham, who published a study of locomotive nomenclature in 1914.

At the time of the abandonment of this policy, the highest number of a named engine was 199, the *Stephen Clement,* a six-wheeled, 16-by-24-inch switch engine bought from the Milwaukee Iron Company of Bay View, and, incidentally, the first engine with six drivers owned by the Milwaukee. Locomotive nomenclature became somewhat complicated for the Milwaukee during the period of consolidation, when other locomotives were added to the stock. Many engines bore names already listed for Milwaukee engines. When the Milwaukee, Watertown and Baraboo Valley Railroad was acquired, five of its seven locomotives were given new names—thus the *Oconomowoc* became the *Minnehaha,* the *Watertown* became the *D. A. Olin,* the *Charles City* became the *Nebraska,* the *Hercules* became the *Minneapolis,* the *Luther A. Cole* became the *L. B. Rock.* Cole was a promoter of the Watertown road, and so were others after whom locomotives were named.

The names of contractors, engineers, officials, cities starred the list of locomotive names on the company's books in 1876. There were the *Winneconne, Abbot Lawrence, Quickstep* (manifestly a speedier than usual engine), *Shakopee, John W. Cary, General Sheridan, Selah Chamberlain, Alexander Mitchell, Rio, John Plankinton, Defiance, Hector,* and *Vermillion,* among scores of other, more prosaic names. The Milwaukee's first engine was named the *Menomonee;* it had been built by the Menomonee Locomotive Works at the corner of Reed and South Water Streets; later it was renamed the *Chandler,* though it ought to have been given some name more appropriate to its begin-

ning when, because the builders had misgivings about the narrow timber floating bridge which connected West Water and Reed Streets, the
engine was delivered on a temporary track laid along Reed Street to
and across the floating bridge to the Milwaukee & Mississippi Rail
Road tracks, and oxen were used to draw the engine across. Even so, it
narrowly escaped diving to the bottom of the river. But names were
bestowed upon engines primarily for other than sentimental reasons,
and the naming of engines after promoters, officials, and other influential persons was abandoned when it was no longer politic.

The company was also becoming aware of the potential revenue in
lumber. Lumbering in upstate Wisconsin was now at its height, and
by 1877 the road was beginning to push toward strategic centers of
lumbering. In that year the road moved north from New Lisbon to
Necedah at a cost to the road of only $45,013.48, "the balance of the
required outlay being contributed by interested parties at New Lisbon
and Necedah." This short, 13-mile line immediately gathered up the
business of several large sawmills in that area which had hitherto been
floating lumber down the Wisconsin and Mississippi Rivers. Years
before, Alexander Mitchell had foreseen the important role the transportation of lumber in Wisconsin was to play, but his advice had not
been heeded when he had urged the construction of a line to Superior
through what was then largely uninhabited land.

The year 1877 was a good one for the company, for it was free of
floating debt, and President Mitchell was proud and happy to report:
"It gives us pleasure to state that during the serious labor disturbances
of last summer, the employees of this Company, without exception,
stood faithfully at their posts and discharged their duties without fal-
tering." Labor, in fact, had thus far given the Milwaukee Road no
trouble; just as the officials of the company strove to give their patrons
the best and most courteous service, so they also made every attempt
to treat their employees with unusual consideration—which accounts
for the fact that the Milwaukee Road's record of labor relations is, in
historical perspective, very good.

Crop successes were matched with crop failures as the decade drew
to a close. An unusually good wheat crop in 1877 was balanced by a
poor crop in 1878. Quite apparently, the officials of the road believed
that the manifest destiny of the company lay westward, for in 1878
the company purchased most of the stock and bonds of the Dubuque
South Western Rail Road in Iowa, extending from Farley southwest-
erly for 50 miles to Cedar Rapids, effecting a connection with the lines
of the Milwaukee Road at Marion, extending from Sabula. This purchase was followed in 1879 by that of the Western Union Company,

a network of roads in Wisconsin and Illinois, and in 1880 by that of the Chicago and Pacific Railroad, which gave the company a line directly west from Chicago to the Rock River, so that, "with connections made," the company owned a direct route from Chicago to the Mississippi at Savanna and had added yet another river bridge at Sabula, Iowa. The purchase of the Southern Minnesota and the Southern Minnesota Railway Extension Companies not only added new miles of track, but also brought to the company 315,000 acres of excellent land, which augmented 120,000 acres gained by the extension of the line from Algona to Sheldon, Iowa, and 130,000 acres by settlement with the McGregor and Missouri River Railway Company, so that the company found it necessary to organize a land department for the disposal of these lands to incoming settlers. In addition to all this, the company expanded its grounds for yard and depot purposes in Chicago and bought facilities for grain storage in that city, as well as blocks of water frontage for dock purposes.

Perhaps because it was closer to the Milwaukee Road than any other paper, the Milwaukee *Sentinel* was always the most sensitive barometer of the road. When the citizens of Chicago protested in 1877, for instance, that the Milwaukee Road was discriminating in favor of Milwaukee, the paper pointed out, after explaining that the company's management had prepared a lengthy and complete table of figures to exhibit its transportation rates, that "Routes between Milwaukee and stations near thereto are fixed so low by the laws of the State of Wisconsin, that the Company would not be compensated for making the additional haul to Chicago at the same price." Likewise, the *Sentinel* busied itself to find ways of encouraging the Milwaukee Road's income; for example, in October, 1878, when an enterprising reporter discovered that the photographer H. H. Bennett of Kilbourn had prepared "a number of Dell views for the magic lantern," it proposed that "The Chicago, Milwaukee and St. Paul Railway Company ought to send somebody with them through the South this winter, to show the people down there something of the wonders of this locality. It would increase the summer business of the Road."

At the same time, the Milwaukee was growing in the estimation of many people and laying the groundwork for that feeling so prevalent among its employees and its patrons which caused them to regard the railway as "our road." The Wisconsin humorist, George W. Peck, soon to be governor of Wisconsin, took notice of all available information about the Milwaukee to turn it to his own uses. Learning of the introduction of a type of stock car called "palace cattle car," he wrote an amusing piece called "Palace Cattle Cars" for *Peck's Sun:*

The papers are publishing accounts of the arrival east of a train of palace cattle cars, and illustrating how much better the cattle feel after a trip in one of these cars, than cattle did when they made the journey in the ordinary cattle cars.

As we understand it the cars are fitted up in the most gorgeous manner, in mahogany and rosewood, and the upholstering is something perfectly grand, and never before undertaken except in the palaces of the old world.

As you enter the car there is a reception room, with a few chairs, a lounge and an ottoman, and a Texas steer gently waves you to a seat with his horns, while he switches off your hat with his tail. If there is any particular cow, or steer, or ox, that you wish to see, you give your card to the attendant steer, and he excuses himself and trots off to find the one you desire to see. You do not have long to wait, for the animal courteously rises, humps up his or her back, stretches, yawns, and with the remark, "The galoot wants to interview me, probably, and I wish he would keep away," the particular one sought for comes to the reception room and puts out its front foot for a shake, smiles and says, "Glad you came. Was afraid you would let us go away and not call."

Then the cow or steer sits down on its haunches and the conversation flows in easy channels. You ask how they like the country, and if they have good times, and if they are not hard worked, and all that; and they yawn and say the country is splendid at this season of the year, and that when passing along the road they feel as though they would like to get out in some meadow, and eat grass and switch flies.

The steer asks the visitor if he does not want to look through the car, when he says he would like to if it is not too much trouble. The steer says it is no trouble at all, at the same time shaking his horns as though he was mad, and kicking some of the gilding off of a stateroom.

"This," says the steer who is doing the honors, "is the stateroom occupied by old Brindle, who is being shipped from St. Joseph, Mo. Brindle weighs 1,600 on foot—Brindle, get up and show yourself to the gentlemen."

Brindle kicks off the red blanket, rolls her eyes in a lazy sort of way, bellows, and stands up in the berth, humps up her back so it raises the upper berth and causes a heifer that is trying to sleep off a debauch of bran mash, to kick like a steer, and then looks at the interviewer as much as to say, "O, go on now and give us a rest." Brindle turns her head to a fountain that is near, in which Apollinaris water is flowing, perfumed with new mown hay, drinks, turns her head, and licks her back, and stops and thinks, and then looking around as much as to say, "Gentlemen, you will have to excuse me," lays down with her head on a pillow, pulls the coverlid over her and begins to snore.

The attendant steer steers the visitor along the next apartment, which is a large one, filled with cattle in all positions. One is lying in a hammock, with her feet on the window, reading the Chicago *Times* article on "oleomargarine, or Bull Butter," at intervals stopping the reading to curse the writer, who claims that oleomargarine is an unlawful preparation, containing deleterious substances.

A party of four oxen are seated around a table playing seven-up for the drinks, and as the attendant steer passes along, a speckled ox with one horn broken, orders four pails full of Waukesha water with a dash of oatmeal in it, "and make it hot," says the ox, as he counts up high, low, jack and the game.

Passing the card players the visitor notices an upright piano, and asks what that is for, and the attendant steer says they are all fond of music, and asks if he would not like to hear some of the cattle play. He says he would, and the steer calls out a white cow who is sketching, and asks her to warble a few notes. The cow seats herself on her haunches on the piano stool, after saying she has such a cold she can't sing, and, besides, has left her notes at home in the pasture. Turning over a few leaves with her forward hoof, she finds something familiar, and proceeds to walk on the piano keys with her forward feet and bellow, "Meat me in the slaughterhouse when the due bill falls," or something of that kind, when the visitor says he has got to go up to the stock yards and attend a reception of Colorado cattle, and he lights out.

We should think these parlor cattle cars would be a success, and that cattle would enjoy them very much. It is said that parties desiring to charter these cars for excursions for human beings, can be accommodated at any time when they are not needed to transport cattle, if they will give bonds to return them in as good order as they find them.

Not long thereafter Peck told a widely circulated anecdote about the Milwaukee Road's La Crosse division in an article called "And He Rose Up and Spake," also originally published in *Peck's Sun*, but subsequently reprinted in various newspapers and in his book, *Peck's Sunshine:*

As a general thing railroad men are "pretty fly," as the saying is, and not very apt to be scared. But a case occurred up on the La Crosse division of the Milwaukee road last week that caused a good deal of hair to stand.

The train from St. Paul east runs to La Crosse, where all hands are changed, and the new gang run to Chicago. On the trip of which we speak there was placed in the baggage car at St. Paul a coffin, and at Lake City a parrot in a cage was put in. Before the train got to Winona other baggage was piled on top, so the coffin only showed one end, and the parrot cage was behind a trunk, next to the barrel of drinking water, out of sight, and where the cage would not get jammed. At La Crosse the hands were changed, and conductor Fred Cornes, as 6:35 arrived, shouted his cheery "All aboard," and the train moved off. The coffin was seen by all the men in the baggage car, and a solemnity took possession of everybody. Railroad men never feel entirely happy when a corpse is on the train.

The run to Sparta was made, and Fred went to the baggage car, and noticing the coffin and the mournful appearance of the boys, he told them to brace up and have some style about them. He said it was what we had all to come to, sooner or later, and for his part a corpse or two, more or less in a car, made no difference to him. He said he had rather have a car load of dead people than go into an emigrant train when some were eating cheese and others were taking off their shoes and feeding infants.

He sat down in a chair and was counting over his tickets, and wondering where all the passes come from, when the Legislature is not in session. The train was just going through the tunnel near Greenfield, and Fred says:

"Boys, we are now in the bowels of the earth, way down deeper than a grave. Whew! how close it smells!"

Just then the baggage-master had taken a dipper of water from the barrel, and was drinking it, when a sepulchral voice, that seemed to come from the coffin, said:

"Dammit, let me out!"

The baggage man had his mouth full of water, and, when he heard the voice from the tombs, he squirted the water clear across the car, onto the express messenger, turned pale, and leaned against a trunk.

Fred Cornes heard the noise, and, chucking the tickets into his pocket and grabbing his lantern, he said, as he looked at the coffin:

"Who said that! Now, no ventriloquism on me, boys. I'm an old traveler, and don't you fool with me."

The baggage man had by this time got his breath, and he swore upon his sacred honor that the corpse in there was alive, and asked to be let out.

Fred went out of the car to register at Greenfield, and the express messenger opened the door to put out some egg cases, and the baggage man pulled out a trunk. He was so weak he couldn't lift it. They were all as pale as a white-washed fence.

After the train left Greenfield they all gathered in the car and listened at a respectful distance from the coffin. All was as still as a car can be that is running twenty-five miles an hour. They gathered a little nearer, but no noise, when Cornes said they were all off their base, and had better soak their heads.

"You fellows are overworked, and are nervous. The company ought to give you a furlough, and pay your expenses to the sea shore."

Just then there was a rustling as if somebody had rolled over in bed and a voice said, as plainly as possible:

"O, how I suffer!"

If a nitro-glycerine bomb had exploded there could not have been more commotion. The express man rushed forward, and was going to climb over into the tender of the engine, the baggage man started for the emigrant car to see if there was anybody from the place in Germany that his hired girl came from, and Cornes happened to think that he had not collected fare from an Indian that got on at Greenfield with a lot of muskrat skins. In less than four seconds the corpse and parrot were the sole occupants of the car. The three train men and a brakeman met in the emigrant car and looked at each other.

They never said a word for about two minutes, when Fred opened the ball. He said there was no use of being scared, if the man was dead he was not dangerous, and if he was alive the four of them could whip him, if he undertook to run things. What they were in duty bound to do was to let him out. No man could enjoy life screwed down in a sarcophagus like that.

"Now," says Cornes, "there is a doctor from Milwaukee in the sleeper. I will go and ask him to come in the baggage car, and you fellows go in and pull the trunks off that coffin, and we will take a screw driver and a can-opener and give the man air. That's doing as a fellow would be done by."

So he went and got the doctor and told him he had got a case for him. He wanted him to practice on a dead man. The doctor put on his pants and overcoat, and went with Fred. As they came into the baggage car the boys were lifting a big trunk off the coffin, when the voice said:

"Go easy. Glory hallelujah!"

Then they all turned pale again, but all took hold of the baggage and worked with a will, while the doctor held a screw driver he had fished out of a tool box.

The doctor said the man was evidently alive, but the chances were that he might die from suffocation before they could unscrew all the screws of the outside box and the coffin, and he said he didn't know but the best way would be to take an axe and break it open.

Fred said that was his idea, and he was just going for the axe when the brakeman moved the water barrel, tipped over the parrot cage, and the parrot shook himself and looked mad and said, "There, butterfingers! Polly wants a cracker."

Cornes had just come up with the axe, and was about to tell the brakeman to chop the box, when the parrot spoke.

"Well, by ——," said the baggage man. The doctor laughed, the brakeman looked out the door to see how the weather was, and the conductor said, "I knew it was a parrot all the time, but you fellows were so anxious to chop into the box that I was going to let you. I never saw a lot of men with so much curiosity." Then they all united in trying to bribe the doctor not to tell the story in Milwaukee.

This kind of good-natured spoofing helped to dramatize railroad life for the general public, and for most of Peck's readers "railroad life" meant the Milwaukee Road.

As the decade drew to its close, the Milwaukee began to advertise widely, even to the extent of placing specialized advertising in such magazines as *The American Angler.* At the same time, the Milwaukee issued literature designed to attract more European emigrants to Wis-

A page from *The American Angler*, June 10, 1882, illustrating the Milwaukee Road's bid for tourist and sportsmen's traffic.

consin. Among the improvements instituted by the Milwaukee in 1879 was the use of evergreen trees for permanent snow fences along its tracks and sidings. The previous year had seen a voluntary attempt on the part of the company to improve working hours and wages, one of those spontaneous moves which accounted for the high degree of amicable relations between the company and its employees.

Despite the opening of the Chicago terminus, the economic position of Milwaukee was strengthened, rather than weakened, as had at first been feared, and now more than ever the home papers gave top space to the doings of the "home Road," reporting in detail everything the road did, whether it ran a special train to the state fair, an excursion train to the reception of General Grant, or accidentally crashed a locomotive into the river, all events which took place between September 10 and October 14, 1879.

By 1880, the Milwaukee Road was flourishing indeed. It owned no less than 3,775 miles of road; only three years before, its total mileage had stood at 1,412. It owned also 425 locomotives, 168 passenger cars (first and second class), 17 sleeping cars, 4 parlor cars, 130 baggage, postal, mail, and express cars, 9,111 box, freight, and caboose cars, 1,419 stock cars, 2,785 flat and coal cars, and 25 wrecking and tool cars. It had run in that year approximately 11,000,000 miles; its net earnings were $5,343,692.93, and the average rate per ton per mile had dropped to $.0176. The cost of the road was now estimated at just under $100,000,000. During the 1870's the Milwaukee Road had emerged under the able guidance of Mitchell and Merrill as one of the largest and most powerful forces in the middle west. As such, it had attracted the unwelcome attention of politicians; it was destined to attract still other attention as the sands of time ran out for the leadership which had demonstrated such business-like acumen in all its dealings.

VI.   Standard Oil Moves In

The river floods have always been a great drawback at North McGregor. I remember the flood of 1896. It came on May 25th, late in the evening, and, shortly before midnight, I heard William Keen, engine dispatcher, shouting with all his might that the eating-house with everything around it was going out. I ran down to the eating-house. Water was all around it, and cries for help were heard everywhere. Engineer J. Straye, Mr. Krohn, the bridge carpenter, and I went up the track and found the water running through the creek at a sixty-mile rate and raised fifteen feet. The cars were afloat.

We tried to get to the round-house, but found the tracks all washed out and cabooses, wooden bridges, box cars, refrigerators, barns and houses piled in a mass all over the tracks. I remember an old hen with a brood of ten chicks, who sat in the hay at the top of a barn, as unconcerned and contented as possible. We got to the round-house about four A.M., walking along the bluffs; the office, store-room, oil-house, sand-house, top of turntable and water take had all disappeared and no trace of them was ever found.

The next day we received car lots of material from Milwaukee. All the roadmasters were on the ground, and ten machinists were sent for. We had fourteen engines to jack up on blocks, take down driving boxes, remove sand and mud, draw pistons to blow mud off steam chests and cylinders, take down air equipment and clean, bore the flues out where the water had been up to the center plates—and we had all those engines ready in seventeen days. It was six weeks before we could run a train on the Iowa and Dakota Division.

—Frank B. Veit

From 1880 forward, the Milwaukee Road expanded and consolidated steadily, save for a brief pause during the small financial panic of 1884. Population in all the regions reached by the rails was now fairly well developed; since increasing numbers of people were flowing into the country west of the Mississippi within the orbit of the Milwaukee Road, there was manifestly no time to be lost in consolidating and in moving out toward new territory. The days of a single objective at a time were over and done; now the road reached for several objectives at once.

The company played a major part in the rapid development of the nation west of the Mississippi. As the Milwaukee Road reached beyond the boundaries of Wisconsin, it accumulated ever more land by grant and purchase. As previously mentioned, the settlement with the McGregor and Missouri River Railway Company, for instance, brought 130,000 acres under the company's control, while the company received from the government 120,000 acres in Iowa by virtue of the extension of the line from Algona to Sheldon, which, according to the annual report for 1880, were acres with "much to recommend them to settlers, and are in good demand." This land immediately posed a problem to the Milwaukee Road; its possession offered possibilities of advancing the company's interest in the territory served by its lines, but the problem involved was that of adequate exploitation to the best advantage of the company. Moreover, the Iowa lands were but a beginning; as the lines of the company reached westward, more lands would doubtless be added.

On September 14, 1881, the Milwaukee Land Company was formed to buy, sell, lease, and improve lands, at first specifically and only in Iowa, but clearly with the intention, and subsequently in fact, of buying up and selling new areas along the road pushing westward. The articles of organization were signed by Messrs. Sherburn Merrill, John W. Cary, P. M. Myers, and B. G. Lennox. Lennox, though but assistant to the president of the company, came to be considered the "highest untitled man in the management," since he was soon one of the most informed men in the Milwaukee Land Company.

The Milwaukee Land Company shortly established itself as an important adjunct to the Milwaukee Road, and, indeed, as a notable assistant in expansion of the areas under its control, and thus to the states where it functioned. It took over timber lands along its lines and sold them to various lumber companies, with the understanding that the companies would use the Milwaukee Road for the transportation of the lumber on these lands. It sold lands to settlers and in many places laid out town sites and helped to populate them. To stimulate the purchase of these lands, the Milwaukee Land Company offered to rebate the cost of breaking all soil broken within one year after the purchase of land from the company. The extent to which this magnanimous offer succeeded in bringing settlers to live along the Milwaukee's right of way is indicated in the annual report of 1881, when Land Commissioner Willis Drummond, Jr., reported to Alexander Mitchell that "Under the system of rebating to settlers for breaking done by them within one year after purchase, the sum of $60,539.51 was credited upon contracts for breaking 24,731.77 acres. This system has proved very successful, having not only induced actual settlement of the lands, but secured the cultivation of an increased acreage."

By the end of 1881, the company had unsold land in the amount of 186,531.74 acres in Iowa and 314,426.72 acres in Minnesota. However, the Milwaukee Land Company was not particularly concerned about the Minnesota land, and was striving only to effect the sale and development of the Iowa land and such land as was subsequently acquired west of Iowa. In another year, however, the Milwaukee Land Company could add to the Milwaukee Road's annual report that "The lands stated in the last report as belonging to the Company have been sold during the year, except about 100,000 acres, mostly in the State of Wisconsin. The net receipts to the treasury of the Company from sales of land during the years 1881 and 1882 are $1,224,364.38; and the amount now due the Company on contracts and mortgages is $1,787,508.90." Less than a year later Dakota lands were being added to the Milwaukee Land Company's control. The annual report of the Milwaukee Road in 1887 pointed to the unique relationship existing between the land company and its parent company:

Your Company's ownership of its extensive system of railways, with its equipment, real estate and other properties, is by a tenure unlike that by which any correspondingly large railway property has ever before been acquired, and is very different from that of corporations that control large systems by lease of the corporate property, or by ownership of a majority interest in the original corporate organizations. It is practically an absolute ownership, in fee, without partners, subject only to mortgage liens; as in the few cases where a corporate property has been acquired under a lease, your Company is owner of the entire share capital of the lessor Company.

The Milwaukee Land Company existed in periods of two decades each; its original establishment was for a period of 20 years, at the end of which time it was destined to be extended for a like period, and so on, until all the lands under its control were disposed of. Its management was to be always composed of the higher executives of the Milwaukee Road, an arrangement which quickly proved eminently satisfactory and was to undergo no change. The immediate objective, however, was the disposal of the Iowa lands, and this the Milwaukee Land Company set about doing while its parent company sought other goals.

For the Milwaukee Road the primary goals were Kansas City, Fargo, and Omaha, and to that end lines across Iowa and Minnesota were completed and extended further into Dakota Territory and Missouri, looking toward a connection with the Union Pacific and other railroads at the Missouri.

The company encountered the usual difficulties of expansion, and ultimately inevitably encountered Indians. As the Milwaukee reached westward, the rails began to push into Indian country at the boundary of the Black Hills. The Indian inspector in charge of the Brule Sioux managed to effect permission from his charges for the Milwaukee's rails to pass through the reservation of their tribe; but beyond the reservation of the Brule Sioux lay the domain of the Sioux chieftain, Spotted Tail. S. S. Merrill and John Lawler, who had laid out the route of the road into the west, felt that the route through Spotted Tail's reservation was the only feasible one, but Spotted Tail was hostile. He had been crowned "King of the Sioux" in 1877 at the suggestion of no less a person than famed General Crook, commander of the Military Department of the Platte, and had shown himself an able and wise leader by bringing together dissenting and restless tribes.

F. W. Kimball, a Milwaukee Road engineer, was sent by S. S. Merrill on two separate expeditions into the reservation, the first time in 1879, the second a year later. He had arranged to set out with a surveying party with a military escort, but, as he related afterward:

. . . before getting out of touch with the telegraph, I was informed that Carl Schurz, Secretary of the Interior, objected to any body of soldiers being on the reservation, and suggested that Indian Police be substituted for the soldier escort. The Indian Police were a body supposed to be chosen from among the better element of the Indians, they were given a little authority, of which they were very fond, and a small monthly stipend. I was asked if I would take them and I agreed, saying that ten would be about the right number—two or three to remain about the camp, two or three to go with me on my explorations ahead of the survey, and some to send back to Fort Hale for our mail. One of their duties was to explain, in case we met occasional bands of redskins, that we had been sent out by authority of the government and they were present by order of the Indian Police.

The Secretary of the Interior's request was not captious; the battle of the Little Big Horn resulting in the massacre of General Custer, who could not obey orders, and his men, was but a few years in the past; Sitting Bull was still at large, and the Indians in the area through which the surveying party for the Milwaukee was making its way had been in attendance at a sun dance. Kimball was well aware of this, and realized that in case of trouble a small soldier escort would be of no account. His experiences were typical:

Upon my arrival at the Lower Agency, I found the agent, and he appointed the ten Indians I had asked for. Then there had to be a pow wow, and they must all know what I wanted them to do, what I would pay, and so forth. It developed a lot of Indian oratory, for most Indians like on such occasions to talk as well as do some of our politicians. It ended that day in nothing being accomplished except that I must give them a feast where they could talk it over. So I bought them a beef and they killed it and had their feast that night. The next day they were quite tractable and we made terms. We were to pay them $1.50 per day and rations. I had ordered provisions for the summer to be sent from Sioux City by one of the Fort Pierre line boats, so had to wait a few days for the goods. Finally they came and we loaded into three covered wagons drawn by two yoke of oxen each, and two horse teams for quicker and lighter work.

Just as we were ready to start, in came a bunch of Indians with a line from the agent at Rosebud saying the Government had instructed him to send them to me. My protest saying I already had a sufficient number of police and did not need them was of no avail, the Government had sent them and they must go. Finally I said all right, come along. In a few minutes in came another band of ten Indians with a similar note from the agent at Pine Ridge (Red Cloud Camp). I saw it was no use to protest, so surrendered, and soon started with thirty Indians instead of ten.

As I wanted to try out some rough country first, I went about fifty miles before starting the survey. I had been at work but a few days, when we came to the single line trail leading from Rosebud camp to Standing Rock, and in prospecting ahead, I had crossed it several times without seeing a sign of Indians; but on the day the surveying party reached it, all our Indian police being with us as we were moving camp, the trail was alive with Indians going home from Standing Rock and other camps, returning from another Sun Dance at Rosebud. They told our Indians they should not be with us, that Spotted Tail was mad, that he had no ears,—that is, he would not listen, and had sent word for them all to come back. This excited our police to such a degree that we had to stop that afternoon and hold a council. I could not change their belief or temper, so I told them to select at least one from each band and I would go across to Spotted Tail's camp with them the next day; but that Stewart would continue the survey while we were gone. But that would not do at all, he must not do anything until we got back. I finally consented and asked how far it was across. They said it was only a little way, but having had some previous experience with an Indian's "little way," was prepared for almost anything. Starting at early sunrise on horse back, we made an all day's ride, probably fifty miles or more, getting to the Agency about 9 P.M., as tired as ever I was in my life. The Agency was locked up for the night, so I sought the Indian trade store, and after devouring some canned goods and crackers, they brought out about twenty buffalo hides and threw them down for me to sleep on, and I tried to sleep, but it was so suffocatingly hot, the windows were all closed to protect the goods from thievery, that I got little rest until toward daybreak.

In the morning I found the agent and stated my trouble. He said he would fix it all right, but after a while Indians came in one by one and talked to him through his interpreter, though not in my presence and I soon found his assurance was not so ready, the outcome of it being that he told me I would better go back and abandon the survey. I asked him if he would go with me to see Spotted Tail, but he would not go or have anything to say to him. It appears Spotted Tail was down in Washington at the time the Indians were sent to me, so he had not been consulted and his dignity had been stepped on. Besides he had been complaining about the agent, who was a past Brig. General of the Civil War, an irascible fellow and not easy to handle. Finally I got him to lend me his interpreter and I went to see Spotted Tail. I found him surrounded by many warriors, but all I could say made no impression on him.

At length, convinced that I could do nothing further, I decided to send back word to Stewart to take the party back to the river and stay there until we could get matters straightened out.

Spotted Tail's hostility was not permanent, however, and it did not extend to white men whom he knew to be honest. It was a missionary friend of Lawler's who finally prevailed upon Spotted Tail and other Indians to go to Washington and sell that part of the land the Milwaukee Road wanted. But Spotted Tail insisted that "Big Eyebrow"— the Sioux name for Lawler—would have to lead them and bring them back. Lawler accordingly took the Indians in a private car to Washington—Spotted Tail, Red Cloud, Bear Bird, Standing Elk, Dead Hand, Dog Back, Little Bear, and White Ghost, with others bearing less colorful names, all dressed in full Indian regalia. Banqueted and royally treated all the way to Washington and back, the delegation, led by Spotted Tail, made no difficulty about the entry of the Milwaukee Road into the Black Hills.

But during this move westward the company neglected no division of its line. On the original old Prairie du Chien division, for instance, it put forth a spur to afford direct rail connection to such towns as Sauk City and Prairie du Sac, which had had highway freight service from the station at Mazomanie, ten miles away. At the same time, the company reached toward the timber and lumber country in northern Wisconsin, purchasing the Chippewa Valley and Superior Railway, thus assuring that not only the Wisconsin River valley lumber but also the annual 300,000,000 feet of Chippewa pine lumber, in addition to shingles, laths, and so forth, would henceforth travel out of the woodlands by rail, instead of down the Chippewa and Mississippi Rivers. Simultaneously, the company was purchasing coal lands in Illinois and Iowa estimated to yield all the fuel needed by the Milwaukee Road for some time.

The Milwaukee was expanding at a hitherto unparalleled rate. This was the decade at the opening of which the staid *Merchant's Guide* of Philadelphia said of the Milwaukee, "It is certainly one of the best, if not the best, built and ballasted roads in the West, and in the matter of its coaches unsurpassed for finish and comfort." Indeed, so rapid was the expansion that within a matter of months the Milwaukee experienced a crying need for cars, and the Milwaukee *Sentinel* was making news of the "car famine": "The Chicago, Milwaukee and St. Paul Company are 1,000 cars short of their present requirements west of the Mississippi. . . . If the Milwaukee possessed all the rolling stock its freighting called for, its earnings would be nearly double the present income. The scarcity of cars oblige it to roll the number at command on the double-quick."

Growing business forced the building of an additional track between Minneapolis and South Minneapolis, and so hard were the freight gangs pushed that, before 1880 came to an end, the company faced a teapot revolt when the freight gang in the South Milwaukee yards talked about striking for a higher rate of pay, causing the company to quell demonstrations, fire the agitators for a strike, and raise the pay of remaining laborers. The rising prestige of the Milwaukee encouraged the company's superintendent, C. H. Prior, to order that all conductors on the Milwaukee's St. Paul–Minneapolis Short Line must henceforth be uniformed, and the company began to issue handsome booklets for its patrons on subjects as diverse as *Gems of the Northwest* and *Skat*, the latter in German for the delectation of attendees at the international skat tourney in Milwaukee.

Before the end of 1881, too, the Milwaukee was experiencing the envy of some of its competitors, which manifested itself in many ways, though perhaps in none more ridiculous than the attempt of the Chicago & Northwestern Company to prevent the Milwaukee from effecting a crossing of the Chicago & Northwestern track at Stockwell's Switch in Lyons, Iowa. When the tracklayers of the Milwaukee reached the crossing, they found a switch engine and a way car of the Chicago & Northwestern across the proposed line of the Milwaukee. Before the obstruction could be moved, the Lyons common council had to be called into extraordinary session. The council ordered the city marshal to move the obstruction at once and allow the Milwaukee the right of way granted it. Aided by citizens, the marshal accomplished his purpose, removing the engineer and brakeman from the locomotive so that the Milwaukee's men could move the Chicago & Northwestern engine and way car well down the track.

In 1882, the Milwaukee concluded a contract with George M. Pullman, transferring a fourth interest in the sleeping cars then owned by the Milwaukee to the Pullman Company, the contract providing that the Pullman Company conduct the sleeping car business for the railroad, and providing also for a division of profits after payment of operational expenses. This was another evidence of the company's rapid expansion, since any such agreement was basically at odds with the company's desire to be free of outside influence. The agreement, however, was destined to last for only eight years, after which the Milwaukee once again resumed full control of its sleeping car business.

In 1882, also, the company once again demonstrated that steadily growing clannishness which existed between employers and employees, as well as among the employees themselves. In the Milwaukee yards, a switch-tender named Gsandtner was killed at his work. He was survived by a daughter Annie, who had long been his helper, though she was but 16 at the time of his death. Yet it was recalled that, four years before, she had begun to help him at his work, and once while he was ill, when he forgot about the switches, Annie had remembered to open them and saved a train from being wrecked. Now the papers reported that at 16 "Switch Annie," as they had begun to call her, "could stand on the track and swing herself onto the footboard of a switch engine with as much grace and ease as any man in the yards." Even at 16 she was picturesque—tall, lithe, attired in a big straw hat, ground-sweeping skirts, and heavy gauntlets. The Milwaukee Road's tradition for family was challenged; there was no son to carry on. But there was Switch Annie, and it was Switch Annie who was officially appointed at 16 to her father's position, immediately bringing an aura of romance to the already famous Milwaukee, so that her little red switch shanty, where she sat knitting between tasks, was for a long time before its removal a place of interest for the curious from outside as well as for the loyal employees of the Milwaukee. She was to throw switches for trains that traveled between Milwaukee and La Crosse and Prairie du Chien for the next 25 years.

Switch Annie and the Milwaukee looked upon service to the Milwaukee as a tradition, just as so many other employees did, notably the Dousman family, famed in the history of Wisconsin. Since 1851, no less than eight members of this family had entered the service of the Milwaukee in one capacity or another. Benjamin A. Dousman of Milwaukee began as an accountant in the Milwaukee's home station while Switch Annie was still helping her father. As the last of the railroading Dousmans, he was destined to be the first Milwaukee employee ever to witness the naming of a Milwaukee sleeping car in honor of his family while he was still in the service of the company.

The increased activity of the Milwaukee in the 1880's was such as to suggest that the company acted as if engaged in a race with time, and, indeed, this was the case, and not unwisely, for the steadily increasing westward flow of settlers was phenomenal. Rails were pushed on the Chippewa Valley & Superior Division from Eau Claire to Chippewa Falls; from Cedar Rapids to Ottumwa, Iowa; and in Dakota no less than 81 miles were constructed to make a continuous line in the James River Valley from Yankton, by way of Mitchell, though Aberdeen to Ellendale, a distance of approximately 250 miles. All this in 1883, and for good reason. In his report of that year, President Mitchell pointed out that

The rapidity of the settlement of Dakota is a marvel of the times. During the last year, over 12,000,000 acres of land were taken up for cultivation by settlers, and from present advices we have every reason to believe that the immigration the present year will equal that of the past. The lines in Dakota, although mostly built in advance of settlements, will at an early day be supplied with an abundance of traffic, the product of the rich prairies, through which they run, now peopled by an energetic and thrifty race of settlers.

The brief panic of 1884 halted the Dakota development only a little, and the company made up for the delay in 1885 by purchasing 117 miles of railroad in Minnesota and Dakota from the Fargo and Southern Railway, thus acquiring an important position in the Red River Valley, a position essential to the protection of its interests in the Dakota Territory. Meanwhile, it pushed construction of the line from

Ottumwa to Kansas City, working deep into northern Missouri toward completion of that line in 1887; it acquired a one-fifth interest in the Belt Railway Company of Missouri, and completed in 1886 a new passenger station at Milwaukee, the original terminus of the road, to be used jointly with the Wisconsin Central Line and the Milwaukee and Northern Railroad.

The Milwaukee Road prospered, and the fruits of Alexander Mitchell's conservative wisdom were now evident. Despite the repeated difficulties of the 1880's, as duly set down in the reports—"The oft-recurring snow blockades of winter and the continuous rains of autumn have been a large expense and a serious interruption to business." (1881)— "The great depression in commercial affairs . . . has prevented the increase of earnings which was expected." (1884)—"Labor troubles have unsettled commercial affairs during a considerable part of the year. Passenger rates in the States of Wisconsin, Iowa and Minnesota have been reduced from four cents to three cents a mile. A large part of the revenue formerly derived from the transportation of wheat and its products from Dakota and Minnesota has been cut off by Lake Superior competition and other causes, which have deprived this Company of the haul from Minneapolis to Milwaukee or Chicago, or have reduced the rates for such haul to so low a point as to make it unprofitable except when it followed the movement of empty cars." (1886)—the company fared well, as is shown repeatedly in the record of earnings, as well as in the formal reports, which continually emphasized in those years that "there has been an increase in earnings," and the "general condition of the property of the Company was never better."

Time, however, was running out for the able duo of Mitchell and Merrill. By the 1880's both men were recognized throughout the nation as railroad giants. In 1882 the Boston *Herald* and other papers devoted columns to biographical and personal material about the two men. The *Herald's* portrait of Merrill was not exaggerated:

Mr. Merrill's passion, almost his life, is the mammoth railroad business which he directs. To it every allegiance, save that of home, is subordinated. He is earnest, persistent, patient; but his patience holds only because "the chips are kept flying" all the time. The record of his work is a record of constant, rapid, brilliant progress. The force of his strong individuality is in no other way shown so well as in the comparison of the rapidly moving railroad work in which Mr. Mitchell and himself are engaged jointly. . . . There is an extension to build, a new feeder line to buy, a strike to contend with, a rate war to fight; and, by the time Mr. Mitchell has concluded what it "would perhaps be well to try and do," Mr. Merrill is doing it, hammer and tongs. With work to perform he knows no fatigue, stops at no obstacle, heeds no voice from any source. Rigid as a disciplinarian, exacting the same prompt obedience to orders that he accords orders coming to him, he is an ideal ruler of men. The almost passionate energy, put into his every personal move, he has the faculty to impart to those about him. . . . At every point on every section of the 4,590 miles of road, and by every employee, high or low, he is known and spoken of respectfully and half affectionately only as "the old man."

The *Herald's* portrait of the Milwaukee Road's president was no less straightforward, but even that paper's earnest praise of Alexander Mitchell could not show in proper perspective the entire background and character of the man who had devoted all his talents and energies to building up the prestige now held by the Milwaukee Road; it could not show how Mitchell had held his railroad together in the difficult early days when he fell heir to the consequences of all the sins of railroad men in dozens of other companies, or how he had kept public good will for his road, or how, by great perseverance and patience, he had made the Milwaukee Road a paying proposition. Mitchell's conservatism had never been permitted to get in the way of any expansion of the road, if the time were opportune, though he did not permit any sentimental interest to influence him, as was shown when, on the occasion of some of his relatives entering the service of the Milwaukee, the president of the company went to the heads of the various departments and issued strict orders that his relatives were not in any circumstances to be looked upon as his protégés and were to be considered on their own merits alone, and any one of them failing to do his full duty must be reported to him. He held to his conservatism unswervingly in political matters alone, though he was a Whig as a banker, and subsequently a Republican, active in the Wide-Awake movement, and finally a Democrat. As a Democrat, he served two two-year terms in congress, though, disliking political life, he was not again a candidate in 1874, when his second term ended. Mitchell and Merrill were colorful and quietly dramatic figures in the history of the road.

But 1883 was, in a sense, their last great year. In that year affairs of the road were going so well that it was possible for Mitchell to make his third trip to Europe, including his native Scotland. When he returned in October, he was met in Chicago by a committee of 25 citizens of Milwaukee appointed to meet him and escort him to Milwaukee "as a fitting expression of pleasure at his safe return from his extended trip to Europe." There were old names long associated with Milwaukee and the Milwaukee Road on the committee, among them E. H. Brodhead, E. D. Holton, S. S. Merrill, H. L. Palmer,

E. O'Neill, C. L. Colby, H. Ludington, J. H. Van Dyke, Horace Chase, J. R. Goodrich, Captain Pabst, and S. T. Hooker.

The Milwaukee *Sentinel,* in its issue of October 27, reported the excursion in detail, including even a section of "rail gossip," which threw a direct light on the qualities of Merrill:

"You know," said one gentleman, "that the St. Paul Road has, or it used to have, a standing order that no one in a parlor car was to go free, not even officials of the Road. I remember one day I was going down, and there was a new conductor for the car on duty. Among those inside was S. S. Merrill, who was talking with two or three ladies, and I noticed the conductor didn't strike that crowd for fare. After a while Merrill strolls out to the conductor's end, and I can imagine what he said, for in a minute or so, in comes Mr. Conductor, and he says as polite as you please: "Mr. Merrill, I'll have to trouble you for your fare." The women looked paralyzed. "What!" they cried, "Do you have to pay fare?" Merrill said he did, and I noticed they went down into their dresspockets, too.

The party returned to Milwaukee in Mitchell's private car, Number 222, attached to the parlor car, named *Aberdeen* out of respect for Mitchell, the special train being under the direction of H. C. Atkins, assistant general superintendent of the road, who, with Senator James R. Doolittle, had joined the welcoming committee in Chicago. In Milwaukee, Mitchell received an ovation from the citizens and suffered himself to be guest of honor at a banquet at the Plankinton.

Within a year the direction of the famous duo came to an end with Merrill's death; Roswell Miller became general manager of the road, Mitchell continuing as president. But Mitchell's health began to decline not long after Merrill's death in 1884, and, though he remained president of the road until his death on April 19, 1887, he became steadily less active.

Roswell Miller, then but 42, succeeded to the presidency of the Milwaukee in 1888. Miller had come to the Milwaukee in 1883 from the Chicago & Western Indiana Railroad, where, as second vice-president and treasurer, he had attracted Merrill's attention. He was a suave, genial man, withal a strict disciplinarian who expected every official and employee to respect his office, very much in the tradition of the army, where Miller had served. Despite his insistence on discipline, he was popular in railroad circles, and his election to the presidency was applauded particularly by residents of Wisconsin because he made his residence in Milwaukee, and continued to do so until the general offices were removed to Chicago at the turn of the century. He was an extremely reticent man, and, while he maintained that his

office ought always to be respected, he was averse to personal distinction, holding that it was the company and not the individual, who was
but a part of it, which was properly to receive the credit for the success which the Milwaukee Road had become. He was adept at putting
off newspaper men without offending the press; he could grant an
interview and say less in more words than any other railroader, and
he had passed the word along the ranks of his subordinates that no
one was to give out any information about him. He had little trouble
in inspiring that confidence and respect he expected and thought
necessary to the successful maintenance of discipline and effective
management. Yet Miller's election was in a way a surprise to financial
circles, where the supposition was that either Philip D. Armour or
John Plankinton would succeed Mitchell. Financial circles had rumored
Armour's opposition to Miller, but in point of fact Armour had written
from Vienna in Miller's support.

At the time of Mitchell's death the Milwaukee Road owned 5,669.95
miles of track, on 3,737 miles of which steel rails had been laid. The
road, which had begun with a loose network of small lines drawn
together by Mitchell with Milwaukee as a central terminus, was now
a great web of rails spread over five states and the Dakota Territory,
with the central terminus of the road gradually shifting to Chicago.
Though it had begun in Wisconsin, the company had more miles of
track in Iowa than in any other state; its mileage was located as follows: 316.15 miles in Illinois; 1,305.05 in Wisconsin; 1,573.20 in Iowa;
1,120.17 in Minnesota; 140.27 in Missouri, and 1,215.11 in Dakota
Territory. The report for that year, 1887, listed 848 passenger and
freight station agencies on the line of the road, in addition to seven
bridges crossing the Mississippi and Missouri Rivers, 1,410 grain elevators and warehouses, most of them owned by the company, and three
coal-mining properties in Illinois and Iowa; and the company was
described as in "absolute ownership in fee" of its property, "without
partners, subject only to mortgage liens."

By that year, however, momentous events were shaping up, events
which were to influence profoundly the destiny of the Milwaukee
Road for decades to come. The growth not only of the Milwaukee but
also of other large railroad companies spurred renewed attempts at
regulation. Several states had sought to regulate interstate commerce
with various laws, one of which, that of the state of Illinois, had been
contested and brought before the United States supreme court in the
case of Wabash vs. Illinois. In 1886 that body had handed down its
decision, which was to the effect that the various states had no right

to regulate interstate commerce or to interfere in any way with traffic moving across their borders.

This celebrated decision was hailed jubilantly by railroad people generally, but it precipitated congressional action, for farmers, large shippers, and labor unions stirred up such a storm of protest that congress opportunely decided that some form of federal legal action must be taken to establish an interstate commerce act, with the result that both chambers finally passed an act designed to foster competition, to forbid rebates and pooling, to make impossible the exacting of higher freight tariffs for short hauls than for long hauls, to prevent any discrimination between persons, places and commodities, and to require reports and accounts of railroads to be made to a commission set up for the purpose of assuring the observance of the provisions of the new law.

The immediate effect in railroad circles was one of consternation and gloom, which was reflected in an uneasy and panicky market, followed in 1888 by the falling of railway rates and a startling decrease in the net earnings of the great roads, notwithstanding an increase in gross revenue. The Milwaukee Road was not willing to give up entirely to pessimism, however, though pointing out that "sweeping changes" seriously disturbed rates which "for many years had been *relatively* adjusted via different routes into common territory; and the readjustment, *relatively*, of such rates" had been very difficult, admitting that "because of these rate disturbances and complications during the eight months of 1887 that the new law was in force, its full effect upon the movement of traffic cannot be satisfactorily determined."

The annual report for 1887 made no attempt to conceal the alarm with which the company viewed the new legislation:

It will take another year's experience to show the extent of the injury that will result to railway property and to the public under the fourth section of the law, relating to long and short haul charges, which is in direct conflict with the last paragraph of section one, requiring that rates "shall be reasonable and just." It will take a lifetime to determine the extent of injury that will result from section five of the Act, which prohibits agreements between transportation lines for an equitable division of traffic or traffic revenue; as it is by such agreements only that reasonable and uniform rates can be permanently secured, to prevent that "undue and unreasonable preference or advantage" in favor of individuals or localities (invariably resulting from railway wars and reductions in rates below cost of service), which the first paragraph of section three, forbidding preferences, was evidently intended to provide against, and if properly enforced will certainly prevent. It is to be hoped that Congress in its wisdom will repeal the two objectionable sections, or so amend the law as to permit railway companies to charge rates for transportation that are in themselves reasonable and just.

The Milwaukee Road waited upon the interpretation of the various sections of the Act while it fought through the courts a legal battle of its own which, though it may now appear to be a minor case, was at the time a *cause célèbre*, giving rise to much newspaper comment. This was the case of William Barnes, Trustee, vs. the Chicago, Milwaukee and St. Paul Railway Company. Barnes was the trustee of the so-called "Third Mortgage," given in 1858 by the La Crosse and Milwaukee Rail Road Company, covering the line of the road from Milwaukee to La Crosse, to secure bonds to the value of $2,000,000. This long-standing dispute concerned the "eastern division" of the one-time La Crosse and Milwaukee Company. In May, 1859, Barnes, as trustee, foreclosed the mortgage by a sale under the power in the mortgage, in pursuance of statute, and at that sale he became the purchaser for the benefit of the bondholders. Thereafter, in connection with them, he organized the Milwaukee & Minnesota Railroad Company, transferring to that company all the property included in the mortgage and purchased by him at the sale resulting out of his institution of proceedings. The La Crosse and Milwaukee Company thus ceased to exist as a corporation, and the new company claimed to be the owner of the property, subject to prior liens, being so treated thenceforth and made a party in all subsequent foreclosure proceedings of the prior mortgages, and being placed in possession of the eastern division of the road as owner until title was extinguished by foreclosure of such prior liens and by purchase by the Milwaukee.

However, in 1878, Barnes had filed a bill in the United States circuit court for the eastern district of Wisconsin, claiming that his former foreclosure, in 1859, of said mortgage was illegal and invalid; that the company formed by him with the assent of the bondholders never acquired title to the property on his first foreclosure, and asking to have the whole of his former proceedings set aside and annulled, to have his mortgage declared an existing and valid lien upon the property, and to have a foreclosure of that property. The Milwaukee Road quite naturally fought this action, standing by the former foreclosure and its results, and the circuit court finally, in 1883, sustained the defense and dismissed the bill. But Barnes, not satisfied, appealed to the United States supreme court, and this body finally handed down its decision in May, 1887, sustaining the decree of the circuit court and barring any further claim under the Barnes mortgage.

The Interstate Commerce Act, together with the mild financial uneasiness of 1887, resulted in a cessation of the expansion plan of the Milwaukee Road. Political uncertainty combined with economic doubt did not make for any encouragment toward further expansion, though the company did carry through its plan to add to its passenger equipment two trains of vestibuled cars for the Chicago–Twin Cities run, each train to consist of seven of the latest, most improved Pullman cars and sleeping, parlor, dining, and combined smoking and library cars, to begin service in May, 1888. The road had reached its Kansas City terminus, and it was planning to conclude a contract with the Union Pacific Railway Company to use the Union Pacific's main tracks from the Milwaukee Road's Council Bluffs terminus to a point in South Omaha, but this was deferred for three years. However, it gradually became clear that, despite the annoyance of various state laws seeking to control interstate commerce, the Federal Interstate Commerce Act was proving more difficult to enforce than it had been to create, largely owing to the impossibility of making any equable decision regarding rates and regulations which would be fair to the public and at the same time not impose an unjust burden upon the railroads. Soon after the enactment of the law, the United States supreme court prevented the commission from fixing rates, deciding that the commission all too often fixed such rates without consideration of every aspect of railroading in hand—that is, without a complete understanding of the complex pattern out of which the company rates had grown in individual cases. Moreover, the companies soon found that their accountings need not be as circumspect and meticulous as they had feared, with the result that, in effect, the people had a law, and the companies still had their railways.

Nevertheless, the increasing evidence of the government's intent to regulate the railroads profoundly stirred financial circles with interests in railroad companies, and it was evident that some action must be taken by them. Late in 1888, Drexel, Morgan & Company, Kidder, Peabody & Company, and others called a conference to discuss plans to control railroads through concentrated financial power. The plan was Pierpont Morgan's, and Morgan was behind the "Private and Confidential Circular" which went out to the heads of the large American railway companies. The initial meeting was held in the library of Morgan's Madison Avenue house in New York on January 8, 1889. Frank Bond, vice-president of the company, attended for the Milwaukee Road, taking his place among such railroad notables as Jay and George Gould of the Missouri Pacific, Chauncey Depew of the New York Central, Charles Francis Adams of the Union Pacific,

A. B. Stickney of the Chicago, St. Paul, & Kansas City, and others. The Morgan-inspired circular had been born out of the natural fear of popular sovereignty of the railroads, but it stated the object of the secret meeting as some plan properly to "maintain public, reasonable, uniform and stable rates," and to enforce the Interstate Commerce Act.

The meeting was chairmanned by Morgan, and it was characterized by plain speaking, most of which, however, did not apply to the Milwaukee Road, which had about it none of the lawlessness associated with the more ruthless exploitation of some of the western railroads. What Morgan told the group, in effect, was that the roads must henceforth be prepared to be run in accordance with principles laid down by their financial backers, and not by expedience. "The purpose of this meeting," said Morgan brusquely, "is to cause the members of this association to no longer take the law into their own hands when they suspect they have been wronged, as has been too much the practice heretofore. This is not elsewhere customary in civilized communities, and no good reason exists why such a practice should continue among railroads." That the financial circles had been aware of such practices in the past must have been obvious; they were aroused not by any moral indignation, but by the fear of popular sovereignty—the control of the people through government. The resulting discussion was, understandably, bitter and direct, but nothing which the railroad men could say could alter Morgan's opinion that a permanent and secret rate-fixing organization was the only alternative to government control.

The second meeting took place two days later, and the discussion was resumed, to end at last in a "gentlemen's agreement" along the lines proposed by Morgan. It seemed almost as if the powerful Morgan and his cohorts had accomplished what the government had not been able to do in its agreement, but this was not so, for railroad men from the Chicago centers did not see eye to eye with Morgan, and, still not trusting the eastern banking interests, formed a pool of their own, which in itself defeated the Morgan plan. But Morgan and the financial interests were not ready to give up trying; they simply bided their time and waited for an opportune moment to move in with some sort of control. This was not long in coming.

Meanwhile, the Milwaukee Road forged serenely ahead. The company was active in the Interstate Commerce Association, which had been formed primarily to deal with "ill-advised and restrictive legislation" on the one hand and "needless railways" on the other. The report of 1889 conceded that the association had "in some cases operated to the detriment of the interests of this Company, without producing any general good. On the whole, however, it has hitherto proved a benefit, although the failure to secure the coöperation of important lines has, from the outset, impaired its usefulness and prevented a full and fair trial of its methods." Yet the company held that the association was the "best form of agreement" yet devised, though "it is idle to expect that any association or agreement for securing stable rates can be a complete success so long as pools are prohibited." The association's hope was that pools might eventually be legalized—"under the supervision, if need be, of the Interstate Commission"—and that contracts enacted by pools would be subject to enforcement by the courts.

To the Milwaukee Road, the Interstate Commerce Association was vastly to be preferred to control from the east. More than any other railroad company, the Milwaukee Road persistently fought clear of outside domination in its affairs, even going so far as to run its own sleeping cars—the only American railroad to do so—and beginning very early to manufacture its own locomotives and freight cars, just as it was a pioneer in the use of vestibule cars and in the adoption of many new inventions. The Milwaukee Road preferred to play a lone hand in the railroad scene, and it seemed impossible that any complete control from outside could ever be established over it.

However, fearful of Morgan control, the officials of the road were less fearful of other influences. Representatives of two major industrial forces in America began to buy into the Milwaukee Road in the 1870's. By the middle of the 1880's Philip D. Armour of Chicago, representing the packing interests, was a director of the road; also, since 1881, the road's board of directors had included William Rockefeller, who represented a far greater industrial empire—Standard Oil. The Armours presumably came into the railroad picture in self-defense, for, with nine great railroads linking Chicago with the rest of America, the traffic in meat was augmented by purchase of live cattle and the concentration of all handling, slaughtering, and dressing in the great Union Stock Yards. Moreover, the packing interests found Gustavus Swift's refrigerator car increasingly necessary to their business; this had been invented in 1874, so that the Armours had already come into the railroad picture by a side door before their association with the Milwaukee Road.

Like Alexander Mitchell, Philip Armour was of Scottish descent. Moreover, long before becoming a director of the road in 1885, he had made Mitchell's acquaintance and become very friendly with him. He was a man of more than ordinary strength and courage, heavy-set, and habitually clean-shaven, though he wore sideburns. He had an unusual capacity for work, often appearing at his desk as early as six o'clock in the morning. His integrity, thrift, energy, and common sense, coupled with benevolence and a curious habit of correctly playing his hunches—which probably derived from a keen business instinct —inspired both respect and affection among his friends and business associates. More than most men, he could count on the co-operation of his own men, and his strong faith in the future sustained him in any crisis. "There is nothing really ever bothers me much," he said on one occasion. "I am of that sort of make-up, that I throw off cares easily. Give me plenty of work, and it is all the tonic I want." Previous to meeting Mitchell, Armour had known James J. Hill, whom he had first met in the late 1850's; he realized quite clearly that the fortunes of his packing business were tied to those of the middle-western railroads, and he picked the Chicago, Milwaukee and St. Paul as the railroad most likely to be of value in his business. Forthwith, he began to buy into it.

Because of his friendship with Mitchell, Armour was said to hold "trumps in the game of railroads which no other player could match." Certainly his friendship with Mitchell gave him an influence in the formation of the road's policies. In common with Mitchell, he looked toward a Missouri River terminus for the Milwaukee Road well before such a terminus was established. He became the second middle-western packer on the board of directors of the Chicago, Milwaukee and St. Paul, following John Plankinton of Milwaukee, though he soon passed all others in ownership of company stock. His influence with his fellow directors, however, did not stem nearly so much from his large interests as from his recognized acumen and the impressiveness of his rigid and simple habits, which were demonstrated soon after he was made a director, when, on a tour of inspection with Marshall Field, George M. Pullman, Norman B. Ream and John J. Mitchell in the president's private car, he replied to a suggestion of cards from his companions: "I have not broken my nine o'clock retiring rule for Mrs. Armour, and I can see no reason to do it for you."

But the control of the Milwaukee Road was not always to remain in the hands of the old families long associated with the company. This was by no means a blow to those who had been in control, for they assumed that the new owners were as much opposed to the combination of J. P. Morgan and James Hill as they themselves were. The new owners were ostensibly two of the nine trustees who made up the great Standard Oil Trust—William Rockefeller and Henry Flagler. Flagler had followed Rockefeller into the Milwaukee Road. Both men were associated with a group of major capitalists—William C. Whitney, Thomas Fortune Ryan, Charles T. Yerkes, Peter A. B. Widener, and

H. H. Rogers—a group of men who moved steadily to acquire control of gas, electric, and railroad companies.

The Standard Oil Trust had been formed in order to protect the interests of Standard Oil, the earlier union of the 40-odd companies controlled by John D. Rockefeller and his partners having been found inadequate as a permanent working plan. By the end of 1882, all the existing stockholders in the oil enterprises had conveyed their shares "in trust" to the nine trustees who became controlling stockholders of all the companies in the Standard Oil system and also a council legally empowered to exercise absolute control without fear of any challenge from anywhere within the vast organization. Quite naturally, with an eye toward greater and greater profits, the trust soon came to feel that it must, short of outright control, keep a listening post of some consequence in every enterprise which directly or indirectly served Standard Oil. The Milwaukee Road was such an enterprise. At first control was not desired; William Rockefeller, as the initial representative of the Standard Oil Trust on the board of directors of the Milwaukee Road, was considered adequate for the best interests of the trust.

Rockefeller, once described as an "amiable mediocrity," was considerably more than that. Amiable he certainly was; in addition, he was well liked, openhearted, jolly, and a good storyteller, but not a talkative man; he liked horses and abhorred pious hypocrites; he was openfaced and not given to deception of any kind. He refused to speak in public and to be interviewed; he never issued statements. Far from being a mediocrity, he was an able, energetic, and intelligent man who foresaw the need for inside information from such companies as the Milwaukee Road long before the trust as a whole acknowledged it. In his own right he was extremely wealthy at the time he bought into the Milwaukee Road and rose to a position on the board of directors. He was not an obstreperous man; despite the fact that his influence was virtually limitless, he made no insistent forays into the management of the Milwaukee Road. It was not, indeed, for several years after he had risen to a commanding position in the company's affairs that it became evident that absolute control potentially, if not actively, might be desirable. This decision was brought about by two related factors above all others—troubled labor conditions in the early part of the 1890's, and the panic of 1893. In addition, there were still a host of problems coming in the wake of the Interstate Commerce Act.

The Milwaukee Road's report of 1890 foreshadowed trouble of various kinds, and subsequent reports elaborated it. Competitive traffic brought about low rates, and the same conditions brought about lower rates on local traffic because of the operation of the long- and short-haul clause of the Interstate Commerce Law. It seemed apparent to the company that "the only result possible under the law, as it now stands, is the absorption of the weaker by the stronger; and that is a painful process which can stop only when there is but one corporation, and competition is absolutely destroyed. Unrestrained competition will, in the end, destroy all competition." That other railroad companies were beginning to react similarly was demonstrated by the withdrawal of some of the most important lines from the Interstate Commerce Association, a withdrawal which considerably weakened the influence of the railways. The agitation about the difficulties experienced by the railroads under the new law, as well as under various regulatory state laws, such as the case of the battle of the Milwaukee Road against the state of Minnesota in the "Milk Case," predisposed people toward retaining all their old prejudices against the railroads without due regard for the merits of the individual cases. The public, inspired by prejudiced politicians anxious to curry favor with the people, as well as by one-sided newspaper accounts, had no opportunity to examine any concrete issue, but played its old game of looking at the railroads as "big business" out to beat the government and, hence, the people.

The "Milk Case" was a case in point. Though the man on the street looked upon the case as evidence of the railroad's attempt to circumvent a law, the case was actually fought to guarantee the railroad company the same protection afforded to any citizen of the United States. It was fought to determine just how far a state legislature could go in fixing transportation rates. The Minnesota statutes authorized the railroad commission to fix compensation to be paid railroad companies for transportation in certain contingencies, and the Minnesota commission, acting under that law, fixed the rates of the Milwaukee Road for the transportation of milk. The company, however, charged that the compensation fixed was not only inadequate, but unreasonably low, and flatly refused to comply with the rate order. The Minnesota commission immediately applied to the Minnesota supreme court for a mandamus writ to compel the Milwaukee Road to adopt the rate the commission had fixed, and the court decreed that the statute authorized the commissioners to fix the rate, that the company could not be heard in an objection that the rate was not reasonable and just because, *ipso facto*, the rate fixed by the commissioners was the only reasonable rate under law, and that the company was bound to obey it, since the court actually had no power to inquire into the question as to the reasonableness of the rate fixed by the commission. This was as intricate a piece of word-juggling and dodging of responsibility as can be imagined; actually, it deprived the Milwaukee Road of the right to be heard in its own defense, and the company had no alternative but to remove the case, by writ of error, to the United States supreme court, which reversed the decision of the Minnesota court, setting forth that, although the legislature had the power to regulate and control railroads, it had no authority to fix compensation below what was reasonable for service rendered, and that the question of reasonable compensation was a judicial one to be decided by the courts on appeal thereto, and not by the legislature, so that any statute attempting to fix compensation of railroads beyond the power of the courts to inquire into its reasonableness was by its very nature unconstitutional and void.

This decision naturally went a long way to free the Milwaukee Road and other companies of the specter of the arbitrary will of state legislatures or of commissioners in the fixing of transportation rates; but at the same time it fed the popular prejudice against railroads to an unwarranted degree and served to keep legislators aware of the advantages of using railroads as whipping boys with which to appease their constituents. But public feeling was fed by more than politicians and the press; as the century drew to a close, unionization of American labor made progress, and with unionization came the inevitable strikes.

The company entered the 1890's with a new contract with the Union Pacific Railway Company, by which it had the right to use the Union Pacific tracks from the Milwaukee Road terminus in Council Bluffs, Iowa, to South Omaha, including the use of the bridge over the Missouri and the Union Station in Omaha. Furthermore, the Milwaukee had vastly increased its rolling stock, its equipment including 776 locomotives, 349 passenger cars, 9 sleeping cars, 9 parlor cars, 10 dining cars, 247 baggage, postal, mail and express cars, 15,648 box cars, 2,499 stock cars, 4,101 flat and coal cars, 468 refrigerator cars, and 514 caboose, wrecking, and tool cars, in addition to which the company owned a three-fourths interest in 45 sleeping cars (which were soon to become its unconditional property) controlled and operated by the Pullman Palace Car Company. The total track mileage had increased to 7,048.97 in seven states, the Dakota Territory having been broken up into North and South Dakota, admitted to the Union in 1889. The Milwaukee Road's main track alone was 5,721.40 miles in length, and the company had acquired by purchase the capital stock of the Milwaukee and Northern Railroad Company, which was of especial value to the Milwaukee Road because it afforded access to the iron regions of the peninsula of Michigan. Moreover, in 1890, the Lisbon, Necedah & Lake Superior Railway Company sold and conveyed its property to the Milwaukee Road for a sum equivalent to the cost of construction to date of sale; and the Milwaukee Road learned that its termination of the Pullman contract was wise, because the earnings of its sleeping cars were "sufficient to pay for the new cars required each year to replace old cars," a profit which had been brought about in part by the company's order removing the customary heavy blankets and substituting white counterpanes for the summer runs. The company, that same year, duly reported that wages had been increased, while at the same time the "standard of a day's work, in train service," had been reduced from twelve to ten hours.

In 1891 labor unionization did not yet appear to be a problem to the Milwaukee Road. The report for that year was still primarily concerned with the difficulties imposed on railroad operation by the controversial provisions of the Interstate Commerce Law. The report declared:

It seems idle to prescribe maintenance of rates in view of the fact that legislation has prohibited pooling—the only satisfactory method of providing for the necessities of railways whose disadvantages prevent them from competing on equal terms with railways that are more favorably situated; and the only efficient means of restraining within safe bounds the destructive competition that results from the existence of too many competitors.

The Interstate Commerce Association had finally died, and in the previous year the Western Traffic Association had taken its place, its governing authority resting in the boards of directors of the various member companies. The Western Traffic Association was not the most ideal solution to the problems besetting the railroads, but, the Milwaukee Road conceded, it had been "of valuable service to railway interests in bringing, for the first time, into the determination of questions arising between competing lines the highest representatives of the companies, as a permanent Board of Control; in terminating the demoralization which existed when the Association was formed; and in since preventing hasty and needless reductions of rates." The Milwaukee Road admitted to the discovery that, Interstate Commerce Law or not, "it is with railways as with individuals: absolute independence of action is impossible; the railway systems are so interwoven that the policy of each is subject to the dictation of its competitors; and more so when each assumes to act independently than when all are restrained by association."

Yet, despite the emphasis on the problems of control and rate regulation, that of wages loomed. "A constant pressure has resulted in a considerable advance in wages," said the report of 1891, "without a corresponding increase in net revenue." During the preceding year, the company paid for labor directly employed in its service $12,463,362.94, and, in addition, a large proportion of material and supplies for labor in production of $5,216,832.80, totaling $17,680,195.74. The Milwaukee Road declared that, since the railways, directly and indirectly, were the largest employers of labor, "labor has more interest in their welfare than capital. It is not unreasonable to expect that the element of labor, which ambitious politicians are so eager to propitiate, will, with a more intelligent appreciation of its own interest, exercise in time a strong influence in securing legislative action relative to railways, which shall be dictated by a just regard for the welfare of so important an interest."

And, went on the report, increased wages demanded increased service, better facilities, higher standards of property. But how can these be supplied, cried the company, "if railway companies are not permitted to earn enough to pay for improving their property," and "how can they borrow unless they can show a reasonable certainty of enough net earnings to pay for borrowed money?" In less than three years, however, the road, having passed one year of surprisingly good earnings and one of depressed earnings, came face to face with its first labor trouble.

In 1893, Eugene V. Debs, an energetic young man who was once a railway shopworker and a locomotive fireman, an officer in the Brotherhood of Locomotive Firemen, and for a time editor of *The Locomotive Fireman's Magazine*, convinced that industrial unions were to be preferred to trades unions, founded the American Railway Union to persuade all railroad men to be members of one organization. Within a year, the American Railway Union listed 150,000 members, and within a year, too, the young union flexed its muscles and brought about an almost disastrous tie-up of railroading from Cincinnati to the west coast. The American Railway Union, however, was secondary in its action, which was a supporting one, and not initiatory; the action had been begun by employees of the Pullman Company, when, in the spring of 1894, the Pullman Company, suffering the effects of the depression of the preceding year, laid off a third of its men and cut the wages of the rest more than 30 per cent without making corresponding reductions in the rent asked for company houses or in the prices of goods sold at company stores.

In the face of this action, the employees of the Pullman Company quit work. Unfortunately for the strikers, the depression had affected virtually all railroads, and there was little demand for new Pullman cars, so that the company was in no hurry to call its men back to work; instead, it cut off credit at the company stores, and this action aroused Debs, always an intensely active defender of the under-privileged, to come to the aid of the strikers with money and the threat of a boycott against the handling of Pullman cars, practically all of which were still controlled by the Pullman Company. Debs' threat failed of its desired effect; so, not to be outdone, he ordered the boycott on June 26, its application to be on all the western railroads. Promptly American Railway Union men began to cut out Pullman cars from their trains and to leave them on sidetracks. As an immediate result, indignant railroad men discharged the boycotting union men, and this in turn resulted in a general strike, almost paralyzing traffic between Chicago and the west.

To the dubious aid of the strikers went immediately a great many hoodlums and many unemployed men who had been inflamed against the railroads; this "aid" was disastrously prejudicial to any cause the strikers had, for the hoodlums crippled engines, burned railroad sta-tions, looted and overturned freight cars, and did all manner of damage; so much, in fact, that President Grover Cleveland was pre-vailed upon to send the federal militia into Illinois over the protest of Governor Altgeld, who called Cleveland's interference an unconsti-tutional action. Cleveland acted on the advice of his attorney general, Richard Olney, a one-time railroad attorney, who secured a sweeping injunction against all strike activities and pointed out to the president that his interference was predicated upon the strikers' interference with the transporting of the United States mail. Ten thousand regulars, made up of cavalry and field artillery, moved into Illinois by July 4, and there the soldiers not only saw to it that the mails were carried, but effectively broke the strike. The confusion wrought by the hood-lums who had joined with the strikers resulted in some popular indignation, enough to permit the arrest of the strike-leaders by federal officers on a charge of conspiracy to obstruct the free transport of the mails and the enjoining of their activities as strike-leaders. Debs, who defied the court order by urging a general strike of all labor organiza-tions, was, with a half dozen other leaders, cited for contempt of court and sentenced to six months in jail.

The Milwaukee Road suffered in common with other railroads, though the Pullman Company no longer had any interest in the Pull-man cars still in use on that road at the time of the strike, since the company had taken over these cars and had added other sleeping cars. In consequence of the strike, therefore, the Milwaukee Road, which had maintained a policy of fairness toward all its employees and had stood out among railroads in not discriminating against union members, was justifiably irate and bitter, especially against the American Railway Union.

In the road's report for 1894, President Miller declared:

The management . . . accepts the fact that labor organizations are not to be prevented, and although their influence has not always been good, it has not discriminated against those who are members, and has not hesitated to confer with their chosen representatives on matters of mutual interest. The brief career of the American Railway Union, however, has demonstrated that there may be organizations which are administered with so little wisdom and so little regard for public or private rights, and are so reckless of consequences, even to their own members, as to be unworthy of recognition. It is not to be expected that an organization which has involved its members in a controversy in which they had no interest, in the effort to establish a principle which could not possibly prevail, and has needlessly cost them their places in times when men are more abundant than work, will take deep root, or long survive its own folly. Nor would it be prudent for railway companies to give any recognition or standing to an organization which has recklessly involved them in the losses consequent upon an effort to enforce a demand which was inimical alike to the interest of the companies, the employees and the public.

The direct interest of the railway companies in this controversy is of secondary importance to the greater interest of the entire industrial system of the country, which is at stake. The railway companies are compelled to contest the right of any organization to place restrictions on their power to fulfill the obligations which are by law imposed upon them. The transportation system of the country must not be used by any organization as a weapon against those with whom it may have controversy.

The company thus set forth a guiding principle which has prevailed, though the report was making no false claim in declaring that the Milwaukee Road had neither discriminated against union members nor hesitated to confer with union representatives. The effects of the Pullman strike and the action of the American Railway Union in support of it precipitated inevitably an incalculable rift between the employers and the employees. The Milwaukee Road alone estimated its loss in traffic receipts during the month of July, 1894, that of the strike, at approximately $500,000—in a year when freight revenues also suffered a large decrease because of the depression. Moreover, there was adjunctive expense, brought about by the damage done by hoodlums who acted in the name of the striking employees but who were actually neither a part of the union nor acting in any official capacity, so that the company's own insurance department, which had been organized February 11, 1893, because the company could not obtain reasonable rates for insurance with a beginning balance at credit of income account of $300,000, had to meet a good many claims it would not have had to meet in ordinary circumstances. These claims were chiefly of damage by fire, directly or indirectly brought about by the property of the company, such as the innumerable fires set by sparks from the locomotive stacks.

In the midst of the labor agitation, the company lost its able general counsel, John W. Cary, who died in March, 1895. Cary, one of the shrewdest railroad lawyers in the United States, had served as head of the Milwaukee's legal department for 36 years. He was a Vermonter, and had been admitted to the Vermont bar in 1844; six years later he located in Racine, and in 1859 he had achieved appointment as an attorney for the company. Soon thereafter he became its general counsel and launched upon a career of conducting all the company's extensive legal actions, almost always winning his cases. In one session of the state supreme court he tried fourteen important cases, winning every one, though opposed by such distinguished attorneys as Caleb Cushing, Henry Cram, and Matt Carpenter. He served a brief term in the Wisconsin assembly in 1872, but he had no love for the political life, though he fathered the law for the government and operation of Wisconsin railways while in the legislature. He was a lawyer first and always, and his loss to the Milwaukee was grievous, as the *Sentinel* recognized in pointing out that Cary had handled "every issue of bonds, of stocks, every act of consolidation" and that the "thousands of contracts . . . and legal questions" were all in Cary's memory; "that is what made his services invaluable to the Company as general solicitor. There is no man able to take his place." However, such able lawyers as Burton Hanson, H. H. Field, and Charles B. Keeler had been trained under Cary and carried on, a staff augmented in 1906 by George R. Peck as general counsel and C. E. Vroman as assistant general solicitor.

The Pullman strike affected the company in other ways. When at last the report of the congressional committee of investigation into the strike was made public, the Pullman Company was severely censured, and, in the course of its report, the congressional committee took occasion to brand the General Managers' Association as arrogant and lawless, which indirectly resulted in a decision of the United States supreme court against all railway associations as a violation of the Sherman Anti-Trust Law, so that in its annual report of 1897, the Milwaukee Road set down that "all attempt at maintenance of such

Associations has been abandoned in the territory" of the road, but
added that no great harm was likely to follow as a result, "inasmuch
as the Associations had ceased to be of any special value; and were
not likely to be, so long as pooling is prohibited by law." The road still
hoped, audibly, that congress might yet learn to permit pooling and
"make it practicable to maintain rates and avoid discrimination."

The Pullman strike, however, was only the beginning of labor
troubles for the railroads, though it was the outstanding example of
the growth of power in labor unions, and perhaps more than any other
labor agitation in the 1890's pointed the way toward realization within
the decade of the immediate goals of the unions—the right to organize,
to strike, and to bargain collectively. The Milwaukee Road made little
attempt to thwart unionization; the officials of the road were justifiably
incensed by the action of Debs' union members against sleeping cars
on their own line, since the road owned its sleeping cars, and there
was no longer any connection between them and the Pullman Company; and the officials quite naturally opposed the subsequent action
of strikers against railroads in general. But the Milwaukee Road did
far less than many other railroads in seeking to delay or sabotage
unionization, and early set forth the only grave doubt about the feasibility of unionization—that of irresponsible leadership, a doubt which
has been echoed with ample justification hundreds of times since
then. In this, then, the road manifested an almost prophetic vision—
it had no fear of unions, it had no quarrel with the principles of unionization, but it had a reasonable doubt of the union leadership, knowing
that by the same average which occasionally brought forth inadequate
leadership of industrial empires, the unions were bound to suffer.

The Milwaukee Road was a very well unified road. There was a
harmony of relationship among its employees, from the highest to the
lowest, which had no equal anywhere in the United States. When Sir
William Van Horne came to the Milwaukee Road in 1880, by way of
the Chicago & Alton Railroad, to serve as general superintendent for
two years, he was so quickly aware of the atmosphere of solidarity
among the employees of the road that he said if a man were kicked
in Milwaukee he protested as far away as the Missouri River. This
clannishness naturally made for good labor relations, and good labor
relations in turn made for a strong loyalty among the employees;
indeed, this loyalty was so exceptional that even in the days of the
1894 strike there were whole divisions of the system where no agitation
was manifest.

Such a feeling among employees, of course, went hand in hand with
the avowed policy of the road to keep clear as much as possible of out-

side domination of its affairs. Unfortunately, events in the United States were not such as to make it easy to avoid outside domination, and the invasion and control of the Milwaukee Road by the Standard Oil Trust, represented by William Rockefeller, and the Harkness interests, represented by Henry Flagler, were a part of the movement of the last two decades of the nineteenth century to centralize control of important industries in a relatively few hands. Thus, J. P. Morgan controlled the country's banking system, Carnegie controlled steel, and the Standard Oil Trust—the Rockefellers and their moneyed associates—controlled oil, iron, copper, and the key railroads. The inevitable struggle, therefore, was between industrial giants, and in this struggle the Milwaukee Road could not hope to remain independent.

The rise of the powerful monopolies and trusts was most often in self-interest, but there was undeniably a motivating fear of control by popular sovereignty. In the case of the railroads, the often unreasoning fear and hatred of them was fed by one popular misconception after another, aided by the nation's press. The railroads looked like fair game to many editors, who thereupon set off after them with a great hullaballoo. Unfortunately, some railroad men did not help the situation in the least. After the farm mortgage scandal in the midwest came instance after instance of criminal ruthlessness from the railroads building westward, while at the same time the rising power of the railroad "barons" stood as a challenge to the public. Moreover, statements like William H. Vanderbilt's "The public be damned!", which was widely reprinted and editorialized upon, simply offered fuel to the feeling against railroads. It made no difference that the famed Vanderbilt quotation was presented as a half-truth; the whole story was that Vanderbilt had been questioned as to why a day coach was being cut out of an extra-fast mail train between New York and Chicago, and he replied that it was not paying. When he was told that the public found it of good use, and when he was asked why he did not then accommodate the public, he answered finally, "The public be damned! I am working for my stockholders. If the public wants the coach, why don't they patronize it?" But, of course, Vanderbilt making good "copy," and his colorful speech affording plenty of ammunition to opponents of the railroads, not one newspaper in ten presented Vanderbilt's statement in its proper context, so that it served to anger still further an already misinformed public. The public, in turn, brought pressure to bear upon politicians, who, already excited by the disclosures of really questionable matters by various state and federal investigating groups, were easily persuaded to enact further restrictive legislation aimed at railroads.

The Vanderbilt furore, however, vitally influenced the immediate future of railroads, for Vanderbilt, bowing before the tremendous popular indignation that the reporting of his statement had aroused, disposed of a part of his holdings in the New York Central line, a sale which was handled by a syndicate headed by J. P. Morgan. This opened the way for Morgan to become a power in railroading, and Morgan lost no time in taking advantage of his position. Within a comparatively short time Morgan had allied himself and his financial power with James Hill, who was in control of the Northern Pacific Railroad, with the result that, through Hill's railroads, Morgan's railway system, Morgan's industries, and Morgan's banks dominated the northern half of the western United States—apart from the north central Mississippi Valley, which became the immediate goal of the Morgan–Hill combination.

The specific goal of the Morgan–Hill combination was entry into Chicago, which no line under Hill's control then had. The Rockefeller interests were determined that such a goal must not be achieved, and, in combination with E. H. Harriman, who had been introduced into the Standard Oil group as a bold and ingenious operator by James Stillman, president of the National City Bank of New York, William Rockefeller and Henry Flagler, as owners of the Milwaukee Road, continued to obstruct Morgan. Morgan had, in fact, offered to buy the Milwaukee Road; Rockefeller and Flagler had refused to sell at any price, not through any devotion to the road, but simply wishing to avoid the competition of Morgan and Hill in Chicago.

Harriman, backed by Stillman and the Standard Oil Trust, climbed rapidly. His boldness, his vision, his genius for reciprocal purchases of stock in related railroads and interlocking directorates—all these factors combined to push him rapidly to the top among railroad leaders. When in 1896 James Hill obtained control of the Northern Pacific Railroad, Harriman countered the following year by getting control of the Union Pacific. The Milwaukee Road, even though allied with Harriman, found itself in the curious position of being suspended, as it were, between two railway systems, upon at least one of which it had to depend to get its west-coast shipments to Chicago. For a railroad which prided itself upon its independence, this situation was certain to rankle.

There was no cessation of the tilting for power between the Morgan–Hill combination on the one hand and the Harriman–Stillman–Rockefeller interest on the other, and to all appearances, late in the 1890's, the Morgan–Hill combination could be kept out of Chicago. However, a chink in the defenses of the Harriman–Stillman–Rockefeller interests developed when the Chicago, Burlington and Quincy Railroad offered an opportunity for new ownership. Harriman moved to capture the Burlington Road, buying stock rather cautiously at first; but his caution proved the undoing of his plan, for Morgan and Hill moved more rapidly and with less caution, and by late 1900 had effective control of the Burlington Road, and thus an entrance into Chicago, the heart of the empire of the middle-western and western railroads, so many of which had opposed Morgan's plan of 1889 for a permanent and secret rate-fixing organization.

The invasion of Morgan and Hill by means of the Burlington Road, which afforded "better lines and better terminals than any other road into these districts and commercial centers," according to the jubilant Hill, drew the lines for continuing battle between the railroad giants of the midwest.

VII. The Milwaukee Looks West

In Milwaukee, I discovered that the Milwaukee Road had tracks which appeared on no printed schedule. Like the "gas track"—where cars whose tanks needed filling by Pintsch gas, for lighting, were put; or the "rosary track," likewise unique, another Milwaukee track named because the cars had to be put there one at a time in correct order.

But perhaps the Milwaukee's most famous "unknown" tracks were those of the "Beer Line," which serves three of the largest breweries in the nation. Its billing station is the Chestnut Street Station at the terminus, and it is located only four blocks from the heart of downtown Milwaukee. Though something like 150 industries are served by the Beer Line—including coal, lumber, paper, electrical, hospital, bedding supplies, foundries, tanneries, manufacturers of boxes, chocolate, ice, shoes, furniture, batteries, automobile parts, and many another article, it is known no less as the Beer Line because of the great breweries it serves. Though the end of the line is but six blocks from the Milwaukee's Union Station in downtown Milwaukee, the actual distance by rail is sixteen miles.

Small wonder that they called it the "Beer Line." Perhaps there was good reason for it, though it was probably neither necessary nor possible to do what the enterprising lads on one section of a line that became part of the Milwaukee later used to do—draw the bung of casks in transit, insert straws, and have a "snifter." In Milwaukee the steins were always handy.

—STEPHEN GRENDON
Through Wisconsin on a Bicycle

THE turn of the century was a time of great change for the Milwaukee Road. From the directors of the road to the lines themselves, change was the order of the day. In 1899 President Roswell Miller relinquished the presidency to Albert J. Earling and moved on to the chairmanship of the board of directors. Earling, another Wisconsin-born railroader, entered the service of the Milwaukee at 17. Born at Richfield, Wisconsin, in 1849, he had been with the Milwaukee since 1866, having begun as a telegrapher and been promoted to train dispatcher; then he became an assistant superintendent for four years, and for two years thereafter he was a division superintendent. From assistant general superintendent he became general superintendent of the Milwaukee lines in 1888, and, two years later, was made general manager, an office he held for five years. In 1895 he was made second vice-president. Earling was another of the young men who had come into the road in the heyday of Mitchell's leadership. He was to become inventor of the block signal system, and he was destined to be one of the most popular of executives for, having risen from the ranks, he kept in touch unfailingly with the men of the Milwaukee, spending many nights in the yards riding switch engines and talking to the men.

Meanwhile, the Milwaukee had inaugurated a new fast mail March 18, 1884, and the road's native city was hailing it; the *Sentinel* editorialized quite as if the heart of the Milwaukee Road were still in its native city and not in Chicago:

Promptly at 11:45 o'clock last evening, the new fast mail train on the Chicago, Milwaukee and St. Paul Railroad arrived in Milwaukee on its initial trip. It stopped here a few minutes, just long enough to change engines, and then proceeded. The train consists of four coaches—three mail and one storage car. It carries no passengers. The trip from Chicago was made on schedule time in one hour, forty minutes. . . . According to the new schedule, the train is due at La Crosse at 4:45 A.M., and at St. Paul at 7 A.M.

The postmaster general had proposed that the Milwaukee Road operate this fast mail train, and the officials of the company acted with such astonishing dispatch that at two o'clock on the morning following the proposal, the train began operation. For eight years, the Milwaukee carried the mail by contract; in 1892, the Post Office Department discontinued the exercising of written contracts, and the famed fast mail as well as other trains on the Milwaukee Road continued to handle the U. S. mails with no contract other than a verbal agreement.

In 1899, too, the Milwaukee inaugurated a tradition which was to last until September, 1922, when death ended the career of Dan Healey, best-known dining car steward in America. Dan was an integral part of the *Pioneer Limited,* the Milwaukee's famed overnight train between Chicago and the Twin Cities, though Dan's run was between Chicago and Milwaukee. He made a round trip daily, serving dinner out of Chicago and breakfast the next morning leaving Milwaukee. The *Pioneer Limited* at the turn of the century and for many years thereafter took two hours and fifteen minutes for the 85-mile trip, in contrast to the present *Hiawatha's* one hour and fifteen minutes. The *Pioneer Limited* was one of the most heavily patronized trains on the Milwaukee Road, and, after the advent of Dan Healey and his famed cuisine, the train was always crowded. Dan was given a free hand in the preparation of menus. Moreover, in addition to great culinary skill, he had a remarkable memory, quickly recognizing previous patrons and rarely forgetting a person's name, an accomplishment which he taught his waiters, some of whom went to Dan's assistance, *sotto voce,* when help was required in identifying a patron. Milwaukee Road diners in the heyday of the *Pioneer Limited* seated 30, as against today's 48, but if patrons of the road entered Healey's car after all seats were occupied, they were entertained while in line at one end of the car by Healey's ready wit, and by complimentary appetizers.

The famed Healey service included the serving of "seconds" at no additional cost, and he always had boxes of candy for ladies to carry away. The price of the elaborate dinner was only $1.00, though later it was raised to $1.25 and $1.50, but at no time did the price actually cover the cost of the *Pioneer Limited's* dinner service. The sumptuous repast provided by Dan Healey is manifest in this typical menu:

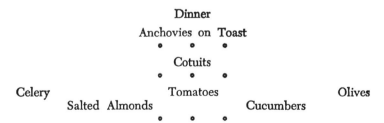

Dinner

Anchovies on Toast

*   *   *

Cotuits

*   *   *

Celery   Tomatoes   Olives

Salted Almonds   Cucumbers

*   *   *

Mullagatawny Soup   Consommé Clear

*   *   *

Boiled Salmon
Egg Sauce

*   *   *

Sweetbread Patties

*   *   *

Roast Beef   Roast Turkey
Pan Gravy   Chestnut Dressing
                                            Cranberry Sauce

*   *   *

New Century Punch

*   *   *

Mashed Potatoes   Brussel Sprouts
Cauliflower in Cream   Sweet Potatoes
                New Potatoes in Cream

*   *   *

Lobster Salad

*   *   *

Mince Pie   Strawberries   Plum Pudding
                                             Brandy Sauce

*   *   *

Tutti Frutti Ice Cream   Assorted Cake

*   *   *

Camembert, Roquefort, and Waukesha Cream Cheese
Bent's Water Crackers, Toasted

*   *   *

Coffee   Chocolate   Tea

*   *   *

Mint Patties

*   *   *

Benedictine

*   *   *

Extra portions served on request—No additional charge

DINNER ONE DOLLAR

Waukesha Imperial Spring Water Used on the Tables of This Car.
Coffee Demi-Tasse served in Buffet Smoking Car free to regular
occupants of sleeping car on presentation of ticket from Dining
Car Conductor.

But at the beginning of the new century, talk in railroad circles was not of fast trains, schedules, or even of profits, though admittedly the Milwaukee was financially the soundest of railroads; concern was for the possible part the Milwaukee might play in the plans of the Morgan–Hill interests and their desire to obtain entry to Chicago.

In the midst of speculation, early in January, 1901, Philip D. Armour died. Armour, for all his conservatism, had been a great and good friend of the Milwaukee; though he was charged with having built many a branch line into some part of Wisconsin where he wanted to go fishing or hunting, even his detractors admitted that if he had urged such construction, it was certain that any such branch was profitable for the Milwaukee. Though he was censured for the use of a private car whenever he wished to travel, Armour developed the shipment of fruits and vegetables by refrigerator cars; before his death he had built over 2,000 such cars. Moreover, Armour had a faculty for paying attention to what seemed to be the most trivial of details; this was demonstrated in a letter he wrote to his sons after his return from John W. Cary's funeral:

Mr. Earling . . . rode home with me from Cary's funeral yesterday, and in the course of conversation related a little incident to illustrate why railroads don't succeed better. It struck me very forcibly, and I think the meat of it will apply to the packing business. He said that while he was in Minneapolis last week he stepped into a little cigar store near the depot and bought a couple of cigars. As he was lighting one, he asked the man whether he was doing a good business. He said, yes; he had all the Milwaukee and St. Paul Railroad trade, and that was a very large volume indeed; in fact, it was practically all the business he had. Then Earling asked him where he bought his cigars, and he replied, "In New York." He then asked him how he shipped them, and he answered, "Via the Burlington Road." "You get all your patronage from the Milwaukee, and yet you give all your patronage to the Burlington?" "Oh, well," said the cigar man, "I never thought anything about that. I have never been asked by any of the Milwaukee people to ship via their road." Of all the great number of employees who supported that tobacco store, not one had ever asked the cigar man to send his business over the Milwaukee Railroad. They were not the commercial men of the Road, of course, but they thought nothing concerned them except their special duties and whatever was doled out to them. Consequently, that is why railroads in a great measure fall short of giving the results to the stockholders that they might give. . . .

Doubtless such observations as this caused President Earling later to call for "more from employees than the mere work they are appointed to do, just as the employees need more from the Company than their money at pay day." Armour's sage advice had been of benefit to the

Milwaukee on many occasions, but, like other major stockholders, he had never actively interfered in the control of the road by virtue of his possession of large blocks of stock.

Since he was reputed to hold Milwaukee Road stock estimated at approximately $4,000,000, Armour's death immediately gave rise to the wildest rumors. The first of them was that James J. Hill would succeed Armour as a director of the Milwaukee; this had hardly been denied when the second rumor, even more explosive, gained currency. This was that the Morgan–Hill interests had already secured control of the road. President Roswell Miller, in Chicago to attend Armour's funeral, issued a statement:

If Mr. Hill and his following have purchased stock, it has been for investment. The preferred stock is all held by investors, and much of it is held in estates; a large percentage of the common is in similar hands. The high prices for the latter have not brought much of it into the market. The reports that Marshall Field's holdings, amounting to $3,000,000, have been secured is absurd. Mr. Field sold most of his stock some time ago, and does not now own over 4,000 shares. Alexander Mitchell also marketed his long ago, and, as for the $5,000,000 said to have been secured from the George Smith estate, I know nothing about it.

In regard to a purported rates "deal" concerning the Erie, Great Northern, and Milwaukee roads, Miller said that it was possible for "certain interests" to get together "for the purpose of strengthening their position with regard to rates and collateral matters," but pointed out emphatically that this did not presume any "change in the official personnel of the Milwaukee."

Railroad stocks were in anything but a bear market, and, with a great deal of speculation going on, they were being bought up indiscriminately. It was widely feared that the profitable Milwaukee stock was being siphoned away by Wall Street men affiliated with the Morgan–Hill interests, and one railroad man echoed these fears when he pointed out that the Milwaukee had been earning "a great deal more than the dividend paid on common stock up to this time, and it has been generally understood that the surplus would ultimately be divided among holders of this stock. It seems rather unfair that those who held the stock for many years, before it began to draw any dividend, should now be at the mercy of great financial combinations which are gobbling up the stock and preparing to get the lion's share of the dividend though they may have been holding the stock only a short time."

What was going on, however, was not what investors feared, though it was destined to have its effect on the Milwaukee all in due time. The flurry in railroad stocks was the direct result of E. H. Harriman's reaction to the gobbling up of the Burlington by Hill and Morgan. His first act, at news of this accomplishment, had been to meet Hill face to face in George F. Baker's home. There, abetted by Jacob Schiff, the Union Pacific's banker, he had charged Hill with secret dealings in obtaining control of the Burlington, and demanded a third interest in the Burlington in return for a third of the purchase money. Hill would not consider Harriman's offer, whereupon Harriman, more enraged than ever, warned him of the consequences and took his leave. Thereafter he laid plans to strike back at Hill and Morgan.

Seeking an opening for an invasion of the Morgan–Hill interests, Harriman concentrated on Northern Pacific, and thereupon inaugurated a chain of events which was to culminate in still more public ire at railroads and the forces manipulating railroad stock. Knowing that half of the Burlington stock had been allotted to Northern Pacific, Harriman set out to buy Northern Pacific. The plan was simple enough in essence; since Harriman still held some stock in the Burlington, he could not only achieve control of the road Morgan and Hill had wrested from him by gaining Northern Pacific's half of the Burlington stock, but he could at the same time turn the tables on the Morgan–Hill eastern interests and oust them from Chicago. Such an end was completely to the interests of the Rockefeller Trust and the Milwaukee Road, now to all intent and purpose a part of the vast Rockefeller empire, though actually control of the road lay in several hands—the Harknesses, in particular, as apart from the Rockefellers—only an alliance of interests binding them together.

Harriman soon learned where Northern Pacific stock was to be had. Furthermore, he knew that the Morgans were certain to take advantage of the situation created by the highly profitable acquisition of the Burlington Road and sell some of the stock they held in Northern Pacific. With Hill, the Morgan interests held $35,000,000, or thereabouts, of the $155,000,000 common and preferred capital stock of the Northern Pacific, which, because of the Burlington acquisition, now commanded a very good price. Harriman quietly drew upon all his resources—the Standard Oil Trust, the National City Bank of New York, the Union Pacific treasury, Kuhn, Loeb & Company,—for $60,000,000, with which, together with such credit as he personally commanded, he began guardedly to buy shares in Northern Pacific.

Harriman had chosen his time well, for Morgan was in Europe and James Hill was in his Seattle office in that spring of 1901. However, Hill was able and shrewd, no less so than his competitors, and the steady rise of Northern Pacific stock indicated that someone was buying, the inferential evidence being that the buyer had unlimited funds at his disposal. He lost no time in traveling east, and early in May he called on his old friend, Jacob Schiff, of Kuhn, Loeb & Company, and through Schiff discovered that Kuhn, Loeb & Company were buying Northern Pacific for Harriman. Schiff made absolutely no attempt to deceive Hill, answering Hill's protest that it was impossible for anyone outside the Morgan–Hill combine to obtain control by saying that Kuhn, Loeb & Company already had a controlling lot of the Northern Pacific stock and that the company would make every attempt to keep a controlling interest in the Northern Pacific. Hill was given to understand that Harriman's move had been prompted by the acquisition of the Burlington Road by the Morgan–Hill combine. Hill promptly cabled Morgan, who in return wired his people to buy 150,000 shares of Northern Pacific stock without regard for the asking price. The battle was thus openly joined.

Schiff had been forehanded in making admissions to his friend, Hill, since Union Pacific, representing Harriman, did not yet have control of Northern Pacific. Events now moved with lightning rapidity. Harriman, realizing that the Northern Pacific could retire the preferred shares, a majority of which were in his hands, telephoned Kuhn, Loeb & Company to increase his holdings of common stock by 40,000 shares. Harriman was at the time sick abed, and Schiff, who was reached only after some delay, felt that further purchases were needless, so that, on Schiff's counsel, Harriman's order was passed over.

Harriman's astuteness would have won him his gamble if he had depended upon someone less conservative than Schiff. Harriman's order was for the additional 40,000 shares of Northern Pacific to be purchased on the morning of May 4. During the night of Sunday, May 5, Morgan's cable reached his office, and, as a result, the Morgan–Hill forces were extremely active in Wall Street Monday morning, while Schiff and Kuhn, Loeb & Company were sitting back. James Keene, leading the fight for shares for the Morgan interests, was so active that by closing time on the Stock Exchange, Northern Pacific common had risen from 110 to 131; on the following day, May 7, the Morgan brokers by their aggressive buying forced common stock up to 149¾.

This dangerous game could have but one inevitable result. Not knowing of the battle between the giants, speculators in Wall Street began to sell Northern Pacific stock short, expecting in due course that such inflationary quotations as those then being chalked up by Northern Pacific common must deflate, and that later they could buy back stock sold short at comfortably and profitably lower prices. What the speculators did not know, of course, was that the shares were being bought for control, and that presently, when stock sold short was recalled, there would be none available for repurchase. By May 9 a frantic situation had developed; rumors of a corner in Northern Pacific had spread, and speculators were making frenzied efforts to cover, bidding the price of Northern Pacific common wildly from $300 to a phenomenal $1,000 a share, with the result that all the securities, stocks, and bonds in the United States were profoundly disturbed and began a bearish decline of from 15 to 40 per cent, thus effectively creating a panic of the first magnitude, world-wide in its impact. From his Paris offices—Morgan, Harjes et Cie,—J. Pierpont Morgan, who was now being blamed for the panic which had ruined thousands of speculators, gave orders to his buyers, and both the Morgan–Hill interests and Harriman realized that the market price of Northern Pacific common must be fixed at not more than $150. Moreover, the now thoroughly angry Morgan, faced with newspaper headlines screaming that he controlled Northern Pacific, blundered to a newspaper reporter, who had inquired of him whether "some statement were not due the public," by snapping, "I owe the public nothing!", words which were quickly enough emblazoned in print from one end of the country to another.

As a result of Schiff's mistake, the Morgan–Hill interests remained in control of Northern Pacific; but, having spent $79,459,000 to buy toward control, Harriman was too potent to be ignored; it was certain that with his concentration of wealth and his intentions on record, Harriman would sooner or later again attempt to obtain control. The situation therefore was one which required constant vigilance on the part of the Morgan–Hill interests. But there was one alternative, and that was an arrangement by means of which "spheres of interest" might be definitely established. It seemed clear to the Morgan–Hill interests that Harriman's gamble was not simply an attempt to strike back at them for their acquisition of the Burlington, but to effect absolute control over every route to the Pacific coast except that of the Great Northern itself and the Santa Fe on the south. To effect that agreement, J. Pierpont Morgan was chosen. The result of Morgan's decision was that William Rockefeller and E. H. Harriman became directors of the Northern Pacific's new board. Furthermore, not satisfied with any "gentlemen's agreement," Morgan decided to form a holding company, the Northern Securities Company, for stock in which the Morgan–Hill and Harriman interests exchanged their Northern Pacific stock, the Harriman interests receiving $82,500,000 of the capital of the new holding company. Both Harriman and William Rockefeller were among the fifteen directors.

Though the Northern Securities Company, formed in mid-November, 1901, was soon under attack as a violation of free competition as defined by the Sherman Act, and ultimately, in 1904, ordered dissolved by the

United States supreme court, the effect it had of partitioning out the territory under dispute—that is, the western half of the nation—crystallized the slowly forming decision of the Milwaukee Road to expand westward. The decision was not easily arrived at, for the period of transcontinental railroad construction had apparently ended with the turn of the century. But there were various factors which combined to present the plan of westward expansion as the only feasible one for the Milwaukee Road.

The financial panic of 1901, followed by the division of the spoils in the Northern Securities Company agreement, made it eminently clear that the Milwaukee Road, without an outlet of its own to the Pacific coast, was certain to be always at the mercy of its competitors. For a road which was one of the largest in the country, this was a patently intolerable situation. There was clearly no reason to hope that "gentlemen's agreements" would be binding; history had demonstrated as much. Furthermore, the Milwaukee Road had to face the fact that there had been a tremendous increase in business throughout the country, and particularly in the vast plains region west of the Mississippi; this, added to the heavy shipping coming into the west by sea, posed a problem of ever-increasing dimensions for the Milwaukee. Often the road's freight was tied up for days in Seattle before it could be moved eastward to some terminal controlled by the Milwaukee; all such delays tied up large amounts of capital, and such amounts pyramided from month to month, preventing this capital from getting into rapid circulation.

Furthermore, the Milwaukee found itself facing a profound change in the character of the country. As a Granger line, it had followed the wheat fields; 32 per cent of its traffic in 1894 was grain, but less than a decade later, though it was actually carrying twice as much grain, that percentage had fallen to 23 per cent. Manufacturing, diversified farming—brought about by the inroads of the chinch bugs upon the wheat crops—and the varied traffic growing out of increasing population and wealth in the areas served by the Milwaukee Road, all had increased steadily. Just as the Milwaukee had originally followed the wheat fields, so now it was bound to follow wherever the traffic was. Westward expansion was the natural direction for the Milwaukee.

Such arguments as could be made against the plan for westward expansion seemed negligible in the early years of the century, particularly when set against the tremendous inconveniences and the uncertainty of arrangements for the use of other lines. The first argument against construction to the west coast was the possibility of a canal across the Isthmus of Panama; this was finally discounted by the considered opinion that either the canal would not be built at all, or, if built, it would be limited to military traffic. The second argument was the undeniable likelihood that Hill and the Northern Pacific to the north, and Harriman and the Union Pacific to the south, might unite to thwart any such expansion program. Already the astute Hill had foreseen that the only possible direction for the Milwaukee Road to take, short of a financially risky detour, was west of the terminal at Evarts, South Dakota, just short of the Missouri River at that point. Directly in the line of the Milwaukee Road's westward route lay the Montana Railroad Company tracks, a short road, called The Jawbone Road, owned by Richard A. Harlow, a mortgage on which was held by Hill; whether by accident or design, this helped to safeguard the interests of the Northern Pacific.

These factors had to be weighed carefully, for if by any overt move the Milwaukee Road revealed its intentions before securing a right of way and terminals, it might quite possibly find its course thwarted by rival interests. Financially, however, the Milwaukee Road was in excellent condition. The early years of the twentieth century were exceedingly prosperous, and the territory along the Milwaukee and to the western coast was growing swiftly. Moreover, the Milwaukee had a reputation for being not only one of the soundest roads financially, but also one of the most enterprising. By 1905, when the actual decision to drive to the west was made, the Milwaukee Road led all American railroads with some 300 electrically lighted cars; it had been the first railroad to light trains electrically, and had achieved the most satisfactory results. It was also one of the first railroads to ship grain in bulk, and it lent itself consistently to experimentation of all kinds.

The territory into which the Milwaukee would be reaching in its westward expansion was prosperous; it was mining country and in part agricultural, a land where many private irrigation projects were under way, and hydroelectric power was being rapidly developed. The assumption that increased revenues would pay for the expansion was justifiable, and, if such revenues were considered in addition to the release of capital now tied up by freight delays, westward expansion must have appeared to be a financially desirable step.

The initial move was made in 1901, when President Earling, acting on the advice of Roswell Miller, chairman of the board of directors, dispatched an engineer over the Northern Pacific line to report on the cost of duplication of that line. Before this report the estimate was that the Northern Pacific line could be duplicated for $45,000,000 or less. Miller, who had served the Milwaukee Road for more than two decades as general manager, president, and chairman of the board, was sufficiently informed and experienced to handle large financial transactions with competence and to be trusted with the determination of financial policies. He had long been dissatisfied with the agreement between the

Union Pacific and the Milwaukee Road, and just prior to 1901 he had resigned from the Union Pacific board because of this dissatisfaction, which arose out of his conviction that the rival Chicago & Northwestern Road had a better arrangement with the Union Pacific.

The Milwaukee Road's common stock in 1901 had advanced from $145 to $158 per share, and early that year 25,000 shares had changed hands on the New York Stock Exchange, partly because of rumors to the effect that James J. Hill was buying into the road with an eye to control, though Hill denied such an end, but hinted that a traffic arrangement between the Milwaukee Road and the Great Northern was possible. But the Milwaukee Road's stock was held to be one of the best securities among railroad stock offerings. The road was beginning to refund and change its divisional bond issues with high interest rates into bonds with lower rates, which were issued on a general mortgage executed over the entire property of the road in 1889. Late in 1902, the common stock of the Milwaukee Road was increased by $25,000,000 by action of the stockholders, giving rise to a rumor that the road planned to build a line to the west coast if the Union Pacific would not permit the Milwaukee to establish passenger and freight service to San Francisco by joint use of the Union Pacific's lines, though in that same month of October, a contract was arranged to effect this goal.

Prior to the actual decision on westward extension, the Milwaukee Road had been consolidating in every direction, making such extensions of its lines as it thought fitting and profitable, improving its equipment, adding heavier power and larger cars, modernizing its plant, and generally bettering its already strong position among the nation's railroads. In its report of June 30, 1901, the length of the road's main track was given at 6,596.32 miles, its westernmost station being at Evarts, South Dakota, the proposed point from which extension to the Pacific coast must begin. Among its equipment were such comparatively new features as vegetable cars, ballast cars, ballast plow cars, steam shovels, and a snow plow. The report noted also that ore docks and terminal facilities had been completed at Escanaba, Michigan, at a cost of $397,864.09.

A year later the Escanaba docks were enlarged sufficiently to double their capacity, indicating the increased revenue of the road from that source. Moreover, the construction of a second main track from Brookfield to La Crosse, Wisconsin, a distance of 182 miles on the La Crosse division, was authorized. Between June 30, 1901, and the same date a year later, the average rate per ton per mile had dropped from 0.861 cents to 0.840 cents. Within yet another year, the company provided increased facilities, additions, and improvements at its West Milwaukee shops, enabling the company "to build at least 50 locomotives per annum

... and effect a saving, at present prices, of at least $3,000 per locomotive." To increase its self-sufficiency, the company continued to acquire coal lands in Iowa and Illinois; to increase its attractiveness to its patrons, the company had added three "cafe observation cars," and later, in its 1905 report, it listed "two composite observation cars."

Meanwhile, in common with other railroads in Wisconsin, the Milwaukee during the summer and autumn of 1903 endured a new form of political attack when the colorful, dynamic governor of Wisconsin, Robert M. La Follette, speaking at county fairs and other gatherings, charged that railroads were discriminating against Wisconsin by compelling farmers, manufacturers, and shippers of Wisconsin to pay higher freight rates than those of other states, particularly Iowa, which had the kind of system of establishing freight rates which the governor sought for Wisconsin. The governor incorporated his charges in his message to the legislature as well. Unfortunately, the governor's figures were not based on fact, and newspapers throughout Wisconsin published comparative lists showing mileage and rates on hogs, cattle, sheep, cheese, tobacco, and other commodities between Iowa and Wisconsin and Chicago, and demonstrating in each case, without the necessity of any further comment, that the rates in Iowa were higher, and not lower, as the governor had charged.

The furore raised by Governor La Follette's charges had some unexpected results. The Hudson *Star-Times* aptly described one of them:

You have all heard of the donkey that kicked so hard that he kicked himself into the side of a wall. This seems to be just what La Follette has done in his railway freight comparisons which he has instituted between the states of Wisconsin and Iowa. He has set discussion to waxing so loud and deep that the actual reverse of his claims has been clearly proven. Facts have shown that Iowa is actually paying a much higher schedule of rates than does Wisconsin. So much so, indeed, that the battle against the railways has for the time being been moved from the Badger state to the land of the Hawkeyes. Iowa now wants a revision of rates so she may compete with Wisconsin in the business world.

In 1904, E. L. Philipp, a one-time ardent supporter of La Follette, and president of the Union Refrigerator Transit Company of Milwaukee, published *The Truth About Wisconsin Freight Rates*, which summarized the newspaper comment on the governor's charges and included comparative tables from many points in Wisconsin, covering all freight moving out of Wisconsin to Chicago. "The right of the State to regulate railways is conceded," wrote Philipp. "The question is, to what extent shall this right be exercised." The proposal for new rate-setting was reminiscent of the days of the Potter Law and the succeeding Granger legislation, but the facts were so at variance with the charges that the Milwaukee was untroubled; its eyes were on the expanding west, on horizons far beyond Wisconsin.

By 1905 capitalization of the company was about evenly divided between capital stock and funded debt; the company was earning more than three times its interest charges and was paying 7 per cent on both classes of stock, leaving a comfortable balance for the property of the company; moreover, it controlled no subordinate lines, having absorbed them in due course of time and made them part of the Milwaukee Road. Its management was quite commonly and justifiably regarded as one of the best in the United States; its distinct policies were widely known and well recognized, and its leaders had worked up from the operator's key through all intermediate steps to the president's chair. Furthermore, the loyalty of the Milwaukee Road's employees, which had already been noted in the troubled time of the American Railway Union strike a decade previously, was consistently remarkable. From more than one perspective, therefore, the time was auspicious for westward expansion.

Yet a step so fraught with possibilities of disaster could not be easily decided. The engineer sent over the Northern Pacific line by President Earling held to his initial preliminary report of $45,000,000, or not much more, to duplicate that line. In August, 1902, Roswell Miller, who was perhaps the man among the directors most determined to see the line through to the Pacific coast, submitted to William Rockefeller a report on a proposed extension to the coast at Eureka, California. Rockefeller, however, did not commit himself; he had an alternate plan in mind, and for some time he mulled it over. As late as July, 1905—fully three years after Miller's initial report was submitted to him—Rockefeller was still in discussions with W. K. Vanderbilt about a Pacific line to be built jointly by the Northwestern and the Milwaukee Roads, a proposal which he favored, but to which Roswell Miller remained cold. Moreover, by 1905, it could no longer be concealed that the Milwaukee Road contemplated westward extension, and there were conflicting reports regarding the position of Harriman and Hill in regard to the plan, though James Hill was on record in a letter to President George B. Harris of the Burlington Road to the effect that (1) if he were head of the Milwaukee Road, or of the Northwestern, for that matter, he would not be satisfied with a connection over some other line, but would build a line to Puget Sound; (2) the Great Northern would be benefited rather than injured by the Milwaukee Road's extension to the coast. However, Hill continued to hold the mortgage on the strategic Jawbone Railroad in Montana.

The decision to go forward with the plan for westward extension was finally made late in 1905, when William Rockefeller, then in Europe, cabled his abandonment of the Northwestern-Milwaukee Road joint extension plan, and Roswell Miller advised President Earling to proceed with arrangements for construction of the line to the west coast. This was on November 4; on November 28 the board formally authorized the building of the Milwaukee Road to Seattle and Tacoma, Washington.

The company moved with dispatch. Before 1905 had ended, the Pacific Railroad Company had been incorporated in Washington in the interests of the Milwaukee Road; though President H. R. Williams of the new company, the former general manager of the Milwaukee Road, denied any connection with the Milwaukee Road, financial circles were well aware of the development. Within a year, three more companies had incorporated under the same name in Montana, Idaho, and South Dakota to build the extension through these states, and all were presently drawing upon the Milwaukee Road for money to aid in construction. Even before the subsidiary company had been organized in South Dakota, the contract for construction of almost 800 miles west of Mobridge —the town where the company had meantime effected the crossing of the Missouri from Evarts—had been let.

The company's decision to reach to the Pacific coast stirred the northwest, particularly the cities of Washington. Spokane was thrown into a flurry of activity of bidding for entry of the Milwaukee, while Seattle, though excited as well, was confident that any road coming to the coast must of necessity enter Seattle. No one questioned the need for the coming of the Milwaukee. In the year of decision, 1905, the Washington papers carried story after story demonstrating the need for greater railroad facilities.

For example, the Spokane *Daily Chronicle* of December 5 said: "In a trip through the Great Northern and Northern Pacific freight yards this morning, there were 13 eastbound freights made up and standing in . . . the yards. The trains could not be taken out on account of lack of power. All the available engines had been pressed into service and even now there is not sufficient power to handle the trains as promptly as desired." And the Seattle *Post-Intelligencer* of November 8 reported:

The traffic officials of the Great Northern state that during the month of October there were twice as many carloads of freight shipped East from this division as during the same month of last year. The business has been so heavy that despite the utmost efforts it is impossible to furnish cars enough to meet the demand. The greatest demand is for cars for the lumber trade, but other shipments to the East are also on the increase. It is a fact

that the state of Washington furnishes more east-bound business to the
transcontinental railroad lines than all of the other states on the Pacific
coast; and that the increase in business is so great that extraordinary efforts
are required on the part of the railroads to furnish facilities for it.

In January, 1906, the *Wall Street Journal* struck the same note:

Seattle foreign exports in 1905 reached $27,856,285, an increase of
$19,690,925. Foreign imports were $9,653,377, an increase of $4,227,575.
Coastwise imports were $28,984,302, an increase of $3,446,043. Coastwise
exports were $37,804,156, an increase of $6,709,743. Total bank clearings
were $301,600,000, an increase of $79,000,000. Builders spent during the
year $6,684,784. Little additional comment is needed to explain why the
earnings of the Union Pacific, Great Northern, Northern Pacific, Canadian
Pacific, and Southern Pacific are constantly increasing, nor to explain why
the Milwaukee . . . and possibly the Northwestern are anxious to reach the
Pacific Coast. . . . The aggregate value of the six leading cities of the
Pacific Coast has probably advanced more in the past twelve months and
will probably advance more in the next twelve months than any other aggregate of property anywhere under the sun.

Curiously enough, the rival roads sounded the same key. A director
of the Union Pacific said that the Union Pacific had known for two years
"that the Milwaukee would be forced to build. . . . By the time the Milwaukee is built through, the traffic . . . will be too much for the Union
Pacific, anyway." James J. Hill made similar comments, and the change
of situation for the Milwaukee was brought home to President Earling
on a visit to Spokane early in 1906, when he learned that the rapacious
lumber barons of Wisconsin had so ravished the Wisconsin timberlands
that the Weyerhausers of Washington had shipped 400 carloads of Washington and Idaho pine to Wausau, Wisconsin. "This seems like shipping
coal to Newcastle," he commented wryly. Wherever he went, Earling
was greeted with enthusiasm; he was feted by chambers of commerce,
businessmen's associations, and city officials, and it was apparent to him
that the cities of the west coast were as anxious to have the Milwaukee
come to them as the officials of the Milwaukee were to come.

In the autumn of 1906, with construction moving along at a rapid
pace, the Milwaukee Road released the proposed route of the westward
extension. The route was to run from Glenham, South Dakota, in a north-
westerly direction over the Missouri River across the southwestern corner of North Dakota, virtually straight west across Montana to Butte, then
across northern Idaho and into Washington to Maple Valley, to connect
with the Columbia & Puget Sound Railroad owned by the Washington
company that was constructing the line to Seattle. The distance was esti-

mated at 2,305 miles from Chicago to Seattle, which made the line 150 miles shorter than the Burlington and the Northern Pacific, and 80 miles shorter than by way of the Burlington and Great Northern. The company also announced that large steel trestles would span deep ravines and rivers, long tunnels would pass through the mountains, and mountain grades would be from 1.66 to 1.81 per cent, as against the Northern Pacific's average of 2.2 per cent.

By September of that year, President Earling formally reported that the cost of the extension, including equipment, would be in the vicinity of $60,000,000, though manifestly this figure allowed for no great variations of the route or for unforeseen difficulties which might be encountered. Construction had been started in April, 1906, and was carried on along the entire right of way between the Missouri River crossing near Glenham, and Butte, Montana. The Missouri River had been spanned by a large steel truss bridge, and the division terminal had been established on the east bank of the river and named Mobridge, its derivation obvious. The approximately 800-mile line between Glenham and Butte included the Jawbone Railroad, the mortgage on which was so firmly held by James J. Hill.

Faced with the necessity of making either a highly needless detour or some kind of arrangement with the owner of the Jawbone, the Milwaukee Road entered into an arrangement to lease the Jawbone, however unsatisfactory this might be, since, if Richard A. Harlow, the owner of the Jawbone and the man for whom Harlowton had been named, failed to pay his mortgage, James Hill might foreclose and become in this fashion the owner of a part of the Milwaukee Road's main track to the west coast. The lease, however, was the only feasible solution at the moment; it was entered into in 1907, and the construction of the road was pushed to the Jawbone and beyond toward Butte with such speed that by summer of the following year the track had been completed to the Montana capital, and the line was opened for passenger and freight operation to Butte on August 30, 1908. The leasing, instead of the absorption, of the Jawbone, however, was not to the liking of the Milwaukee Road.

The Jawbone had a colorful history. Courtland Du Rand, a Minnesotan, now owner and operator of the Big Elk Ranch near Martinsdale, Montana, came west just in time to go to work grading for the Jawbone. "A dollar a day for the team, plus their oats, and a dollar a day plus board for myself," he wrote, remembering those months in 1898 when he was 16 and anxious to make his mark in the world. "I worked that whole season and waited another year to get my pay. That's why the railroad was nick-named the Jawbone Road—on account of its not paying its bills. As long as they fed us and the horses, they said we didn't need any money; we couldn't spend it anyway." The Jawbone, added Du Rand, was built by every available man in the region, and some of them were of such a character that the sheriff of the county had to be constantly on call:

There was one colored fellow, husky and robust, and a fighter. He kept picking on everybody who came into a certain bar. Every time a new man came in, he'd say, "Fellow, you've got to have a drink with me." The average young man said he never drank, and he'd get a reply, "You've got to have a drink with me. I'll make you."—and that always started a fight.

He was broken of this habit when one day the Sheriff from White Sulphur Springs, 45 miles away, was sent for. As he got into town he took off his badge, and made himself look just like one of the working boys around town. He was a powerful young fellow, being 210 pounds or more, and he had a baby face. Most strangers picked on him because he looked to be simple about fighting. The men led him to the "fighter" at the bar. The colored man jumped on him and said, "Young fellow, step right up and have a drink with me." When the Sheriff said that he never drank, the "fighter" answered, "Step up and take a drink or take off your coat because I'm going to lick you until you do." The Sheriff, with his simple expression, said, "All right, I'll just have to be licked," and he let the big fellow start in on him. Then the Sheriff let loose; he used lefts and rights, and he was so powerful he broke two ribs and dislocated the other's jaw—they fed him milk and bread for a week in the hospital. He had an eyebrow half peeled off, he had a split ear, and that colored boy was a perfect patient for the next month, and plenty tame.

The country was wild; the men took their recreation in shooting grizzly bears and antelope, carrying guns, belts, cartridges, and lariats on the train from Martinsdale; they shot antelope from the windows of the coach. They then hung the game on high poles at night and dried it in strips, well salted, so that they had food for weeks. They fished from the train as well. The pace of the Jawbone a-building, however, was far slower than that of the Milwaukee which was to incorporate it.

In view of its status at that time, the Jawbone was the object of considerable speculation. If Harlow defaulted on his mortgage payments and Hill subsequently foreclosed, the Milwaukee Road would be in part at least in no better a position than it had been when working over the lines of another company's road, and actually in a more annoying position, considering that the owner of the Jawbone would be very advantageously placed for creating difficulties for the Milwaukee Road. It was manifest that Hill would not turn the mortgage over to anyone connected with the Milwaukee Road, even though Hill was anxious to negotiate a loan at this time. When, in 1909, Hill went to England to negotiate the loan, the Milwaukee Road gained possession of the Jawbone. Harlow's mortgage had been made payable to Hill or the Great Northern *at any time;* very quietly the Milwaukee Road advanced to Harlow sufficient money to pay off his mortgage to the Great Northern at its St. Paul office. Once Harlow had accomplished this, the Milwaukee Road bought the Jawbone, through the Chicago, Milwaukee and Puget Sound Railway Company of Washington, to whom the deed was made out January 15, 1910. The Chicago, Milwaukee and Puget Sound Railway of Washington was the name assumed by the Pacific Railroad of Washington when, late in 1908, it took over the Pacific Railroads of Idaho, Montana, and South Dakota. This acquisition of the Jawbone Railroad chagrined Hill, but the terms of the mortgage had been clear, and there was nothing to be done to regain any ground lost to the Milwaukee Road in the transaction.

In 1906, however, the Jawbone was beyond the Milwaukee's grasp; though its ultimate disposition was speculative, the Milwaukee had no other recourse but to proceed with construction as rapidly as possible. Construction was pushed in many places along the way to the Pacific, with a speed which dwarfed the most extensive progress of the earlier transcontinental roads in their push across the continent west of the Mississippi.

Typical of Milwaukee power in the late 1800s, the 539, an "American" type, and its crew pose for the photographer.

The Clear Creek trestle provides a great view of its loop on the West Saint Paul Pass Tunnel near Taft, Idaho. This shot is unobstructed due to the 1910 forest fire which devastated the area. Charred tree trunks are visible within the new growth.

Building a trestle to cross the Judith River in Montana in 1913.

The famous Eagle's Nest Tunnel in 16-Mile Canyon in central Montana.

*Gas-electric railcars such as this one in Iowa served
Milwaukee Road branch lines in the 1920s.*

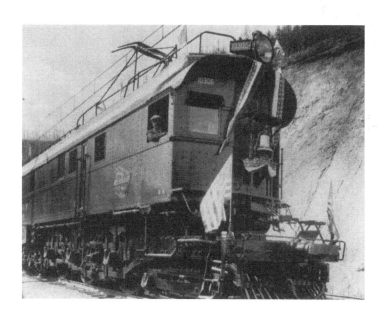

*President Warren Harding at the controls of a Milwaukee Road
locomotive in 1923.*

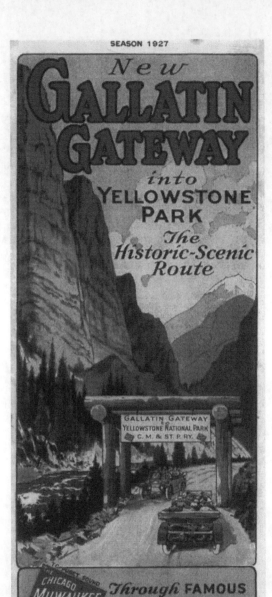

New
GALLATIN GATEWAY
into
YELLOWSTONE
PARK

The
Historic-Scenic
Route

GALLATIN GATEWAY
&
YELLOWSTONE NATIONAL PARK
C. M. & ST. P. RY.

Through FAMOUS
GALLATIN CANYON

CHICAGO
MILWAUKEE
AND ST. PAUL

With completion of the
Puget Sound extension,
the Milwaukee Road
worked hard to promote
tourism to Yellowstone
National Park. In 1927 the
company issued this public
folder describing the
New Gallatin Gateway
through the park.

*Typical of locomotive power in the 1930s, this Milwaukee Road Class I2
awaits its next assignment at Milwaukee in 1936.*

*A 1935 view of the Milwaukee Road's depot in Milwaukee.
Erected in 1886, this depot was replaced by a new structure in 1965.*

*In this posed shot, the new 1935 Hiawatha shows off
its modern design.*

*By 1938, new Hiawathas appeared with an even more striking
design than the first models.*

A 1938 capsule view of Milwaukee Road locomotive power at the Milwaukee Shops, covering fifty years of locomotive progress.

Passengers leaving the Hiawatha *upon its arrival in Milwaukee in 1939.*

Although passenger traffic boomed during World War II, the Milwaukee Road still produced advertising materials, including specialized timetables printed on ink blotters. As with most wartime publications, the company urged the public to "buy more war bonds and keep them."

Fairbanks-Morse locomotives led new train sets for Olympian Hiawatha service in 1948.

The Milwaukee Road took great pride in its passenger service between Chicago and the Twin Cities. This wartime folder glowingly describes its Hiawatha trains.

At the time of the centennial of the Milwaukee Road,
the company distributed this ink blotter promoting not only its passenger service,
"Route of the Hiawathas," but also industrial locations along its far-flung network of
main and secondary lines.

The morning Hiawatha on the Minnesota side of the Mississippi River
near Winona, sometime in the early 1950s.

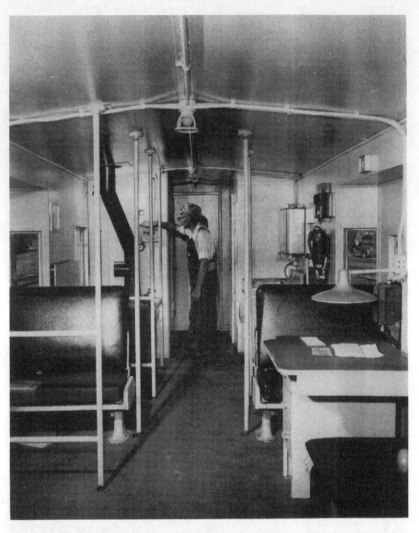

*This interior shot of a new 1956 caboose shows the conductor's office
and the crew's home on the road.*

Like other railroads, the Milwaukee kept perishables from spoiling with refrigerated trailers that operated whether the train was on the road or in the yards.

The Milwaukee was also a seagoing railroad. Here, the tugboat Milwaukee *awaits completion of loading before moving its cargo among Seattle, Bellingham, and Port Angeles, Washington.*

Two "Little Joes" lead a freight across the Clark Fork River in Montana.

The Milwaukee Road's famous bi-polar locomotives served faithfully for over fifty years. This unit is seen pulling the Olympian *in Washington's Cascade Mountains shortly after the Milwaukee built its line to the Pacific Northwest.*

The vast forests of the Pacific Northwest were sources of revenue for the Milwaukee Road.

*A Milwaukee freight pauses at the depot in Savanna, Illinois,
before heading west into Iowa and its final destination, Kansas City.*

VIII. To the Pacific

The Milwaukee has been moving the great 100-car Ringling Brothers, Barnum and Bailey circus for years. Like the Milwaukee, the great Ringling Brothers circus is indigenous to Wisconsin, having come out of Baraboo in the early 1880's.

On the second district of the Milwaukee Division one of Ringling Brothers, Barnum and Bailey's playful pachyderms, in the best tradition of the circus, made the people forget their troubles.

The circus was on its way from Milwaukee to Davenport over our rails when it reached Davis, Illinois, on the morning of September 11th. There were orders out on the train order stand at the station, awaiting the engineer and conductor of the special.

As the locomotive rolled by, the engineer reached out, slipped his arm through the fork and pulled in his copy, leaving one for the conductor in the caboose. But Jumbo, peeping out of his car back in the middle of the train, had seen what the engineer did and apparently decided he would try it himself. It looked like just the kind of fun his face was made for.

So, snaking his trunk out of the car, he awaited his moment. As he approached the stand, he took careful aim and popped his long trunk right through the loop. Then he pulled his copy in to see what it said.

Luckily, Operator R. V. Stickler saw the entire show and, grabbing the triplicate copy, set it up in time for the conductor to take it as the caboose went by.

—*The Milwaukee Magazine*
October, 1944

Proportionately, the construction of the coastward line did not take as long as the preliminary explorations and surveys. The construction was a highly organized work, and great improvements in methods had been made since the time the initial lines of the Milwaukee Road were laid a half century earlier; there was none of the tentative pushing out along one division after another, with all the delays and uncertainties of that method, for work was advanced on several divisions along the entire route of the line at once. The Mobridge to Butte line was typical in its construction, save for added difficulties found on more western divisions in crossing mountainous terrain.

The Mobridge–Butte line was divided into four primary sections; the first, or Dakota, section ran from Mobridge to Montline, a distance of 196 miles; the second, or eastern Montana, section, from Montline to Melstone, 225 miles; the third, or Musselshell, section, from Melstone to Lombard, 200 miles; and the fourth, or Rocky Mountain, section, from Lombard to Butte, 97 miles, a total of 718 miles. Each section had an engineer of construction in direct charge of it, but all engineers reported to the chief engineer at the Chicago office. Each engineer of construction organized an office consisting of draftsmen and clerks with their headquarters for the four designated sections at Minneapolis, Miles City, Helena, and Butte, respectively. After the primary surveys, maps and profiles had to be prepared, quantities had to be calculated, invoices for construction material—timber, iron, and so on—had to be made, all of which entailed a large personnel.

The entire route from Mobridge to Butte was let to McIntosh Brothers of Milwaukee; they in turn sublet the work in sections of varying length, requiring adequate bonds from each firm to which work was awarded. By the time the road was ready for construction, of course, the plan to move to the Pacific coast was well known, and there was no lack of available contractors to submit competitive bids.

The various sections of the Mobridge–Butte route presented different problems. The Dakota section, for instance, lay in a country almost entirely devoid of settlement; therefore it had no roads, and it offered no supplies of any kind, so that hay, oats, provisions for the men, lumber for buildings, tents, camp supplies, coal, grading machines, scrapers,

178

wagons, dump cars, rails, and so forth had to be hauled for the entire length of 196 miles from the railhead at the Missouri River. To add to this difficulty, the prairie country through which most of this section passed was crossed by a good many streams, which required the construction of bridges and the special grading of roads for the transportation of heavy equipment. Therefore the Dakota section was divided among three division engineers, each of whom was responsible for 65 miles of line, and each of whom worked with six or more resident engineers, each in turn having four or five men, so that for every 200-mile section there were approximately 40 men concerned with the engineering features alone.

The eastern Montana section, likewise divided into three divisions of approximately 75 miles each under similar engineering units, presented some further variation in the problems encountered. The region extending from the Little Missouri River to the valley of the Yellowstone, near Fallon, a distance of 65 miles, supported only a few scattered cattle and sheep ranches, and was to all intent and purpose unsettled country, the only products to be utilized being beef and mutton. Construction began near Fallon largely because Fallon was on the Northern Pacific; supplies could be hauled to Fallon on that railroad, and from there by team.

However, the Milwaukee Road ran through a region of an unusual number of river and creek valleys, making more bridges necessary, and adding materially to the construction cost. Moreover, the construction of bridges depended far more on weather than on roads. When, for instance, in June, 1906, a cloudburst filled the headwaters of Sandstone and Fallon Creeks, along the valleys of which grading was in progress, flood waters swept down the full width of the valley by night, carrying away food and wood, drowning horses and mules, as well as two men, and sweeping away tents, hay, oats, and materials. The effect was almost demoralizing, since many men on the line lost close to their entire capital, invested in teams and grading outfits, and they were held to the job only on liberal terms of payment for work partly completed even if that work had not yet been accepted by the engineers. That single flood cost the road a month of time and brought about a revision of the location of some 12 miles of road in the valley of the Sandstone, with the consequent loss of such grading as had been done and paid for on the abandoned line.

The second division of the eastern Montana section extended from Cato to the present site of Cartersville, a distance of 75 miles, the eastern end of which offered no difficulties to contractors, since the Northern Pacific unloaded outfits and supplies at Terry. But from the moment that the Yellowstone River was reached, construction difficulties mounted.

Three crossings of the Yellowstone River were necessary: the first was made five miles west of Terry; the second crossing, or "Tusler Crossing," 25 miles further along; and the third, five miles west of Miles City.

It was the 25 miles between the first and second crossings which gave the construction crews and contractors the greatest trouble. There were no bridges at all across the Yellowstone to give access to the line on the north bank, opposite the side where the Northern Pacific railway had its course, so that all grading outfits, teams, steam shovels, and so forth had to be conveyed across at considerable expense and trouble. Supplies for men and animals could be brought on the Northern Pacific to the nearest point of construction and then taken across the river in small boats. But the larger pieces presented greater difficulties. A steam shovel, for instance, used to excavate at the Bonfield Bluffs, was hauled across the Yellowstone by cable and capstan along the river bottom through deep water, costing the life of a McIntosh foreman. A ferry was built for cars, rails, and other machinery; and a large part of the roadbed at Bonfield Bluffs had to be built in the swift current of the river, forcing the selection, excavation, and deposit of large masses of solid rock on the river side of the embankment, an operation taking place in midwinter and thus necessitating the maintenance of a special body of men to cut ice so that rock could reach its proper position at the foot of the slope. Large portions of the road had to be protected by riprap and wing dams against the Yellowstone's predatory rises, for, wherever no riprapping had been done, high water always caused considerable damage and the loss of thousands of yards of material.

The third division of the eastern Montana section, from Forsyth to the first crossing of the Musselshell River, once again differed radically from the two preceding divisions of this section, for it lay in unsettled country through which all supplies had to be hauled from Forsyth. The company experienced unforeseen difficulty in finding oats and hay for teams, and the grading had to be done in gumbo soil that was impassable even after slight rains, and by grading machines almost entirely —a cumbersome procedure. Furthermore, water was scarce, coal was nonexistent save for what could be hauled from Forsyth, and the cost of the 65-mile division was proportionately great.

The Musselshell section posed yet another kind of problem in each of two divisions. The initial division led through a more heavily populated area where many ranches had been established along the irrigated valley of the Musselshell; therefore, while supplies for teams working along the line could be purchased in part, and while the Musselshell River gave good water and the valley's cottonwood trees furnished fuel, the channel changes made in the Musselshell to save bridging entailed not only large amounts of riprapping, but brought about serious complications in irrigation systems, in many cases requiring the construction of inverted siphons to carry irrigation ditches across the roadbed and of entirely new systems of dams, head gates, and ditches to satisfy the demands of the owners, and, as an aftermath, required the company's right-of-way agents to spend months of time and thousands of dollars in the work of settling claims for damages.

The second division required the construction of practically a new line from Harlowton to Lombard, close to the Montana Railroad. The new line, particularly in Sixteen Mile Canyon, a relatively narrow passageway, vastly increased the cost and difficulties of construction, since the Montana Railroad wished to continue operation of its trains without interruption. Yet many crossings were necessary, and heavy rockwork involved blasting operations which hurled masses of rock on the right of way of the Montana despite every precaution that could be taken; therefore, extra hands were necessary to move obstructions so that the passage of trains would not be impeded. In addition, many tunnels had to be built, so that this comparatively short section was one of the most costly on the entire coast route.

Finally, the Rocky Mountain section brought the road to the Continental Divide, up to which, on this division, construction engineers experienced no greater annoyance than the difficulty of hauling supplies despite lack of roads. From Piedmont, at the foot of the Divide, to Butte the line required mountain work and gradient, crossing the Continental Divide at Pipestone Pass and piercing the summit through a tunnel. Extremely hard and solid rock was encountered for large portions of this division, necessitating the hauling of large quantities of explosives by team from Butte and the construction of roads to the principal camps from the Butte–Whitehall highway. The tunnel work required, in addition, the construction of boardinghouses, and took longer than contractors had estimated, though at Butte some delays were brought about by unions which strove, with comparatively little success, to foment trouble among the men. However, from Butte to the Continental Divide, construction proceeded eastward at the same time, so that transportation of construction material, particularly tunnel lining and steel trestles to supplant temporary timber trestles, was accordingly expedited.

The completion of track to Butte did not by any means spell the end of work on the initial 718 miles of the coastward line, for, while grading had been made as permanent as possible, culverts and bridges had often been constructed of temporary timbers across long and deep ravines; many of these ravines were subsequently filled and many others were replaced with steel. Moreover, the Mobridge bridge and the three steel bridges across the Yellowstone River were not constructed by contract, but by company men themselves and were completed, despite all the obstacles afforded by the swift and deep river, by the time track-laying outfits reached the bridges. Since the three Yellowstone bridges had an aggregate length of 3,300 feet, it is possible to arrive at a rough estimate of the enormous tonnage involved in the raising of both temporary and permanent structures—all of which was hauled over spur tracks built by the Northern Pacific to points opposite the bridge sites. In addition to the construction of these bridges, the company had to order the building of reservoirs and dams and to dig wells in order to assure the water supply along the line, a procedure involving extensive study of watersheds.

Track-laying on the Mobridge–Butte section was begun, naturally enough, on the basis of expedience—that is, at points nearest contacts with the Northern Pacific. Therefore, on this 718-mile distance, track was laid from Mobridge west, from Cato both east and west, from Miles City west, from Harlowton east, and from Lombard west, daily track being laid reaching an average distance of 1.75 miles—a far cry indeed from the average achieved on that first infinitesimal distance from Milwaukee to Waukesha! Curiously enough, though the country west of Mobridge was either unsettled or sparsely settled, track-laying was often impeded by the influx of settlers, whose cars and wagon trains moved steadily into the region along the Milwaukee Road's extension, even as the officials of the road had foreseen, so that the line, constructed through largely "unsettled" country, had in but a few years time the appearance of traveling through settled area for its entire distance from Mobridge to Butte, excepting only such lands as belonged to Indian reservations and were not open to settlers, like the Standing Rock Indian Reservation and the reservation of the Crows in the vicinity of Miles City.

Inevitably, the railroad's movement westward not only stimulated the growth of settlements, but helped to create them. The tendency to establish and name towns followed the Milwaukee Road west. In Iowa there were Britt, named after an engineer of the Milwaukee; Garner, named after another railroad man; Hull, which grew out of winter quarters of Milwaukee Road gangs; Luana, named after the wife of a pioneer who gave the Milwaukee land for a right of way on condition that the station would be named after his wife; Ruthven, named for Robert and Alex Ruthven, who gave half their land to the Milwaukee in return for locating the town platt there; Sanborn, after George W. Sanborn, a Milwaukee division superintendent; Van Horne,

founded in 1881, after Sir William Van Horne, then general superintendent of the Milwaukee; and Whittemore, named after the engineer who was in charge of Milwaukee Road construction west of
Algona, Iowa, in 1878. In South Dakota there were Alexandria, named
after the daughter of Alexander Mitchell; Bowdle, in tribute to a
Milwaukee Road employee whose job was to secure town sites; Faith,
named after the daughter of Percy Rockefeller; Gayville, which got its
name after Elkanah Gay, a conductor, who was the first person to
locate there after the railroad was built; Kimball, after a Milwaukee
Road surveyor; Langford, after a Milwaukee Road director; Lennox,
after S. S. Merrill's private secretary; Marion, after Merrill's daughter;
Oldham, named incredibly after a pile of smoked hams abandoned
at the site by a construction crew; Pukwana, named by a Milwaukee
Road engineer after an Indian legend; Stickney, named by the Milwaukee Land Company after a Milwaukee employee; Tulare, named
after a pair of tall-tale-telling bachelors who entertained passengers
and crews of stalled trains (Tulare coming from Two Liars through
Tu-Lair); and Isabel, after another daughter of Percy Rockefeller.

As the Milwaukee moved into North Dakota, more new towns sprang
up, among them Rhame, named after the chief civil engineer of the
Milwaukee, and the only town of that name in the United States;
Marmarth, after Margaret Martha Fitch, granddaughter of President
Earling; Reeder, after a Milwaukee Road employee, an engineer later
connected with the Puget Sound lines; and Montline, named because
of its location at the state line between Montana and North Dakota.
Similarly, in Idaho, Avery was named for Avery Rockefeller; Ramsdell
for a construction engineer; and Jersey, a station named by Milwaukee
Road men. The naming of such stations, towns, and small cities continued to the west coast. The country was colorful, however, and
certain settlements were there long before the Milwaukee Road came
through—towns like Two Dot, Montana.

Two Dot, twelve miles west of Harlowton on the Milwaukee's main
line, got its name from George R. (Two Dot) Wilson, a New Yorker
who had become a successful cattle-buyer by the time he was sixteen,
but restlessly set out to work his way to Whitewater, Wisconsin, from
which town nine years later he joined a wagon train for Montana.
There he worked for a while cutting and hauling wood and for a little
while longer on a claim near Virginia City. But in a few years he was
back at cattle-buying, and soon at cattle-raising and selling. His brand
was a pair of dots on each hip of his animals—cattle, sheep, and horses
ranging over thousands of acres in Meagher and Sweetgrass Counties.
Men like Two Dot Wilson had gone a long way to civilize the country

in which they lived, and welcomed the railroads when they came. In return, the Milwaukee, in common with other railroads, helped to perpetuate their memories.

It was often a problem to name locations on the new lines built by the Milwaukee. Obviously, side tracks, passing tracks, and places for the unloading of materials had to be established, and some of them were expected to grow into communities. In naming them, however, the Milwaukee had to consider the Post Office Department, which, to avoid duplication of names, had to approve the naming of new communities. Occasionally the naming of a town resulted in amusing incidents; for instance, after the naming of Bonfield because of the beautiful fields visible from the right of way, a lady wrote to the Milwaukee to say that her name was Bonfield, and that she had the history of every member of the Bonfield family in America, but wanted to know as to which member of her family inspired the name of the Milwaukee station. The company tactfully told her that, because of incomplete records, it was impossible to answer her inquiry.

Despite all the assistance settlers gave to the construction crews of the Milwaukee, the going was rugged. W. W. Hunt of Yankton, South Dakota, who worked as a telegrapher on the Iowa & Dakota division, recalled the conditions of working at his trade when, in 1907, he was sent to Scenic, South Dakota, as a telegrapher:

I found a box car set out to use as a telegraph office. That car and the section house were the only buildings there were. I climbed up into the car and found a rough desk or table with a set of telegraph instruments installed on it. There was a half inch of coal dust on the floor and there wasn't a broom around. However, Mr. Boland, the roadmaster, showed up and had the section men clean it out. After supper there was no place to go and nothing to read, so very early I asked to be shown to my bed. The Indian woman who was the section foreman's wife brought me a blanket and pointed to the floor. . . . The Company at that time was graveling the west half of the Black Hills Division. The gravel pit was near the Cheyenne River and Scenic was at the top of the hill east of the river. Pusher engines pushed the gravel trains to Scenic; that was one reason the dispatcher needed an operator at Scenic, as the pusher engines needed orders to return to the pit. Train and enginemen from all over the Milwaukee system were out there to help do the job. At first I worked almost continuous time. Had a cot sent to me and put it back of the telegraph table. . . . When my wife came out, the Company set out another car, lined the floor and walls of both cars with sheeting, put building paper on the ceilings, and made a vestibule between the cars. We used one end of the first car as a bedroom and the other as the office; the second car was our living room, dining room and kitchen. . . . Homesteaders came in, and we began to get freight. R. P.

Edson, the division superintendent, came along one day and asked me if I knew station work, which I did. He had the agent at Murdo send me some stationery, and I opened the station.

Considering the time of its construction, the westward line of the Milwaukee Road offered very good wages. For one thing, many railroads were expanding and improving, so that the Milwaukee Road's westward expansion had to be made in the face of a rising demand for seasoned railroad workers. Thousands of men had to be shipped in at great expense, and many of them were restless, so that there was a constant fluctuation of personnel as men left to look for other jobs and new men had to be imported to take their places. Furthermore, since the work had to be pushed regardless of season, there was necessarily always a seasonal loss of those men who had sufficient funds to take off for warmer parts of the country as winter approached. Teamsters, for instance, demanded and received $1.75 a day, and other labor was paid proportionately. Some parts of the line were graded almost entirely by Indians, though these parts occurred only in the vicinity of reservations, since the Indians did not like to move far from their homes.

Beyond Butte, the line was pushed as insistently to meet the eastward advance from Puget Sound. The road had to cross no less than five mountain ranges between Harlowton and Seattle—the Belt Mountains, the main range of the Rockies, the Bitter Roots, the Saddle Mountains, and the Cascades. It had to proceed without any concessions of land or free right of way of any consequence, buying land for gravel pits outright and purchasing outright also all real estate necessary for roadbed, station grounds, and terminal facilities. Construction beyond Butte was divided into divisions in much the same way as was the initial stretch from Mobridge to Butte, and work was let by contract, Winston Brothers handling all work between Butte and Avery, H. C. Henry all territory west of Avery. While work on the Mobridge–Butte stretch was proceeding, work had also begun at Huson and Haugen in Montana, west of Butte, and at Lind, Murdock, Seattle, and Tacoma in Washington.

Difficulties of construction continued to arise, now here, now there. The tunnel at Pipestone Pass was only the first of the larger tunnels; it was followed by the St. Paul Pass tunnel, completed in March, 1909, by Winston Brothers, and by the Snoqualmie tunnel, driven by company men and completed January 17, 1915, though the coast line was opened before then for traffic over a temporary line.

The Snoqualmie Pass operation was one which harked back to the middle of the preceding century in railroad history. Originally an Indian trail long before white men invaded western North America, its name derives from an Indian word signifying that the origin of the Indians is the moon. The Snoqualmie Pass was the object of explorations carried on at the direction of the Engineer Corps of the U. S. Army in 1853-1854, explorations for the express purpose of determining the location of possible routes for a transcontinental railroad from the Mississippi and the Missouri Rivers to Puget Sound. The explorations were conducted on orders of the secretary of war in the cabinet of President Pierce, Jefferson Davis, who was later to become president of the Confederacy, and of Isaac Stevens, first governor of Washington Territory. Two explorations were in the direct charge of Captain George B. McClellan, later to become widely known as one of the Union generals in the prosecution of the Civil War.

McClellan, however, manifesting that same lack of vision and daring which marred his career as a Civil War general, took a negative view of the possibility of negotiating the Snoqualmie Pass. Though he plotted two possible locations for railroad tunnels near the Pass, he expressed clear doubts that the route was practicable, since, he had been given to understand by the Snoqualmie Indian guides who accompanied his party, snowfalls of 25 to 35 feet in the Pass during the winter would constitute effective barriers to rail travel; instead, McClellan recommended the 150-mile longer Columbia River valley route. His report did not convince or satisfy Stevens; so he sent Lt. Abiel W. Tinkham to make a further reconnaissance. Tinkham, with Yakima Indian guides, left Fort Walla Walla on January 7, 1854, and arrived at the summit of the Snoqualmie two weeks later; thereafter, instead of turning back as McClellan had done, he continued through the Pass, descending the Snoqualmie River to Seattle, and recording an average of two feet of snow on the eastern approaches to the Pass, and four to seven feet in the Pass itself. His report was more favorable than McClellan's, but it was left to the Milwaukee Road to justify the daring foresight of Isaac Stevens and Lieutenant Tinkham. In the construction of the famed Snoqualmie tunnel, as many as 700 men were employed, a maximum number to be engaged on a single project.

While train service to Butte, Montana, had been inaugurated late in August, 1908, and passenger service early in October, it was less than a year before freight service had been opened all the way to Seattle and Tacoma, and local passenger train operation was begun between Seattle, Tacoma, and Malden, Washington, early in June, 1909, followed a month later by service east to St. Joe, Idaho, and, another month later, to Avery, with local passenger service between Butte and Avery beginning on the same date, August 15, 1909.

Actually, difficulties of construction notwithstanding, this tremendous accomplishment was achieved in less than three years, beginning September, 1906, and ending May 14, 1909, when the last spike was driven four miles west of Garrison, Montana. By August 15, 1909, local passenger service had been established over the entire length of the line, from Mobridge to the west coast, though it was not until May 28, 1911, that the company put its through trains into operation, when the *Olympian* and *Columbian* service was inaugurated. The company had every right to feel proud of its achievement, but there was no inclination anywhere to rest upon any laurels, for the extension to the west coast had cost far more than all early estimates had led the officials to believe, and there was a pressing necessity for making the extension pay for itself as soon as possible.

To that end, the Milwaukee Road lost no time in the purchase or construction of branch-line feeders. As early as March, 1909, exploration and surveys had been begun for the Cheyenne, Moreau, and Cannon Ball branches in North and South Dakota, an aggregate branch distance of 301 miles; construction had started within the year, and on May 31, 1910, trains began operating on the Moreau branch; on the other branches, trains were in service before the year had ended. The purchase of the Jawbone Road added the 64-mile Harlowton–Lewiston branch and the 5-mile Ringling–Dorsey line in 1910. In that same year construction had begun on the Grass Range, Roy, and Winifred branches in Montana, and operation of trains was begun on the 71-mile St. Marie's branch. After surveys in 1908, construction was begun early in 1910 also on the Plummer, Spokane, and Coeur d'Alene branches, 46 miles in length, to connect with the Idaho and Washington Northern Railway, which was purchased in 1915 and thus added to the expanding empire of the Milwaukee Road. In that year, still further construction, new operation, or surveying went forward; for instance, the Gallatin Valley Railway, a subsidiary line, 51 miles in length, was built between Three Forks and Bozeman Hot Springs; the 48-mile Warden branch was begun in March and began operating in December; the Everett, Washington, branch, 55 miles long, was completed in November, 1911, and opened to service; and operation of trains was started on the McKenna Gate branch, 34 miles long, in August, 1910.

The construction of branch lines was economically sound, for the westward movement of settlers was as great as it had ever been after the Civil War. In 1906, for example, it was possible for an engineer to report but one ranch on Sandstone Creek from Marmarth to Ismay, Montana, and one other between Ismay and Terry; by the time the Milwaukee Road had its branch lines in operation, this was flourishing agricultural country, with the bench lands adjacent to Sandstone, Correll, and Fallon Creeks being well settled and well irrigated, though here and there great ranches still existed, since these had been grants and were never government land open to the influx of settlers. This land was producing excellent crops of wheat, oats, rye, and other grains, all beginning to move eastward along the Milwaukee Road. As it was with the Sandstone Creek valley, so it was with other areas along the new railroad tracks—a farming population moved in, villages came into being, and an unsettled country became in the space of a few years a well populated area, its people engaged in plumbing the natural resources of the new land, from the raising of grain to the development of coal fields, all contributing to the revenue of the Milwaukee Road.

Recognizing the importance of having someone from the west upon the board of directors, the road, after the death of Henry H. Rogers, added John D. Ryan to the board in 1909 at the suggestion of William Rockefeller. Rogers was one of the Rockefeller men and one of the most astute directors, in financial matters particularly, ever to serve on the Milwaukee Road's board of directors. Ryan was president of the powerful Anaconda Mining Company, and had a lively interest in water power; his familiarity with the country through which the new extension of the Milwaukee Road must operate made him a desirable addition to the board, particularly since Rockefeller himself had long before bought a considerable interest in Anaconda. Ryan was also very much alive to another factor that bore directly upon problems of the railroad in mountain operation: he was keenly interested in railroad electrification, partly to secure a new use for copper, partly to afford an outlet for the vast undeveloped water power he and his associates directly or indirectly controlled. The General Electric Company had electrified a short line from Butte to Anaconda under the aegis of the Anaconda Copper Company, and the General Electric Company was already engaged in making studies regarding electrification of the Milwaukee Road.

Even before Ryan's coming to the board of directors, President Earling had considered that it might be advisable to electrify a portion of the line to the west coast, and to that end he had made provisions for power sites along the new line. Earling's intention was evidently to establish the road's own power stations, but Ryan's experience easily convinced Earling and the other officials of the road that, if electrification were decided upon, it would be better for the road to make arrangements with existing power outlets, since companies like the Montana Power and Washington Power Companies already had extensive systems and all basic facilities for servicing the Milwaukee Road.

Several factors entered directly into the matter to balance the scales in favor of electrification. Primarily, there was the problem of the mountain grades. The road to the west coast included, unavoidably, many long grades and short-radius curves, particularly in the four large mountain ranges—the Belts, Rockies, Bitter Roots, and Cascades; many of the grades were of 1 per cent or more, that ascending the west slope of the Belt Mountains maintaining a 1 per cent grade for a distance of 49 miles, while the west-bound grade between Beverly and Boylston, in Washington, ran for 19 miles at 2.2 per cent.

Many of the curves reached a curvature of 10 degrees, and, particularly in winter weather, the grades and curves made the movement of trains a difficult and uncertain venture, since temperatures sometimes went down as low as 40 degrees below zero, causing engine failures or simple inability to make enough steam to operate. Moreover, though the steam locomotives operating on the road were of the most recent construction for that time, most of them oil burners, the locomotives had an average run of only 113 miles, owing to the inadvisability of chancing longer runs in such relatively difficult terrain. Steam locomotives also caused many delays because of hot brake shoes and wheels on the grades, coaling, taking on water, cleaning fire, and waiting for steam, as well as delays brought about by weather conditions. There was also the cindery smoke with which the passengers had to contend, particularly in the tunnels, of which there were 45 on the passenger main line and 15 on the freight line between Plummer Junction and Marengo and branch lines, longest of which were the St. Paul Pass tunnel, 8,771 feet in length, and the Snoqualmie Pass tunnel, of 2¼ miles, though the Snoqualmie tunnel was not completed until after the decision to electrify had been made—work on the tunnel, designed to save 3.6 miles of line, a rise and fall of 443.5 feet, and 1,239 degrees of curvature, being carried on in 1913 and 1914.

The company, convinced that electrification would lower costs and improve service, began by ordering preliminary surveys made under the direction of Reinier Beeuwkes. The project was not something to be rushed into without adequate inquiry, since the electrification of any considerable distance of main line was an historic step and was thus far unprecedented in the history of American railroads. Beeuwkes and his party returned with specifications for electrification so accurately drawn up in every detail that a changeover could be made without any significant interruption of regular schedules. After considering the advantages of electrification, particularly in regard to the time and labor that could be saved in mountainous country, the company hesitated no longer, and late in 1912 made a 99-year contract for power for the Rocky Mountain division with the Great Falls Power Company of Montana, a half interest in which was controlled by Ryan and his associates, and, four months later, entered into a similar contract with the Thompson Falls Power Company, another company in which Ryan had an interest, for the adjoining Missoula division. Both these power companies were taken over shortly thereafter by the Montana Power Company, which was likewise of vital interest to Ryan, since he exchanged his stock in the two predecessor companies for stock in Montana Power. Ryan was thus in a unique position; as a member of the board of directors of the Milwaukee Road, he took no part in the discussions of that board relative to power, except to point out the advantages of using existing facilities as much as possible; but, dealing with President Earling, he did act for the power companies in framing the contracts for the Milwaukee Road.

It was decided to electrify first the stretch of the Milwaukee Road extending from Harlowton, Montana, to Avery, Idaho, 438 miles in length, and work on electrification was begun in April, 1914. Plans called for the building of conversion stations or substations at 30-mile intervals along the proposed electrification route. Electrical energy in the form of 100,000-volt, three-phase alternating current could be transmitted to these substations, where its tremendous pressure was reduced and converted into direct current at 3,000 volts, which could be applied directly to a heavy copper cable paralleling the track throughout the electrified zone and connected at intervals to the trolley on two copper wires, half an inch in diameter, supported over the center of the track about 25 feet above the rail and directly feeding the locomotive the energy needed for its propulsion by means of a pantograph through various control devices to the motor. Locomotives were equipped with control cabs at both ends, and, important for the steep grades, with regenerative braking.

Regenerative braking permitted the recovery of energy on descending grades by reversing the customary function of electric motors, utilizing the momentum of the train to drive them as generators. Such regeneration recovered from 40 per cent to 60 per cent of the energy required to pull a train up a grade, resulting in a return of approximately 12 per cent of the entire power drawn from the power company, so that the road would, in actual functioning, only borrow some of its power. In contrast to the smooth passage of electrically propelled locomotives and trains over the mountain grades, the steam-locomotive-drawn trains required a great deal of skill; for the control of a 2,500-ton train, for instance, traveling at 17 miles an hour down a 2 per cent grade, 4,700 horsepower had to be dissipated. Small wonder that brake shoes became red hot! Smoother operation and the elimination of smoke and cinders were certain to impress travelers.

On November 30, 1915, the first train operation using an electric locomotive took place on the Milwaukee Road's Rocky Mountain division, when a train of business cars was hauled from Three Forks to Deer Lodge, 112 miles. Just a week later, train Number 16, the east-bound *Olympian,* was hauled from Butte to Three Forks, 70 miles over the Continental Divide, by an electric locomotive, thus becoming the first passenger train on the line to be electrically operated. A year later the electrification of the section between Harlowton and Avery was in effect completed, and the entire distance of 438 miles was being run by electrically operated locomotives. Within a short time, a matter of weeks, it was evident that the results of electrification were all that had been anticipated, and the board of directors, meeting on January 25, 1917, authorized further electrification between Othello and Tacoma, Washington, a distance of 207 miles, and in March entered into a 98-year contract with the Intermountain Power Company, another Ryan Company (later incorporated into the Washington Power Company), for power to be furnished the Coast division, of which the Othello-Tacoma run was a part.

The company discovered almost immediately that the operating efficiency—especially of freight trains—under electrification was astonishing. Compared with the performance of steam-operated locomotives, the tonnage per train was virtually doubled, and the maintenance expense, owing to the regenerative braking process, was significantly reduced, while at the same time safety of operation was increased. Over-all efficiency was increased to such an extent that, in the initial eight years of operation, the road estimated that a saving of $12,400,000 had been effected by electrification.

Meanwhile, the company had not been idle on other fronts. While the extension to the coast was in progress, the Milwaukee Road continued other construction and improvements. In the year the westward extension was begun, the company was beginning branch lines in North and South Dakota and in Wisconsin; it bought a short road from Oglesby to Granville in Illinois; it constructed second main tracks in Wisconsin and Minnesota; it completed the elevation of tracks in Chicago; it improved its shops in West Milwaukee, Dubuque, Minneapolis, and Savanna; it began new shop construction in West Milwaukee, and built an additional ore dock at Escanaba, Michigan. This work, begun in 1906, was continued in 1907 and 1908, while the westernmost lines of the company were reaching to Butte, Montana.

In 1909, the Milwaukee Road began its first marine operation with a barge running between Seattle and Ballard over Puget Sound. The operation, which was to expand to include several barges and the tug *Milwaukee,* capable of handling full trains, reached its peak in October, 1944, when 3,869 carloads were handled in and out over the Tacoma loading apron. Originally only ties, shingles, and similar freight were handled, as against the average thousand cars of all freight that the Milwaukee sends to sea every month today. The barge line in 1909 served primarily the lumber and shingle mills along the coast; its initial operation to the Ballard district of Seattle was soon expanded by service to Port Townsend and Bellingham. The tug *Milwaukee* was added in 1913.

The entire marine operation was undertaken because the almost island topography among the ports made rail service by water far more feasible than rail service by land. The seafaring skill required of the Milwaukee Road employees for such work was for decades under the guidance of Captain Peter Shibles, the skipper who inaugurated the tug *Milwaukee's* service on the Sound. The operation in skilled hands was readily made to seem simple, but it required the utmost care on the part of Captain Shibles and his crew of 14 men to place the barge so that a "yard goat" could couple on to an outside string of five cars and pull it across the loading apron into the yard. Within 15 minutes the barge could be fully loaded with three five-car strings. Blocking and jacking cars was likewise not child's play, since the *Milwaukee* and its barges, run on a seven-day schedule, could encounter any kind of weather, and often did. Shibles, a veteran deep-water skipper, knew the Sound very well; in thick weather he navigated by echo, since he was acquainted with every headland from which the sound of the whistle bounced back, just as he knew the tides, the eddies, the currents along the way. His habit of leaning out of one window to listen weathered one side of his face a deep mahogany. The barge service was destined to expand steadily, since it was recognized at once that no amount of rails built between ports could possibly do the work of the barge service for even quadruple the operation expense of the barges and their tugs.

As a transcontinental road, the Milwaukee lay open on several fronts to the kind of diverse troubles and disasters which are far more likely to be the lot of widespread empires than of lesser lines. Nevertheless, the Milwaukee had comparatively little major trouble to deal with in its vast empire; this perhaps was due less to luck than to the caliber of the Milwaukee's employees, to whom the Milwaukee, for all its movement to the coast, was still "our road." However, the company could not hope to escape all difficulties. In November, 1909, one of the company's mines, the St. Paul at Cherry, a six-year-old town in southern Illinois, caught fire because of the carelessness of an employee in the mines, who set fire to a car of six bales of hay being sent down the main shaft. Smoke and an obstruction in the passage made it impossible to hose the burning bales. The car was thereupon shunted down to the third vein, with instructions to the miners in that vein to prepare to put the fire out with their hose. Unfortunately, the car stuck in the shaft; by the time it was loosened and sent on down and the fire in the hay had been put out, the shaft itself had caught fire. The fire spread rapidly, trapping 263 men in the second vein and 160 in the third. Word of the disaster trickled out of Cherry during that night, so that by Sunday, the following day, the town was the goal of doctors, reporters, the Red Cross, and officers of the company, among them President Earling, who, greatly distressed, made every effort to do whatever was possible for the stricken. Between 250 and 300 men lost their lives in the disaster, though 20 trapped men at first given up for dead managed to survive and were brought up eight days later.

Less than a year thereafter, in August, 1910, the Milwaukee was involved in a major forest fire. The Milwaukee had not reached far into the Wisconsin or Minnesota forests at the time of the Peshtigo and Hinckley fires, back in 1871 and 1894, respectively; but now the lines of the road passed through forest territory in many places. The great Idaho fire of 1910 raged through many counties of northern Idaho and northwestern Montana, and the Milwaukee Road operated through three of those counties: Benewah and Shoshone in Idaho, and Mineral County in Montana. Thousands of acres of valuable timber were destroyed, though the loss of life was not comparable to that in the Wisconsin and Minnesota fires, of which the Peshtigo, with the burning over of 3,280,000 acres and the death of almost 1,500 people, was the greatest disaster of its kind in the history of the nation.

Beyond question, the men of the Milwaukee did a large share of the work necessary to prevent the death toll from rising. Telegraphers warned of the advance of the fire. As the flames advanced toward Avery, on the Milwaukee Road, two trainloads of Avery people were moved to Tekoa, Washington, though here and there Milwaukee bridges were burning, and three of the Milwaukee's bridges near Malden, Washington, burned out. On the night of August 20, Engineer John Mackedon, returning from a trip to the mountaintop with but one assistant in his engine, drew up at the Milwaukee Road's station at Falcon, which was on fire, to find several hundred men, women, and children gathered on the platform of the depot. The moment he stopped, his engine was besieged by people who climbed aboard or clung to it wherever they could find a place to take hold. Mackedon realized that he could not possibly carry them all on his engine; so, despite the fact that cars on a side track were aflame, Mackedon cut an empty from them and left Falcon with the car and the engine packed with the survivors of the flaming town.

In an article on the fire published in *Railroad Man's Magazine* for May, 1911, Harry Rusch of Avery described the heroic efforts of Milwaukee Road men—how Conductor Harry B. Vandercook and Engineer Blondell, missing Superintendent C. H. Marshall when they sought refuge in one of the Milwaukee's tunnels after escaping fire-swept Falcon, decided to go back down the mountain for him:

The huge timbers of the bridges were burning beneath them, but they still kept on until they had rescued the official from certain death. Their return trip up the mountain to the tunnel was terrible. The bridges were all ablaze. After crossing them they were compelled to stop and extinguish the flames that threatened to demolish their caboose. They remained in the tunnel eight days until the bridges were rebuilt. . . . When asked about his experience, Engineer Blondell replied: "Why, all that you could see of a bridge was a wall of flame, but we crossed it. I hooked her up, threw her wide open, and then we lay down on the deck to protect ourselves from the heat. We expected that every minute would be our last on earth."

In addition to the role of the men on the trains, others also played courageous parts. Ralph W. Anderson, foreman at the roundhouse at Avery, saved that town by summoning all his Japanese employees and all other Milwaukee Road personnel in the vicinity to build a backfire on both sides of the St. Joe River, thus saving Avery by sending the fire around the town.

These isolated instances were repeated elsewhere on the main and branch lines of the Milwaukee. The Idaho fire extended north and south from the Canadian boundary along the Bitter Root Mountains for a distance of something like 500 miles; the pall of smoke overhead was so dense that all cities and towns throughout the Pacific northwest experienced several very dark days; it extended so far to sea that the British ship *Dunfermline*, 500 miles west of San Francisco, reported smoke, which obscured observations for a period of almost a fortnight thereafter. The excessively dry summer and the high winds of that month demonstrated the extreme hazard of fire, with the result that since that time Milwaukee Road operating and track maintenance crews are constantly alert for fire danger. Fire patrols follow trains, and all passengers and train crews are impressed with the need for precautions against carelessness.

In the four years between 1906 and 1910 the company had grown from 7,043.54 miles of track to close to 10,000 miles, though the report dated June 30, 1910, lists only 7,296.55 miles as the length of the main track, manifestly not taking account of the fact that, pending formal and public assimilation at a later date, the company did actually control and own the subsidiary companies organized to build various sections of the line to the west coast. No capital stock was issued in 1910, and the funded debt of the road decreased, though its general mortgage bonds increased to $26,897,000, and its road and equipment were valued at $280,828,179.04. In its equipment, the Milwaukee Road had, by 1910, expanded into one of the largest of great railroads; it owned 1,199 locomotives, 518 passenger cars, 100 sleeping cars, 24 parlor cars, 20 dining cars, 6 observation cars, 435 baggage, mail, and combination cars, 29,329 box cars, 3,503 stock cars, 8,739 flat, coal, and ore cars, 1,844 refrigerator and vegetable cars, 1,453 ballast cars, 607 caboose cars, 692 work train, wrecking, and tool cars, and 16 business cars. The team of Earling and Miller were still at the head of the company, and its directors included some significant names in the nation's financial history— Walter P. Bliss, Frank S. Bond, A. J. Earling, Charles W. Harkness, John D. Ryan, Donald G. Geddes, Roswell Miller, William Rockefeller, John A. Stewart, J. Ogden Armour (who had replaced Philip on the occasion of Philip's death in 1901), Frederick Layton, L. J. Petit, and Percy A. Rockefeller—nine out of thirteen from New York, or listing New York as their address, so that the invasion of the Rockefeller forces was manifestly complete.

In only a short time, when full operation of the west-coast line began, the Milwaukee Road had become, as A. C. Kalmbach called it, "the Northwest passage," for it was hauling raw silk, wood, oil, tea, cotton, porcelain, and wool from China or Japan; pelts from Siberia; and hemp and cocoanut oil from the Philippines, in addition to the varied products of the great northwest—all kinds of finished lumber, crude oil, grain, wool, livestock, zinc, fish, agricultural products, wood pulp, paper, posts, piling, manganese, copper, copper products—the traffic the far-sighted officials of the Milwaukee Road had foreseen when they made the historic decision to reach westward to the Pacific.

IX. Receivership and Reorganization

On hand to meet The Marquette *every morning when it pulls into Mason City, Iowa, at 7:45 is Minnehaha, the station cat, whose breakfasts for the last ten years have been served with the compliments of the Milwaukee Road. She insists on fresh meat—rejecting cold, pressed meats—and she never fails to show up and see what's on the menu.*

Minnehaha waits until the dining car is placed and then makes her approach, never making a mistake about which is the diner. She is very cagey about letting anyone touch her and no one is even allowed near her two kittens, who stay at home in the freight house while she makes forays for food. On the Milwaukee's hardy fare, she raises two families a year.

—The Milwaukee Magazine
November, 1946

Despite the justifiably promising future seen for the Milwaukee Road at the time the decision to build westward to the coast was made, and despite the fact that the Milwaukee Road was exceeded by no other railroad in the soundness of its financial status at that time, events were destined to prove too much for every resource and ingenuity the road could muster. Though critics of the Milwaukee Road subsequently indicted the road's leadership for the westward expansion and blamed the ultimate collapse of the road upon the extension of the line to the west coast, this was too simple an explanation of the debacle, which was brought about by a number of factors, none of which was apparent at its outset, and no one of which alone would have humbled the strongest railroad empire in the land.

Nevertheless, westward expansion proved to be the most important of these factors. For one thing, the line to the west coast had cost out of all proportion to the estimate. The maximum estimate figured by President Earling had been $60,000,000; the actual cost had come to $256,968,126, inclusive of $22,990,254 for electrification. If the income of the Milwaukee Road had continued in proportion to its income in the initial decade of the century, the road could have surmounted this drain on its resources. Unfortunately, however, factors affecting the income of the road were beyond the road's control, and, since the expense of operation and interest charges on bonds exceeded the income of the road, it remained only a matter of time before major trouble resulted.

The financing of the westward expansion was accomplished by issuing bonds and stocks to the general public; the bonds were sold until 1918 in blocks, and were in various issues, all of which were bought up readily because the credit and reputation of the management were of the soundest. There were several important issues—the Chicago, Milwaukee and Puget Sound 4's due in 1949; the 25-year gold 4's due in 1934; the convertible gold 4½'s due in 1932; the 15-year European loan 4's due in 1925; and the gold 4's due in 1925, in addition to general and refunding 4½'s and 5's, in the amount of $72,219,000, due in 2014. The European loan issue amounted to $13,076,000, and the gold 4's due in 1925 amounted to $35,100,000; since both fell due in 1925, they were the first of the westward expansion issues to be met, and, in view of the circumstances in the Milwaukee Road's history during the second decade of the century, the ability of the road to meet these obligations was the subject of considerable speculation in financial circles throughout the country.

The issuance of these bonds was a complicated procedure and resulted in an equally complicated structure. The Puget Sound 4's, for instance, were issued against a first mortgage on the westward extension, and an ultimate amount of $155,000,000, issued by this subsidiary company to the Milwaukee Road for funds advanced, went into the company's treasury. The European loan was sold in France just prior to World War I; even in France the reputation of the Milwaukee Road was well known, and the bonds sold freely and easily; but during the war the Milwaukee Road redeemed the European loan issue with the sale of gold 4's in this country, a sale handled exclusively by Kuhn, Loeb & Company and the National City Bank of New York. In 1913, the company executed a general and refunding mortgage on its property, thus making the debentures heretofore issued into mortgage bonds, and, after this, began to borrow on the new mortgage to raise the additional money needed to pay for branch lines and electrification. Thus, from June 30, 1909, to December 31, 1917, there was an increase of $266,096,000 in the company's funded debt in public hands.

The initial factor in the overwhelming cost of the westward extension of the Milwaukee Road was an augmenting of construction costs; to this was added the necessity of paying more for such land as the company did not already own when knowledge of its proposed road to the coast was publicly confirmed, resulting in what Percy Rockefeller later called "very vicious competition"—the attempt of rival railroad interests to purchase land desired and needed by the Milwaukee Road with the manifest intention of blocking the road out of the territory toward which the line was being extended. The company had "to pay a great deal more for the property, on account of the competitive conditions, than had been anticipated," in the words of Percy Rockefeller.

Later, when the building of the westward extension—customarily then referred to as the Puget Sound Railway—was being investigated by the Interstate Commerce Commission, it was maintained that "ordinary caution" should have impelled President Earling and his board of directors to be aware of the possibility of increased land prices and to add it to their estimates, but this criticism was unwarranted, for the addition of such intangibles to any estimate of any nature whatsoever would readily make any venture prohibitive. President A. J. Earling had been eminently cautious; he had taken years to accede to Roswell Miller's proposal for the westward expansion, and his agreement had come only after

William Rockefeller's nod. Earling, though a cold, somewhat austere man with little sense of humor, was devoted to the Milwaukee Road and functioned ably enough as its president, despite the opposition of J. Ogden Armour, who opposed the Standard Oil interests and who looked upon Earling as a Rockefeller-Harkness man. No more blame could logically be attached to Earling than to any other man in direct or indirect control, for the events which conspired against the road were not entirely foreseeable.

The fact that construction on the road to the west had been of a permanent nature wherever possible had also added considerably to the costs; other transcontinental roads had used much temporary construction at first, and subsequently laid down permanent installations as long-range improvements. Moreover, there was yet another factor in the cost of construction which critics of the westward expansion doggedly over-looked in comparing the cost of the Puget Sound line to that of other transcontinental roads, and that was the scrupulous fairness of the Milwaukee Road in the matter of wages—an important factor which was not a major consideration of the road's rivals who were earlier to reach the west coast. Yet even these additional costs did not seem to be insurmountable problems for a railroad company which in 1905 and for some years thereafter had earned roughly four times its interest charges, and even in 1912 was earning twice its interest charges. The increase in revenues from 1900 to 1909 amounted to 46 per cent, and in the latter year operating expenses were only 64.66 per cent of revenues.

But the increase in revenues did not continue, a situation that again was due to a variety of factors. The building boom which had opened the century in the Pacific northwest reached its peak in 1909; the lumber industry, which had increased its output by 200 per cent in the century's first decade, likewise remained relatively stable after 1910; Washington lumber and the metal output of Idaho and Montana were not shipped exclusively on the Milwaukee Road, for the competition that had been inaugurated by rival roads in land purchases obtained a share of this business, and this competition in turn contributed to an inadequate rate structure for all the railroads involved. But the greatest blow to fall upon the transcontinental railroads was the opening of the Panama Canal in 1914 to traffic of all kinds; the hope that the canal would be restricted to military traffic had proved baseless. Though the opening of the canal was a shock to all transcontinental roads, it was a grievous blow to a road as heavily indebted as the Milwaukee.

All these factors were necessarily not immediately conclusive, and their effect was bound to be a cumulative one. Meanwhile, having expanded into one of the greatest railroad systems in the world, the Milwaukee

Road found itself faced with increased maintenance expenses at a time when most of its resources had gone into building westward. Needing to maintain its right of way and also to buy more rolling stock, the company elected to improve its property before adding more rolling stock than was absolutely necessary. In the second decade of the twentieth century, the Milwaukee was constructing second main tracks in several places—from Huxley to Madrid, Iowa; from Bristol to Aberdeen, South Dakota, for instance; it was installing automatic block signals from Milwaukee to North La Crosse, Minneapolis to Aberdeen, Kittitas to Cle Elum, and so forth; it was eliminating grade crossings in Minneapolis, elevating tracks in Chicago and Milwaukee; it was extending lines in Michigan, Montana, Washington; it was still building logging roads in northern Wisconsin and constructing grain tanks in Milwaukee—all this while electrification of the road was proceeding in the west, and the Snoqualmie tunnel was being completed, to be placed in operation in mid-January, 1915.

Moreover, other activities on a wide front continued unabated. With the issue for April, 1913, the company began publication of *The Milwaukee Magazine,* edited by Mrs. Isabelle Carpenter Kendall, onetime stenographer in the office of the division freight agent in Milwaukee, and later in the office of A. J. Earling, then second vice-president and general manager. During the westward extension, Mrs. Kendall was on assignment gathering local color and pictures for the road's advertising department, an experience which stood her in good stead when she began work on the magazine, for she demonstrated at once a keen sense of news and a flair for color and drama in the lives of Milwaukee Road men and women. Mrs. Kendall, who served as editor until her retirement in 1940, was also one of the organizers of the Milwaukee Road's Women's Club, organized to promote better acquaintance for mutual enjoyment and helpfulness among the families of Milwaukee employees; she served this organization initially as treasurer, then as acting president general, and as its second president general for ten years, succeeding Mrs. H. E. Byram, the first president general.

Just as the establishment of *The Milwaukee Magazine* and the Milwaukee Road's Women's Club served to strengthen the bonds among Milwaukee Road employees, so the company continued to improve its material property. In addition to the customary repair and maintenance which went on, of course, over every division, the company on October 19, 1916, launched the larger section of a two-part pontoon bridge, the largest of its kind in the world, though a 396-foot pontoon bridge built between Wabasha, Minnesota and Trevine, Wisconsin, in 1895 and rebuilt in 1931 is the longest single pontoon bridge. The two-part pontoon bridge at Prairie du Chien reached a length of 485 feet, though the portion of the bridge launched in 1916 was 276 feet long, and was under construction for just short of a year in shipyards especially prepared for the task not far from Prairie du Chien, under the supervision of Chief Carpenter Neal Gregory. The bridge was launched over the west channel of the Mississippi to link Prairie du Chien and North McGregor, Iowa. Scarcely two months later, just before Christmas, 1916, the Union Pacific's old single-track bridge across the Missouri River between Council Bluffs, Iowa, and Omaha, Nebraska, which the Milwaukee used, was replaced with a new double-track bridge costing $1,000,000. The old bridge, long inadequate for the traffic rolling across it, was replaced by rolling it from its piers on to falsework, and the new bridge was then maneuvered into place by a similar process in an operation requiring less than an hour's time, and regarded as the most striking and efficient bridge removal ever performed.

With the almost complete electrification of the road in the Bitter Root Mountains, the Milwaukee invited two of its erstwhile rivals to make a tour over the electrified district. Presidents Hill of the Great Northern and Hannaford of the Northern Pacific were duly impressed at the efficiency of electric hauling of freight up the steep grades, but doubtless their reaction was tempered by the knowledge of the tremendous cost of the project.

Th second decade of the century also witnessed a major change in transportation other than that by rail. With the increasing improvement of the automobile and the greater number of automobiles being made available, year after year, travel by horse-drawn vehicles was declining, with the inevitable result that grade-crossing accidents began to mount steadily, forcing the Milwaukee, with other railroads, to spend more and more money for safety education.

The Milwaukee, on the eve of war in 1917, urged its employees to do everything possible to preserve the national economy, exhorting employees to knit and crochet articles of clothing—the *Magazine* carried full directions for knitting an army sock—and to enlarge home gardens, President Earling offering his personal prize of $1,500 to amateur gardeners for the largest yield per acre in any single commodity and for the best all-around vegetable garden.

By 1917, the company had undergone considerable change. Roswell Miller had died in 1913, Charles W. Harkness in 1916, after 30 and 20 years respectively with the company. The president's special report of December 31, 1916, took official cognizance of the increase in operating expenses:

It will be noted that the operating revenues for the twelve months ending December 31, 1916, exceed those of any previous period, being $110,609,688.86, an increase over the previous year of $13,561,638.36, or 13.9%. In connection with this, however, special attention is directed to the radical increase in operating expenses, due primarily to increases in the cost of fuel and other materials used in the maintenance and operation of the property, which averaged about 30% during the year and have steadily advanced since; also to a great many increases necessarily granted to labor during the year, and other increases resulting from congestions due to embargoes, all of which it will be noted produced an increase in operating expenses of $11,593,518.20, or 18.65%.

President Earling also took note of an 8.85 per cent increase in taxes, and of the Adamson Law, which, passed by congress and sustained by the United States supreme court, increased the wages of enginemen, trainmen, and allied employees "in excess of $2,000,000 per annum," a figure which would add proportionately to the operating expenses of the Milwaukee Road for 1917. The report, given in May, 1917, listed capital stock as $233,722,383.87, as against a funded debt of $490,547,154.66.

Moreover, President Earling's alarm was an additional burden, for he had been ill for some time, and his illness was cited by his opposition, J. Ogden Armour, as another reason to replace him with Harry E. Byram, brought from the Burlington Road to succeed Earling as president, an end which was accomplished in 1917 when Earling became chairman of the board of directors and took a place on the executive committee among William Rockefeller, Percy Rockefeller, John D. Ryan, and John A. Stewart.

In 1917, the road's operating expenses were 75.44 per cent of revenue, and its earnings fell from three times its fixed charges in the decade just past to only slightly over one and one-quarter times the fixed charges of 1917. What seemed to loom for the Milwaukee Road was not pleasant to contemplate, but before a crisis could develop, the United States entered World War I, and in December, 1917, the government established the U. S. Railroad Administration and seized all of the country's railroads. Seizure was followed by passage of the Federal Control Act on March 21, 1918, which authorized the president of the United States to come to an agreement with each railroad company to arrange the amount of annual compensation to be paid to the company, such amount not to "exceed a sum equivalent to the average annual operating income for the three years ending June 20, 1917," and to assure the companies involved that their property would be kept in good repair and returned in substantially the same condition at the termination of federal control. The officials of the company managed to obtain an agreement with the director general of the railroads which provided for an annual compensation just short of $28,000,000, which included $2,000,000 extra for the extension to the west coast and almost half a million more for the electrification. Moreover, President Harry Byram was named federal manager of the road until it was returned to the company in 1920.

Government control, while it staved off major financial trouble, was by no means a boon. Seizure at the end of 1917 included the taking over of all cash on hand and such balances as were due from agents, so that the company was forced to borrow funds in order to meet current expenses and other corporate requirements. Arbitrarily, the director general assigned to the Milwaukee Road 100 heavy freight locomotives and 5,000 box cars, a third of which were to be constructed by the company in its Milwaukee shops. Because of the high wartime prices current, the board of directors protested and succeeded in reducing the number of cars from 5,000 to 3,000. Moreover, because the director general insisted that all members of the corporation which were selected to work with his organization in the operation of the property sever their connection with the company, President Harry Byram gave way to R. M. Calkins.

The report for 1918 highlighted another aspect of federal control, when President Calkins pointed out:

The results of Federal operation and control of the railways of the country have dispelled whatever doubt may heretofore have existed as to the necessity for needed changes in the laws governing their operation under private management, and, prior to the adjournment of the last Congress, the Senate Committee on Interstate Commerce held numerous hearings on the subject to obtain the views of the public, the railway owners, the executive officers, and the employees.

In addition, the Milwaukee Road was given some unpleasant publicity, which played directly into the hands of railroad-baiters, when its director, John D. Ryan, then director of aircraft production in Washington, was accused of maneuvering contracts so that the Milwaukee Road and other National City Bank interests were enriched at the expense of the federal government, which, through Ryan's influence, bought inferior American spruce at a high price instead of superior Canadian spruce, such as the British Bristol plane people were using, at a lower price. Though the Milwaukee Road had no direct connection with Ryan's Bureau of Aircraft Production, it benefited, as did the National City Bank, by Ryan's predilection for accepting the advice of financial interests over that of experienced lumber experts, and the resultant publicity was yet another burden to be borne.

However, under federal control, the Milwaukee Road, in common with other railroads, received one small benefit, though it was one which had long been overdue. Late in 1918 the Interstate Commerce Commission decided that the transportation of mail should be paid on a space basis, rather than on the weight basis then current. Not only was the company's revenue increased thereby, but the new rates were made retroactive to November 1, 1916, so that the company's back pay for handling the U. S. mail amounted to almost $750,000.

The government operated the railroads at a tremendous loss, and its operation of the Milwaukee Road was no exception. When the property of the company was returned early in 1920, the operating expenses had crept up from the 1917 high to 97.94 per cent of revenues. Under federal operation, there was a deficit of $51,000,000, to say nothing of a net loss before interest charges of close to $10,000,000. The company's rolling stock was sadly depleted and depreciated, despite government allocation of cars and locomotives; this condition had been evident during the war, when every effort was made to maintain maximum efficiency in the interests of the prosecution of the war, but it was at once distressingly plain when the company was faced with the urgent need to replenish rolling stock at a time when it had not the money with which to do so.

Even the Transportation Act of 1920—though it included a government guarantee that railway operation income for the six-month period from March 1 to September 1, 1920, should not be less than half the amount named as annual compensation in the agreement between the company and the director general of railroads, thus cushioning the adjustment—with its promise of some adjustment of rates by the Interstate Commerce Commission, did nothing for the company in the way of adding to or improving its rolling stock, for the 1920 report cites receipt of a guaranty advance totaling $14,297,702, "of which amount $6,471,457 was used in payment of increases in wages to its employees from May 1, 1920 to August 31, 1920, in accordance with the decision of the United States Railway Labor Board, and the balance, $7,826,245, was used for interest payments on the Mortgage Bonds and Equipment Trust Notes of the Company." The equipment trust notes resulted from a federal mortgage placed on the road's equipment, a form of raising money the company had hitherto avoided, and a direct result of federal operation of the road during the war.

By 1920, though badly in need of new rolling stock, the Milwaukee Road owned a total of 68,634 cars, which included 1,917 steam locomotives, 62 electric locomotives, 62,189 freight cars, 635 coaches, 134 combination passenger cars, 99 passenger and baggage cars, 7 gas-electric motor cars, 17 buffet-observation cars, 202 standard sleeping cars, 36 tourist sleeping cars, 1 tug boat, 8 barges, and 2,736 service cars exclu-

sive of derrick, steam shovel, and wrecking cars. The funded debt had
risen to $529,562,654.66 as against capital stock value of $233,722,383.87,
and the valuation of road and equipment was put at $658,157,161.47.
The Milwaukee's revenue trains ran 37,547,198 miles, and its freight
cars, 738,287,812 miles during the year. The road had also acquired the
100 Mikado-type locomotives and the 4,000 box cars allocated by the
United States Railroad Administration under an equipment trust agreement with the government, and it was waiting upon the government's
Bureau of Valuation for service of tentative valuation. Harry E. Byram,
relieved of his position as federal manager of the road by the termination of federal control, returned to the Milwaukee as president.

That the condition of the Milwaukee Road in 1921 was serious no one
could gainsay; that it was hopeless was a moot point. Clearly, President
Byram did not consider it hopeless, for he continued to pursue policies
which in no way reflected any belief that the road's financial structure
was becoming top-heavy. One of the factors about wartime operation
which had impressed Byram as federal manager of the Milwaukee Road
was the fuel difficulties experienced during the war years. The Milwaukee Road was more or less at the mercy of distant mines on other lines,
and, in attempting to improve this situation, President Byram was persuaded to believe that the Chicago, Terre Haute & Southeastern Railway
Company was a desirable acquisition, because that company gave the
Milwaukee Road direct access to coal fields in southern Indiana.

In 1921 the Milwaukee Road leased this railroad for a period of 999
years, thus acquiring 360 miles of main track. But by the terms of the
lease, the Milwaukee Road acquired something considerably less desirable—an existing indebtedness of $19,500,000 and the obligation to pur-
chase 43,000 shares of capital stock outstanding at $10 a share. Moreover,
in 1922, the Milwaukee Road made another acquisition which was rather
a liability than an asset when it took over the Chicago, Milwaukee &
Gary Railway Company, owning about 95 miles of track which extended
around Chicago in northern Illinois, thus giving the road direct connection with the newly added Terre Haute lines without the necessity of
passing through Chicago terminals. President Byram hoped to save substantially by direct access to fuel and the more ready interchange of business with eastern roads outside the Chicago terminals. Unfortunately,
however, by its terms of acquisition, the Milwaukee Road agreed to pay
interest and principal on the debt encumbering the Gary Company—
$3,000,000.

Whatever the hopes of President Byram and others agreeing to the
acquisition of these two roads, those hopes were not fulfilled. The roads
were both in financial difficulties of their own when they were taken

over by the Milwaukee Road; both had been in such difficulties for some time, and one of them was using a portion of track belonging to the United States Steel Corporation. This was the Gary line, which had been called a railroad of "two tails without a middle," and for use of that middle the Gary line had made a disadvantageous contract with the steel corporation. Despite the best efforts of the Milwaukee Road's management, it could not be hoped that these two additional roads brought into the system could operate even to meet expenses, let alone at a profit. Up to 1925, the Terre Haute line was operated at an aggregate deficit in net income of over $4,000,000, and the Gary of over $930,000. Difficult as the Milwaukee Road's financial plight had been before their acquisition, it was manifest that these roads had only increased the Milwaukee's financial burden.

The fact was that Byram, though an excellent operator, was simply not qualified to handle such negotiations as those for the acquisition of the Terre Haute and Gary Roads; the replacement of the far more able Earling by Byram, at the dogged and mysterious insistence of J. Ogden Armour, who was soon in any case to divest himself of his Milwaukee Road holdings, was a serious blunder, though it is doubtful that any other president could have staved off disaster. But President Byram was by no means solely at fault, as subsequently the Interstate Commerce Commission pointed out when it concluded: "This investigation has shown that many of the directors knew comparatively little about the affairs of their company, that many of them did not even attend the meetings of the board with any regularity, and that some of them were affiliated with interests which conflicted in one way or another with the interests of the railroad company." The directors of the Milwaukee Road at the time were H. E. Byram, Donald G. Geddes, George G. Mason, Samuel McRoberts, E. L. Philipp, J. Ogden Armour, E. S. Harkness, Samuel H. Fisher, Mortimer N. Buckner, John D. McHugh, William E. S. Griswold, C. H. MacNider, and Franklin M. Crosby, of whom only Harkness, Fisher, and Buckner represented substantial interests.

Yet the fundamental reasons for acquisition of these two lines were sound enough. Intangible factors operated once more to nullify any potential gain not only on these two short lines, but on the entire Milwaukee Road as well. Each of these factors was in itself small, but each contributed its share toward the debacle that was to follow. From April to September of 1922, for instance, a coal-miners' strike suspended operations of the mines on company lines, depriving the company of its normal earnings on coal transported for commercial use and at the same time causing the company to pay more for locomotive fuel for its own use, thus creating an additional expense of $2,195,000. From July to

September, 1922, a shopmen's strike was in effect, not only seriously interrupting traffic and repair work, but bringing about additional expense of $2,225,000 attributable to the strike. Furthermore, the Milwaukee Road had to submit to reductions in freight rates taking effect in January and July, 1922, reductions which in turn reduced earnings for that year by almost $12,000,000, though this was offset in part by a decrease of $3,705,000 in wages because of reduced numbers at work, owing to the shopmen's strike for increased wages that July. In the strike, 16,400 men left the service, while 1,400 remained to work long hours under great difficulties to maintain service on the railroad.

Reduction in freight rates came at a time when the road had to meet other challenges. Rate reductions affected agricultural products particularly, but at the same time the metal industries of Montana curtailed operations because prices had declined markedly, particularly of zinc and copper, after the end of World War I. In addition to this, the country through which the rails of the Milwaukee Road passed was slow to recover from the brief depression of 1921, and bank failures in this region were frequent for years after 1921. As another aftermath of the war, the rates for shipment by water were reduced, and more tonnage than ever before began to pass through the Panama Canal, practically all diverted from the transcontinental railroad lines. Coincident with this change, passenger traffic fell off because of the increasing use of automobiles, trucks, and transcontinental busses. The Milwaukee Road's passenger-traffic revenue in 1924, for instance, stood at approximately $22,000,000, in contrast to $31,000,000 in 1920, a steady decrease averaging over $2,000,000 every year.

In mid-1922, the Milwaukee Road also suffered the loss of one of its wisest counselors when William Rockefeller died in Tarrytown, New York, after serving on the board of directors 40 years. The board memorialized "his courtesy and kindliness to his fellow directors, his marked loyalty and personal interest" in the affairs of the road, a loyalty not shared by all others, for, within three years thereafter, no Milwaukee Road stock was owned by either Percy Rockefeller or J. Ogden Armour, though the Harkness family holdings were intact and were represented on the board by Samuel Fisher. At the same time that the board of directors was deprived of William Rockefeller's advice, it added new members whose knowledge of railroading was not nearly to be compared with that of Rockefeller.

President Byram's operating experience served him well, however. Operating expenses of the road from 1921 through 1924 were brought under control and adequately decreased over the period of federal operation, but this factor was not enough to offset inadequate operating income, and the consistently rising interest charges could not be overcome. Early in 1924, the company floated a new issue of securities, $14,000,000 in gold 6's, due in ten years, secured by $20,000,000 in general mortgage bonds held in the company's treasury. This enabled the company to pay the banks the $5,000,000 due them at the end of 1923, for even then the banks were convinced that, owing to its financial structure, the Milwaukee Road could not escape receivership. During 1922, the company had renewed a $10,000,000 note to the government and sold several issues of equipment trust certificates aggregating over $23,000,000, so that badly needed rolling stock might be bought; the lack of such rolling stock had undoubtedly contributed to the decrease in operating income, a lack which President Byram had recognized at once on his coming into the Milwaukee Road just prior to World War I and which he had been trying to remedy ever since, despite the adverse financial situation under which the road continued to operate.

Though the company's report for 1923 contained some encouragement ("For the first time since December 31, 1917, the operations have yielded an income sufficient to meet interest obligations, and, while the income is insufficient for a dividend to stockholders, yet the improvement in net earnings since the end of Federal control and the substantial gain over previous years indicates continuing progress."), by the end of 1924 the plight of the Milwaukee Road was such that it could not very well be concealed. The 1924 report conceded that "The unfavorable business conditions in some of the territory served, the continued decrease in passenger travel, and the impossibility of meeting water competition through the Panama Canal, have had their effect in the current year in decreasing revenue." At the end of 1924, the company's capital stock outstanding amounted to $233,379,383.87, as against $107,511,300 less than 20 years before; at the same time the Milwaukee Road's long-term debt liability had increased from approximately $115,500,000 in 1905 to $443,982,796.42, so that by 1925 the capitalization of the company was 65 per cent funded debt and only 35 per cent capital stock. While in 1923 the report of President Byram had listed a net income of $207,686.10, the report a year later listed a net deficit of $1,868,605.94.

Early in 1925, at the behest of the road's bankers, Kuhn, Loeb & Company and the National City Bank of New York, and of President Byram and the board of directors, engineers examined the property and books of the Milwaukee Road and reported succinctly that the deficit and also over $25,000,000 expended for equipment and improvements had been financed by the liquidation of materials and sup-

plies, the reduction of current assets, the securing of bank credits, and
the increase of the funded debt, indicating that at the same time that
its property was depreciating—and such depreciation was not always
deducted—the Milwaukee Road was borrowing money and paying
unearned interest by drawing on its last assets. The engineers were
Coverdale and Colpitts, who were acknowledged experts in the examination of this kind of property. The interest of the National City
Bank and of Kuhn, Loeb & Company was subsequently challenged,
particularly since it was revealed that, well before 1923, Charles E.
Mitchell, president of the National City Bank, had become dubious
about the Milwaukee Road's future and had recommended that the
road's junior bonds be sold; this had been opposed by William Rockefeller, however, and was not done until 1923.

The bank and Kuhn, Loeb & Company took a major interest in the
Milwaukee Road as its bankers, even though neither organization held
any considerable amount of Milwaukee Road securities. When, in
mid-1924, President Byram asked four directors to form a special committee with him for the purpose of arriving at some solution to the
problem of how the road could meet approximately $47,000,000 in
bonds maturing in 1925, the committee, both in August and in December, met with Mitchell of the National City Bank and with Jerome J.
Hanauer of Kuhn, Loeb & Company. These banks had been the financial agents and advisers of the Milwaukee Road for many years, and,
since the westward expansion, they had handled all Milwaukee Road
securities. The committee and the bankers considered every plan; the
bankers were forced to point out that any exchange of the maturing
securities for new ones would involve the necessity for admitting that
no one could assure the bondholders that interest and principal would
ultimately be paid. This was tantamount to admission that no course
but "a readjustment of the financial structure of the Company" could
be taken.

President Byram was reluctant to agree. He made application for
help to the Interstate Commerce Commission, which promised to release such of the old general mortgage bonds of 1889 as were held
by the government for security for the notes in government hands,
since Byram and the board of directors thought it might be possible
to issue these bonds to refund the 1925 maturities. But it was plain
that, unless some way could be found to reduce interest and increase
operational income at the same time that expenses were lowered, any
such course as that now proposed by the management would be only
a delaying action, affording temporary relief and merely staving off
what seemed to be an inevitable readjustment. President Byram also

made direct application to the federal government for a loan, but, however sympathetic men in the government were with the plight of the Milwaukee Road, there was no statute then in existence which would make it possible for the government to make such a loan. As late as January, 1925, Byram made an appearance before the senate Interstate Commerce Committee in support of the Gooding Bill, projected to reduce the rate of interest on government loans. This was at a time when the Milwaukee Road owed the United States $55,000,000, and, while passage of this bill into law would also have afforded the Milwaukee Road something more than purely temporary relief, congress adjourned without passing the bill.

President Byram and the board of directors were extremely unwilling to face the inevitability of receivership. This was quite possibly not alone because of the fear that ineptitude and carelessness might be exposed on the part of some of them, but because they were not fully aware of all the factors involved, and they did not know at what point in the preceding decade of the road's history receivership had become "inevitable," holding almost to the last in the belief that refinancing could have been prevented by means of retrenchment and relief. What President Byram and the board of directors may not have known any more than the Harkness directors were certain facts later brought out in an investigation by the Interstate Commerce Commission; these facts pertained to the largest stockholding interests—and thus a controlling force—of the Milwaukee Road. Four large stockholding interests were dominant. William Rockefeller held a maximum of 150,000 shares; J. Ogden Armour, 125,000; the George O. Smith interests in England had invested almost $20,000,000 in bonds and stocks; and, finally, E. S. Harkness held approximately 100,000 shares. Of these interests, the Smith investment was the first to be liquidated, beginning during the course of World War I. Between 1920 and 1924, the Armour interest was liquidated, and, subsequent to William Rockefeller's death, the Rockefeller interest was in turn disposed of, between 1922 and 1925.

Of the four guiding interests, therefore, only the Harkness interest remained in 1925, represented on the board of directors by Samuel Fisher, the Harkness attorney, though Mr. Fisher resigned and was replaced by Mr. Gates in February of that year. Apart from Percy Rockefeller, who had resigned in 1921, a year before his father's death, some interests were still represented on the board of directors though their holdings had been liquidated. Of his resignation, Percy Rockefeller later explained that because of his uncertainty about the precise meaning of the Clayton Act—against interlocking directorates—he had

resigned from the directorate of the Milwaukee Road in order to remain one of the directors of the National City Bank. Whatever the
motive of the liquidation of Milwaukee Road stock by the George O.
Smith interests, it is difficult to escape the conclusion that the Rockefeller and Armour liquidations were accomplished because of some
doubt about the future of the company and its ability to meet its towering obligations.

In view of all these tributary factors, the absurdity of maintaining
that the underlying factor in the Milwaukee Road's difficulties was the
extension to the west coast emerges clearly; critics of the road might
as readily have charged that if no charter had been granted to the
Milwaukee & Waukesha in 1847, the Milwaukee Road would not have
been in difficulties in 1925.

As a result of its subsequent investigation of the causes leading up
to the financial troubles of 1925, the Interstate Commerce Commission
held that actual control of the Milwaukee Road had passed to its
bankers by January, 1925. This President Byram stoutly denied, maintaining that the directors of the road held the initiative and had
merely consulted the bankers. Despite President Byram's denial, however, the facts brought forth in the testimony clearly showed that
Kuhn, Loeb & Company and the National City Bank had accepted
the fact of receivership and had gone about planning for the appointment of receivers even before the board of directors of the company
had voted the receivership. The bankers were responsible not only for
the employment of Coverdale and Colpitts, as examiners of the Milwaukee Road, but also for drawing up a set of questions for the engineers to answer. However, at no point in their activities did the
bankers keep President Byram or the road's directors in ignorance of
their procedure, and Jerome Hanauer of Kuhn, Loeb & Company
made it clear to President Byram that, if the Coverdale and Colpitts
report was unfavorable, receivership was not to be avoided. The
bankers were governed by the conviction that the road's deficit was
certain to rise, in the end reaching astronomical heights; and the engineers estimated that in five years the Milwaukee Road's deficit would
be over $28,000,000.

However, the conduct of Kuhn, Loeb & Company, particularly in
the transaction in which they acted for the Milwaukee Road to buy
the French issue bonds through the issue of 4 per cent gold bonds,
was by no means above censure. The Interstate Commerce Commission disclosure, after a thoroughgoing investigation, that Kuhn, Loeb
& Company and the National City Bank divided a profit of 5 per
cent, when a commission of 2 per cent would have been generous,

instead of turning over just profits to the Milwaukee Road, for which they were acting, drew from the commission a tart censure: "They had acted as bankers for the St. Paul as far back as 1880; since 1909, they and the National City Bank had exclusively handled vast sums for the St. Paul; and yet at this opportunity to render an important banking service, the banker-railroad relation was suspended and profits greater than regular banking compensation were received." Since these profits were received at the expense of the Milwaukee Road, manifestly their loss added another factor to the mounting stream which was to wear down the company's financial structure. The bankers, therefore, recognizing that after Roswell Miller's death in 1913 the Milwaukee Road had no one of generally wide competence and experience to handle large financial transactions, took advantage of that situation to serve not the road but themselves.

The Interstate Commerce Commission enquiry demonstrated beyond cavil that, though the activity of the bankers for the Milwaukee was highly questionable, both in the fees assessed in connection with the reorganization and in the unethical fixing of the receivership in conjunction with Judge Wilkerson, whose conduct also was not above reproach, some of the fault must be shared by the directors and the executive head of the company. Specifically, the commission charged that the affairs of the Milwaukee were mismanaged by virtue of the fact that directors did not attend meetings as they were required to do and were not fully cognizant of all company affairs, and that these affairs should have been brought to their attention. The charge also included President Byram's inept acquisition of defunct railroad companies when the Milwaukee itself was in precarious financial condition, partly because of the secret disposal of stock by certain large interests associated with the directorate. The commission likewise held that the contracts for electric power for the western extension were unwise and unnecessarily costly in that the contracts obligated the Milwaukee to pay for power it did not use. An Interstate Commerce Commission investigation of the huge $6,500,000 receivership fees the banks assessed against the company was begun, but was restrained by an injunction sustained by the United States supreme court.

The Coverdale and Colpitts report was ostensibly the deciding factor in the matter of a receivership. On March 17, 1925, the board of directors of the Milwaukee Road met to consider the engineers' report. There was not much question about what had to be done, though there was so much discussion as to how the decision was to be registered that Director E. L. Philipp, former governor of Wisconsin, finally said with blunt impatience, "I don't see why we should spend

so much time choosing language to say you cannot pay your debts."
The board of directors thereupon voted to go into receivership, and
on the following day, by order of the United States district court,
Judge Wilkerson presiding, H. E. Byram, Mark W. Potter, and Edward
J. Brundage were appointed receivers of the property and franchises
of the Chicago, Milwaukee and St. Paul Railway Company. On the
following day, Milwaukee common stock sold at a low of 5, and the
preferred at a low of 8.6, in contrast to 199⅝ and 218, respectively,
two decades before.

Without delay, the National City Bank and Kuhn, Loeb & Company, managers of the reorganization, working with three security
holders' committees, began to devise a plan to reorganize the financial
structure of the Milwaukee Road whereby fixed charges would henceforth remain without earnings and yet provide adequate working
capital as well as as much protection, proportionately, as possible to
the holders of the different kinds of securities. Within three months
a plan was ready, but it was immediately opposed by groups of bondholders and stockholders, and, as a result of their opposition, the
bankers made some alterations. By mid-November, the new proposal
was announced, emerging as a carefully worked out arrangement
which would allow for the greatest advantage to the reorganization,
opposed to which its inequities were not in proportion. The major
terms of the proposed reorganization were as follows:

Equipment trust certificates, divisional issues, and general mortgage
bonds issued on the lines of the Milwaukee Road prior to the westward extension, amounting in total to $181,370,400, were to remain
undisturbed.

Two government notes totaling $35,000,000 and a timber loan of $2,-
200,000 were to be paid in cash, while a third government note of
$20,000,000 was to be paid with $17,000,000 in cash and $3,000,000
in preferred stock.

All bonds secured by the general and refunding mortgage of 1913,
and those issued on the first mortgage on the westward extension,
totaling $230,950,796, were to be exchanged for 50-year mortgage
bonds at 5 per cent, due in 1975, to the extent of 20 per cent of the
holdings, and for the 75-year 5 per cent adjustment mortgage income
bonds, due in 2000, to the extent of 80 per cent of the holdings, with
interest on these junior bonds to be cumulative beginning in 1930.

Preferred stockholders were to be assessed $28, and common stock-
holders $32, for which they were to be given all but $4 of their assessments in 50-year 5 per cent mortgage bonds. The assessments were
made for the purpose of raising $70,000,000 in cash to pay up the

government and timber obligations and to supply a working capital with sufficient money left over to add equipment, to improve the property of the company, and to cover the expenses of the receivership and reorganization, expenses which ultimately came to a towering $6,500,000. Stockholders were to receive a share of new stock for a share of old, since new mortgage bonds in the amount of $106,-888,980 and new income bonds in the amount of $184,760,640 were to be issued.

The reorganization managers called for the deposit of stock and bonds, and by the beginning of 1926 the majority of them (slightly over 60 per cent of the stock and close to 80 per cent of the junior bonds) had been deposited by their holders. Those bondholders who dissented were organized by Edwin C. Jameson, president of the Globe and Rutgers Fire Insurance Company of New York, representing approximately $18,000,000 worth of junior bonds, and thereafter the Jameson Committee fought the reorganization managers' plan from one point to another, contributing to the delay in the road's getting out of receivership and into reorganization. But the courts and the Interstate Commerce Commission, while fully cognizant of the inequities of the plan, generally supported the proposal which had been drawn up by Jerome Hanauer, and in April, 1926, the district court of Chicago entered a decree ordering the sale of the Milwaukee Road, the successful bidder for which must present a reorganization plan for approval by the court at the same time that it approved the sale. The sale of the property was set for November of that year, and, in the circumstances, with no other plan of reorganization ready—none of the dissenting groups having anything but modifications of the managers' plan to offer—it was inevitable that Kuhn, Loeb & Company and the National City Bank of New York would be the only bidders, and thus the road's bankers would come into actual control of the property, already having on deposit a great majority of the stock and bonds.

The sale, possibly the greatest of its kind, involving such valuable property, attracted a great deal of attention. The party of bidders and other interested persons was followed across country. The Chicago *Tribune* reported the arrival of representatives of the New York bankers in its issue of November 20, 1926:

Jerome J. Hanauer, operating head of Kuhn, Loeb & Company, and author of the reorganization plan, and Pierpont V. Davis, vice president of the National City Bank, were the financiers of the party from New York. Robert T. Swaine and Donald C. Swatland, attorneys for the reorganization committee were the ones who deposited $20,000,000 in certificates from their vest pockets and handed the papers to Attorney Herbert A. Lundahl, special master who will conduct the sale for the Federal court. Frederick H. Ecker, chairman of the bondholders' committee, will join the party in St. Paul. H. E. Byram, receiver and operating head of the Road, and Mark W. Potter and Edward J. Brundage, receivers, were 'also in the westbound group.

The sale was held in Butte, Montana, November 22, and, though the representatives of the bankers were prepared for opposition bidding, since the price for the property had been set at $122,500,000, none developed. The entire proceedings at Butte took but 40 minutes, most of which were taken up by the reading of the legal notice of sale and the reading of bids for the reorganization managers, whose nominees were the only bidders. Kuhn, Loeb & Company and the National City Bank bought in the property of the Milwaukee Road for $140,000,000, and, pending the decision of the courts and the Interstate Commerce Commission, were in control of the road. Despite opposition, the court approved the reorganization plan and the sale early in 1927, and, though the Jameson group fought approval through to the United States supreme court, the managers and their plan were upheld, the Interstate Commerce Commission handing down a 7 to 4 decision in January, 1928, though aware of the inequities of the plan and pointing out that such reorganization as this must be judged on the basis of its majority of security holders, on a practical and not an ideal basis.

On March 31, 1927, the Chicago, Milwaukee, St. Paul and Pacific Railroad Company, a Wisconsin corporation, was organized to acquire the property of the Milwaukee Road (specifically, the Chicago, Milwaukee and St. Paul Railway Company), and, after the authorization of the Interstate Commerce Commission early in 1928, the reorganized company entered into possession and operation of the Milwaukee Road as of midnight, January 13, 1928, with Henry A. Scandrett, who had resigned a vice-presidency of the Union Pacific, as the new president of the road, and former President Byram as chairman of the board of directors.

Apart from Scandrett and Byram, the executive committee included Walter W. Colpitts, Frederick H. Ecker, Samuel H. Fisher, George E. Roosevelt, and Robert T. Swaine, all people who had been active in the reorganization; and the board of directors included Messrs. Byram, Colpitts, Ecker, Fisher, Roosevelt, Swaine, and Scandrett, in addition to M. N. Buckner, W. P. Chrysler, D. G. Geddes, Joshua Green, W. W. K. Sparrow, Mark W. Potter, and W. D. Van Dyke. The capital stock of the new road was listed as $256,884,450.19, and the funded debt at $459,378,289, while the net income for 1928 was subsequently reported as $9,250,332.91.

The new organization had every right to hope that the forecasts of the engineers who had examined the road prior to its receivership might be fulfilled; the engineers had concluded that, within ten years, operating revenues would increase by 25 per cent, even making every allowance for the continuing decline in revenue from passenger traffic; yet, within the ten-year period, by 1935, the Milwaukee Road was to enter a petition for bankruptcy and go into a second reorganization from which it did not emerge until a decade later. As of 1928, however, the outlook for the newly reorganized Milwaukee Road was brighter than it had been at any time during the previous decade.

The twenties, however large a part the struggle against bankruptcy played, also brought to the Milwaukee new experiences which went down into the histories of the era. Though the heyday of the train-robbers who terrorized the railroads in their westward expansion during the nineteenth century had passed even before the present century dawned, the Milwaukee Road on the night of June 12, 1924, experienced the largest loss by robbery in the history of rail travel in the United States. The goal of the bandits was approximately $3,000,000 that was leaving Chicago's Federal Reserve Bank for Milwaukee and banks of the northwest on the regular fast mail, Number 57, carrying no passengers. Moreover, the robbery might have been completely successful if it had not been for one of those unaccountable mishaps which so often thwart the plans of men.

Brilliantly planned, execution of the robbery was almost as well done, save for the single mistake that led to capture of the robbers. The exploit was a daring one, and it originated not in the brain of a professional gangster, as was at first suspected, but in the agile mind of Postal Inspector William J. Fahy. What turned Fahy into the path of crime is one of those mysteries which is never solved and is perhaps insoluble; for Fahy had a distinguished career behind him. He had sent "Big Tim" Murphy to Leavenworth for the Dearborn Station mail looting; he had sent Vincenzo Cosmano to prison for six years for the Pullman robbery in Chicago; and his brilliant work in robberies at Grand Rapids and Harvey was frequently cited to give substance to his reputation as the sleuth who had solved almost every important mail robbery in the Chicago district for the preceding five years.

It was Fahy, however, who planned the robbery. He knew of the regular shipments of the Chicago Reserve Bank, made as registered mail, which went into the bank's own pouches, as distinguished from other mail. Presumably, too, Fahy knew the approximate amount of each shipment, and, once having arranged for accomplices to commit the robbery, he had only to wait for an opportunity which promised adequate reward. This opportunity came on June 12, 1924, on the night of which Number 57 pulled out of Chicago carrying one of the largest shipments of money ever sent from the Chicago Federal Reserve Bank at one time. As events showed, the robbery had been in Fahy's mind for months before it was committed.

Fahy's accomplices were James Murray, alias J. Mahoney, a onetime beer-runner and political lieutenant in the old nineteenth ward of Chicago; Brent Glasscock, a notorious underworld gunman also known as "Old Missou No. 2"; Willis Newton, a Kansas City gangster; Jesse, Joseph, and Willie Newton, Texas bad men, brothers of Willis; and Herbert S. Holliday, another gangster with some experience in robbing the mails. Fahy suggested a robbery first to Murray, who immediately fell in with his plans; through Murray, Fahy got in touch with Glasscock. Glasscock said later, when on trial, that he had known Murray since 1917, but "it was in February, 1924, that he suggested a mail robbery to me. Murray told me he could get tips on big shipments from a friend. So I made an appointment to meet Murray in a restaurant. He drove up with another man, and he said to me, 'This is Fahy,' and the man he introduced told me he was a postal inspector."

Glasscock lost no time in proposing that he be given "dope for robberies." "I am the man who can tell you that, all right," said Fahy, according to Glasscock's testimony. "I can go anywhere in the mail cars, in the registered mail departments, around the trucks, into the offices, and any place I like. I know now there are big money shipments going out right along. Why, there's a $100,000 payroll that goes to Georgetown on the eleventh and twenty-sixth of every month!" Glasscock, impressed finally by Fahy's mention of "millions" on Number 57, took a trip to Kansas City and picked up Willis Newton, while Fahy, for his part, visited George Evenger, a clerk on Number 57, and asked him a great many leading questions about the guarding of the train, even going so far as to enter the third car on the train, much to Evenger's astonishment. Fahy was thus prepared to lend maximum aid to the robbers, and, ironically, had the robbery gone off without a hitch, he and he alone would have been in charge of the investigation, thus being able to render valueless any clues which might turn up.

So daring was Fahy, being sure of himself, that he actually brought Brent Glasscock and Willis Newton to the Union Station in Chicago to show them how the mail was handled and to point out to them that the registered mail all went into the third car of the train. He added, "There are only three guns on the train, and they're carried by the chief clerks; but they won't shoot—they don't know how." Nevertheless, Glasscock, being an old hand, realized that no one's actions could be predicted in advance and decided on the use of gas. The bandits armed themselves therefore with formaldehyde, designed to smother the mail clerks. It was Glasscock, too, who picked out sparsely settled Rondout, Illinois, as the setting for the robbery.

The bandits met that day in front of the Art Institute, on Chicago's crowded Michigan Boulevard. Holliday and Willis Newton made the initial move; they went to the Union Station, flashlights in their pockets, slunk along the shadows of the train shed, and leaped out after engine and tender had hitched onto the first car of Number 57, intending to ride the brake beams to their holdup rendezvous, 30-odd miles from Chicago. Coincidentally, they encountered two tramps there, but, by posing as yard detectives, sent the tramps scurrying. Before boarding the train in this unorthodox fashion, Newton had been told by Fahy, who was watching the loading of the train that night, precisely where the most valuable pouches had been placed. Meanwhile, Glasscock and Joe, Willie, and Jesse Newton drove to Rondout in two fast Cadillacs.

As the train neared Rondout, Holliday and Willis Newton crawled over the tender unobserved, and, shoving guns into the faces of Fireman E. J. Dibble and Engineer Steve R. Waite, they took charge of the train, which was then traveling at 60 miles an hour and slowing for the lonely Buckley Road crossing, where the rest of the gang waited. Holliday and Willis Newton watched for the signals of Glasscock and the remaining Newton brothers, and, seeing flashlights winking, in turn responded by turning the locomotive's headlight off and on. The train was accordingly stopped, and the bandits converged on the mail cars, raucously demanding that the mail clerks open the doors.

Their demand refused, the robbers threw their homemade formaldehyde bombs at the car windows. The bombs broke the glass and fell inside despite the bars across the windows. The clerks had no alternative; in order to avoid suffocation, they opened the doors and dropped into the glare of the red flare where the robbers stood wearing gas masks. The engineer and fireman were marching down the tracks to join them. Glasscock forced a gas mask on the chief mail clerk, Louis Phillips, pushed him back into the third car, and jumped up after him. "I want the Federal Reserve shipments to Milwaukee, Minneapolis, St. Paul, Helena, Butte, Seattle and Spokane. I also want a sack consigned to Roundup, Montana." The sacks were thrown out of the train.

The success of this daring robbery depended on a safe getaway. Until then, the operation, so carefully planned, had gone smoothly, but now there was a slip. One of the cars had driven up alongside the train to receive the mail sacks, and a brakeman, insisting on the need for going to the end of the train to fix a signal to prevent a following train from running into Number 57, had just been permitted to walk to the end of the train—from which he went on in the darkness to the nearest farmhouse to telephone the report of the holdup. Then occurred the slip fatal to Fahy's brilliant plan. Willie Newton, ordered to move toward the back of the train on the right side to stand guard there and presumably also to check on the whereabouts of the missing brakeman, started off on the left side. Discovering his error, he promptly began to cross between the cars, gun in hand, and, in the uncertain light, he was seen by another of the bandits, who, assuming that each member of the gang was in his appointed place, took it for granted that Willie was a mail clerk or a member of the train crew who had somehow armed himself and was now coming in to attack; forthwith he shot four times, each time inflicting a wound. Willie fell under the cars and began to moan. Coming out of the robbed mail car, the mail clerk, Phillips, noticed him, spoke to him, and identified him as a member of the gang, whereupon the robbers were in a quandary. In any other circumstances, Willie Newton would have been killed; but, since three of his brothers were participating in the crime, killing Willie was out of the question; he was picked up and thrown into a car driven by his brother.

The two cars roared away from the scene of the robbery, going directly to Ottawa, Illinois, where the group had arranged to store "contraband whisky" in a paint shop owned by an uncle of Murray. There Murray joined them, and he and Joe Newton brought Willie back to Chicago and took him to the flat of a friend of Murray's, Walter McComb, on Washtenaw Avenue. At the paint shop, the loot was separated into two piles, negotiable and nonnegotiable. The nonnegotiable loot was put into one of the cars and abandoned near Joliet, on the way to Chicago. Near Kansas City, the loot was split into seven shares by Glasscock and Holliday, one for each of the robbers, and one for Fahy and Murray together. The loot was then hidden in various places—in jars buried in a field outside Kansas City, along an Oklahoma road, in a Wilmette barn, in a Tulsa home.

Meanwhile, law-enforcement officers had converged on Rondout. The Milwaukee road's superintendent of police, L. J. Benson, was calling on Chicago's chief of detectives, Michael Hughes, when the news of the robbery came through; they went out to Rondout together. Captain William Shoemaker, head of the Chicago crime squad, and his men likewise went out to the scene. So did Postal Inspector William J. Fahy; he came in time to pose for news photographers, holding one of the gas masks which had been left behind, and he made a great show of carefully studying the ground, even going so far as to wire the department in Washington that he was confident he could solve the mystery.

Unfortunately for Fahy's carefully laid plan, the discovery of a pool of blood along the tracks, plus the evidence of the mail clerk, Phillips, enlisted the widespread aid of the Lake County sheriff's office as well as of the Chicago police, for manifestly the wounded bandit must get medical attention somewhere, and, judging by the amount of blood lost at the scene, aid could not be too long delayed. Had it not been for this, the entire work of tracing the bandits would have been under the direction of Fahy himself, whose strategic position would permit his failure easily enough.

In Chicago, a doctor was called for Willie Newton. From then on, capture of the gang was only a matter of time. The doctor ultimately responded to the routine call for information about all wounded persons treated, and Willie was arrested at the Washtenaw Avenue flat of Walter McComb. In a near-by restaurant, Willis and Joe Newton were arrested. Jesse Newton, told by Holliday that his three brothers had been arrested by Captain Shoemaker, fled Chicago for Fort Worth. James Murray, the man who had approached McComb on behalf of "his old friend," Willie Newton, was found ignominiously under a bed. The flurry of arrests brought in the astounding underworld tip to "work on Fahy," as a result of which the incredulous but now suspicious police trapped Fahy by means of a ruse. Postal inspectors gave Fahy false information that there was a scheme afoot to trick Murray into selling some of the stolen bonds; Fahy transmitted this information to Murray and was seized.

The remainder of the gang was caught in surprisingly short order. Jesse Newton had gone to Mexico, but was enticed back across the border and arrested; Holliday, trailed from a hiding place in Kansas City, was arrested while he was driving through Little Rock, Arkansas, with his mother and a niece; Glasscock, known to be a sufferer from chronic stomach trouble, was arrested while leaving Battle Creek Sanitarium; he was carrying $30,000 in currency and $50,000 in unset diamonds. Tried before Judge Adam C. Cliffe in federal court, Glasscock, the Newtons, and Holliday pleaded guilty, Murray, McComb, and Fahy denying guilt. Glasscock and the Newtons testified for the prosecution. Fahy and Murray got 25 years each; Glasscock and Willie and

Willis Newton, 12 years; Joe Newton, 3 years; and Jesse Newton, a year and a day. McComb was acquitted. All but about $100,000 of the stolen loot was recovered.

Thereafter the Post Office Department supplied gas masks to mail clerks in the registered mail cars, and placed a riot gun on each car to distribute a stream of bullets into the paths of besieging bandits. Fahy futilely protested his innocence even after his release from prison after serving his full term, less time off for good behavior; his death in 1943 ended what might once have been a distinguished career in government service, had it not been for the lure of easy money.

The Milwaukee Road, fortunately, experienced no repeat performance of the Rondout robbery even on a minor scale. But the next year, in 1925, it again encountered the spectacular when an earthquake caught train Number 15 in famed Sixteen-Mile Canyon just out of Barron, Montana. The train was traveling in two sections on that Saturday, June 27, 1925, and carried, apart from a heavy complement of passengers, the assistant master car builder, F. D. Campbell, who was on a personal inspection tour in Washington, Idaho, and Montana. Campbell, who was riding in the first section of the train, took such good note of what took place that he was able to give an excellent account of it subsequently.

The earthquake occurred late in the afternoon. Campbell had observed something peculiar and strange to Montana—horizontal chain lightning streaking the sky below a bank of gray, hazy clouds from which some rain fell desultorily. An hour later, when the train was just out of Barron, at a little past six o'clock of a still-light summer evening, and while he was in conversation with Conductor Sterling of the first section of Number 15, Campbell related, "we experienced what we considered a sun kink under the train and ran ten car lengths before the train was brought to a stop." They looked back, but could see nothing but dust, black clouds, and, curiously, rocks "coming down on the railroad track and bounding into the Missouri River." Campbell and Conductor Sterling got off and walked back along the train. At the second sleeper, *Racine,* they found a pedestal and an oil box entirely gone; the next car, the *Waubay,* had badly dented gas boxes, and some other damage of less importance; the *Council Bluffs* was dented where a rock had struck it, its battery box was damaged, and its oil box and pedestal were broken; on the *Columbia* the end cylinder, nonpressure head, and guides were broken; while on the open-air observation car, *Alta Vista,* a pedestal and one tie rod were broken. The train had been stopped at 6:19; it was an electrified portion of the western line of the Milwaukee Road, and the power was off, thus leaving the train stranded.

What had happened was not clear to Campbell or Conductor Sterling, any more than it was to the curious employees and passengers on Number 15. But, as the two men walked back toward the head end of the car, the second earth tremor took place; this left them in no doubt as to what had stopped the train. "With the moving of the ground and the upheaving of the land, the shock was so great that a person could not stand," Campbell reported. There was also a "terrifying roar of tremendous rocks falling down the side of the mountain." Though the passengers were badly frightened, it was necessary to keep them in the cars because the region was infested with rattlesnakes.

The train, however, was near open country and at some distance from the mountain, though several rocks did come down, bounding over the train and into the Missouri. The first concern of the Milwaukee Road's employees was for the passengers. Campbell wrote later:

We had an unusual load of passengers; the tourist had a large number of regular army men on the way to Alaska. The ladies' coach was filled up with women and children. The four sleepers were comfortably loaded with people from all over the country and England, and there were many Baptist ministers on their way to the convention at Seattle—old and young people, and quite a number of children. We took extra precaution in the cars of the passengers and had wonderful assistance from the regular army soldiers, especially after the second shock, when we had obtained a handcar and, with the assistance of the officers and soldiers, were able to pull it around the train and over the rocks, so that we could proceed to Eustis to get into communication with the outside world.

The trip toward Eustis was informative; the handcar could not, in fact, get into Eustis, for not only were all wires down and communication and power cut off, but rocks of one to fifteen tons in weight were on the track, and "rails were so bent that they could not be used; they looked like hairpins."

The party returned to the train and set out for Barron, in the opposite direction. On the way they estimated that the rock which had struck the first section of Number 15 weighed at least 2,500 pounds. They also learned that the second section of Number 15 had had an almost miraculous escape; this section had just cleared the tunnel before the bridge across Sixteen-Mile Creek east of Barron when the first shock stopped them, while immediately behind them the tunnel went down on both ends and the roof collapsed in the middle with sufficient weight to crush the train and all its occupants had the shock taken place but a few moments before.

But the earthquake was not over, by any means; it was no brief disturbance. With almost meticulous method, Mr. Campbell kept a record of the shocks, which began at 6:19 P. M. June 27 and did not end until 5:00 A. M. June 29. Number 15 was therefore stranded in the midst of an earthquake for 35 hours, in the course of which there were no less than 31 shocks of varying degrees of intensity. The road's employees, including the methodical Campbell, stood guard for that Saturday night, waiting upon the daylight to take steps to supply the train.

Early Sunday morning, the resourceful conductor, Sterling, remembered that a former section boss who had become a rancher was living half a mile east of the place where Number 15's first section was marooned; from him, they obtained an auto delivery car and went to Three Forks for other supplies, having already got water and ice from Barron, for the June day promised to be hot, and was. The trip to Three Forks, among further tremors, was illuminating. "There were large cracks in the earth from one to eighteen inches, and when we dropped rocks down them, we could hear them going down for God knows how many feet," according to Campbell. "At places it was necessary to place planks across, in order to get over with an automobile." Fortunately, they had had the foresight to bring the planks. At Three Forks, the magnitude of the quake was plainly evident, for many buildings were down, particularly those of brick. It was evident, too, that chasms were opened in the bed of the Missouri, for the waters rapidly receded, though they rose again during Sunday and thereafter remained at their customary height.

Ironically, while the earthquake damaged open country property of the Milwaukee Road, it left intact "one point that had been watched for years, with the expectation that the rocks would come down," while other, supposedly solid cliffs collapsed. Though the earth settled at bridge bulkheads, bridges were left in good solid condition. Yet the train was not able to move throughout Sunday, though early Sunday morning some communication was made with Deer Lodge, and information as to the condition of Number 15 was put through, in preparation for wrecking and repair forces. By Monday morning, H. B. Earling, vice-president, and F. N. Hicks, western traffic manager, arrived from the west, together with other personnel of the road. A steam engine pulled Number 15 to Eustis, from which the train proceeded to Three Forks under its own power. Leaving Three Forks at 10:21 Monday morning, the train reached Seattle at long last at 9:30 the following morning, June 30, delivering a load of passengers who were "very much pleased" at the way in which the road's employees had taken care of them in one of the most unusual situations in which any train ever found itself.

X. The Milwaukee Carries On

Suddenly, the train—slowly from under
the web of city streets, the ramps, the streaming cars:
slowly, like a great beast gathering in its black length the
  thunder
to hurtle away into the dark countryside under stars—
the train with its headlight probing, and the brakeman
  standing beside,
swinging his red lantern, slowly coming forth, drawing
  away
into deeper dark, the world outside—

going far into night, far into day,
the train along the gleaming track
chuffing, steaming, crying, the lit windows looking out
  everywhere,
going somewhere in the night and never coming back,
free in the country dark of the city's strident lair—

the train going far to childhood, oh far
to youth, to love, far to anguish, far over the land
past yesterday, tomorrow, and forever, oh far . . .
like a great beast in the dark night,
the train—making its long-drawn lonely cry,
slowly into the sleeping land, the unwary heart, into the
  bright
of coming day, into the world of men to be born, to love,
  to die. . . .

—Chicago: Night Train

During all the legal battles that marked the course of the two decades begun in 1925, the Milwaukee Road continued to function as a major rail transportation system. Receivership and all that goes with it is necessarily remote from the public, even such parts of the public as are certain to be affected monetarily by that receivership. Meanwhile, the Milwaukee Road carried on, at first under the legally appointed receivers, and then under the reorganized management.

The receivers—Byram, Potter, and Brundage—were free of a major handicap which had burdened the management prior to receivership; that was the obligation to pay interest on defaulted bonds. The opportunity was thus presented to the ex-president of the Milwaukee Road, now its operating head, to bring about the improvements he had hoped to make immediately after his accession to the presidency in 1917. All kinds of property improvements were promptly made; during World War I and immediately thereafter, when the road had attempted to retrench in order to meet its obligations, shops, yards, roundhouses, elevators, and other property of the company went without repair; now the receivers directed that all the fixed property of the road not in acceptable shape should be repaired without delay. At the same time, the receivers, doubtless impelled by Byram's always-strong belief that adequate rolling stock was an important key to prosperity, not only added rolling stock and economized on its use, but inaugurated the operation of roller-bearing trains, an improvement which was so successful in every way that it was soon scheduled for every important passenger train on the Milwaukee Road. The *Pioneer Limited* was the first of the Milwaukee trains to be equipped with roller-bearing cars; that was in 1927, and soon thereafter the *Olympian* and the *Arrow* were equipped with roller bearings.

The use of roller-bearing cars was another indication of the progressiveness that distinguishes the history of the Milwaukee Road. The company had conducted exhaustive tests and had proved to its own satisfaction that cars mounted on plain bearings had approximately seven to eight times as much frictional resistance as similarly weighted cars mounted on roller bearings. Thus, after four-fifths of a century of struggling with hotboxes, the hotbox as a problem was all but elimi-

228

nated at low speeds, where the advantage of roller bearings showed most markedly.

The company completed new mechanical coaling stations, erected a new depot at La Crosse, Wisconsin, and established automatic train control on the La Crosse division between Portage and La Crosse and other points. Automatic train control, followed by centralized traffic control and inductive train communication, was a far cry from the equipment of the early days of the Milwaukee. That an operator, simply by switching lights on a control board, could command train movement for 60 miles or more was certainly not visualized by the founders of the Milwaukee, but no amount of automatic control could ever do away with the manual signs and signals which play so important a part in the life of the Milwaukee railroader—two thumbs up stands for "on the spot," though the signal is used also to designate that the men are railroad men; one thumb up toward the mouth signals a need for water or for going for water for the engine; hands swung over the stomach from neck to abdomen mean that the tank is full, the track is full, or the coach is full—though on one occasion a man new to his job, not being as familiar as he might have been with the signals, alarmed a fellow trainman by the grave gesture of putting his hand to his throat in what his fellow trainman took to be a cutting motion, so that he thought the new man was contemplating suicide before it dawned on him that he was trying to signal full coach.

Some rate reductions had to be faced; since 1921, the reduction in ton-mile earnings had amounted to 18 per cent, owing entirely to two general rate reductions made by the Interstate Commerce Commission; but at the same time this decline had been offset in part by another increase of 15 per cent in railroad rates on mails, an increase ordered in August, 1928, but made retroactive to May 9, 1925. All these improvements were made from operational income, and there was no necessity for receiver's notes. Moreover, improvements continued unabated with the accession of the new management, when H. E. Byram retired from the presidency to become chairman of the board. The new president, Henry A. Scandrett, came to the Milwaukee as its president early in 1928 from the Union Pacific, where he had ascended to the vice-presidency from a beginning as a claim adjustor in 1901.

Throughout 1929, the company continued to improve the property of the Milwaukee Road—large amounts of new rails were laid; bridges were rebuilt and strengthened; station, office, shop, and enginehouse facilities were repaired; tracks were elevated in the vicinity of cities, particularly Milwaukee and Chicago; yard tracks and sidings were extended; a new and modern station was built at Prairie du Chien; and during the year the company bought 1,700 automobile cars. Though increased motor vehicle competition continued the decline in passenger and now also in milk revenue, the company applied to the Interstate Commerce Commission for authority to acquire and operate the property of the Chicago, Milwaukee & Gary Railway Company, stock of which had been acquired in 1922. The application was granted two months later, and ownership and operation was begun on April 1, 1930.

However, the period of postwar prosperity was coming to its end. The depression, which was first felt in the United States in 1929, struck hard at the railroads. By the end of 1930 the company was forced to concede that the decline in revenues had been extremely severe. Total operating revenues were reduced 16.8 per cent—freight revenues 15.7 per cent and passenger revenues 24.3 per cent—while the net railway operating income fell 39.28 per cent. To meet this shrinkage in revenues, the management strove to improve operating efficiency and reduce costs without repeating the error of the war years and the years immediately before of depreciating the physical condition of the property. In mid-year, however, the Interstate Commerce Commission ordered a general readjustment of rates on grain and grain products in the western district, and this order resulted in a further reduction in revenues.

Yet improvements continued, though no longer at the rate inaugurated during the years of the receivership. The company started the construction of a waste and oil reclamation plant in Milwaukee, to cost $90,000, and designed to bring about economies large enough to justify the investment. New engine terminal facilities were erected at Sioux Falls, South Dakota, and double-track construction was begun between Polo and Birmingham, Missouri, in conjunction with the Rock Island Railroad. All these ventures were consistent with the policy of improving the property of the Milwaukee Road begun during the three-year receivership.

The depression alone was not the only difficulty which the Milwaukee Road, in common with other railroads, had to fight in 1930 and 1931. The Interstate Commerce Commission handed down decisions which, at best, were quixotic. Western trunk line carriers had made application in 1929 to the commission for an increase in class rates. On May 6, 1930, the commission handed down its decision, to become effective December 3, 1931, providing for general increases on short-haul traffic, and decreases on long-haul traffic. Since the railroads had their maximum competition with motor-truck carriers in short-haul traffic, the decision was clearly not designed to afford much increased revenue. On July 1, 1930, the Interstate Commerce Commission issued a decision requiring a general readjustment of rates on grain and grain products within the western district. These rates became effective on August 1, 1931, and it was estimated that, if the order from the commission were complied with, the loss to the western district carriers as a whole would be in the vicinity of $20,000,000 annually. The Milwaukee Road joined other roads in a suit to enjoin the order of the commission, and this resulted in the decision of the United States supreme court nullifying the commission's order and restoring grain rates in effect prior to August, 1931. The court's decision was given early in January, 1932, and the old rates were restored on the twentieth of the following month.

During the depression, the Interstate Commerce Commission was besieged by the railroads of the nation. The Milwaukee Road was one of the railroads petitioning the commission in June, 1931, for a 15 per cent advance in freight rates; though the application was dismissed, the commission did authorize emergency rate increases on certain commodities from January 4, 1932, to March 31, 1933, provided that revenues obtained therefrom be pooled to create a fund out of which loans might be made to roads failing to earn fixed charges and without other resources to pay such charges. As President Scandrett pointed out ruefully, in the 1931 report: "If these emergency rates had been in effect during 1931 on intrastate and interstate traffic, they would have increased the revenues approximately 3%, or $2,750,000." This Marshalling and Distributing Plan of 1931 resulted in the formation of the Railroad Credit Corporation, organized and administered by the participating carriers. Acknowledging the plight of the railroads, the government made it possible during 1932 for distressed carriers to borrow money from the Reconstruction Finance Corporation, pending approval of the Interstate Commerce Commission.

The 1931 report pointed up the distress of the Milwaukee Road. President Scandrett made no secret of the difficult position of the company:

The unprecedented industrial depression which began in the latter part of 1929 continued with increasing severity throughout 1931. Because of this, aggravated by the unusual drought last summer, which extended in varying degrees from Minnesota through the States of North Dakota, South Dakota, and Montana, the revenues of the Company for the year 1931 were reduced substantially below those of 1930. . . . With the continued severe decline in passenger revenues, due to the competition of motor vehicles and the smaller amount of travel as a result of the depression, every effort was made, and is still being made, to reduce the cost of passenger train service by the elimination of train miles. Because of the requirements to provide certain local service, it has not been possible so far to reduce the mileage in direct proportion to the loss of revenues.

The loss in revenues was indeed grievous. The report pointed out that the total operating revenues for 1931 showed a decrease of 21.8 per cent, and listed a net deficit of $13,812,759.02. Instead of the 5.75 per cent fixed by the Interstate Commerce Commission as a fair rate of return on the investment in the road and its equipment, the Milwaukee Road received 1.07 per cent, a deficiency of $36,349,000. Some measures manifestly had to be taken to prevent total collapse, and the Milwaukee Road could no more act alone in the crisis than could any other major road.

On January 14, 1932, a committee of nine railroad presidents under the chairmanship of Daniel Willard met with a committee representing the Railway Labor Executive Association for the purpose of discussing wages. After 17 days of discussion and negotiation, they agreed on an arrangement to begin in February and to extend for one year, effecting a 10 per cent reduction in salary and wages for all employees represented by the committee. The deduction likewise extended to salaries of all officers and employees whose compensation exceeded $300 per month.

But this reduction in wages was offset by the continuing depression, with its decrease in revenues, though the Milwaukee Road had acquired a fourth interest in the line of the Longview, Portland and Northern Railway Company extending from Vader Junction to Longview Junction, Washington—22.86 miles, including terminals—at a cost of $1,066,265, an acquisition authorized by the Interstate Commerce Commission. This was a line which ran into a growing industrial district in southwest Washington, on the Columbia River, and was taken over late in 1931. At best, too, any wage reduction was certain to be temporary, and the agreement of early 1932 was extended late in the same year to October 31, 1933.

Passenger-train revenue decreased by 28.1 per cent in 1932, and the company could discontinue many unprofitable trains and decrease passenger train miles only by 31.1 per cent. This was but one of the ways in which the company sought to reduce operating expenses. In its self-scrutiny, the road became ever more acutely aware of the inroads state and local taxing bodies were making upon its income, particularly in contrast to the service being done motor trucking in the building of highways from public moneys. In 1913, for instance, the Milwaukee Road received in railway operating revenues 17.5 per cent for each dollar invested in the road and its equipment; and for each such dollar invested, the company paid .72 cents in taxes other than federal. In 1932, two decades later, the revenue stood at 11.25 cents, and payment in taxes at 1.05 cents. Taxes other than federal amounted to 4.1 per cent of the total revenue in 1913, and 9.3 per cent of the total revenue for 1932. Added to the federal taxes paid, the aggregate tax bill of the Milwaukee Road—and of other railroads in its class— lent considerable weight to the railroads' complaint that they were being taxed proportionately heavier for operating over their own, privately owned lines than their competitors were being taxed for operating over state, local, or federally owned roads. And taxes likewise contributed to the deficiency of $45,340,000 in 1932 in the fair rate of return which had been estimated by the Interstate Commerce Commission.

By 1932 the Milwaukee Road was once again in the position of having to borrow money. From the Railroad Credit Corporation, into which, in accordance with the Marshalling and Distributing Plan of 1931, the company had paid $1,702,897.82 of emergency revenue, the Milwaukee Road borrowed $2,000,000 to apply to partial payment of interest due August 1, 1932, giving as security a note due on demand on or before July 26, 1934, a pledge of the distributive share to which it would be entitled in any distribution of the funds being administered by the Railroad Credit Corporation, a triparty agreement assigning to the corporation all the cash receipts of the Milwaukee Land Company in excess of its current operating expenses and taxes, and the pledge of the equity of all collateral at any time pledged by it with the Reconstruction Finance Corporation, subject to any loan now or hereafter made by the latter corporation. At the same time, the Milwaukee Road applied to the Reconstruction Finance Corporation for such part of $10,996,331 as would not be loaned by the Railroad Credit Corporation. Some further temporary relief was given railroads when the Interstate Commerce Commission, aware of the railroads' plight, authorized the continuance of emergency rate increases up through September 30, 1933, except on nonferrous ores and concentrates. Yet the net deficit continued to be very high; the 1932 report listed it at $23,269,677.88.

Late in April, 1932, the Milwaukee bowed to the inevitable in regard to a quaint aspect of the past when it applied to the Interstate Commerce Commission for authority to abandon a narrow-gauge line, 35.7 miles long, extending westward from the main line at Bellevue,

Iowa, to Cascade, in the same state. This was the only narrow-gauge line operated for any length of time by the Milwaukee. It was built between June, 1879 and January, 1880, and it was acquired by the Milwaukee late in 1880. It had a gauge of 3 feet, and a succession of ascending and descending grades, some of which were in excess of 2 per cent, with a maximum of 2.8 per cent uncompensated. It had numerous curves in excess of 8 degrees with a maximum of 12½ degrees. Its cuts and fills were very narrow, and 75 per cent of the right of way was only 33 feet wide. It was laid with about half and half 56 and 60 pound rail. There were 6 villages on the line, serving a tributary population of about 8,000 people. At the Bellevue terminus, it was necessary to maintain transfer facilities, and all through freight had to be transferred at that point to standard-gauge cars. The line's equipment consisted of 4 light locomotives and 110 cars of various kinds. The locomotives were from 31 to 49 years old, and handled from 110 to 145 gross tons over the ruling grades in either direction. Most of the cars were old and of wooden construction, the majority of them dating back to 1880. The branch was operated at a substantial loss for four years previous to the Milwaukee's application for authority to abandon, an abandonment authorized March 8, 1933, though the Milwaukee did in June enter into an agreement with a newly incorporated common carrier, the Bellevue and Cascade Railroad Company, under which the Milwaukee agreed to sell the line together with all rights of way, roadbed, tracks, equipment, station grounds, buildings, and facilities for $18,000, payable in 120 equal monthly installments. But operations of this new company were not successful and ultimately it was sold to the Joseph Schonthal Company of Columbus, Ohio, for $37,500. This company acquired the property by deed from the Milwaukee early in 1936, and four months later took up the line. The Milwaukee relinquished it reluctantly, but without alternative in the face of the road's increasingly precarious position.

Though 1933 was a slightly better operating year than its immediate predecessors, owing in part to the Chicago World's Fair—at which the Milwaukee Road was the only one to exhibit a modern passenger coach, built in its own shops, and establishing a precedent in providing more space between seats for coach passengers: a forecast of the de luxe coach trains of the future—there was little hope that conditions might better. The depression and all its attendant difficulties prevailed. The Milwaukee Road made some voluntary reductions in rates on less than carload traffic, primarily to meet truck competition, but these reductions were offset not only by the increased passenger traffic created by the Chicago Fair, but also by a marked increase in forest products and general carload revenues. Yet the company obtained another two-year loan from the Railroad Credit Corporation, this time of $1,710,000, and its share of distribution from that corporation for 1933 was $207,714.

In mid-June, 1933, President Roosevelt approved the Emergency Railroad Transportation Act, providing for the appointment of a federal co-ordinator of transportation and designed to promote or require action on the part of carriers and subsidiaries to be subject to the Interstate Commerce Act; to assist at financial reorganization of carriers, within legal boundaries, so as to reduce fixed charges to the extent required by the public interest and to improve carrier credit; and to provide for study of all means of improving conditions of transportation "in all its forms and the preparation of plans therefor." This action, designed to help railroads, actually did them a disservice, since it eliminated the obligation of the commission to fix rates that would yield a fair return upon the aggregate value of railway property; though the commission had striven to be equitable in its rate-fixing, rates had not been adjusted in proportion to the fluctuation between earnings and fixed charges. Thus a rate fixed in 1927 was wholly inadequate in subsequent years because the business of the Milwaukee Road, in common with that of many other railroad companies, fell off to such an extent that the company could not earn its fixed charges, no matter to what expedient the management had recourse.

Despite the increase of revenues, the deficit continued to increase; at the end of the year it stood at $14,412,141.21, and, while prospects for 1934 seemed somewhat better, the situation was grim. On October 13, 1934, application was made to the Reconstruction Finance Corporation for a loan of $4,000,000 as of December 28, 1934, for the purpose of maintaining minimum working capital and meeting fixed interest payments on funded debt maturing on January 1 and February 1, 1935, and for an additional loan of $5,000,000 as of June 28, 1935, for the maintenance of minimum working capital and to meet fixed interest charges and principal payments on equipment trust obligations maturing July 1 and August 1, 1935. Upon this application, only $3,500,000 was borrowed, $2,700,000 of which was received December 31, 1934, and the remaining $800,000 on January 31, 1935. On March 25, 1935, the board of directors voted to defer payments on $900,000 principal amount of equipment trust certificates which matured April 1. At the same meeting the board considered application for a further loan from the Reconstruction Finance Corporation, but voted against such a loan, "except in connection with a plan for the reorganization of the capital structure of the Company." So once more reorganization

appeared to be the only way to avoid an accumulating deficit, year
after year, and, however reluctantly, the directors of the Milwaukee
Road began to consider it.

Meanwhile, business in general began slowly to improve. Even a
drought of unprecedented proportions did not materially affect the
increase in shipments of agricultural products. At the Chicago terminals, passengers arrived in large numbers for the continuation of
the Century of Progress, though not sufficiently to affect passenger
revenue materially, particularly since the lowered passenger fares
effected late in 1933 were extended to September 30, 1935, from their
initial expiration date of May 31, 1934. The company profited by the
repeal of the misguided prohibition amendment, for out of industrial
sites leased to 122 industries not theretofore located on the Milwaukee
Road's lines, a majority were liquor establishments.

In April, the Conference Committee of Railroad Managers and the
Railway Labor Executives Association agreed to restore the 10 per cent
reduction from basic wage rates established February 1, 1932, in a
sliding scale—2½ per cent July 1, 1934; 2½ per cent January 1, 1935;
and 5 per cent April 1, 1935; it was also agreed that no notice of any
change in the basic rates should be served prior to May 1, 1935.
At the same time, such corresponding deductions as had been made
from basic rates in 1932 were restored to other employees up to a
maximum of $400 monthly. Thus, once again, to offset the slight
increase in revenues, there was this increase in the cost of labor; and,
to add to this, there were marked increases in the cost of material
and supplies as a result of the establishment of codes under the
National Industrial Recovery Act, as well as additional maintenance
work and accruals to cover the company's contribution to the National
Railroad Pension Fund, as required by the Railroad Retirement Act.
In final analysis, therefore, while the operating revenues of the company increased 2.8 per cent, the operating expenses during the same
period crept up by no less than 7.8 per cent, despite everything the
company could do to keep expenses down.

The increasing competition of highway traffic, with its emphasis on
speed, meanwhile, was of mounting concern to the company. Convinced that speed was not the sole property of highway-born traffic,
and equally certain that the railroads must match the progress of such
traffic with technological advances of their own, the company encouraged the inventive ingenuity of its employees, particularly in the shops.
In mid-year, too, the management agreed to a suggestion that a trial
run be made in an effort to establish a new sustained speed record
by steam for a distance of 50 miles or more. The test was made with

a five-car steel train of roller-bearing equipment pulled by a four-year-old steam locomotive on a regular run between Chicago and Milwaukee, a distance of 85 miles, and was under the direction of Assistant General Manager Norman A. Ryan. The men operating the train included several veterans—Engineer William Dempsey of Milwaukee had had 35 years of service with the Milwaukee; Conductor Charles Albright of Evanston and Fireman Ward Kirby of Milwaukee were likewise old-timers with the road; Peter Mick and Frank Peterson were the brakemen. They were accompanied on the run by A. G. Hoppe, engineer of tests; George B. Haynes of Chicago, passenger traffic manager; John C. Prien of Milwaukee, general agent, passenger department; R. D. Miller of Milwaukee, assistant superintendent of the Milwaukee division; and Bob Scott of Waukegan, formerly of Milwaukee, who had been with the road for 56 years and who had once made the run from Chicago to Milwaukee with 13 cars and, as he put it, "got her over ninety that time and the Company turned around and issued a bulletin that no engineer should do it again." The train carried its regular complement of about 150 passengers, none of whom knew that the train was making a test speed run save a small group of Chicago and Milwaukee newspaper and press association representatives who had been invited to make the trip but who were requested not to give it advance publicity.

The previous American sustained speed record had been made by the Lehigh Valley Road, when one of its trains averaged 80 miles an hour for a stretch of approximately 44 miles between Alpine and Geneva, New York, in 1897, and the world record was held by a Great Western train in England, which ran 77.2 miles at 81.6 miles an hour in 1932.

The train drew out of Chicago promptly at 9:00 A.M., July 20, 1934, under the guidance of Engineer Dempsey, who "let out" his locomotive to gain steadily increasing speed. By the time it reached Morton Grove, Illinois, it was clocking 87 miles an hour; beyond that town, it reached 90; at Northbrook, it was running smoothly at 92, and it entered Rondout, Illinois, at 97 miles an hour, soon thereafter reaching 99. At Gurnee, Illinois, the speedometer showed 100 miles an hour, and for two miles over the Root River in the vicinity of Oakwood, Wisconsin, the train's speed was clocked at 103. As a result, the test train of the Milwaukee Road established a new world's sustained speed record for passenger train travel, averaging 92 miles an hour for a distance of 53.58 miles, between Deerfield, Illinois, and Lake, Wisconsin.

The Milwaukee *Sentinel* editorialized two days later that the run was important because, "It will do the steam road worlds of good to have evidence that it can still hold its own in speed, safety, comfort and economy. What the railroads badly need is to catch up on time lost when, given over to despair, they stopped progressing." But hope that trains might run regularly on a 70-minute schedule between Milwaukee and Chicago was not permitted to rise, for G. B. Haynes pointed out to reporters during the run that the maintenance of such a speed is neither easy nor economical. "It costs heavily to keep the tracks open for fast trains, and it delays the movement of freight. Moreover, highway crossings are a great handicap. The public would have to be educated to trains operating at such speeds or there would be an increase in crossing fatalities." Haynes conceded that, though the test run demonstrated that a steam locomotive would go as fast as motorized power, it was still a moot question "whether motorized or steam power is preferable for fast passenger train movement."

But speed was the object, nevertheless. Even as Haynes cautioned against hope, the Milwaukee Road was building the famed *Hiawatha*, its first streamlined train, and experiments were begun under the direction of K. F. Nystrom in developing high-speed passenger car trucks, though the *Hiawatha* rode on a four-wheel equalized truck with helical and elliptical springs. Safety, improved riding qualities, reduced weight, lower noise level, and elimination of friction surfaces were the acknowledged ends of Nystrom's experiments, which were begun in 1934 and carried on for a decade. In a comparatively short time the *Hiawatha* was regularly making the 85-mile run between Chicago and Milwaukee in 75 minutes, attaining 100 miles per hour, the limit permitted, at points en route.

The first, preview run of the new *Hiawatha* was made on May 15, 1935, from Milwaukee to New Lisbon, with representatives of all departments on board. That trial run was an exciting experience; it was reported in glowing terms in the June issue of *The Milwaukee Magazine*:

At 91 m.p.h. everyone remarked that it didn't seem as though the *Hiawatha* was traveling much faster than about 45. At 100 m.p.h. a shout went up. One hundred and one, they calculated; 103.5, then 105, 105.5; faster and faster it went until at 109 miles per hour the *Hiawatha* decided that that was a very comfortable pace and continued along at that speed for five or six miles without a change, but as interest began to wane in seeing 109 miles per hour marked up as mile after mile went by, Ed. Donahue, the man at the throttle, gave it another notch and in very short order there were figures of 110.5, 111.3 and then 112.5 m.p.h.

That's the speed that the *Hiawatha* attained, not as a speed test, but just by way of getting from Watertown to New Lisbon at a pace at which it could travel comfortably.

Anyone who saw Mr. J. T. Gillick, Vice-President in charge of Operation, as the train was performing need never ask him what he thought of it. His beaming countenance was a full and complete answer to the unasked question. It was not necessary for him to tell anyone how happy he was.

Upon arrival at New Lisbon, Mr. Gillick dispatched a telegram to Mr. Scandrett and Mr. Pierpont [chief traffic officer at that time] as follows: "Left Milwaukee 9:40 a. m. Stopped at Watertown to look at engine, which was running cool. With this stop passed Portage 11:03 a. m., one minute less than schedule. Maximum speed 97.3 miles per hour. Arrived New Lisbon 11:33 a. m. Schedule calls for 34 minutes. Maximum speed 112.5 m. p. h. Train rode beautifully. Jones [L. M. Jones, at that time superintendent of sleeping and dining cars] has a cup and glass of water on table that has not spilled yet."

Engineer Donahue epitomized the train's performance, remarking, "the faster it ran, the better it rode."

The *Hiawatha* captivated the imagination of children and adults all along its line of travel; people drove out in cars and parked to watch the train flash past, handsome in its color scheme of maroon and gold. The streamlined locomotive was an innovation, since it concealed behind its encasing metal jacket the sandbox, the feedwater heater, air pumps, pipes and steam locomotive accessories, and the steam dome, presenting a sleek appearance which, even motionless, suggested speed. Its swift, flashing movement along the Milwaukee's rails appealed to modern railroad fans just as the early locomotives appealed to their adherents. For more than one fan, S. Kip Farrington epitomized the feeling of powerful flight which many travelers experience on the *Hiawatha* in his "Hiawatha—Speed Queen of the Milwaukee," in *Railroading from the Head End.*

Five years later, the *Midwest Hiawatha* was placed in operation between Chicago and Omaha, Sioux City, and Sioux Falls. It duplicated the performance of the earlier *Hiawatha,* and the attraction it held for the imaginative was poignantly revealed in a letter from John Geesaman, a sailor marooned at first in the Aleutians and then in the Marianas. He wrote home to ask about the *Hiawatha,* remembering his unfailing thrill at sight of "this brilliant splash of orange, gray and maroon as it flies down the main line," and confessed: "I saved that picture of my pet stream-liner at Western Avenue so that whenever I get homesick, I just break it out." When John got out of service, the Milwaukee treated him to a ride in the cab of the *Midwest Hiawatha.* The *Midwest Hiawatha* was followed in service by the *Olympian Hiawatha* seven years later.

The company continued to fight excessive taxation as well as to decrease operating costs as much as possible. The state of Washington had overtaxed operating property of the Milwaukee Road for a six-year period, from 1926 to 1932, and the Milwaukee fought the excessive valuations upon which the taxes were based. Though the litigation took some time, the decision handed down by the tax commission in 1934 brought about a reassessment of the property and reduced the aggregate taxes for the disputed years by $1,171,564. Similarly, the road fought the Federal Retirement Act, providing for a retirement and pension system for railroad employees of carriers subject to the Interstate Commerce Act, and providing for retirement to be' compulsory at the age of 65, though extension by mutual agreement for periods of one year to the age of 70 was permissible. The United States supreme court declared the Federal Retirement Act unconstitutional early in 1935.

Late in 1934 a community of interest brought about the formation of the Association of American Railroads, combining the duties and activities of the American Railway Association and the Association of Railway Executives, "in order to promote trade and commerce in the public interest, further improve railroad service, and maintain the integrity and credit of the railroad industry." President Scandrett became one of the directors, and its financial and credit advisor was Fairman R. Dick, a director of the Milwaukee Road. The railroads likewise acted in concert to petition the Interstate Commerce Commission for authority to increase freight rates to conform proportionately to operating expenses, but this petition was denied, though certain surcharges were allowed for a period ending June 30, 1936.

The Milwaukee in the winter of that hectic year not only fought taxation, but also, more prosaically and more expensively, it fought snow. Snow, one of the costliest enemies of railroading, has cost the Milwaukee millions for its removal. But perhaps no winter ever gave the Milwaukee so much trouble as that of 1935–1936, when Wisconsin newspaper headlines like "Trains Are Stalled in Snow Mountains" and "Drifts and Bitter Winds Nip Romance of Rails" were no whit exaggerated. Though the winter of 1946–1947 afforded at least one major blizzard which ranked with the worst experienced by the Milwaukee Road, the trouble with snow in January and February of 1936 was unequaled.

The Milwaukee division took the brunt of the snowy assault in those months. Superintendent J. H. Valentine of that division had the foresight to wire Aberdeen, South Dakota, to send rotary plows to Portage, Wisconsin, and from mid-January to mid-February, the superintendent found one of the biggest tasks of his entire career in railroading on his hands, for one blizzard after another struck and struck hard. With the number of his maintenance men more than doubled, Superintendent Valentine took his own turn in the caboose attached to a Prairie-type locomotive hooked to the first rotary which came into Portage from the west, and pushed out of Portage toward Fox Lake at the maximum rotary plow speed of four miles an hour. A second locomotive from Horicon hooked on and pushed to Milwaukee.

From that time on until late February, the Milwaukee division's wires were kept hot with word of trains stalled in drifts. There were never so many drifts on the Milwaukee division in the history of the road. On one occasion, so thickly did the snow come down in sub-zero weather, driving in from the Great Lakes on a howling wind, that train Number 56, stopped by a red block near Sturtevant, while Number 2, following a plow unit, was stopped by the plow unit's pause for water, became snowbound in the short time it took to take on water, and, as a result, the *Olympian,* having already left for Chicago, had to be stopped, and the *Pioneer Limited* then set out after another rotary to take on passengers from stalled Number 56. The trains met in a well of snow as high as the locomotives, while snow six feet in height made a wall between the trains, a wall through which a hole had to be shoveled so that passengers could reach the *Limited.*

This was early in February, 1936. On the fourth of that same snow-bound month, the *Southwest Limited* was marooned over night near Sturtevant, holding up the southbound *Hiawatha* for hours and tying up traffic along the entire Milwaukee division, a memorable experience for passengers and crew. The Milwaukee *Journal* interviewed the crews on their arrival in Milwaukee. "You couldn't see a thing," said Fireman William Hayes. "It was like driving through a sea of milk and foam. Drifts were as high as the coaches, and the engine pounded through, hitting the drifts hard, but finally slowed down to a walk. There was plenty work shoveling coal with snow coming into the cab, melting, getting you soaking wet."

"But we'd have made it just the same," said Engineer Bert McCormick, "if we hadn't busted that super-heater unit. I heard it go, like an air pipe. 'Where's that air leaking?' I yelled, and then I saw the steam gage dropping like a shot. Then I knew we were through."

Conductor Krause added, "At Savanna we were supposed to pick up a coach from Omaha, but it never did show up; nobody even knew where that train was. We heard the whole blooming Iowa Division was snowed in, with not a wheel turning."

Before that winter ended, Superintendent Valentine had learned to

regard as commonplace reports of snowdrifts 9 to 18 feet high and
100 to 3,000 feet in length, and in such numbers as to establish all-time
records—23 between Atwater and Berlin, Wisconsin; 18 between Ripon
and Oshkosh, Wisconsin; 10 between Rush Lake and Winnieconne,
10 more between Horicon and Portage—drifts enough to stall as many
as 17 freight trains at a time. Superintendent Valentine's experience
was duplicated on other divisions. Not until February 20 were all the
lines of the Milwaukee Road open again, after an unprecedented
battle which had added millions of dollars to the maintenance cost of
the Milwaukee.

In April, 1936, *The Milwaukee Magazine* carried the story, referring
to the winter just past as "the great winter," adding that "the storms of
1881 and 1888 which have been the boast of the elders around the
switch shanty stoves for these many years will now pale into insignifi-
cance in the light of this nearer perspective." Perhaps the highest and
most difficult drift blocking the Milwaukee Road was on the Iowa and
Dakota division, at Lawler, Iowa, a drift 25 feet deep and 1,000 feet
long.

Next to snow removal, the Iowa and Dakota division found that the
most pressing need was for the delivery of coal to beleaguered communities all along the line; so hard pressed were some South Dakotans
that they were forced to cut down valuable shade trees for fuel until
the Milwaukee could get through with coal. Ironically, train Number 3, coming into Mason City during the worst of the February
blizzards, encountered a stalled bus and picked up the driver and all
his passengers. So efficiently did the men of the Milwaukee work that
in more than one case the Milwaukee lines were the only rail lines
open, a fact that did not go unnoticed among the shipping fraternity.

Only two years previously, in 1933, the Milwaukee had had to cope
with unprecedented rainfall and floods in the Pacific northwest. Rainfall in the initial fortnight of December of that year was equal to any
previously recorded for an entire month; moreover, rivers were already
high because of thawing snow, and the result was that the Milwaukee
Road suffered land and snow slides that washed out tracks and flooded
yards. The heaviest slide occurred near Ragnar, in the Cascades,
though serious washouts impeded traffic on both sides of the Bitter
Root Mountains. A slide near Drexel held up train Number 16 in late
December for five days at Drexel, though most of the passengers
eventually hiked to St. Regis and went on by train from there. The men
of the Milwaukee, though some of them were themselves marooned,
saved others trapped by high water. One crew, seeing a house in
danger near the St. Joe River, and discovering that the family was

away on a holiday, broke into the building and saved all the furnish-
ings, including the kitchen stove and the water heater, taking them
to the substation just before the house disappeared down-river. Slides
at Ragnar had impeded traffic in February, 1932, when 500 feet of
track were washed out to a depth of 120 feet.

Track washouts occurred periodically on the lines of the Milwaukee.
Just as in its first few years of existence, when the Milwaukee to
Prairie du Chien line was the only main line of the Milwaukee, floods
washed out sections of the line near Boscobel, so in June, 1947, the
midnight passenger train through Boscobel was blocked by water
before reaching Wauzeka, and, trying to return to Boscobel, found
the road over which it had just traveled also cut off by water. Washouts between Lone Rock and Blue River on the same division prevented work trains from reaching the marooned train, and traffic between Lone Rock and Marquette, Iowa, had to be rerouted. The train
was stalled for more than 12 hours before it was able to go on. Washouts throughout June, 1947—of roadbed and bridges—and the flooding
of stations occurred commonly throughout flood-battered Iowa.

Ottumwa, Iowa, on the Kansas City division, was inundated, with
a third of its area under water and a quarter of its citizens made
homeless, when the Des Moines River overflowed its banks, not only
once, but four times within the month of June, 1947. The Milwaukee
Road tracks were covered with water for miles, damage extending
as far west as Tama, Iowa, more than 50 miles northwest of Ottumwa,
and to Powersville and Lucerne, 65 miles south of Ottumwa. At
Ottumwa, the Milwaukee's Sherman Street station was commandeered
by the Red Cross as a point of assembly for evacuees, but the station
itself was inundated before evacuation work could be completed.
Superintendent F. R. Doud, Trainmaster Novak, section foremen, and
laborers were on duty continuously for days in the Ottumwa area,
and approximately 25 per cent of the Milwaukee Road's employees
in the Ottumwa area were forced to evacuate their homes. The various
Milwaukee Road service clubs came speedily to their aid. Service
was interrupted for several days at various places in Iowa as a result
of each of the four floods.

These 1947 floods, following upon torrential rains, succeeded a
winter of deep snow comparable to that of 1936–1937. A blizzard
struck the midwest on the night of January 29, and, in what Assistant
General Manager H. C. Munson called "the worst snow-storm in
Milwaukee's history," the road's native city, the whole east end of the
La Crosse & River division, and the entire line from Sturtevant, Wisconsin, to Channing, Michigan, was snowed under. Nineteen inches

of snow fell with paralyzing suddenness at a time when the Milwaukee Road's volume of industrial business in its native city was unprecedentedly high. Though passenger service was back to normal in two days, it took ten days for freight service to be re-established. Only the swift recruitment of extra workmen and equipment at a cost of $160,000, and the dogged loyalty of employees, many of whom came to work on skis, enabled the Milwaukee to dig out from under drifts as deep as twenty feet in many places.

The pictures of the storm published in *The Milwaukee Magazine* caused many an old-timer on the Milwaukee to recall the Minnesota blizzards of 1880–1881, when snow started to fall on October 15, 1880, and did not stop until drifts were as high as telegraph poles, to be followed by snow almost daily thereafter, blockading parts of the Milwaukee line for weeks. "We had orders to sell our rail ties to the people for fuel, a limit of ten ties per family," recalled C. J. Cawley, agent at Pipestone, Minnesota. "Sugar and kerosene ran out around March 1, and there were very few groceries obtainable. The equipment of the snow fighters of those days was a pick and shovel and the duration of service was four months in the open. As the winter wore on, the snow in the cuts had to be taken out in tiers, with men on each level throwing the snow up and out . . . finally cutting a block of snow about as large as a box car, slipping a cable around it, and pulling it out with an engine." A Paul Bunyan winter.

The Milwaukee's worst communications tie-up was caused by neither snow nor flood, but by ice, when on February 22, 1922, an ice storm extending from Winona, Minnesota, to Lake Michigan completely paralyzed wire service on large parts of the River, La Crosse, Wisconsin Valley, Northern, and Superior divisions. Rain started to fall steadily early in the morning and fell all day with the temperature at around freezing, without accompanying wind, so that ice formed evenly on everything. Telegraph wires at some points reached a diameter of five inches, and many of them broke, or their weight pulled off crossarms and even broke off poles, though the absence of wind saved most poles. Tracks filled in with ice, level from rail to rail, and at Plymouth, Wisconsin, a traveling salesman who tired of waiting for a train already 36 hours overdue bought a pair of ice skates, strapped his suitcase to his back, and skated the 59 miles to DePere. Wire service between Milwaukee and Green Bay was not restored for six days, because the general iciness of the roads made it impossible to clear wires with any rapidity, one crew of five linemen being able to clear one wire for only six miles in sixteen hours.

The chasm between operating expenses and operating revenues

widened persistently, and the Milwaukee's net deficit at the end of 1934 was $16,247,620.86; the meeting of the board of directors in March, 1935, was but the prelude to the filing of a petition in bankruptcy on June 29, 1935, subsequent to which the court before which the petition was filed directed the company to continue in possession and control of its properties and to operate them until such time as the court might render a different decision. In October of that year, the trustees of the property were appointed: Henry A. Scandrett, Walter J. Cummings, and George I. Haight, and their appointment was ratified by the Interstate Commerce Commission late in December, in time for the trustees to file their bonds and take title to and control of the property of the Milwaukee Road on the first of January, 1936.

The petition in bankruptcy was inevitable. Circumstances beyond the control of the management of the Milwaukee Road pointed the way to a further reorganization, and not all the determined struggling for an advantageous position in the face of mounting operating expenses and decreasing revenues could alter the position of the Milwaukee Road. Nor was such relief as an increase of 7 per cent of the previous total line-haul transportation on interstate carload traffic, authorized by the Interstate Commerce Commission to become effective in mid-April, 1935, of any signal importance; by this time all such measures were too picayune to stave off bankruptcy and reorganization. Yet the company did not halt its efforts to increase revenues and decrease expenses during the anticipation and the period of the bankruptcy. In 1935 it established a permanent, basic one-way fare of 3 cents per mile in sleeping and parlor cars, and of 1% cents per mile for coach travel. In 1935, too, the Milwaukee entered the high-speed service race with the establishment of a new daytime train service between Chicago and the Twin Cities, one train each way, when, on May 29, it inaugurated the streamlined *Hiawatha*, which made the run of 410 miles to St. Paul in 6½ hours. Yet operating revenues increased only 5.3 per cent while expenses went up 9.7 per cent, the rate of return earned on investment in road and equipment was .65 per cent, and the road's net deficit rose to $18,008,748.17.

In no way deterred by bankruptcy and reorganization proceedings, the management continued to authorize further improvements in a determined effort to meet competition. The *Hiawatha* proved to be very popular, and during 1936 its eight cars were replaced with nine cars of Cor-ten steel, of improved streamlined design, roomier, and so much lighter that the nine-car train weighed less than the eight cars replaced. An additional *Hiawatha* run was necessary to Minocqua,

Wisconsin, to take care of the summer-resort travel, showing that the speed and comfort of streamlined trains tended to increase passenger traffic. The Milwaukee likewise joined with all the western carriers to begin early in 1936 a "pick up and delivery service," by which the railroads picked up less than carload freight by motor truck at the shipper's place of business and delivered it to the consignee's place of business without charge for the extra service at each end.

The reorganization proceedings, however, rapidly became a protracted struggle for advantage among various interests. In the reorganization proceedings, all creditor and stockholder groups appeared and sought to obtain as much participation under the plan as possible. The group of institutional investors vied with a protective committee organized by the holders of preferred stock of the Milwaukee Road and headed by H. C. Orton and Robert E. Smith. The initial plan of reorganization filed with the Interstate Commerce Committee on January 10, 1938, was only one of several plans which were ultimately to come before the Interstate Commerce Commission, each to be argued in turn, so that reorganization was delayed year after year for more than ten years after the initial petition in bankruptcy had been entered. It soon became apparent that reorganization under the original plan filed in 1935 was not possible. Late in 1938, the protective committee, having objected to the reorganization plan of the institutional investors and the trustees, proposed that the Chicago, Milwaukee, St. Paul and Pacific and the Chicago & Northwestern, which had gone into receivership only a day before the Milwaukee Road, be merged into one railroad system on a basis of participation by both bond and stockholders, and claiming that operating economies of more than $10,000,000 annually would result from such a merger; the plan was put forward by common stockholders of the Northwestern as well, since adverse business conditions did not make for the likelihood of any speedy consummation of a reorganization. But this plan, which would have combined the two systems into one of almost 20,000 miles, met with no more approval than did earlier plans, and the struggle for control continued in the background while the Milwaukee Road strove to pull itself out of repeated deficits. Yet this plan became the basis for the plan that was eventually to be approved by the commission as the one having the largest support among the institutional investors, a group with large holdings of senior bond issues.

While in 1937 the rate of return on investment in road and equipment had been 1.22 per cent, in 1938 it was only .72 per cent, despite the fact that the gap between operating revenues and operating expenses had narrowed, operating revenues decreasing 7.64 per cent as against a decrease of 7.42 per cent in operating expenses. Increasingly, in 1938, as in most of the years of the Milwaukee Road's existence, the company found it necessary to adjust to more new laws, such as the Federal Fair Labor Standards Act and the Railroad Unemployment Insurance Act, the latter removing unemployment insurance for railway employees from the jurisdiction of the various states and vesting it exclusively in the federal government.

In mid-1938, the Milwaukee Road sustained the most serious accident in its history when the westbound *Olympian*, with 11 cars, just after midnight on June 19, 1938, struck a bridge over Custer Creek near Saugus, Montana, and was derailed because a flash flood had undermined the concrete and steel structure and thrown it out of line. The engine, mail car, express car, 2 coaches, 2 tourist cars, and a sleeping car were hurled into the raging water, resulting in the death of 44 passengers and 4 employees on duty, as well as injury to 57 passengers, 13 employees on duty, and 5 off duty. The bridge, which was 180 feet long, was one of the structures that had been built to replace an earlier bridge of piles at that crossing; it spanned a creek which was normally dry for 9 months out of every year, and which, when at normal height, seldom exceeded 4 feet.

The disaster was caused by a cloudburst which had taken place in the Custer Creek valley several miles north of the bridge between four in the afternoon and some time past ten the night of June 18. The tremendous volume of water thus sent rushing down the valley of Custer Creek lacked sufficient force to collapse the bridge, but, striking the region in a dry season, it washed away and undermined the earth around the piers, which were of reinforced concrete, thus impairing the alignment of the bridge and derailing the train. Only two hours before the accident another train had crossed the Custer Creek bridge without any employee's having reason to suspect that the rising volume of water was undermining it. Despite the fact that the Custer Creek disaster followed 20 years during which the Milwaukee Road had operated without loss of life of a revenue passenger in a train accident, many of those newspapers constitutionally inimical to railroads published condemnatory editorials from the pens of men who always profess to be informed on all matters, suggesting that the accident was due to inadequate inspection and maintenance of the bridge. H. A. Scandrett, acting as trustee for the Milwaukee Road, answered all such editorials immediately, giving a complete history of the Custer Creek bridge, pointing out that "The management, confronted with the necessity of either failing to pay interest on its debts or skimp its maintenance to a point which might have resulted in unsafe operating conditions, chose unhesitatingly the former course, and three years ago placed the property in bankruptcy." An exhaustive investigation by the Interstate Commerce Commission absolved the Milwaukee Road of all blame, categorically stating that "This accident was caused by the undermining of the piers of a bridge, due to a cloudburst."

The accident, however, proved a test of the quality of the Milwaukee Road's service, and the road passed that test with flying colors. Everyone involved, from the Chicago office to those at the scene of the accident itself, worked with tireless speed to effect rescues and to communicate all available information to those waiting to hear from relatives and friends known to have taken the *Olympian*. This was as true of a sleeping car porter who worked with incredible agility to rescue passengers from drowning and of a section man, himself injured, working desperately to recover bodies in a partially mud-filled car, as it was of the Public Relations Department in Chicago, where public relations officers were apprised of the accident by telephone early Sunday morning, June 19, and promptly took the hitherto unprecedented step of telephoning the Chicago papers and the press associations to give them all the facts at hand, in keeping with the company's new policy. The office was then kept open continuously for two days and nights, and, with the help of other offices, answered inquiries by telephone, telegrams, and in person from individuals asking about relatives on the train, and from newspapers demanding all further information as it became available, thus demonstrating a notable sense of duty to the public on the part of the Milwaukee Road.

In 1938 the Milwaukee became the first railroad to eliminate elliptic springs in passenger car trucks, and to use helical springs instead, such as were in use in freight cars. This novel departure from precedent was made in May, and was the result of K. F. Nystrom's repeated experiments at the shops in Milwaukee. The Milwaukee's Karl Fritjof Nystrom, Fellow in the American Society of Mechanical Engineers, chairman in 1946 of the Railway Division of American Society of Mechanical Engineers, had come to the Milwaukee Road from the Grand Trunk (Canadian National) in 1922 as engineer in charge of car construction. He had many accomplishments to his credit, and the *Hiawatha* also owed its existence in large part to him. When in 1934 the first welded steel passenger cars were being built for the *Hiawatha,* and it was felt that the Milwaukee shops were not yet sufficiently organized or equipped to undertake such a program, Nystrom talked to a mass meeting of the men and explained that the problem was theirs as much as it was his and the management's. Working together to the limit of their skill and efficiency, he said, they could put the Milwaukee at the head of the car-building industry, and could demonstrate to a skeptical industry that welded cars were the cars of the future. As a result, the cars were delivered on the date promised.

An energetic, inventive, Swedish-born master car builder, Nystrom set out immediately upon his coming to the Milwaukee to concentrate the Milwaukee's important fabrication work in Milwaukee. He induced the company to replace the wooden car repair shops, burned in 1918, with a new car building shop in 1930—legend has it that permitting a party of company officials, led by President Henry A. Scandrett, to stand in the cold to watch the repairmen working in the cold had a good deal to do with the company's decision. Nystrom pioneered the all-welded car and built railroad cars at costs substantially below that of the nation's standard builders. He conceived the plan of assembling the underframe of a railroad car upside down for faster and easier assembly; he built the largest capacity steel box cars within the clearance limits of the Association of American Railroads; the freight-car building program begun in 1935 developed in ten years into the biggest program yet undertaken in the Milwaukee shops or any similar shops, in twelve years turning out 14,586 freight cars. Nystrom's value to the Milwaukee grew from year to year, since he held over a hundred personal patents ranging from major designs to a grain-tight box-car door, but the *Hiawathas* remain one of his major achievements.

The Milwaukee's oldest employee died in 1938. Certain critics of the Milwaukee Road once called it a slow road because it was "filled with old men." But the "old men" of the Milwaukee were often on the job because they preferred work with the Milwaukee to retirement. Of these men, John M. Horan, known as "Soda Ash Johnny," was the oldest. He was over 100 years old when he died, and his seventy-fifth anniversary with the Milwaukee had been celebrated in a private dining car of the Milwaukee Road at Milwaukee. Moreover, at 100 he had completed almost 83 years of service with the Milwaukee Road, for at that advanced age, still mentally alert and steady on his feet, he carried on as a boiler-washer inspector, walking daily from his home to his office, a distance of six blocks, descending the viaduct of 120 stairs on his way home. He had earned his nickname because he had originated the use of soda ash in the treatment of water in locomotive boilers. He also developed the system of locating washout plugs now widely used.

Soda Ash Johnny began working for the Milwaukee April 17, 1855, as a loader of wood into the wood-burning locomotives of that day. Next he melted tallow for candles and prepared the tallow for locomotive cylinder lubrication. During his 83 years of service he worked as a machinist, an engineer, and a general shop foreman at Yankton, South Dakota, where he developed the improvements for which he became famous among railroad men. He was also a traveling inspector. Upon reaching the age of retirement, he refused to accept a retirement pension, preferring to remain an active railroad man. His position on the Milwaukee Road was unique among laborers of such advanced age, and on March 19, 1930, Ripley saluted him in his panel, *Believe It Or Not*. Milwaukee Road officials feted Soda Ash Johnny on his one hundredth birthday, January 22, 1938; he died ten days later.

Soda Ash Johnny in his life demonstrated the affection Milwaukee Road men hold for the Milwaukee. Men of the Milwaukee work consistently for the road, whether they are section men or retired superintendents, like William Dolphin, one-time superintendent of Milwaukee Road dining cars, who invented and patented a nonsloshing, nonspilling coffee cup for the dining cars—a cup looking very much like any common cup, but containing an inside lip which acts as a breakwater to prevent coffee going over the rim.

And when these men have ceased to work for the Milwaukee, they look back into memory and thus carry on a vicarious existence with the road still. Charles Lapham, who joined the Milwaukee as a surveyor in 1879 (the son of Dr. Increase A. Lapham, who had surveyed the original route of the Milwaukee and Waukesha in 1849) and who built the railroad's first bridge across the Mississippi and relocated the channel of the Menominee River, in addition to more prosaic surveying tasks, looked back over his years with the road in an article that he wrote a decade ago for the Milwaukee *Journal:*

Railroading isn't the same any more. It's gone tame. There were times when the road's expansion was blocked by common councils, lawyers, and everybody else. Those were the days when competition was bitter between young railroads. We were always fighting to get into new territory, and speedy action was necessary to stop the other fellow from beating us to it. Once we wanted to lay a track across a street near what is now our freight depot at Fowler Street. The politicians wouldn't let us, and we were desperate because we couldn't afford to wait very long. We got everything ready—rails, ties, etc.—and went there at four-thirty one Sunday morning with a big gang. We worked as quietly as we could on such a noisy job, and just as fast as we could, and we laid those tracks right across the street. We got across before anyone knew what was going on. There was a row over it, but, being Sunday, they couldn't get an injunction to stop us. And after we got the tracks in, I guess they thought we might as well leave them there. . . .

Another time we got wind at Madison that the Illinois Central wanted to extend up from Madison into the north woods to tap the lumber business. The Milwaukee Road and the Northwestern ran side by side along a lake where there was just room between their tracks for a third track, and the Illinois Central plan was to sneak in and lay its tracks right down the middle before we could stop them. But we fixed them. We went in there and laid the track ourselves one Sunday. There were telegraph poles in the way, but we just spaced the ties out and left the poles standing in the middle of the new track until later in the week, when we took them out.

George Cooper, for 58 years an employee of the Milwaukee Road, recalled the early days of the road in an article written for the Milwaukee *Evening Wisconsin,* back in 1913. The days Cooper recalled were the earliest—when the Milwaukee was but 65 miles in length, running from Milwaukee through Prairieville (now Waukesha) to Whitewater. On a winter day in 1855, when a snowstorm trapped the wood-burning locomotive and three cars, the conductor left his train and went into Davis's drug store at Prairieville to send a message to Milwaukee, 20 miles away, asking for help. The telegraph operator took the message and charged the conductor $2.50, whereupon the conductor cried aloud to heaven to witness this robbery. "Well, you charged me $1.25 to ride out from Milwaukee," replied the operator and collected his fee. The telegraph operator was Cushman K. Davis, later senator from Minnesota and a member of the peace commission settling the terms of the Spanish-American war in Paris. One of the "boys" on the run was Fred D. Underwood, later president of the Erie Railroad. "Fred Underwood and I were braking together in western Wisconsin at the same time," said Cooper. "Sir William Van Horne, who went up to Canada and became a great man on the Canadian Pacific, was with the Milwaukee in the old days. He was a reserved man, different from Mr. Merrill, who always shook hands with me and asked, 'How are you, George?' "

The success of the streamlined trains brought about a new daytime fast train service effective January 21, 1939, between Chicago and Minneapolis consisting of two trains named *Morning Hiawatha;* the northbound train made 18 intermediate stops and yet reached Minneapolis in 8 hours, while the southbound, with 10 fewer intermediate stops, reached Chicago in 6 hours, 50 minutes. The trains were drawn by new streamlined locomotives purchased in 1938, and the cars were all of modern steel construction, made in the company's shops at Milwaukee. The new service was instantly successful, and its substantial earnings amply justified the road's experiments toward increasing speed, particularly on its passenger trains.

At the same time, the road helped to promote and advance water conservation and irrigation development projects in all the northwestern states. This assistance was designed ultimately to increase the agricultural tonnage carried by the Milwaukee. Furthermore, the road co-operated with the United States Bureau of Reclamation in the planning and settlement of 213 farms on the Sun River Project near Great Falls, Montana. This kind of aid was but a forerunner of the service that was to be offered within a few years, when the involvement of the United States in World War II came about.

The result of these moves in the direction of improved service was evident in the annual report, for in 1939 the deficit was reported at $14,427,382.63, as compared to $17,996,269.77 the previous year, and by the end of 1940 the deficit had gone down to $8,826,521.54.

Reorganization of the Milwaukee Road continued to be argued before the Interstate Commerce Commission throughout 1938 and 1940. On February 12, 1940, the Interstate Commerce Commission approved a plan of reorganization for the company, to be made effective as of January 1, 1939, determining the total capitalization of the company, including the Terre Haute bonds and taking the nonpar value of common stock at $100 per share, as $548,833,321, and the annual charges at $12,532,528. The plan provided for no disturbance of the liens of the Terre Haute bonds, except for a modification altering the terms of the bonds so as to bear fixed interest at the rate of 2.75 per cent per annum, and contingent interest in addition at the rate of 1 per cent per annum, and nullified the guaranty on the income bonds assumed by the debtor, adding that, if the bondholders of the Terre Haute failed to accept the suggested modifications, the lease should be terminated. Equipment obligations were to remain undisturbed; loans from the Reconstruction Finance Corporation would be partly paid off in cash then in the hands of the trustee of the company's first and refunding mortgage, the remainder to be discharged by the issuance of new first mortgage bonds bearing 4 per cent interest. The reorganization in respect to holders of bonds and stock of the Milwaukee Road was equitable enough to satisfy the Interstate Commerce Commission, though the commission issued a supplemental order early in June, 1940, modifying the plan already approved and reaffirming its belief that the equity of the debtor's stockholders had no value. Though the district court of the northern district of Illinois, eastern division, began hearings on the modified plan in September and approved the plan in November, with some minor corrections and clarifications, the opposing interests appealed to the United States circuit court of appeals, thus still further prolonging the reorganization and resulting in the return of the reorganization plan to the Interstate Commerce Commission once again.

Meanwhile, the status of the Milwaukee Road, though it remained in trusteeship, was altering. The war in Europe had already brought about an increase in operating revenues, and the passage of the Transportation Act of 1940, setting forth a policy of providing fair and impartial regulation of railroads and motor and water carriers, establishing a board of investigation and research to investigate the relative economy and fitness of such carriers, and providing for payment by the government of full tariff rates for the transportation of persons or property, other than for military or naval purposes, was a major sign that the federal government was fully cognizant of its own responsibilities toward the railroads. The Milwaukee Road quickly fulfilled the one provision demanded by filing a release from claims against the government arising out of land grants, and the immediate result of the Act for the Milwaukee Road was the increase of mail revenue by approximately $120,000 annually.

The establishment of widely scattered ordnance plants by the federal government benefited the Milwaukee Road in 1941, though in some cases the road found itself in the amusing position of having to re-lay tracks just taken up, as in the instance of the Sauk City–Prairie du Sac country along the Wisconsin River, where, after a futile attempt on the part of Prairie du Sac to retain a separate station for itself, the company finally managed to establish a single station for the twin villages, but had hardly done so before it had to re-lay the tracks taken up and extend them up beyond Prairie du Sac to the fertile prairie north of the twin villages, where the government began late in 1941 to construct the Badger Ordnance Works, one of the largest of such projects in the United States. This construction was on a spur off the first major line of the Milwaukee Road, the Milwaukee–Mississippi line, and this spur, which had consistently carried a single daily train of 6 to 10 cars, now began to haul trains, sometimes twice daily, of 40 cars and more. But the extension of the Sauk City–Prairie du Sac branch and the increased traffic on it represented but one such development, and all of them were spurred by the entry of the United States into the war December 7, 1941.

The road's major achievement in this aspect of the war effort was the service given to the atomic project at Hanford, Washington. The Hanford project involved the abandonment not only of the town of Hanford but of an area of 600 square miles in that region. Hanford was at the end of a 46-mile spur off the main tracks of the Milwaukee Road; the spur was known as the Hanford branch, and the town's

1,800 people received word by telegraph one day of the order to re-move, without previous warning. The Milwaukee Road performed an herculean task; not only did it relocate 1,800 people, but between April 1, 1943, and July 31, 1945, the Milwaukee carried in 41,633 car-loads of freight, a shipment equal to a single train 333 miles long. As an adjunct to Hanford, the government-created town of Richland Village sprang up eight miles away, and in the course of two years grew into a city of 60,000 people.

The Milwaukee likewise played an important part in the develop-ment of the world's largest naval ammunition depot at Crane, Indiana, and subsequently in the handling of the tremendous tonnage moving in and out of Crane. The war affected the Milwaukee in other ways. Prior to the attack on Pearl Harbor, approximately 27,000,000 tons of commerce moved annually through the Panama Canal; but after the attack, commercial shipments stopped completely, and a major share of canal traffic was shifted to the railroads serving the west coast. In addition, the Milwaukee, in all manner of ways, from editorials in *The Milwaukee Magazine* over President Scandrett's signature to posters all along the lines, lent its support actively to war savings bond cam-paigns and scrap drives: "4,000 lbs. of scrap and fittings were removed from under buildings. . . . There have been 98,650 lbs. of shop-made tools taken from the blacksmith shop and converted into scrap . . . also from the shops, 1,849 lbs. of brass recovered . . . also 36,559 lbs. of miscellaneous scrap recovered from the roundhouse and shops. . . . One section foreman and his crew of four men recovered 9,500 pounds of other than company scrap. . . ."—and similar war efforts. The Mil-waukee took up over 1,000,000 lineal feet of rail, and recovered over 10,000,000 pounds of scrap metal before the end of 1942.

The results of this increased activity were economically predictable. The Milwaukee Road finished 1941, for instance, with a net income of $5,531,333.80, despite having granted wage increases to all operat-ing and nonoperating employees. Most of the increases were retro-active, though they were in part offset by the Interstate Commerce Commission's granting of temporary freight rate increases to "expire six months after the termination of the present war." The establish-ment of the Office of Defense Transportation by the executive order of President Franklin D. Roosevelt, under the direction of Joseph B. Eastman, chairman of the Interstate Commerce Commission, speedily resulted in the realization of the aims of that office, which were of tremendous benefit to all carriers, since the subjection of every other consideration to the prosecution of the war made for the development of measures designed to secure the maximum use of existing transportation facilities, to provide such additional facilities and equipment as necessary to expedite the services required, and to coordinate services to achieve the maximum in expeditious movement of men, material, and supplies to the points of need.

Though the Milwaukee Road was soon suffering from lack of equipment, just as in World War I, a condition prevailing on every railroad during the war, its experiments in the Milwaukee shops served it in good stead. It made further improvements in passenger trucks in 1941 by allowing the movement of the wheels with the journal boxes to float freely with the equalizer, thereby eliminating friction, wear, and disturbances between the journal boxes and the truck frame. By 1942, the road was already acutely aware of the strictures of wartime operation. "The loss of thousands of trained men to the armed forces and the shortage of critical materials, coupled with the greatest traffic volume in the history of the Railroad, made 1942 a year of many difficulties," set forth the annual report. "That these were surmounted is due to the hard, conscientious and intelligent work of the men and women of the Milwaukee Road, and the Trustees are happy to record this acknowledgment of their loyal, devoted service." By the end of that year, 3,237 employees had joined the armed forces, and, while the total corporate deficit stood at $163,482,052.23, the road's net income for 1942 was $12,174,831.

Reorganization was still before the courts and the Interstate Commerce Commission. Opposing interests had carried the battle against approval of the plan announced in 1940 to the United States supreme court in 1942, and on March 15, 1943, the court rendered its opinions, approving the provisions of the plan of reorganization, including the provision excluding the stockholders from participation, and making but two exceptions—first, that there had been no determination as to whether the general mortgage bondholders or the 50-year bondholders had a first lien on the so-called "pieces of lines east," which dispute, the court held, should be resolved by the district court; second, that, since junior interests participate under the plan, the commission and the district court should determine what the general mortgage bonds and the 50-year bonds should receive in addition to a face amount of inferior securities equal to the face amount of their old bonds as equitable compensation for the loss of their senior rights. The decision of the supreme court meant, however, a new period of legal delay while the Interstate Commerce Commission and the district court took the supreme court's direction under advisement, a period during which the opposition did not admit defeat, but persisted in its efforts to thwart the reorganization except on its own terms.

The 1943 report of the trustees set forth simply, "The expanded production for the war effort, and the resulting heavy increase in traffic, produced the largest gross revenue in the history of the Railroad." The threat of a strike late in 1943 and the refusal of three of the operating brotherhoods to arbitrate brought about a presidential order of seizure of the railroads through the War Department, possession beginning December 27, 1943. But government control was short-lived, for the emergency board's recommendations were ultimately accepted by the three dissenting operating brotherhoods, and a settlement was arranged with the 15 nonoperating unions by granting wage increases of from 4 cents to 10 cents an hour; control ceased at midnight January 18, 1944. During 1943, the Milwaukee Road so bestirred itself in projects designed to aid the war effort, from increasing the production and processing of foods to aiding in victory garden work, that the National Victory Garden Institute awarded the Milwaukee Road a bronze plaque and a citation for outstanding service. In April, too, the Milwaukee Road's Milwaukee Motor Transportation Company, organized in December, 1942, with a capital stock of $50,000, owned by the trustees of the road, began operations with the acquisition of motor equipment; it operated to meet competitive motor truck service and to supplement the rail service to smaller towns along the Milwaukee Road in Wisconsin and Michigan. On the other hand, equipment began to show the wear and tear resulting from increased use, and particularly from such use demanded by the Office of Defense Transportation, requiring the heavier loading of cars and the use of refrigerator cars for loads usually carried in box cars. As a result of the "largest gross revenue in the history of the Road," the Milwaukee Road's net income came to $29,413,623, while its total corporate deficit shrank to $134,756,006.85.

Revenues for 1944 were even larger than those for 1943, and a larger volume of freight was handled in that year with a decrease in train miles. Yet 6,350 employees were in the armed forces of the United States, and 103 of them had already given their lives; the company sent a $10 check and a letter of Christmas greetings to each employee in military service, insofar as military addresses were obtainable. The pinch of wartime operation increased. "During a considerable part of the year there was a shortage of box and refrigerator cars, which continued into 1945, and was accentuated by the severe weather conditions in the Northeastern part of the country, resulting in the tying up of Western roads' cars in that territory," said the trustees in their annual report for 1944. And, "Throughout the year there was a shortage of trained and experienced employees which, coupled with the inability to obtain materials, made it necessary to curtail maintenance and improvement programs." At the same time, payments for loss and damage rose to their highest level since 1930, owing largely to increased commodity prices, shortages of suitable materials for packing and crating, inexperienced employees, and heavier loading of cars.

The various newly established departments of the Milwaukee Road functioned consistently to aid the war effort, and ultimately to serve the road. The Agriculture and Mineral Development Department, for instance, was active throughout the year in the organization of soil conservation and grazing districts, and it worked with federal, state and private interests to effect adoption of an integrated plan for the development of the entire Missouri River basin, including irrigation, flood control, and navigation. The Public Relations Department, organized in and active since 1923, began in 1943 a more intensive program of employee-public relations. An advisory committee comprising officials representing the general departments was appointed by President Scandrett to hold regular meetings to develop ways and means of interesting employees in better service and more courteous and considerate contacts with the public. To this program rallied the 60 employee service clubs, organized in 1938. At the same time the department began a much closer contact with the press and conducted a campaign designed to educate the public by arranging for and making talks, publishing the monthly *Milwaukee Magazine*, conducting war bond, Red Cross, and community fund campaigns, and supervising the activities of employee service clubs.

The long-drawn-out reorganization proceedings began to culminate when, in mid-year of 1944, the district court approved a modified plan of reorganization certified to the court by the Interstate Commerce Commission subsequent to the ruling of the United States supreme court. When this plan was submitted to all creditors entitled to vote thereon, the percentage voting in favor of it was extremely high—holders of Milwaukee & Northern Railroad Company first mortgage bonds, 100 per cent; of the consolidated mortgage bonds, 99.39 per cent; of the Gary first mortgage bonds, 93.56 per cent; of the Milwaukee Road's general mortgage bonds, 99.28 per cent; of the 50-year mortgage bonds, 99.25 per cent; of the convertible adjustment mortgage bonds, 87.88 per cent; of all other claims allowed by the special master or the court, 99.82 per cent; while the Reconstruction Finance Corporation and the Federal Emergency Administration of Public

Works were 100 per cent in favor of the plan. The court held a hearing to determine whether or not the plan should be confirmed, and on February 23, 1945, entered an order and decree confirming the reorganization plan. The road's total capitalization was set at $535,-965,396. In mid-March the district court approved the appointment of a reorganization committee, consisting of James M. Barker, William C. Cummings, William H. Mitchell, Elmer Rich, and Henry F. Tenney, and, since the confirmed plan of reorganization included an alternate distribution of securities if the Reconstruction Finance Corporation's claim should be paid in full with cash, the district court, finding the cash position of the trust estate sufficient to pay the claim in full, authorized the payment of $10,442,827.50, with accrued interest of $92,773.77.

Nevertheless, final approval was destined to be still further delayed by an almost fortuitous circumstance, when Representative Chauncey W. Reed of Illinois introduced legislation into congress authorizing the immediate return of railroads undergoing reorganization to the control of their old stockholders, if annual earnings for the preceding seven calendar years were sufficient to pay the fixed charges. The bill was introduced late in 1945, and the opposing stockholders of the Milwaukee Road hoped to utilize the Reed Bill to gain control of the road and prevent its reorganization, or at least stave off approval of the reorganization until they might effect a saving of their investment. However, after more than a decade of bankruptcy and reorganization proceedings, Judge Michael L. Igoe, late in 1945, handed down a decision directing consummation of the reorganization of the Chicago, Milwaukee, St. Paul and Pacific Railroad, answering protests from the Transportation Association of America, based on the pending Reed Bill, by pointing out that "It would have cost anywhere from $50,000 to $200,000 to have put the decision off. If we had waited until action was taken on the bill, this Road might be in receivership another ten years."

Officers of the reorganized company included Henry A. Scandrett as president, T. W. Burtness as secretary, and Leo T. Crowley as chairman of the board of directors. There was, in effect, no alteration in the management, which boded well for the Milwaukee Road, since its management, in common with its employees, had done a particularly noteworthy job of running the company, first, against all the factors of prewar competition, and secondly, during the war emergency. Even while the reorganization was going through its final stages, the Milwaukee Road was expanding, improving, growing, experimenting as never before; indeed, the last decade of its first hundred years saw a resurgence of almost dramatic leadership in the Milwaukee Road such as had been shown in no other decade of its history, not even the expanding decade of the 1880's.

For instance, in 1945 the company began work on modernization and improvement of shop facilities at its extensive shops in Milwaukee, a program which is still in progress at an estimated cost of $4,300,000, savings resulting from which are expected to amortize the investment within a five-year period. A new entry into Kansas City was effected in the construction of a new double-track line jointly with the Chicago, Rock Island and Pacific Railway Company; this line included construction of a new steel bridge over the Missouri River, dedicated as the *President Harry S. Truman Bridge*, and opened to traffic in mid-1945; this bridge replaced the old bridge, exclusively owned by the Milwaukee Road, and was projected to carry 50 to 60 trains a day. The company established centralized traffic control systems between Faribault and Mendota, Minnesota; between Glencoe and Granite Falls, Minnesota; between Delmar and Puder, Illinois; and on the new double-track line between Birmingham and Kansas City, Missouri, thus completing 295 miles of lines, or 18 sections, on which the system had been established, and carrying on a program begun but two years before. The road also installed space radio equipment on several trains, designed to provide for communication between the head and rear end of freight trains; the cabooses were also equipped with walkie-talkie sets, so that the conductor or brakeman might remain in constant communication with the engineer, even if he should leave the caboose. Moreover, all the departments which functioned so ably during the wartime emergency not only continued but expanded their efforts.

The Milwaukee Road ended 1945 with road and equipment valuation of $799,137,296.12, capital stock of $324,495,400, and a funded debt of $191,155,833.74. The net income for 1945 stood at $14,077,911. In its brochure, *Facts, 1945*, the Milwaukee Road set forth its hopes for the postwar years:

Now that the war is over, we are faced with the less desperate but economically serious problems of peace. One of these is the decline in revenues. For the first three months of 1946, our freight revenues were about $7,000,-000 less than for the same period in 1945. In March, 1946, passenger revenues began to fall off. . . . By hard, unremitting effort, we can reasonably expect to obtain our share of the freight and passenger traffic available in the future. A second important factor in the operation of the railroad is the increase in costs with which we are faced. . . .

But the Milwaukee Road was quick to enter into the Rail Travel Credit Plan, which enabled travelers to obtain tickets through the use of credit cards good for transportation, sleeping and parlor car tickets, and payment of excess baggage charges, a plan developed by the Railroad Passenger Interterritorial Committee and inaugurated on eastern roads late in 1946; the Milwaukee was one of 45 railroads to put the plan into effect on April 1, 1947. The Milwaukee Road, too, worked in co-operation with the Hertz Drivurself System and similar services to implement a new rail-auto travel plan, which became effective July 1, 1947, a plan designed to offer travelers the combined advantages of both rail and automobile transportation at reasonable prices, inaugurating such service initially in 20 cities on the Milwaukee Road. At the same time, the Milwaukee, ever striving to maintain the best possible relations between the traveling public and employees, distributed cards bearing requests for a frank expression regarding food and service on the road's dining cars. Within a few weeks 1,159 cards had been returned by travelers on the Milwaukee, with the heartening information that 655 guests described the Milwaukee dining cars' food as "excellent" and 421 as "good," and 1,120 found the Milwaukee's general service to be "good."

In 1947 the Milwaukee Road's car building program, calling for 5,025 freight cars and several hundred passenger cars in 1947, and 4,622 in 1948, put the company far out ahead of all others in the United States which build their own rolling stock. The program focused attention anew on the Milwaukee shops, where 60 of the 72 cars for the six new trains which began service to the west coast June 29, 1947, as the *Olympian Hiawatha*, were built from the track up. The Milwaukee's K. F. Nystrom, with his inventive ingenuity and his devotion to the road, attracted delegations of railroad men and mechanical engineers from virtually every country in the world. The Milwaukee's shops lie in the valley of the Menominee River about three miles west of downtown Milwaukee, occupying approximately 160 acres between the road's main line and the river. Built originally on marshland that had to be filled in, the shops were considered at their establishment in the late seventies to be sufficiently far from town, so much so that the company soon inaugurated train service between downtown Milwaukee and its new shops.

The men of the Milwaukee shops had every opportunity to display their inventiveness. J. N. Barr, for instance, onetime superintendent of motive power, developed the wheel-treating process, an early type of passenger-car vestibule, and several types of snow plows. Many others contributed minor time-saving devices, though no Milwaukee shopman approached the inventive achievements of Nystrom. At peak capacity in the 1890's, the shops completed a new engine every three days; in the 1920's, the shops reached a capacity of 28 new freight cars daily. The 1947 car-building program, however, exceeded any previous program projected as well as all previous records; up to mid-June of 1947 the shops had built 17,636 freight cars.

Beginning July 1, 1947, a retirement plan was adopted by the Milwaukee, establishing 65 years as the retirement age for general and local officers, with the proviso that those now 65 might remain with the railroad until they reached 70. Even before the adoption of the new plan, retirements occurred with increasing frequency throughout the road's personnel. At Bridgeport, Wisconsin, Harry Lathrop retired on November 20, 1946, after 67 years with the Milwaukee. Lathrop was one of the most picturesque of Milwaukee Road agents, known far and wide as "the poet-agent," for he was the author of *The Yankee Abroad, Memories of Wisconsin and Other Poems*, and other books. His birthday in 1856 coincided with the coming of the Milwaukee to Bridgeport on the original line to Prairie du Chien; he grew up a rail fan, and went into service of the Milwaukee in 1878 in Mazomanie as a clerk, transferring soon thereafter to Sauk City as the first agent at that station. By 1903, however, he was back at Bridgeport as agent in his native village, and there he remained in active service until he reached the age of 90, when his son Lewis took over.

On January 1, 1947, Assistant Superintendent William Mack Thurber of Dubuque, Iowa, retired, terminating one of the longest family service records in the road's history. His service began as a telegrapher on the old Prairie du Chien division, from which he moved to Genoa as operator and to Savanna as assistant dispatcher, thereafter becoming chief dispatcher of the Illinois division, trainmaster at Dubuque, and superintendent of the Dubuque, the Iowa and Dakota, the La Crosse, and the Illinois divisions. Assistant Superintendent Thurber's 48 years, added to the previous service records of other members of his family, totaled 241 years, underscoring once more the strong sense of solidarity among the families of the Milwaukee Road employees, and the invariable feeling for the Milwaukee as being "our road."

In May, 1947, President Henry A. Scandrett retired, and his successor was Charles H. Buford, an Arkansan who came to the Milwaukee in 1907 as an instrument man, from which post he rose to become engineer of the Milwaukee's track elevation project in Chicago prior to 1917. Thereafter he served as trainmaster, superintendent, general superintendent, assistant general manager, general manager, vice-president in charge of the operations and maintenance department of the Association of American Railroads in Washington, and finally, in March, 1946, he became executive vice-president of the Milwaukee. During his career with the road, Buford had been located in several Wisconsin towns—La Crosse, Milwaukee, Green Bay, and Wausau. He was one of seven railroad men to be awarded President Truman's Certificate of Merit and the Certificate of Appreciation of the Bureau of Naval Personnel of the U. S. Navy, conferred for distinguished service to the nation in the field of transportation during the war.

The Milwaukee, after a hundred years of service against odds imposed by government control, saw a changing sentiment in the final year of its first century. Newspapers throughout the country were beginning to question the wisdom of a government policy which the railroads had always called the "subsidy racket." In mid-1946, the *Railway Employees Journal* editorialized on the authorization by congress of $500,000,000 for federal aid to airport construction. The *Journal* did not pull its punches:

Railroads have built elaborate and expensive passenger terminals, entirely at their own cost, at most of the country's important centers. In many instances railroads have to haul passengers an average distance of from 50 to more than 100 miles to earn an amount equal to the per passenger cost of terminal service alone. There is certainly no fairness in furnishing the airlines, free of cost to them and at public expense, with airports to enable them to compete more effectively with railroads. . . . In the twenty years between the two great wars . . . the greater part of money spent on development of other means of transportation (more than was spent on the railroads in all the years of their history) came out of government treasuries and was raised by taxation. Yet when the second great war came, the country depended upon the railroads to carry upwards of 90% of the transport load essential to victory. . . . The railroads maintain their own tracks and roadways, at an annual cost that absorbs upwards of one-eighth of their revenues. Inland waterways, paid for with government money when built, are maintained at a public expense that averages about twice as much per channel mile as it would cost to maintain a mile of railroad. . . . Waterway, airway and highway carriers are able to offer rates lower than they could afford if they were required to pay the full cost of their services from rates and fares, as the railroads are.

The Milwaukee *Journal's* editorial was typical of informed newspaper comment on the subsidy issue:

We tax the railroads, but subsidize their competitors. . . . The inconsistency is plain. The result is becoming plain. It will be that railroads cannot make their costs. We shall let them first run down and then go broke. Since we still must have them, this will mean bailing them out at public expense.

This is a blind policy, neither fair to the railroads as commercial enterprise, most of them well operated under the strictest kind of regulation, nor in our own interest. Our alternatives have become clear. Either we must subsidize the railroads or require that other forms of transportation—busses and trucks, waterways and especially airways—pay an increasing share of the enormous sums which construction and maintenance are costing the taxpayer.

The result of the blind and vicious policy of using the railroads as whipping boys, begun almost a century ago, was beginning to show. The subsidy of competitive transportation considerably antedated the airways traffic; it began with highways and went on with waterways in a fantastically lopsided manner which aroused no particular ire on the part of those watchdogs of the public welfare who had been whipping the railroads for decades. Their pat answer had always been, of course, that the railroads had received 131,000,000 acres of land free from the government, at an estimated value of $.94 an acre, or $123,-000,000; that, they maintained, was equal to any subsidy. But what none of them ever brought out was that, in return for lands granted, the land-grant railroads, and their competitors as well, ever since the time of the land grants, carried government troops and all government property used for military purposes for one-half standard rates. Prior to 1941, those railroads also carried government property used for nonmilitary purposes for one-half rate and U. S. mails for four-fifths of the standard rates. Not until December, 1945, when congress passed the Boren Act, were the land-grant rate provisions repealed, as of October 1, 1946. Land-grant rate deductions totaled more than $1,180,-000,000, or ten times the value of the lands granted to the railroads—a blunt fact which never interested the railroad-baiters. Of this figure, the Milwaukee bore more than its proportionate share. The Milwaukee and its predecessor companies were granted 833,879 acres in Iowa and Minnesota only; up to January 1, 1947, reduced rates cost the Milwaukee $49,741,626, or almost $60 an acre.

In the closing years of its first century, the Milwaukee Road began to rebuild 900 cabooses, eliminating the cupolas that were so long a feature of the caboose, and installing side bays instead, thus permitting a roomier and more easily heated car in place of the partitioned car of earlier days. The cabooses, familiar in red for many years, were repainted, most of them, in aluminum and black, a combination easier to see in the glow of an oncoming headlight, and then to red and orange. The modern caboose has not only the latest type of stove for heating and cooking, but also side seats six feet long, usable as beds; and there are three clothes lockers, a washstand and water supply, a refrigerator, a tool locker, and a toilet, all under plywood ceilings designed for greater warmth in winter and greater insulation against heat in summer.

The Milwaukee Road ended its first century with marked changes in the character of the freight carried on its trains, in comparison to that carried in its initial decade. Manufactured articles now made up 34.1 per cent of revenue tonnage, while agricultural products, including grain and livestock, made up 25.7 per cent, less than coal, ore, and the products of mines, which stood at 27.6 per cent. Lumber and forest products accounted for 10.9 per cent, and the final 1.7 per cent was made up of less than carload lots. The road moved 52,326,187 tons of freight in 1945, at an average revenue per ton-mile of less than 1 cent—9³⁄₁₀ mills—while the average haul per ton was 347 miles, as against an average passenger mile revenue of $.0171. The road carried 11,-343,310 passengers an average distance of 191 miles per passenger.

As it closed its first century, the Milwaukee operated 10,733 miles of road, and owned in addition the Milwaukee Land Company, engaged in the sale of timber and land, and the Republic Coal Company. In its first hundred years, the Milwaukee had pioneered perhaps more extensively than any other major railroad—in the electrification of its lines to the coast, in the use of electric lights on trains west of Chicago, in the operation of all-steel trains, in the use of roller bearings and of steam-heated passenger trains, and in the introduction of all-welded passenger cars and all-steel, all-welded freight cars of all types, having built, from war's end in 1945 to the end of 1946, approximately 15,000 such cars. Moreover, the Milwaukee's record continued into 1947; when the shortage of cars aroused government protest in mid-1947, the railroad companies' car-building shops, working under the same adverse conditions as non-company-owned car-builders, had built in the month of August alone 27 per cent of all cars delivered instead of the 15 per cent they were to build. Of this percentage the Milwaukee had supplied its customary preponderant share.

From uncertain beginnings, through an almost constant barrage of opposition from legislative sources as well as from misinformed or deliberately misled men in the street, the Milwaukee Road grew to a position of national prominence, with its orange coaches and familiar trade-mark famous from coast to coast, and the quality of its courtesy and service exceeded by no other railroad in the land. Despite its periods of travail, the Milwaukee was fortunate to have within its ranks the men of vision to guide its fortunes, and, after looking back over its first hundred years, it could look forward with confidence to its second century.

Appendix A

Wisconsin

1. Milwaukee & Mississippi Rail Road Company.
   Incorporated February 11, 1847, as:
   (a) Milwaukee and Waukesha Rail Road Company.
   Name changed to Milwaukee & Mississippi Rail Road Company February 1, 1850.
   Consolidated May 18, 1853, approved June 25, 1853, with:
   (b) Madison and Prairie du Chien Rail Road Company.
   Incorporated March 24, 1852.
   To form Milwaukee and Mississippi Rail Road Company (3).
2. Southern Wisconsin Rail Road Company.
   Incorporated April 7, 1852.
   Sold February 13, 1856, to Milwaukee and Mississippi Rail Road Company (3).
3. Milwaukee and Mississippi Rail Road Company.
   Formed by consolidation of Milwaukee & Mississippi Rail Road Company (1) and Madison and Prairie du Chien Rail Road Company (1b) May 24, 1853.
   Foreclosed October 12, 1860; purchased January 18, 1861, by bondholders.
   Deeded January 21, 1861, to:
   (a) Milwaukee and Prairie du Chien Railway Company.
       Organized January 18, 1861, by purchasers of Milwaukee and Mississippi Rail Road Company (3).
       Sold December 31, 1867, to Milwaukee and St. Paul Railway Company (13).
4. La Crosse and Milwaukee Railroad Company.
   Formed January 23, 1854, by a consolidation of:
   (a) La Crosse and Milwaukee Rail Road Company, incorporated April 2, 1852, and
   (b) Milwaukee, Fond du Lac and Green Bay Railroad Company.
       Formed June 27, 1853, by consolidation of:

(c) Milwaukee and Fond du Lac Railroad Company,
incorporated February 21, 1851, anc

(d) Milwaukee, Fond du Lac and Green Bay Railroad
Company, incorporated April 2, 1853.

Consolidated September 23, 1856, with Milwaukee and Watertown
Railroad Company (6) to form La Crosse and Milwaukee Rail
Road Company (8).

5. Milwaukee and Horicon Rail Road Company.
Incorporated April 17, 1852.
Sold June 23, 1863, to Milwaukee and St. Paul Railway Company
(13).

6. Milwaukee and Watertown Railroad Company.
Incorporated March 11, 1851.
Consolidated September 23, 1856, with La Crosse and Milwaukee
Railroad Company (4) to form La Crosse and Milwaukee Rail
Road Company (8).

7. Racine and Mississippi Rail Road Company.
Formed by a consolidation March 31, 1855 (Wisconsin), and February 14, 1855 (Illinois), of:

(a) Racine, Janesville and Mississippi Rail Road Company.
Incorporated April 17, 1852.
Consolidated February 23, 1854, with:

(b) The Rockton and Freeport Rail Road Company.
Incorporated February 10, 1853.

Consolidated March 29, 1856, with:

(c) Savanna Branch Railroad Company.
Incorporated January 21, 1851.

To form Racine and Mississippi Railroad Company (11).

8. La Crosse and Milwaukee Rail Road Company.
Formed September 23, 1856, by a consolidation of La Crosse and
Milwaukee Railroad Company (4) and Milwaukee and Watertown Railroad Company (6).
Line: Portage to La Crosse deeded to Milwaukee and St. Paul Railway Company (13) May 5, 1863.
Line: Milwaukee to Portage deeded to Milwaukee and St. Paul
Railway Company (13) March 5, 1867.
Note: Line: Milwaukee to Portage operated from January 4, 1866,
to March 5, 1867, by:

(a) Milwaukee & Minnesota Railroad Company.
Incorporated May 24, 1859.
Sold to Milwaukee and St. Paul Railway Company (13)
March 5, 1867.

Line: Brookfield to Columbus sold December 24, 1857, to:

(b) Madison, Fond du Lac and Michigan Railroad Company.
Formed August 7, 1856, by a consolidation of:

    (c) Madison, Fond du Lac and Michigan Railroad
        Company, incorporated March 31, 1855, and
    (d) Beaver Dam and Baraboo Railroad Company,
        incorporated March 31, 1855.
Name changed May 13, 1858, to:
    (e) Milwaukee, Watertown and Baraboo Valley
        Railroad Company.
    Name changed March 16, 1861, to:
        (f) The Milwaukee and Western Rail-
            road Company.
            Deeded June 8, 1863, to Mil-
            waukee and St. Paul Railway
            Company (13).

9. Watertown and Madison Railroad Company.
    Incorporated March 17, 1853.
    Quitclaimed October 12, 1858, to Milwaukee, Watertown and Bara-
    boo Valley Railroad Company (8e).

10. Mineral Point Rail Road Company.
    Incorporated April 17, 1852.
    Deeded November 12, 1861, to:
        (a) The Mineral Point Railroad.
            Incorporated November 18, 1861.
            Deeded July 1, 1880, to Chicago, Milwaukee and St. Paul
            Railway Company (23).
            Deed executed September 29, 1880.
            Deed included property of Dubuque, Platteville and Mil-
            waukee Railroad Company (15).

11. Racine and Mississippi Railroad Company.
    Formed March 29, 1856, by consolidation of:
        (a) Racine and Mississippi Rail Road Company (7), a consoli-
            dation of The Rockton and Freeport Railroad Company
            (52), and
        (b) Savanna Branch Railroad Company (7c).
    Wisconsin division deeded to The Western Union Rail Road Com-
    pany (17) June 5, 1867.
    Illinois division deeded to The Western Union Rail Road Company
    (17) August 25, 1868.

12. Ripon and Wolf River Railroad Company.
    Incorporated March 31, 1856.
    Sold October 30, 1863, to Milwaukee and St. Paul Railway Com-
    pany (13).

13. Milwaukee and St. Paul Railway Company.
    Incorporated May 5, 1863.
    Name changed February 11, 1874, to Chicago, Milwaukee and St.
    Paul Railway Company (23).

14. Fox Lake Railroad Company.
    Incorporated March 10, 1859.
    Acquired June 14, 1859:
    (a) Fox Lake and Wisconsin River Railroad Company.
        Incorporated March 5, 1857.
    Acquired by Chicago, Milwaukee and St. Paul Railway Company
    (23) July 3, 1884.
15. Dubuque, Platteville and Milwaukee Railroad Company.
    Incorporated March 15, 1861, as:
    (a) Platteville and Calamine Railroad Company.
    Name changed April 6, 1867, to Dubuque, Platteville and Milwau-
    kee Railroad Company (15).
    Deeded August 6, 1880, to Mineral Point Rail Road Company (10).
16. The Madison and Portage Railroad Company.
    Incorporated February 25, 1870.
    Acquired August 9, 1870:
    (a) Sugar River Valley Railroad Company.
        Incorporated March 29, 1855.
        Deeded August 9, 1870, to The Madison and Portage Rail-
        road Company, in part.
        Remaining property deeded to Chicago, Milwaukee and
        St. Paul Railway Company (23) August 1, 1880.
    Leased March 24, 1871, to Milwaukee and St. Paul Railway Com-
    pany and Chicago, Milwaukee and St. Paul Railway Company,
    until April 16, 1880.
    Consolidated June 19, 1873 (Wisconsin), June 30, 1873 (Illinois) with:
    (b) The Rockford Central Railroad Company (74).
        Incorporated March 9, 1869.
    To form:
    (c) Chicago and Superior Railroad Company June 19, 1873 (Wis-
        consin), and June 30, 1873 (Illinois).
        Deeded April 16, 1880, to Chicago, Milwaukee and St.
        Paul Railway Company (23).
17. The Western Union Rail Road Company.
    Formed (Illinois: January 27, 1866; Wisconsin: February 3, 1866)
    by a consolidation of:
    (a) The Northern Illinois Rail Road Company (54), a consoli-
        dation (June 13, 1865) of:
        (1) The Northern Illinois Railroad Company (54b),
            incorporated February 24, 1859, and
        (2) The Mississippi Railroad Company (63), incorpo-
            rated (Illinois) February 15, 1865.
    and
    (b) The Western Union Railroad Company.
        Formed by a consolidation of (Illinois: January 27, 1866;
        Wisconsin: January 31, 1866):

(1) The Western Union Railroad Company (56), incorporated (Illinois) February 21, 1863, and
(2) The Western Union Railroad Company, incorporated (Wisconsin) April 1, 1863.
Consolidated April 8, 1876, with:
(c) Watertown Rail Road Company.
Incorporated in Illinois, November 14, 1874.

To form:
(d) The Western Union Railroad Company.
Articles of consolidation filed (Illinois) April 8, 1876.
Leased June 24, 1879, to Chicago, Milwaukee and St. Paul
Railway Company for 999 years.
Sold to Chicago, Milwaukee and St. Paul Railway Com-
pany (23), September 1, 1901.

18. The Milwaukee and Northern Railway Company.
Incorporated February 24, 1870.
Acquired July 12, 1870, property of:
(a) Milwaukee and Superior Railroad Company.
Incorporated March 4, 1856.
In 1857 this company built 5.0 miles of track from North
Milwaukee toward Cedarburg but the track was re-
moved in 1858.
Deeded June 9, 1880, to The Milwaukee and Northern Railroad
Company (30).

19. The Oshkosh and Mississippi River Railroad Company.
Incorporated March 30, 1866.
Acquired January 24, 1871:
(a) Winnebago Rail Road Company.
Incorporated April 2, 1853.
Sold February 17, 1893, to Chicago, Milwaukee, and St. Paul Rail-
way Company (23).

20. The Wisconsin Union Railroad Company.
Incorporated April 11, 1866.
Sold December 12, 1872, to Milwaukee and St. Paul Railway Com-
pany (13).

21. Wisconsin Valley Railroad Company.
Incorporated March 16, 1871.
Sold October 19, 1880, to Chicago, Milwaukee and St. Paul Railway
Company (23).

22. Prairie du Chien and McGregor Railway Company.
Incorporated October 10, 1872.
Operated for Chicago, Milwaukee and St. Paul Railway Company,
under contract, July 1, 1873, to October 18, 1894.
Sold October 18, 1894, to Chicago, Milwaukee and St. Paul Rail-
way Company (23).

23. Chicago, Milwaukee and St. Paul Railway Company.
Name of Milwaukee and St. Paul Railway Company (13) changed
to Chicago, Milwaukee and St. Paul Railway Company February
11, 1874.
Deeded December 31, 1927, to:
(a) Chicago, Milwaukee, St. Paul and Pacific Railroad Company.
Incorporated March 31, 1927.
24. Pine River Valley & Stevens Point Rail Road Company.
Incorporated August 5, 1872.
Sold October 12, 1880 (also deed dated December 31, 1880) to
Chicago, Milwaukee and St. Paul Railway Company (23).
25. Necedah and Camp Douglas Rail Road Company.
Incorporated October 13, 1874.
Sold June 25, 1878, to Chicago, Milwaukee and St. Paul Railway
Company (23).
26. Fond du Lac, Amboy & Peoria Railway Company.
A consolidation (articles of consolidation filed: Illinois, June 9,
1875; Wisconsin, January 26, 1876) of:
(a) The Fond du Lac, Amboy & Peoria Railway Company, in-
corporated October 10, 1874, and
(b) Fond du Lac and Whitewater Railway Company, incorpo-
rated December 26, 1874.
Acquired October 4, 1878:
(c) Iron Ridge and Mayville Railroad Company.
Incorporated April 10, 1865.
Sold December 31, 1883, to Chicago, Milwaukee and St. Paul
Railway Company (23).
27. Viroqua Railway Company.
Incorporated May 24, 1878.
Sold to Chicago, Milwaukee and St. Paul Railway Company (23)
deeds dated November 6, 1880, and December 31, 1880.
28. Janesville, Beloit and Rockford Railway Company.
Incorporated March 10, 1880.
Conveyed by deed March 29, 1882, to Chicago, Milwaukee and
St. Paul Railway Company (23).
29. The Menasha & Appleton Railway Company.
Incorporated July 12, 1879.
Conveyed June 10, 1880, to The Milwaukee and Northern Railroad
Company (30).
30. The Milwaukee and Northern Railroad Company.
Incorporated June 5, 1880.
Acquired property of The Menasha & Appleton Railway Company
(29) June 10, 1880.
Consolidated September 12, 1887, in Wisconsin, and September 2,
1887, in Michigan, with The Menominee Branch Railroad Com-
pany (35) and:

(a) Republic Branch Railroad Company (50).
Incorporated September 28, 1881.
To form Milwaukee and Northern Railroad Company (38).

31. The Wisconsin and Michigan Railroad Company.
Incorporated January 31, 1881.
Sold January 6, 1887, to Milwaukee and Northern Railroad Company (38).

32. Chippewa Valley and Superior Railway Company.
Incorporated June 15, 1881.
Sold November 9, 1882, to Chicago, Milwaukee and St. Paul Railway Company (23).

33. Wisconsin, Pittsville and Superior Railway Company.
Incorporated September 2, 1882.
Sold June 30, 1891, to Chicago, Milwaukee and St. Paul Railway Company (23).

34. The La Crosse and Onalaska Short Line Railroad Company.
Incorporated May 22, 1883.
Deeded July 10, 1903, to Chicago, Milwaukee and St. Paul Railway Company (23).

35. The Menominee Branch Railroad Company.
Incorporated July 9, 1883.
Consolidated September 2, 1887 (Michigan), and September 12, 1887 (Wisconsin), with The Milwaukee and Northern Railroad Company (30) and Republic Branch Railroad Company (30a) to form Milwaukee and Northern Railroad Company (38).

36. Markesan & Brandon Railway Company.
Incorporated August 9, 1882.
Deeded July 10, 1903, to Chicago, Milwaukee and St. Paul Railway Company (23).

37. Milwaukee, Dexterville and Northern Railway Company.
Incorporated August 27, 1884.
Sold June 30, 1891, to Chicago, Milwaukee and St. Paul Railway Company (23).

38. Milwaukee and Northern Railroad Company (of Wisconsin and Michigan).
Incorporated in Wisconsin September 12, 1887; in Michigan, September 2, 1887.
A consolidation of:
The Milwaukee and Northern Railroad Company (30).
Republic Branch Railroad Company (30a).
The Menominee Branch Railroad Company (35).
Sold June 26, 1893, to Chicago, Milwaukee and St. Paul Railway Company (23).

39. Oconto and South Western Railway Company.
Incorporated August 6, 1889.

Sold June 17, 1890, to Milwaukee and Northern Railroad Company (38).

40. Milwaukee, Menominee Falls and Western Railway Company.
      Incorporated October 26, 1885.
      Name changed December 11, 1891, to The Milwaukee and Superior Railway Company (45).

41. Lisbon, Necedah & Lake Superior Railway Company.
      Incorporated November 16, 1889.
      Sold June 30, 1891, to Chicago, Milwaukee and St. Paul Railway Company (23).

42. The Wisconsin Midland Railroad Company.
      Incorporated March 4, 1887.
      Deeded November 5, 1897, to Chicago, Milwaukee and St. Paul Railway Company (23).

43. Kickapoo Valley and Northern Railway Company.
      Incorporated June 4, 1889.
      Sold November 25, 1899, to:
      (a) Wisconsin Western Railroad.
            Incorporated November 21, 1899.
            Sold January 26, 1909, to Chicago, Milwaukee and St. Paul Railway Company (23).

44. The Wood County Railroad Company.
      Incorporated June 21, 1883.
      Passed into hands of The Sherry Cameron Company, who conveyed all its real estate property and railroad from Arpin to Vesper to Chicago, Milwaukee and St. Paul Railway Company (23), October 31, 1891.

45. The Milwaukee and Superior Railway Company.
      Name of Milwaukee, Menominee Falls and Western Railway Company (40) changed to The Milwaukee and Superior Railway Company (45) December 11, 1891.
      Sold October 18, 1900, to Chicago, Milwaukee and St. Paul Railway Company (23).

46. Janesville and Southeastern Railway Company.
      Incorporated March 1, 1900.
      Deeded September 18, 1901, to Chicago, Milwaukee and St. Paul Railway Company (23).

47. The Mazomanie, Sauk City and Prairie du Sac Rail Road Company.
      Incorporated December 21, 1880.
      Sold May 28, 1886, to Chicago, Milwaukee and St. Paul Railway Company (23).

48. Eastern LaFayette and Mississippi Railway Company.
      Incorporated March 24, 1871.
      Transferred to Chicago, Milwaukee and St. Paul Railway Company (23) December 29, 1880.

A. The Bird and Wells Lumber Company.
    Incorporated June 16, 1888 (not a common carrier).
    Sold part of logging railroad to Milwaukee and Northern Railroad
    Company (38) September 21, 1892.
B. Marinette, Tomahawk and Western Railway Company.
    Incorporated October 9, 1894.
    Line: Grundy to McInnes sold to Chicago, Milwaukee and St. Paul
    Railway Company (23) September 9, 1903.
C. La Crosse and Southeastern Railway Company.
    Incorporated September 14, 1904.
    Line: Westby to Chaseburg sold to Chicago, Milwaukee, St. Paul
    and Pacific Railroad Company (23a) August 5, 1933.
D. Stange Lumber Company.
    Not a common carrier. Timber operator.
    Line: Star Lake to Knutson sold to Chicago, Milwaukee and St.
    Paul Railway Company (23) 1926.

Michigan Peninsula

49. Ontonagon & Brule River Railroad Company.
    Incorporated September 10, 1880.
    Sold June 20, 1890, to Milwaukee and Northern Railroad Com-
    pany (38).
50. Republic Branch Railroad Company.
    Incorporated September 28, 1881.
    Consolidated September 2, 1887 (Michigan), September 12, 1887
    (Wisconsin) with The Milwaukee and Northern Railroad Com-
    pany (30) and The Menominee Branch Railroad Company (35).
51. The Wisconsin and Michigan Railroad Company (31).
    Incorporated January 31, 1881.
    Deeded January 6, 1887, to The Milwaukee and Northern Railroad
    Company (30).

Illinois

52. The Rockton and Freeport Railroad Company.
    Incorporated February 10, 1853.
    Consolidated February 23, 1854, with Racine, Janesville and Mis-
    sissippi Rail Road Company (7a).
    Name changed February 14, 1855 (Illinois), to Racine and Missis-
    sippi Rail Road Company (7).
53. Savanna Branch Railroad Company.
    Incorporated by articles of association dated January 21, 1851,
    adopted by directors January 23, 1854.

Consolidated March 29, 1856 (approved February 14, 1857) with
Racine and Mississippi Rail Road Company (7).
54. The Northern Illinois Rail Road Company.
Formed by a consolidation June 13, 1865, of:
(a) The Mississippi Railroad Company, incorporated February
15, 1865, and
(b) The Northern Illinois Railroad Company, incorporated February 24, 1859.
Consolidated January 27, 1866 (Illinois), and February 3, 1866
(Wisconsin), with The Western Union Railroad Company (17b).
55. Racine and Mississippi Railroad Company (See 7 and 11).
Formed by a consolidation March 29, 1856, of:
(a) Racine and Mississippi Rail Road Company (7) and
(b) Savanna Branch Railroad Company (53).
Illinois division deeded to The Western Union Rail Road Company
(17) August 25, 1868.
56. The Western Union Railroad Company.
Incorporated February 21, 1863.
Consolidated January 27, 1866, with The Western Union Railroad
Company (Wisconsin) (17d).
57. Chicago and Pacific Railroad Company.
Incorporated February 16, 1865, as:
(a) Atlantic and Pacific Rail Road Company.
Name changed to Chicago and Pacific Railroad Company (63)
April 30, 1872.
Leased April 2, 1880, to Chicago, Milwaukee and St. Paul Railway
Company (23) for 999 years.
Deeded June 13, 1898, the "remaining interests" to Chicago, Mil-
waukee and St. Paul Railway Company (23).
Conveyed in "fee simple" to Chicago, Milwaukee and St. Paul Rail-
way Company by deed dated April 2, 1900.
58. Chicago, Milwaukee and St. Paul Railway Company (Illinois corpo-
ration).
Incorporated April 3, 1872.
Leased to Milwaukee and St. Paul Railway Company (13) Decem-
ber 12, 1872, for 999 years.
The Deering Line transferred to The Chicago, Evanston and Lake
Superior Railway Company (65) by deed dated June 13, 1898.
Deeded "remaining interests" to Chicago, Milwaukee and St. Paul
Railway Company (23) May 5, 1896.
Conveyed in "fee simple" to Chicago, Milwaukee and St. Paul Com-
pany (23) by deed dated April 2, 1900.
59. Illinois, Iowa and Minnesota Railway Company.
Incorporated December 9, 1902.
Leased June 29, 1908, to Chicago, Milwaukee & Gary Railway Com-
pany (61) for 49 years.

Deeded October 20, 1908, to Chicago, Milwaukee & Gary Railway Company (61).

60. Rockford Belt Railway Company.

Incorporated February 4, 1905.

Leased June 29, 1908, to Chicago, Milwaukee & Gary Railway Company (61).

Deeded October 20, 1908, to Chicago, Milwaukee & Gary Railway Company (61).

61. Chicago, Milwaukee & Gary Railway Company.

Incorporated March 2, 1908.

Control acquired January 1, 1922, by Chicago, Milwaukee and St. Paul Railway Company (23).

Deeded March 31, 1930, to Chicago, Milwaukee, St. Paul and Pacific Railroad Company (23a).

62. Central Illinois and Wisconsin Railway Company.

Incorporated October 16, 1880.

Leased March 7, 1882, for 99 years to Chicago, Milwaukee and St. Paul Railway Company (23).

Deeded August 1, 1900, to Chicago, Milwaukee and St. Paul Railway Company (23).

(a) Line: Rockton to Rockford.

Deeded January 11, 1905, to Chicago, Milwaukee and St. Paul Railway Company (23).

(b) Line: Rockford to Davis Junction.

63. The Mississippi Railroad Company.

Incorporated February 15, 1865.

Consolidated June 13, 1865, with The Northern Illinois Railroad Company (54b) to form The Northern Illinois Rail Road Company (54).

64. Warsaw, Rock Island and Galena Railroad Company.

Incorporated February 10, 1849, as:

(a) Warsaw and Rockford Railroad Company.

Acquired, by special act of the Illinois legislature, powers, rights, privileges, and franchises of:

(1) Nauvoo and Warsaw Railroad Company, incorporated February 24, 1847.

Name changed February 21, 1863, to Warsaw, Rock Island and Galena Railroad Company (64).

Sold line between Port Byron and Galena to The Northern Illinois Railroad Company (54b) by deed dated January 27, 1865.

Deeded November 18, 1872, to The Western Union Rail Road Company (56).

65. The Chicago, Evanston and Lake Superior Railway Company.

A consolidation (formed by articles of consolidation dated December 22, 1885, filed December 2, 1890) of:

(a) The Chicago and Evanston Railroad Company, incorporated
February 16, 1861, and

(b) Chicago and Lake Superior Railroad Company, incorporated
October 6, 1883.

Leased December 1, 1887, to Chicago, Milwaukee and St. Paul
Railway Company (23) for 999 years.

Deeded June 14, 1898, "remaining interests" to Chicago, Milwaukee
and St. Paul Railway Company (23).

Conveyed in "fee simple" to Chicago, Milwaukee and St. Paul Railway Company (23) by deed dated April 2, 1900.

66. Cook, Lake and McHenry Counties Railway Company.
Incorporated April 25, 1899.
Deeded July 19, 1901, to Chicago, Milwaukee and St. Paul Rail-
way Company (23).

67. Davenport, Rock Island and Northwestern Railway Company (Illinois).
Incorporated May 8, 1896, as:
(a) Rock Island and Eastern Illinois Railway Company.
Name changed July 30, 1900, to Davenport, Rock Island and
Northwestern Railway Company (67).
Deeded July 30, 1901, to Davenport, Rock Island and Northwestern
Railway Company (Iowa) (92).

68. Moline and Peoria Railway Company.
Incorporated September 25, 1900.
Deeded July 30, 1901, to Davenport, Rock Island and Northwestern
Railway Company (92).

69. Ashdale and Thomson Railway Company.
Incorporated January 30, 1902.
Deeded July 20, 1903, to Chicago, Milwaukee and St. Paul Railway
Company (23).

70. Rochelle and Southern Railway Company.
Incorporated October 1, 1902.
Deeded December 15, 1913, to Chicago, Milwaukee and St. Paul
Railway Company (23).

71. Oglesby and Granville Railway Company.
Incorporated September 14, 1905.
Deeded December 15, 1913, to Chicago, Milwaukee and St. Paul
Railway Company (23).

72. Bureau County Mineral Railway Company.
Incorporated September 12, 1904.
Deeded January 29, 1909, to Rochelle and Southern Railway Com-
pany (70).

73. Chicago, Terre Haute and Southeastern Railway Company of Illinois.
Incorporated November 30, 1910.
Deeded December 22, 1910, to Chicago, Terre Haute & Southeast-
ern Railway Company (Indiana) (81).

74. The Rockford Central Railroad Company.
 Incorporated March 9, 1869.
 Consolidated December 6, 1871, with The Madison and Portage
  Railroad Company (16).
  Articles filed in Wisconsin June 19, 1873.
  Articles filed in Illinois June 30, 1873.
75. The Libertyville Rail-Way Company.
 Incorporated November 27, 1878.
 Conveyed by deed to Chicago, Milwaukee and St. Paul Railway
  Company (23) March 7, 1881.
76. Chicago Suburban Railway Company.
 Incorporated July 13, 1882.
 Leased to The Chicago, Evanston and Lake Superior Railway Com-
  pany (65) June 11, 1888, for 999 years.
 Conveyed by deed to The Chicago, Evanston and Lake Superior
  Railway Company (65) June 13, 1898.

Indiana

(Corporate History of Chicago, Terre Haute & Southeastern
Railway Company)

 Leased June 15, 1921 (effective July 1, 1921), to Chicago, Milwaukee, St. Paul and Pacific Railroad Company (23a) for 999 years.
77. Evansville & Richmond Railroad Company.
 Incorporated September 10, 1886.
 Deeded June 4, 1897, to Evansville & Richmond Railway Company
  (78a).
78. Southern Indiana Railway Company.
 Incorporated May 27, 1897, as:
  (a) Evansville & Richmond Railway Company.
 Name changed December 1, 1897, to Southern Indiana Railway
  Company (78).
 Deeded November 30, 1910, to Chicago, Terre Haute & Southeast-
  ern Railway Company (81).
79. The Bedford Belt Railway Company.
 Incorporated March 30, 1892.
 Deeded December 1, 1910, to Chicago, Terre Haute & Southeastern
  Railway Company (81).
80. The Chicago Southern Railway Company.
 Incorporated September 26, 1904.
 Deeded December 1, 1910, to Chicago, Terre Haute and Southeast-
  ern Railway Company of Illinois (73).
81. Chicago, Terre Haute & Southeastern Railway Company.
 Incorporated November 26, 1910.

Leased June 15, 1921 (effective July 1, 1921), to Chicago, Milwaukee and St. Paul Railway Company for 999 years.

Leased January 1, 1946, to Chicago, Milwaukee, St. Paul and Pacific Railroad Company (23a).

Iowa

82. Dubuque Western Railroad Company.
    Incorporated September 10, 1855.
    Deeded April 30, 1861, to Dubuque Marion and Western Railroad Company (83).

83. Dubuque Marion and Western Railroad Company.
    Incorporated February 13, 1860.
    Sold June 22, 1863, to Dubuque South Western Rail Road Company (84).

84. Dubuque South Western Rail Road Company.
    Incorporated June 26, 1863.
    Deeded February 22, 1881, to Chicago, Milwaukee and St. Paul Railway Company (23).

85. McGregor Western Railway Company.
    Incorporated February 12, 1863.
    Acquired Minnesota Central Railway Company (118) June 22, 1867.
    Deeded August 5, 1867, to Milwaukee and St. Paul Railway Company (13).

86. Dubuque and MacGregor Railway Company.
    Incorporated March 20, 1868.
    Name changed February 18, 1869, to Dubuque and Minnesota Railway Company.
    Name changed March 29, 1871, to Chicago, Dubuque and Minnesota Railroad Company.
    Deeded September 20, 1877, to Dubuque and Minnesota Railroad Company (87b).

87. Chicago Clinton Dubuque and Minnesota Rail Road Company.
    Formed by a consolidation February 28, 1878, of:
    (a) Clinton and Dubuque Railroad Company.
        Incorporated September 13, 1877.
        Deeded March 6, 1878, to Chicago Clinton Dubuque and Minnesota Rail Road Company (87), and
    (b) Dubuque and Minnesota Railroad Company.
        Incorporated September 13, 1877.
        Acquired Chicago, Dubuque and Minnesota Railroad Company (86) September 20, 1877.
    Deeded October 19, 1880, to Chicago, Milwaukee and St. Paul Railway Company (23).

88. Chicago, Clinton and Dubuque Railroad Company.
    Incorporated January 31, 1870, as:
    (a) The Dubuque Bellevue and Mississippi Rail Way Company.
    Name changed November 6, 1871, to Chicago, Clinton and Dubuque Railroad Company (88).
    Deeded September 20, 1877, to Clinton and Dubuque Railroad Company (87a).

89. Chicago, Bellevue, Cascade and Western Railway Company.
    Incorporated January 30, 1878.
    Deeded June 29, 1880, to Chicago Clinton Dubuque and Minnesota Rail Road Company (87).

90. Waukon and Mississippi R. R. Company.
    Incorporated April 15, 1875.
    Deeded June 29, 1880, to Chicago Clinton Dubuque and Minnesota Rail Road Company (87).

91. Waukon & Mississippi Railroad Guaranty Company.
    Incorporated December 9, 1876.
    Deeded June 29, 1880, to Chicago Clinton Dubuque and Minnesota Rail Road Company (87).

92. Davenport, Rock Island and Northwestern Railway Company (Iowa corporation).
    Incorporated January 20, 1884, as Davenport, Rock Island and Railway Bridge Company.
    Name changed January 28, 1895, to Davenport and Rock Island Bridge, Railway and Terminal Company.
    Name changed June 10, 1898, to Davenport, Rock Island and Northwestern Railway Company.
    Leased February 27, 1901, to Chicago, Milwaukee and St. Paul Railway Company (23) and Chicago, Burlington and Quincy Railroad Company for joint possession, use, and operation in common with the grantors for a term of 999 years.

93. Davenport, Clinton and Eastern Railway Company.
    Incorporated April 2, 1895.
    Deeded July 30, 1901, to Davenport, Rock Island and Northwestern Railway Company (92).

94. Des Moines North Western Railway Company.
    Incorporated June 25, 1875, as:
    (a) Des Moines, Adel, and Western Rail Road.
    Name changed October 7, 1880, to Des Moines North Western Railway Company (94).
    Deeded May 19, 1888, to Des Moines and Northwestern Railway Company (98a).

95. Milwaukee, Chicago, Cassville and Montana Railroad Company.
    Incorporated June 22, 1871.
    Sold to Iowa Eastern Railroad Company (104) March 23, 1872.

96. The Cedar Rapids & St. Louis Railroad Company.
    Incorporated March 6, 1871.
    Deeded May 24, 1888, to Chicago, Milwaukee and St. Paul Railway Company (23).
97. St. Louis, Des Moines and Northern Railway Company.
    Incorporated May 21, 1881.
    Sold one-half interest in road from Clive to Des Moines to Des Moines North Western Railway Company (94) January 23, 1882.
    Sold total interest in road from Clive to Waukee to Des Moines North Western Railway Company (94) January 23, 1882.
    Conveyed to Des Moines and Northern Railway Company (98b) November 23, 1889.
98. Des Moines, Northern & Western Railway Company.
    Formed December 28, 1891, by a consolidation of:
    (a) Des Moines and Northwestern Railway Company, incorporated December 6, 1887, and
    (b) Des Moines and Northern Railway Company, incorporated December 23, 1889.
    Deeded to Des Moines, Northern and Western Railroad Company (100); deed not dated, but notarized on February 23, 1895, and February 25, 1895.
99. Maquoketa, Hurstville and Dubuque Rail Road Company.
    Incorporated August 3, 1888.
    Deeded June 15, 1903, to Chicago, Milwaukee and St. Paul Railway Company (23).
100. Des Moines, Northern and Western Railroad Company.
    Incorporated March 15, 1895.
    Sold May 1, 1899, to Chicago, Milwaukee and St. Paul Railway Company (23).
    Second deed dated June 19, 1907, to correct omission in original deed.
101. McGregor and Sioux City Railway Company.
    Incorporated January 23, 1868.
    Deeded May 1, 1869, line from Calmar to Nora Springs to Milwaukee and St. Paul Railway Company (13).
    Name changed November 1, 1869, to McGregor and Missouri River Railway Company (102).
102. McGregor and Missouri River Railway Company.
    Line: Nora Springs to Algona deeded to Milwaukee and St. Paul Railway Company (13) February 1, 1870.
    Remaining property, rights, and franchises deeded to Chicago, Milwaukee and St. Paul Railway Company (23) February 4, 1880.
103. The Sabula, Ackley & Dakota Rail Road Company.
    Incorporated June 25, 1870.
    Deeded July 2, 1872, to Milwaukee and St. Paul Railway Company (13).

104. The Iowa Eastern Railroad Company.
     Incorporated April 1, 1872.
     Acquired property and franchises of Milwaukee, Chicago, Cassville and Montana Railroad Company (95) by deed dated March 23, 1872.
     Deeded March 30, 1882, to Chicago, Milwaukee and St. Paul Railway Company (23).
105. Sioux City and Pembina Railway Company.
     Incorporated January 29, 1876.
     Consolidated October 28, 1879, with Dakota Southern Railroad Company (127a).
106. The Davenport and North Western Railway Company.
     Incorporated July 5, 1876.
     Acquired by deed December 1, 1876:
     (a) Davenport and St. Paul Rail Road Company.
         Incorporated August 26, 1868.
     Deeded July 1, 1879, to Chicago, Milwaukee and St. Paul Railway Company (23).
107. Mason City and Minnesota Railway Company.
     Incorporated July 18, 1870.
     Deeded January 9, 1871, to Milwaukee and St. Paul Railway Company (13).
108. Des Moines Western Railway Company.
     Incorporated August 25, 1871.
     Conveyed to Des Moines, Adel and Western Rail Road (94a), April 17, 1878.
 E. The Minneapolis and St. Louis Railway Company.
     Line: Storm Lake, Iowa, to Rembrandt, Iowa (13.19 miles), sold to Chicago, Milwaukee, St. Paul and Pacific Railroad Company (23a) 1936.

Minnesota

109. The Caledonia and Mississippi Railway Company.
     Incorporated December 3, 1873.
     Sold June 29, 1880, to Chicago Clinton Dubuque and Minnesota Rail Road Company (87).
110. The Caledonia Mississippi and Western Rail Road Company.
     Incorporated April 2, 1879.
     Sold June 29, 1880, to Chicago Clinton Dubuque and Minnesota Rail Road Company (87).
111. Minnesota & North Western Railroad Company.
     Incorporated May 23, 1857.
     Name changed September 17, 1872, to Central Railroad Company of Minnesota (112).

Reorganized July 14, 1873, as Central Railroad Company of Minnesota (112).

Deeded June 1, 1874, to Central Railroad Company of Minnesota (112).

112. Central Railroad Company of Minnesota.

Incorporated May 23, 1857, under name of Minnesota & North Western Railroad Company (111).

Name changed to Central Railroad Company of Minnesota September 17, 1872.

Deeded June 1, 1874, to Central Railroad Company of Minnesota (new company), which was organized by the bondholders on July 14, 1873.

Deeded November 22, 1879, to The Southern Minnesota Railway Company (113).

113. The Southern Minnesota Railway Company.

Incorporated March 9, 1877.

A reorganization of Southern Minnesota Railroad Company (114).

Acquired Southern Minnesota Railroad Company (114) by deed dated March 3, 1877.

Acquired Central Railroad Company of Minnesota (112) by deed dated November 22, 1879.

Acquired The Southern Minnesota Railway Extension Company (115) by deed dated January 1, 1880.

Sold April 13, 1880, to Chicago, Milwaukee and St. Paul Railway Company (23).

114. Southern Minnesota Railroad Company.

Incorporated March 2, 1855, as:

(a) The Root River Valley and Southern Minnesota Rail Road ‘ Company.

Name changed to Southern Minnesota Railroad Company (114), May 23, 1857.

Sold March 4, 1864, to Southern Minnesota Railroad Company.

A reorganization of the old company.

Acquired by The Southern Minnesota Railway Company (113) by deed dated March 3, 1877.

115. The Southern Minnesota Railway Extension Company.

Incorporated January 21, 1878.

Deeded January 1, 1880, to The Southern Minnesota Railway Company (113).

116. Milwaukee & Minnesota Railroad Company.

Incorporated May 24, 1859.

Sold March 5, 1867, to Milwaukee and St. Paul Railway Company (13).

117. Minneapolis and Cedar Valley Railroad Company.

Incorporated March 1, 1856.

Conveyed March 10, 1862, to Minneapolis, Faribault and Cedar Valley Railroad Company (118a).

118. Minnesota Central Railway Company.

Incorporated March 10, 1862, as:

(a) Minneapolis, Faribault and Cedar Valley Railroad Company. Name changed to Minnesota Central Railway Company (118) February 1, 1864.

Deeded June 22, 1867, to McGregor Western Railway Company (85), except land grants.

Line: Austin to Iowa state line conveyed to Milwaukee and St. Paul Railway Company (13) February 15, 1870.

119. Minnesota Midland Railway Company.

Incorporated January 15, 1867.

Deeded February 12, 1883, to Chicago, Milwaukee and St. Paul Railway Company (23).

120. Minnesota and Pacific Railroad Company.

Incorporated May 22, 1857.

Sold to The Saint Paul and Pacific Railroad Company (121a), March 10, 1862.

121. The Saint Paul and Chicago Railway Company.

Incorporated March 10, 1862, as:

(a) The Saint Paul and Pacific Railroad Company.

Name of branch south of St. Paul changed to The Saint Paul and Chicago Railway Company (121), March 20, 1867.

Sold, except land grants, January 3, 1872, to Milwaukee and St. Paul Railway Company (13).

122. Hastings and Dakota Railway Company.

Incorporated February 20, 1857, as:

(a) Hastings, Minnesota River and Red River of the North Railroad Company.

Name changed March 5, 1867, to Hastings and Dakota Railway Company (122).

Sold and deeded June 29, 1872, line: Hastings to Glencoe, Minnesota, except land grants, to Milwaukee and St. Paul Railway Company (13).

Sold January 1, 1880, line: Glencoe to Ortonville, Minnesota, except land grants, to Chicago, Milwaukee and St. Paul Railway Company (23).

Deeded January 1, 1880, completed road and proposed line in Dakota to Chicago, Milwaukee and St. Paul Railway Company (23).

Quitclaimed December 28, 1882, railway between Minneapolis and Benton to Chicago, Milwaukee and St. Paul Railway Company (23).

123. The Stillwater and Hastings Railway Company.

Incorporated April 9, 1880.

Sold March 1, 1882, to Chicago, Milwaukee and St. Paul Railway
Company (23).
124. Duluth, St. Cloud, Glencoe & Mankato Railway Company.
Incorporated April 19, 1888, as:
(a) The Duluth Glencoe and Southwestern Railway Company.
Name changed to Duluth, St. Cloud, Glencoe & Mankato Railway
Company (124), January 10, 1900.
Deeded to Chicago, Milwaukee and St. Paul Railway Company
(23), December 21, 1910.
125. Fargo & St. Louis Air Line Rail Road Company.
Incorporated July 14, 1883.
Deeded September 10, 1883, to Fargo and Southern Railway Com-
pany (128).

Dakotas

126. Dakota and Great Southern Railway Company.
Incorporated August 14, 1883.
Deeded October 1, 1886, to Chicago, Milwaukee and St. Paul Rail-
way Company (23).
127. Sioux City and Dakota Rail Road Company.
Formed October 28, 1879, by a consolidation of:
(a) Dakota Southern Railroad Company.
Incorporated April 1, 1872, and
(b) Sioux City and Pembina Railway Company (105).
Incorporated January 29, 1876.
Deeded February 22, 1881, to Chicago, Milwaukee and St. Paul
Railway Company (23).
128. Fargo and Southern Railway Company.
Incorporated June 25, 1881.
Sold and deeded June 16, 1885, to Chicago, Milwaukee and St.
Paul Railway Company (23).
129. Chicago, Milwaukee and St. Paul Railway Company of South Dakota.
Incorporated August 25, 1906.
Conveyed by deed to Chicago, Milwaukee and St. Paul Railway
Company of Washington (141), December 26, 1908.
130. White River Valley Railway Company.
Incorporated January 19, 1905.
Deeded April 18, 1910, to Chicago, Milwaukee and St. Paul Rail-
way Company (23).

Montana

131. Montana Railroad Company (Jawbone Railroad).
Incorporated September 4, 1894.

Deeded January 15, 1910, to Chicago, Milwaukee and Puget Sound Railway Company (142).

Deeded December 24, 1912, to Chicago, Milwaukee and St. Paul Railway Company (23).

132. Gallatin Light, Power & Railway Company.
Incorporated April 5, 1892.
Deeded December 18, 1897, to Bozeman Street Railway Company.
Acquired by Gallatin Valley Electric Railway (133a), November 27, 1909.

133. Gallatin Valley Railway Co.
Incorporated March 23, 1908, as:
(a) Gallatin Valley Electric Railway.
Name changed to Gallatin Valley Railway Co. (133) September 9, 1910.
Acquired by Chicago, Milwaukee and St. Paul Railway Company (23) December 31, 1918.

134. Bozeman Street Railway Company.
Incorporated December 1, 1897.
Conveyed by deed to Gallatin Valley Electric Railway (133a) November 27, 1909.

135. Great Falls Terminal Railway Company.
Incorporated July 3, 1912.
Conveyed by deed to Chicago, Milwaukee and St. Paul Railway Company (23) November 5, 1914.

136. Chicago, Milwaukee and St. Paul Railway Company of Montana.
Incorporated December 18, 1905.
Sold December 26, 1908, to Chicago, Milwaukee and St. Paul Railway Company of Washington (141).

137. Big Black Foot Railway Company.
Incorporated January 13, 1910.
Conveyed by deed December 30, 1916, to Chicago, Milwaukee and St. Paul Railway Company (23).

Idaho

138. Idaho & Washington Northern Railroad.
Incorporated April 1, 1907.
Deeded January 25, 1916, to Chicago, Milwaukee and St. Paul Railway Company (23).

139. Chicago, Milwaukee and St. Paul Railway Company of Idaho.
Incorporated January 23, 1906.
Sold December 26, 1908, to Chicago, Milwaukee and St. Paul Railway Company of Washington (141).

140. Idaho and Western Railway Company.
Incorporated December 27, 1909.

Sold and deeded December 6, 1912, to Chicago, Milwaukee and Puget Sound Railway Company (142).

Washington

141. **Chicago, Milwaukee and St. Paul Railway Company of Washington.**
Incorporated October 13, 1905, as:
(a) The Pacific Railway Company.
Name changed to Chicago, Milwaukee and St. Paul Railway Company of Washington (141) January 10, 1906.
Name changed to Chicago, Milwaukee and Puget Sound Railway Company (142) January 2, 1909.

142. **Chicago, Milwaukee and Puget Sound Railway Company.**
Name of Chicago, Milwaukee and St. Paul Railway Company of Washington (141) changed to Chicago, Milwaukee and Puget Sound Railway Company (142) January 2, 1909.
Deeded January 1, 1909, one-half interest in line: Black River Junction to Tacoma to Oregon and Washington Railroad Company.
Deeded December 24, 1912, to Chicago, Milwaukee and St. Paul Railway Company (23).

143. **Bellingham Bay and British Columbia Rail Road Company.**
Incorporated June 21, 1883.
Deeded October 21, 1912, to Bellingham and Northern Railway Company (145).

144. **Bellingham Terminals & Railway Company.**
Incorporated May 3, 1909.
Deeded to Bellingham and Northern Railway Company (145) October 21, 1912.

145. **Bellingham and Northern Railway Company.**
Incorporated October 17, 1912.
Deeded December 31, 1918, to Chicago, Milwaukee and St. Paul Railway Company (23).

146. **Milwaukee Terminal Railway Company.**
Incorporated April 8, 1908.
Chicago, Milwaukee and St. Paul Railway Company (23) acquired control December 31, 1918.

147. **Tacoma Eastern Railroad Company.**
Incorporated July 14, 1890.
Acquired December 31, 1918, by Chicago, Milwaukee and St. Paul Railway Company (23).

148. **Seattle, Port Angeles and Lake Crescent Railway Company.**
Incorporated November 27, 1911, as:
(a) Port Ludlow, Port Angeles and Lake Crescent Railway.
Name changed December 19, 1911, to Seattle, Port Angeles and Lake Crescent Railway Company (148).

Conveyed by deed to Seattle, Port Angeles & Western Railway
Company (149) January 25, 1915.

149. Seattle, Port Angeles & Western Railway Company.
Incorporated January 20, 1915.
Acquired December 31, 1918, by Chicago, Milwaukee and St. Paul
Railway Company (23).

150. Pacific & Eastern Railway Company.
Incorporated October 22, 1906.
Deeded May 1, 1913, to Puget Sound & Willapa Harbor Railway
Company (152).

151. Olympia Southern Railway Company.
Incorporated July 1, 1913.
Deeded September 16, 1913, to Puget Sound & Willapa Harbor
Railway Company (152).

152. Puget Sound & Willapa Harbor Railway Company.
Incorporated April 9, 1913.
Deeded December 31, 1918, to Chicago, Milwaukee and St. Paul
Railway Company (23).

153. Priest Rapids Railway Company.
Incorporated July 11, 1907.
Sold January 8, 1910, to Chicago, Milwaukee and Puget Sound
Railway Company (142).

154. Seattle Southeastern Railway Company.
Incorporated September 13, 1906.
Sold February 13, 1912, to Chicago, Milwaukee and Puget Sound
Railway Company (142).

Appendix B

CHRONOLOGICAL HISTORY OF DEVELOPMENT OF THE MILWAUKEE ROAD WITH KEY TO CONSTRUCTING AND PREDECESSOR COMPANIES

Year	TERMINI From	TERMINI To	Road Miles	Key to Constructing Company Named in Corporate History Index
1847			None	1
1850	Milwaukee, Wis.	Elm Grove, Wis.	10.00	1
1851	Elm Grove, Wis.	Waukesha, Wis.	10.70	1
1852	Waukesha, Wis.	Milton, Wis.	41.50	1
1853	Milton Jct., Wis.	Janesville, Wis.	8.10	2
	Milton, Wis.	Stoughton, Wis.	18.50	3
1854	Stoughton, Wis.	Madison, Wis.	15.50	3
	Chestnut St., Milwaukee, Wis.	North Milwaukee, Wis.	6.29	4
1855	North Milwaukee, Wis.	Horicon, Wis.	44.68	4
	Horicon, Wis.	Waupun, Wis.	15.00	5
	Brookfield, Wis.	Watertown, Wis.	31.80	6
	Racine, Wis.	Delavan, Wis.	46.73	7
1856	Delavan, Wis.	Beloit, Wis.	22.58	7
	Horicon, Wis.	Portage, Wis.	47.59	4
	Waupun, Wis.	Ripon, Wis.	15.00	5
	Madison, Wis.	Boscobel, Wis.	71.00	3
1857	Milwaukee, Wis.	Cedarburg, Wis.	5.00	18a
	Ripon, Wis.	Berlin, Wis.	12.00	5
	Boscobel, Wis.	Prairie du Chien, Wis.	28.00	3
	Janesville, Wis.	Monroe, Wis.	34.00	3
	Portage, Wis.	New Lisbon, Wis.	43.03	8
	Watertown, Wis.	Columbus, Wis.	18.80	8
	Watertown, Wis.	Sun Prairie, Wis.	24.48	9
	Mineral Point, Wis.	Illinois State Line	31.28	10
	Wis.-Ill. State Line	Warren, Ill.	1.01	10
	Beloit, Wis.	Durand, Ill.	16.60	11
1858	New Lisbon, Wis.	North La Crosse, Wis.	61.30	8
	Durand, Ill.	Davis, Ill.	4.40	11
1859	Davis, Ill.	Freeport, Ill.	14.10	11
	Farley, Ia.	Sand Springs, Ia.	13.80	82

Year	TERMINI From	TERMINI To	Road Miles	Key to Constructing Company Named in Corporate History Index
1860	Sand Springs, Ia.	Anamosa, Ia.	16.90	82
	Rush Lake Jct., Wis.	Omro, Wis.	9.56	12
1861	Kittredge, Ill.	Lanark, Ill.	3.60	54b
	Freeport, Ill.	Kittredge, Ill.	15.40	54b
1862	Lanark, Ill.	Savanna, Ill.	17.90	54b
	Port Byron, Ill.	Rock Island Jct., Ill. (East Moline)	9.66	64
1863	Anamosa, Ia.	Springville, Ia.	10.70	83
	Springville, Ia.	Marion, Ia.	10.80	84
1864	Columbus, Wis.	Portage, Wis.	28.20	13
	Milwaukee, Wis.	Brookfield,[1] Wis.	13.00	13
	Mendota, Minn.	Westcott,[2] Minn.	6.70	118
1865	Savanna, Ill.	Thomson, Ill.	9.68	54b
	Thomson, Ill.	Fulton, Ill.	7.27	54
	Extension at Berlin, Wis.		.30	13
	Marion, Ia.	Cedar Rapids, Ia.	5.00	84
	Mendota, Minn.	Minneapolis, Minn.	9.00	118
	Westcott, Minn.	Faribault, Minn.	39.80	118
1866	Fulton, Ill.	Port Byron, Ill.	21.74	54
	Fox Lake,[3] Wis.	Fox Lake Jct., Wis.	2.70	14
	Faribault, Minn.	Owatonna, Minn.	15.20	118
	McGregor, Ia.	Cresco, Ia.	62.30	85
	La Crescent, Minn.	Houston, Minn.	18.00	114
	Mendota, Minn.	St. Paul, Minn.	5.56	118
1867	Houston, Minn.	Rushford, Minn.	10.00	114
	Owatonna, Minn.	State Line, Minn.	60	13
	State Line, Minn.	Cresco, Ia.	22.35	13
1868	Calamine, Wis.	Belmont, Wis.	9.60	10a
	Omro, Wis.	Winneconne, Wis.	5.33	13
	Rushford, Minn.	Lanesboro, Minn.	19.78	114
	Hastings, Minn.	Carver, Minn.	47.60	122
	Stock Yards, Milwaukee, Wis.	Merrill Park, Milwaukee, Wis.	.80	13
1869	Merrill Park, Milwaukee, Wis.	North Milwaukee, Wis.	6.17	13
	Sun Prairie, Wis.	Madison, Wis.	12.00	13
	St. Paul, Minn.	Hastings, Minn.	20.12	121
	Ramsey, Minn.	Albert Lea, Minn.	21.50	114
	Calmar, Ia.	Nora Springs, Ia.	64.00	101
	Conover, Ia.	Decorah, Ia.	8.77	13
1870	Madison, Wis.	Portage, Wis.	33.01	16
	Eagle, Wis.	Elkhorn, Wis.	16.59	17
	Belmont, Wis.	Platteville, Wis.	7.54	15
	North Milwaukee, Wis.	Cedarburg, Wis.	13.70	18

[1] Via West Allis.
[2] Now Radio Center.
[3] Operated line as horse car line from 1866 to 1884.

| Year | TERMINI | | Road Miles | Key to Constructing Company Named in Corporate History Index |
	From	To		
1870	Sabula, Ia.	Preston, Ia.	20.00	103
	Nora Springs, Ia.	Algona, Ia.	61.60	102
	Austin, Minn.	State Line, Minn.	11.34	118
	Hastings, Minn.	Red Wing, Minn.	21.00	121
	Winona, Minn.	Weaver, Minn.	19.40	121
	Albert Lea, Minn.	Winnebago, Minn.	41.50	114
	Lanesboro, Minn.	Ramsey, Minn.	54.50	114
	Mason City, Ia.	State Line, Minn.	27.95	107
1871	Ripon, Wis.	Oshkosh, Wis.	19.08	19
	Reed St., Milwaukee, Wis.	Ill. State Line	37.59	20
	Cedarburg, Wis.	Hilbert Jct., Wis.	63.30	18
	Hilbert Jct., Wis.	Menasha, Wis.	15.70	18
	Preston, Ia.	Delmar Jct., Ia.	13.00	103
	River Jct., Minn.	State Line, Ia.	24.93	86
	Dubuque, Ia.	State Line, Iowa-Wis.	92.08	86
	Red Wing, Minn.	Weaver, Minn.	43.20	121
1872	Savanna, Ill., Island Extension		2.00	17
	Delmar Jct., Ia.	Marion, Ia.	54.00	103
	Davenport, Ia.	Delaware, Ia.	89.33	106a
	Eldredge, Ia.	Maquoketa, Ia.	32.38	106a
	Elk River Jct., Ia.	Midland Jct., Ia.	2.00	88
	Western Ave., Chicago	Wis.-Ill. State Line	45.40	58
	Dubuque, Ia.	Sabula Jct., Ia.	44.10	88a
	Turkey River Jct., Ia.	Garber, Ia.	15.14	86
	Carver, Minn.	Glencoe, Minn.	26.70	122
	Beulah,[4] Ia.	Stulta, Ia.	14.49	104
	Winona, Minn.	Bridge Jct., Minn.	24.40	121
	Sioux City, Ia.	Vermillion, S. D.	29.58	127a
1872–73	Watertown, Wis.	Hampton Coal Mine	4.25	17c
1873	Hilbert Jct., Wis.	Green Bay, Wis.	27.00	18
	Tomah, Wis.	Grand Rapids,[5] Wis.	45.04	21
	Halsted St., Chicago	Elgin, Ill.	36.07	57
	Delaware, Ia.	Fayette, Ia.	38.92	106a
	McGregor, Ia.	Prairie du Chien, Wis.	1.26	22
	Vermillion, S. D.	Yankton, S. D.	26.20	127a
1874	Green Bay, Wis.	Fort Howard, Wis.	0.80	18
	Grand Rapids,[6] Wis.	Wausau, Wis.	42.70	21
	North La Crosse, Wis.	La Crosse, Wis.	1.30	23
	Wells, Minn.	Mankato, "D" St., Minn.	38.90	112
	"D" St., Mankato, Minn.	Maple St., Mankato, Minn.	1.10	112

[4] Built narrow gauge.
[5] Now Wisconsin Rapids.
[6] Wisconsin Rapids.

Year	TERMINI From	To	Road Miles	Key to Constructing Company Named in Corporate History Index
1875	Elgin, Ill.	Byron, Ill.	52.40	57
1876	Wausau, Wis.	One mile north, Wis.	1.00	21
	Lone Rock, Wis.	Richland Center,⁷ Wis.	16.22	24
	La Crosse, Wis.	La Crescent, Minn.	2.69	23
	Elk Point, S. D.	Calliope, Ia.	25.90	105
1877	New Lisbon, Wis.	Necedah, Wis.	13.02	25
	Iron Ridge, Wis.	Fond du Lac, Wis.	29.52	26a
	Waukon, Ia.	Waukon Jct., Ia.	22.95	90
	Wabasha, Minn.	Theilman, Minn.	20.21	119
1878	Viroqua Jct., Wis.	Melvina, Wis.	12.91	27
	Glencoe, Minn.	Montevideo, Minn.	82.60	122
	Algona, Ia.	Hull, Ia.	100.00	23
	Winnebago, Minn.	Jackson, Minn.	43.00	115
	Theilman, Minn.	Zumbrota, Minn.	40.00	119
	Calliope, Ia.	Sioux Falls, S. D.	44.70	105
	Waukee, Ia.	Adel, Ia.	6.70	94a
	Garber, Ia.	Wadena, Ia.	29.60	87b
1879	Springville, Ia.	Paralta, Ia.	2.10	23
	Melvina, Wis.	Viroqua, Wis.	19.26	27
	One mile north of Wausau, Wis.	Merrill, Wis.	12.53	21
	Adel, Ia.	Panora, Ia.	21.00	94a
	Bellevue, Ia.	Cascade, Ia.	35.77	89
	Caledonia, Minn.	Preston, Minn.	43.77	110
	Reno, Minn.	Caledonia, Minn.	14.00	109
	Montevideo, Minn.	Ortonville, Minn.	45.30	122
	Hull, Ia.	Marion Jct., S. D.	61.40	23
	Marion Jct., S. D.	Running Water, S. D.	62.34	23
	Jackson, Minn.	Flandreau, S. D.	95.00	115
1880	Janesville, Wis.	Beloit, Wis.	13.86	28
	Brodhead, Wis.	Albany, Wis.	7.00	23
	Menasha, Wis.	Appleton, Wis.	4.70	29
	Byron, Ill.	Kittredge, Ill.	27.50	23
	Savanna, Ill.	Sabula Jct., Ia.	3.00	23
	Fayette, Ia.	Jackson Jct., Ia.	25.12	23
	Midland Jct., Ia.	Clinton, Ia.	8.05	23
	S. Minneapolis, Minn.	Benton Jct., Minn.	28.00	23
	Milbank, S. D.	3 miles south of Wilmot, S. D.	14.00	23
	Marion Jct., S. D.	Mitchell, S. D.	44.00	23
	Rock Valley, S. D.	Hudson, S. D.	9.38	23
	Minneapolis, Minn.	St. Paul, Minn.	8.30	23
	Flandreau, S. D.	Madison, S. D.	29.00	23
	Ortonville, Minn.	Bristol, S. D.	69.45	23
1881	Monroe, Wis.	Shullsburg, Wis.	33.74	23
	Mazomanie, Wis.	Prairie du Sac, Wis.	10.37	23

⁷ Narrow gauge—wooden rail.

Year	TERMINI From	To	Road Miles	Key to Constructing Company Named in Corporate History Index
1881	Menasha, Wis.	Neenah, Wis.	0.80	30
	Fort Howard, Wis.	One mile south of Stiles, Wis.	24.40	31
	Bristol, S. D.	Aberdeen, S. D.	38.80	23
	3 miles south of Wilmot, S. D.	11 miles north of Wilmot, S. D.	14.00	23
	Mitchell, S. D.	Chamberlain, S. D.	67.11	23
	Aberdeen, S. D.	Ellendale, N. D.	40.51	23
	Aberdeen, S. D.	Ashton, S. D.	32.60	23
	Rockton, Ill.	Rockford, Ill.	15.15	62
	Rondout, Ill.	Libertyville, Ill.	3.00	58
	Sioux Falls, S. D.	Sioux Falls Jct., S. D.	32.13	23
	Madison, S. D.	Howard, S. D.	21.70	23
	Panora, Ia.	Fonda, Ia.	70.00	94
	Lakeland, Minn.	Lakeland Jct., Minn.	2.00	123
1882	One mile south of Stiles, Wis.	Coleman, Wis.	15.10	31
	Beaver Dam Jct., Wis.	Beaver Dam, Wis.	2.09	23
	Wabasha, Minn.	Eau Claire, Wis.	48.30	32
	Red Cedar Jct., Wis.	Cedar Falls, Wis.	20.67	32
	Galewood, Ill.	Dunning, Ill.	2.98	76
	Des Moines, Ia.	Clive, Ia.	6.78	97
	Clive, Ia.	Waukee, Ia.	7.50	97
	Clive, Ia.	Boone, Ia.	34.97	97
	Marion, Ia.	Council Bluffs, Ia.	260.00	23
	Wadena, Ia.	West Union, Ia.	13.60	23
	Spencer, Ia.	Okoboji, Ia.	17.06	23
	Northfield, Minn.	Cannon Jct., Minn.	31.98	23
	Mitchell, S. D.	Letcher, S. D.	15.00	23
	Ontonagon, Mich.	McKeever, Mich.	20.00	49
	Stillwater, Minn.	Hastings,[8] Minn.	24.78	23
	Yankton, S. D.	Scotland, S. D.	26.88	23
1883	Babcock, Wis.	Pittsville Jct., Wis.	8.12	33
	Pittsville Jct., Wis.	Vesper, Wis.	8.42	33
	Pittsville Jct., Wis.	Pittsville, Wis.	1.85	33
	Eau Claire, Wis.	Chippewa Falls, Wis.	14.30	23
	Coleman, Wis.	Wausaukee, Wis.	22.20	31
	North La Crosse, Wis.	Onalaska, Wis.	3.76	34
	Okoboji, Ia.	Spirit Lake, Ia.	3.12	23
	Aberdeen, S. D.	Ipswich, S. D.	26.00	23
	Ashton, S. D.	Letcher, S. D.	80.93	23
	Howard, S. D.	Woonsocket, S. D.	38.70	23
1884	In Chippewa Falls, Wis.[9]		1.63	23
	Wausaukee, Wis.	Amberg, Wis.	9.86	31
	Ellis Jct., Wis.	Marinette, Wis.	20.40	31

[8] Except 2 miles from Lakeland Jct., to Lakeland.
[9] Acquired ½ interest from Chippewa Falls & Western Ry. Co.

| Year | TERMINI | | Road Miles | Key to Constructing Company Named in Corporate History Index |
	From	To		
1884	Marinette, Wis.	Menominee, Mich.	1.80	35
	Brandon, Wis.	Markesan, Wis.	11.49	36
	Ortonville, Minn.	Fargo, N. D.	116.97	128
	Cedar Rapids, Ia.	Ottumwa, Ia.	90.81	23
	In Decorah, Ia.		.27	23
1885	Chicago, Ill.	Calvary, Ill.	10.09	65a
	10th Ave., Clinton, Ia.	CRI&P Switch, Ia.	.04	23
1886	Clinton St., Milwaukee, Wis.	8th Street, Milwaukee, Wis.	1.15	23
	Amberg, Wis.	Menominee River, Wis.	20.12	31
	Calvary, Ill.	Evanston, Ill.	1.60	65
	Glencoe, Minn.	Hutchinson, S. D.	13.45	23
	Andover, S. D.	Harlem, S. D.	55.64	126
	Stulta, Ia.	Elkader, Ia.	4.71	23
	Ellendale, N. D.	Edgeley, N. D.	23.77	23
	Ipswich, S. D.	Bowdle, S. D.	31.00	23
	Scotland, S. D.	Mitchell, S. D.	47.67	23
	Tripp, S. D.	Armour, S. D.	20.45	23
	Madison, S. D.	Lake Preston, S. D.	30.12	126
	Sioux City, Ia.	Rodney, Ia.	37.27	23
	Deering Line, Ill.		0.84	58
	Lake Preston, S. D.	Bristol, S. D.	72.90	126
1887	Davenport, Ia.	West Davenport (within city)[10]		23
	Dexterville, Wis.	Progress, Wis.	15.00	37
	Merrill, Wis.	Minocqua, Wis.	54.23	23
	Mather, Wis.	Alva, Wis.	13.63	23
	Albany, Wis.	New Glarus, Wis.	15.78	23
	Eureka, S. D.	Orient, S. D.	67.00	23
	Lake Preston, S. D.	Bristol, S. D.	72.90	126
	In Running Water, S. D.		.51	23
	Ottumwa, Ia.	Kansas City, Mo.	202.54	23
	Rodney, Ia.	Manilla, Ia.	53.00	23
	Menominee River, Mich.	Champion, Mich.	56.70	50
1888	Alva, Wis.	Goodyear, Wis.	2.54	23
	Lapham Jct., Wis.	Zeda, Wis.	3.00	23
	Progress, Wis.	2½ miles north, Wis.	2.50	37
	Evanston, Ill.	Wilmette, Ill.	1.70	23
	In Decorah, Ia.		.96	23
	Marion Cut Off, Ia.		2.19	23
1889	2½ miles north of Progress, Wis.	Lynn, Wis.	4.95	37
	Green Bay, Wis.	East River, Wis.	.61	38
	Oconto Jct., Wis.	Oconto, Wis.	11.94	39
1889	Vesper, Wis.	Arpin, Wis.	5.50	44
	McKeever, Mich.	Sidnaw, Mich.	26.00	49

[10] Acquired joint ownership interest from Davenport, Iowa and Dakota R. R. Co.

Year	TERMINI		Road Miles	Key to Constructing Company Named in Corporate History Index
	From	To		
1889	Hopkins, Minn.	Lake Minnetonka, Minn.	7.84	23
	Maquoketa, Ia.	Hurstville, Ia.	2.23	99
1889–91	Wausaukee, northwesterly, Wis.		2.78	A
1890	Elnora, Ind.	Westport, Ind.	102.00	77
	Necedah, Wis.	Babcock, Wis.	20.00	41
	Lynn, Wis.	2 miles northwest, Wis.	2.16	41
	In Fond du Lac, Wis.		2.30	42
	Granville, Wis.	Sussex, Wis.	11.50	40
1891	Bellingham, Wash.	Sumas, Wash.	22.81	143
1892	Wauzeka, Wis.	Soldiers Grove, Wis.	34.25	43
	Wausaukee, Wis.	Girard Jct., Wis.	14.87	38
	2 mi. NW of Lynn, Wis.	Romadka, Wis.	3.18	23
	N. P. Depot, Bozeman, Mont.	Grand Ave. and Main St., Bozeman, Mont.	1.30	132
	Grand Ave. & Main St., via 9th St., Bozeman, Mont.	College, Bozeman, Mont.	1.20	132
1893	Bedford, Ind.	Oolitic, Ind.	4.00	79
	11 miles north of Wilmot, S. D.	Sisseton, S. D.	9.20	23
	Channing, Mich.	Sidnaw, Mich.	47.05	38
1895	Minocqua, Wis.	Star Lake, Wis.	18.80	23
1896	Nekoosa Spur, Wis.		2.92	23
	Ringling, Mont.	Dorsey, Mont.	3.63	131
1897	Sussex, Wis.	North Lake, Wis.	8.58	45
	Soldiers Grove, Wis.	La Farge, Wis.	17.72	43
	Lombard, Mont.	Summit, Mont.	49.40	131
1898	Prairie du Chien, Wis.	No. McGregor, Ia.	1.50	23
1899	Fonda, Ia.	Spencer, Ia.	43.48	23
	Rockwell City, Ia.	Storm Lake, Ia.	38.58	23
1900	Sumas, Wash.	Glacier, Wash.	21.21	143
	Storm Lake, Ia.	Rembrandt, Ia.	13.19	E
	Kelso, Mich.	Crystal Falls, Mich.	6.87	23
	Bowdle, S. D.	Glenham and Evarts, S. D.	40.91	23
	Napa, S. D.	Platte, S. D.	82.00	23
	Summit, Mont.	Harlowton, Mont.	45.50	131
	Libertyville, Ill.	State Line, Ill.-Wis.	29.33	66
	Janesville, Wis.	State Line, Ill.-Wis.	34.57	46
1900–02	Tacoma, Wash.	La Grande, Wash.	36.60	147
1900–03	Elnora, Ind. (Including Branch Lines)	Terre Haute, Ind.	97.00	78
1901	Browns, Ia.	Green Island, Ia.	11.90	23
	Otis, Wis.	Heinman, Wis.	7.60	23
	Grundy, Wis.	McInnes, Wis.	19.25	B
	Grand Ave. & Main St. via 7th Ave., Bozeman, Mont.	College, Bozeman, Mont.	1.28	134

Year	TERMINI From	To	Road Miles	Key to Constructing Company Named in Corporate History Index
1903	Terre Haute, Ind.	Ill.-Ind. State Line	34.00	78
	Preston, Minn.	Isinours, Minn.	4.46	23
	Cutler Jct., Wis.	Boulder Jct., Wis.	1.05	23
	Zumbrota, Minn.	Faribault, Minn.	33.47	23
	Muscatine, Ia.	Rutledge, Ia.	76.30	23
	Davenport Connection, Ia.		0.64	23
	Ashdale, Ill.	Ebner, Ill.	15.10	69
	Steward Jct., Ill.	Burlington St., Mendota, Ill.	22.08	70
	5th St., Mendota, Ill.	Ladd, Ill.	12.28	70
	CB&Q RR Crossing, Ill.	Seatonville Jct., Ill.	2.26	70
	Oglesby, Ill.	Granville, Ill.	10.50	71
	Hampton, Wash.	Lyndon, Wash.	5.31	143
	Track at Linton, N. D.		1.10	23
	Eureka, S. D.	Linton, N. D.	48.43	23
	Farmington, Minn.	LeSueur Center, Minn.	35.37	23
	Woonsocket, S. D.	Wessington Springs, S. D.	15.58	23
1904	La Grande, Wash.	Park Jct., Wash.	13.02	147
	Kapowsin, Wash.	Electron, Wash.	2.02	147
	Park Jct., Wash.	Ashford, Wash.	5.71	147
	Chicago Heights, Ill.	Ill.-Ind. State Line	114.00	80
	Heinman, Wis.	Gleason, Wis.	3.56	23
	LeSueur Center, Minn.	Benning, Minn.	20.11	23
	Ladd, Ill.	Cherry, Ill.	3.13	72
	Harlowton, Mont.	Lewistown, Mont.	61.96	131
	Westby, Wis.	Chaseburg, Wis.	15.82	C
1905	Park Jct., Wash.	Mineral, Wash.	4.10	147
	Rockford, Ill.	Aurora, Ill.	59.00	59
	Joliet, Ill.	Delmar, Ill.	37.00	59
	Chamberlain, S. D.	Oacoma, S. D.	3.90	130
	Oacoma, S. D.	Reliance, S. D.	12.90	130
	Reliance, S. D.	Presho, S. D.	23.50	130
	Velasco, Wis.	Cutler Jct., Wis.	15.24	23
	McInnes, southward, Wis.		1.55	23
	Armour, S. D.	Stickney, S. D.	20.67	23
	Boulder Jct., Wis.	Papoose, Wis.	11.50	23
1906	Presho, S. D.	Murdo, S. D.	35.48	130
	Mineral, Wash.	Tilton, Wash.	6.50	147
	Mineral, Wash.	Ladd, Wash.	2.97	147
	McInnes, southward, Wis.		6.33	23
	Evarts Jct., Cut Off, S. D.		0.56	23
	Glenham, S. D.	E. Bank of Mo. River, S. D.	11.72	23
	Renner, S. D.	Madison, S. D.	33.08	23
1907	Tilton, Wash.	Glenavon, Wash.	2.70	147
	Murdo, S. D.	Creston, S. D.	110.97	130
	Creston, S. D.	Farmingdale, S. D.	10.39	130

Year	TERMINI From	To	Road Miles	Key to Constructing Company Named in Corporate History Index
1907	Farmingdale, S. D.	Rapid City, S. D.	22.11	130
	Green, Mich.	White Pine, Mich.	11.16	23
	Albert Lea, Minn.	St. Clair, Minn.	39.46	124
	McGuires, Idaho	Newport, Wash.	44.10	138
	Coleman, Idaho	Clagstone, Idaho	6.54	138
	P. & E. Jct., Wash.	Willapa, Wash.	8.56	150
1908	Salsich Jct., Wash.	McKenna, Wash.	15.30	147
	Boulder Jct., Wis.	Blue Bill, Mich.	14.50	23
	Mont. State Line	Harlowton, Mont.	333.30	136
	Lombard, Mont.	Colorado Jct., Mont.	93.70	136
	Cliff Jct., Mont.	Deer Lodge, Mont.	26.40	136
	Deer Lodge, Mont.	State Line, Idaho	188.50	136
	State Line, Idaho	State Line, Wash.	98.10	139
	Mo. River, S. D.	State Line, N. D.	91.76	129
	State Line, N. D.	State Line, Mont.	102.53	129
1909	Tacoma, Milwaukee Waterway, Wash.		0.07	146
	Elm Grove, connection, Wis.		0.51	23
	Idaho State Line	Maple Valley, Wash.	307.87	142
	Tacoma Jct., Wash.	Tacoma, Wash.	2.08	142
	Black River Jct., Wash.	Tacoma Jct., Wash.	26.30	142
	3 Track Transfer Landing (Seattle), Wash.		0.14	146
	Cedar Co. Landing (Ballard), Wash.		0.11	146
	Front St. 3 Track Landing (Tacoma), Wash.		3.68	146
	Commerce St. (Tacoma), Wash.		0.24	146
1909–10	Bagley Jct., Wash.	Selleck, Wash.	2.30	154
	Bellingham, Wash.	Squalicum, Wash.	5.80	144
1910	Cowlitz Jct., Wash.	Morton, Wash.	8.01	147
	McKenna, Wash.	Helsing Jct., Wash.	33.23	142
	Selleck, Wash.	Enumclaw Jct., Wash.	13.79	142
	Warden; Wash.	Marcellus, Wash.	46.96	142
	St. Maries, Idaho	Purdue, Idaho	50.00	142
	Bovill, Idaho	Elk River, Idaho	20.71	142
	Moreau Jct., S. D.	Isabel, S. D.	59.40	142
	Trail City, S. D.	Dupree, S. D.	83.20	142
	McLaughlin, S. D.	New England, N. D.	132.64	142
	Newport, Wash.	Ione, Wash.	51.60	138
	Three Forks, Mont.	Bozeman, Mont.	38.32	133
	Bozeman Hot Springs, Mont.	Salesville, Mont.	4.98	133
1910–12	Tracks at Seattle, Wash.		1.48	142
1911	Dupree, S. D.	Faith, S. D.	23.41	142
	Cedar Falls, Wash.	Everett, Wash.	54.84	142

Year	TERMINI From	To	Road Miles	Key to Constructing Company Named in Corporate History Index
1911	In Tacoma, Commerce St., Jct. with N. P. Ry., Wash.		1.23	146
	Ione, Wash.	Metaline Falls, Wash.	9.50	138
	Belgrade, Mont.	Belgrade Jct., Mont.	5.41	133
1912	Tanwax Jct., Wash.	Western Jct., Wash.	2.09	147
	Tiflis, Wash.	Neppel, Wash.	15.57	142
	Beverly, Wash.	Hanford, Wash.	45.91	142
	Lewistown, Mont.	Hilger, Mont.	17.85	142
	Center St., Spokane, Wash.	N. P. Xing, Spokane, Wash.	1.73	142
	Dishman, Wash.	Coeur D'Alene, Idaho	25.43	140
	Plummer, Idaho	Manito, Wash.	19.92	140
	Pt. Blakely, 1 Track Landing, Wash.		0.09	146
	Eagle Harbor, 1 Track Landing, Wash.		0.17	146
	Bellingham, 3 Track Landing, Wash.		0.22	146
1913	Bozeman, Mont.	Menard, Mont.	25.00	133
	Bonner, Mont.	Potomac, Mont.	11.47	137
	In Great Falls, Mont.		3.45	135
	New Jct. at Cologne, (for Benton Cut Off), Minn.		1.73	23
1914	Maytown, Wash.	Doty, Wash.	38.50	152
	Crystal Falls, Mich.	Iron River, Mich.	20.92	23
	Lewistown, Mont.	Grass Range, Mont.	35.98	23
	Lewistown, Mont.	Great Falls, Mont.	136.85	23
	Hilger, Mont.	Roy, Mont.	25.10	23
	Roy Jct., Mont.	Winifred, Mont.	23.10	23
	Colorado Jct., Mont.	Cliff, Mont.	14.30	23
	Merrill, Wis.	New Wood, Wis.	18.25	23
	Port Angeles, Wash.	Majestic, Wash.	23.60	148
1915	Doty, Wash.	P. & E. Jct.	16.06	152
	Willapa, Wash.	Raymond, Wash.	2.75	152
	Snoqualmie Tunnel Line, Wash.		4.64	23
	Tacoma, Bouffelin Mill Landing, Wash.		0.20	146
	Tacoma, N. W. Woodenware Landing, Wash.		0.07	146
	Pt. Townsend, Wash.		0.39	146
1915–16	Port Angeles, Wash.	Discovery Jct., Wash.	38.20	149
1916	Goshen, Wash.	Welcome, Wash.	11.29	145
	Great Falls, Mont.	Agawam, Mont.	66.70	23
1916–17	Majestic, Wash.	Twin Rivers, Wash.	6.77	149

	TERMINI		Road	Key to Construct-ing Company Named in Cor-porate History
Year	From	To	Miles	Index
1917	Grass Range, Mont.	Winnett, Mont.	22.98	23
	Colorado Jct., Mont.	Butte, Mont.	1.11	23
1918	Bensenville, Ill.	Techny, Ill., Cut Off	3.70	23
1923	Fordson Jct., Minn.	Fordson, Minn.	4.45	23
1926	Hollendale Line, Minn.		6.94	23
	Bonner Jct., Mont.	Sunset, Mont.	13.25	23
1930	At Morton, Wash.		.51	23a
1934	Sunset, Mont.	Cottonwood, Mont.	13.75	23a
1941	Sauk City, Wis.	Badger Ordnance, Wis.	9.00	23a
1943	Granger, Ia.	Woodward Jct., Ia.	7.14	23a

DECREASES IN MILES OF ROAD

Year	From	To	Miles of Road
1895	Mather, Wis.	Goodyear, Wis.	16.01
	Lapham Jct., Wis.	Zeda, Wis.	2.66
1901	Menomonie, Wis.	Cedar Falls, Wis.	4.35
1902	Wabasha, Minn.	Midland Jct., Minn.	6.00
1904	South Stillwater, Minn.	Stillwater, Minn.	2.16
1907	At Glenham, S. D.		3.18
1909	Evarts Jct., S. D.	Evarts, S. D.	5.30
1918	Madrid, Ia.	Phildia, Ia.	2.97
	Rock Valley, Ia.	Hudson, Ia.	9.38
	Northfield, Minn.	Cannon Falls, Minn.	13.87
	North La Crosse, Wis.	Onalaska, Wis.	3.62
	Milwaukee, Wis., Cement Line		1.06
	Pittsville Jct., Wis.	Arpin, Wis.	13.70
1919	Boulder Jct., Wis.	Papoose, Wis.	10.80
1920	Magenta, Wis.	Central Jct. (Chippewa Falls), Wis.	11.15
	Coleman, Idaho	Clagstone Junction, Idaho	6.15
1922	Woodward, Iowa	Phildia, Ia.	4.37
1923	Lynn, Wis.	Romadka, Wis.	5.23
	Gratiot, Wis.	Warren, Wis.	7.10
	Cogswell, N. D.	Harlem, N. D.	5.11
1926	The New Wood Line	(Remainder, Merrill-New Wood taken up 1943)	3.36
1926–29	Boulder Jct., Wis.	Michigan State Line	9.00
1926	Wausaukee, Wis.	Girard Jct., Wis.	17.70
	Bluebill, Mich.	Wisconsin State Line	4.00
	Tomah, Wis.	Norway, Wis.	12.71

LINES ABANDONED, WITH AND WITHOUT ABANDONMENT
OF SERVICE

January 13, 1928, to December 31, 1946

Year	From	To	Miles of Road
1928	Tanwax Jct., Wash.	Tidewater, Wash.	2.08
1930	Springfield, S. D.	Running Water, S. D.	6.57
	Troy Center, Wis.	Eagle, Wis.	4.97
	Worthington, Ia.	Farley, Ia.	6.90
	Kirkland, Ill.	Camp Grant, Ill. (CM&G RR)	15.14
1931	Disque, Wash.	Deep Creek, Wash.	15.30
	Long Grove, Ia.	De Witt, Ia.	9.01
	Velasco, Wis.	Boulder Jct., Wis.	16.99
	Lynn, Wis.	Lindsey, Wis.	6.79
1932	Elkhorn, Wis.	Troy Center, Wis.	11.48
	Ontonagon, Mich.	White Pine, Mich.	19.35
	Hopkins, Minn.	Lake Minnetonka, Minn.	7.29
1933	Bellevue, Ia.	Cascade, Ia. (Narrow Gauge)	35.72
	Dexterville, Wis.	Lindsey, Wis.	15.71
1934	Wabasha, Minn.	Zumbro Falls, Minn.	35.50
	Babcock, Wis.	Norway, Wis.	15.84
1935	Farmington, Minn.	Hastings, Minn.	17.67
	Doering, Wis.	Kalinke, Wis.	14.90
1936	Brampton, N. D.	Cogswell, N. D.	7.49
	Scotland Jct., S. D.	Tyndall, S. D.	11.16
1937	Kapowsin Jct., Wash.	Electron, Wash.	2.01
1938	Turkey River Jct., Ia.	West Union, Ia.	58.25
	Eldridge Jct., Ia.	Long Grove, Ia.	3.15
	Menno, S. D.	Scotland, S. D.	8.95
1939	Wauzeka, Wis.	La Farge, Wis.	52.13
1940	Oxford Jct., Ia.	Dixon, Ia.	22.72
	Sauk City, Wis.	Prairie du Sac, Wis.	.92
	Coal Creek Branch, Ind.	Windsor Jct., Ind.	5.26
1941	Renner, S. D.	Colton, S. D. (Wholly Owned)	14.05
	Colton, S. D.	Wentworth, S. D. (Jointly Owned with G. N.)	15.60
1943	Blackhawk, Ind.	Hymera, Ind.	8.52
	Otis, Wis., to Gleason to	Doering, Wis.	16.79
	Goshen Jct., Wash.	Kulshan, Wash.	11.29
	Merrill, Wis.	New Wood, Wis.	14.89
	* Vernita, Wash.	Hanford, Wash.	25.10
	Hymera, Ind.	Hawton, Ind.	4.34
1944	Woodruff, Wis.	Star Lake, Wis.	16.84

* Sold to U. S. Government account, being in a war project.

LINES ABANDONED SINCE JANUARY 13, 1928,
ACCOUNT CO-ORDINATION

Service Not Abandoned:

Year	From	To	Miles of Road
1933	Oconto Jct., Wis.	Oconto, Wis. (Using C&NW)	10.16
	Bagley Jct., Wash.	Enumclaw, Wash. (Using NP)	10.30
1934	Ayres, Ill.	Ebner, Ill. (Using CB&Q)	8.49
1935	Chehalis, Wash.	Dryad, Wash. (Using NP)	18.55
	Colton, S. D.	Madison, S. D. (Using GN)	16.21
1937	Cannon Jct., Minn.	Cannon Falls, Minn. (Using CGW)	14.04
	Lewistown, Mont.	Choteau, Mont. (Using GN)	16.11
1940	Monroe, Wash.	Lowell, Wash. (Using GN)	13.58
1945	Spokane Bridge, Wash.	Coeur d'Alene, Idaho (Using GN)	6.12
	Birmingham, Mo.	Suburban Jct., Kansas City, Mo. (Using line jointly with CRI&P RR Co.)	6.34

CHICAGO, MILWAUKEE, ST. PAUL AND PACIFIC RAILROAD COMPANY

Finance and Accounting Department

Common Stock 1874 to 1945

Year Ending December 31	Common Stock Outstanding December 31	Dividends Declared During Year	Rate (%)	Paid On
1874	$15,399,261.00			
1875	15,399,261.00			
1876	15,399,261.00			
1877	15,404,261.00			
1878	15,404,261.00			
1879	15,404,261.00	$385,106.42	2½	$15,404,261.00
1880	15,404,261.00	539,149.14	3½	15,404,261.00
		539,149.14	3½	15,404,261.00
1881	20,404,261.00	539,149.14	3½	15,404,261.00
		539,149.14	3½	15,404,261.00
1882	27,904,261.00	714,149.14	3½	20,404,261.00
		714,149.14	3½	20,404,261.00
1883	30,904,261.00	976,649.14	3½	27,904,261.00
		1,081,649.14	3½	30,904,261.00
1884	30,904,261.00	1,081,649.14	3½	30,904,261.00
		1,081,649.14	3½	30,904,261.00
1885	30,904,261.00	463,563.92	1½	30,904,261.00
		772,606.53	2½	30,904,261.00
1886	30,904,261.00	772,606.53	2½	30,904,261.00
		772,606.53	2½	30,904,261.00
1887	39,680,361.00	772,606.53	2½	30,904,261.00
		974,569.02	2½	38,982,761.00
1888	39,868,961.00	974,569.02	2½	38,982,761.00

Year Ending June 30	Common Stock Outstanding June 30	Dividends Declared During Year	Rate (%)	Paid On
1889	$39,868,961.00			
1890	39,868,961.00			
1891	46,027,261.00			
1892	46,027,261.00			
1893	46,027,261.00	$919,153.82	2	$45,957,691.00
		919,153.82	2	45,957,691.00
1894	46,027,261.00	919,153.82	2	45,957,691.00
		919,153.82	2	45,957,691.00
1895	46,027,261.00	920,545.22	2	46,027,261.00
		460,272.61	1	46,027,261.00
1896	46,027,261.00	460,272.61	1	46,027,261.00
		920,545.22	2	46,027,261.00
1897	46,026,600.00	920,545.22	2	46,027,261.00
		920,545.22	2	46,027,261.00
1898	46,026,600.00	1,380,798.00	3	46,026,600.00
		1,150,665.00	2½	46,026,600.00
1899	46,923,600.00	1,150,665.00	2½	46,026,600.00
		1,168,315.00	2½	46,732,600.00
1900	47,146,600.00	1,173,090.00	2½	46,923,600.00
		1,178,440.00	2½	47,137,600.00
1901	55,821,800.00	1,178,665.00	2½	47,146,600.00
		1,414,458.00	3	47,148,600.00
1902	58,183,900.00	1,674,654.00	3	55,821,800.00
		1,745,517.00	3	58,183,900.00
1903	58,183,900.00	2,327,356.00	4	58,183,900.00
		2,036,436.50	3½	58,183,900.00
1904	58,183,900.00	2,036,436.50	3½	58,183,900.00
		2,036,436.50	3½	58,183,900.00
1905	58,183,900.00	2,036,436.50	3½	58,183,900.00
		2,036,436.50	3½	58,183,900.00
1906	58,183,900.00	2,036,436.50	3½	58,183,900.00
		2,036,436.50	3½	58,183,900.00
1907	82,910,000.00	2,036,436.50	3½	58,183,900.00
		2,901,850.00	3½	82,910,000.00
1908	83,107,100.00	2,908,748.50	3½	83,107,100.00
		2,908,748.50	3½	83,107,100.00
1909	115,946,000.00	2,908,633.00	3½	83,103,800.00
		2,908,633.00	3½	83,103,800.00
1910	115,946,000.00	4,058,110.00	3½	115,946,000.00
		4,058,110.00	3½	115,946,000.00
1911	115,946,000.00	4,058,110.00	3½	115,946,000.00
		4,058,110.00	3½	115,946,000.00
1912	115,946,000.00	4,058,110.00	3½	115,946,000.00
		2,898,650.00	2½	115,946,000.00
1913	115,946,000.00	2,898,650.00	2½	115,946,000.00
		2,898,650.00	2½	115,946,000.00
1914	116,850,100.00	2,898,517.50	2½	115,940,700.00
		2,921,252.50	2½	116,850,100.00

Year Ending June 30	Common Stock Outstanding June 30	Dividends Declared During Year	Rate (%)	Paid On
1915	117,356,100.00	2,921,252.50	2½	116,850,100.00
		2,921,252.50	2½	116,850,100.00
1916	117,406,000.00	2,347,122.00	2	117,356,100.00
		2,935,150.00	2½	117,406,000.00

Year Ending December 31	Common Stock Outstanding December 31	Dividends Declared During Year	Rate (%)	Paid On
1916	$117,406,000.00	$2,935,150.00	2½	$117,406,000.00
1917	117,406,000.00	2,935,150.00	2½	117,406,000.00
		2,348,120.00	2	117,406,000.00
1918	117,406,000.00			
1919	117,406,000.00			
1920	117,406,000.00			
1921	117,406,000.00			
1922	117,406,000.00			
1923	117,406,000.00			
1924	117,406,000.00			
1925	117,406,000.00			
1926	117,406,000.00			
1927	117,406,000.00			
1928	137,709,450.19			
1929	138,429,595.78			
1930	136,649,794.62			
1931	136,973,393.23			
1932	136,838,627.55			
1933	136,710,933.17			
1934	105,175,913.33			
1935	105,158,522.37			
(No par value) 1936	105,133,461.24			
1937	105,127,554.26			
1938	105,100,524.72			
1939	105,098,771.19			
1940	105,102,990.28			
1941	105,088,721.00			
1942	105,088,833.54			
1943	105,104,384.45			
1944	105,099,757.40			
* 1945	212,321,400.00			

* No par value—stated value, $100 per share.

CHICAGO, MILWAUKEE, ST. PAUL AND PACIFIC RAILROAD COMPANY
Finance and Accounting Department
Preferred Stock 1874 to 1945

Year Ending December 31	Preferred Stock Outstanding December 31	Dividends Declared During Year	Rate (%)	Paid On
1874	$12,274,483.00	$859,213.81	7	$12,274,483.00
1875	12,274,483.00			

Year Ending December 31	Preferred Stock Outstanding December 31	Dividends Declared During Year	Rate (%)	Paid On
1876	12,274,483.00	2,148,034.53	17½	12,274,483.00
1877	12,279,483.00	429,606.90	3½	12,274,483.00
1878	12,279,483.00	429,781.90	3½	12,279,483.00
		429,781.90	3½	12,279,483.00
		429,781.90	3½	12,279,483.00
1879	12,279,483.00	429,781.90	3½	12,279,483.00
		429,781.90	3½	12,279,483.00
1880	12,404,483.00	429,781.90	3½	12,279,483.00
		429,781.90	3½	12,279,483.00
1881	14,401,483.00	434,156.90	3½	12,404,483.00
		453,266.90	3½	12,950,483.00
1882	16,447,483.00	504,051.90	3½	14,401,483.00
		528,691.90	3½	15,105,483.00
1883	16,540,983.00	575,661.90	3½	16,447,483.00
		578,934.40	3½	16,540,983.00
1884	16,540,983.00	578,934.40	3½	16,540,983.00
		578,934.40	3½	16,540,983.00
1885	21,540,900.00	578,934.40	3½	16,540,983.00
		578,934.40	3½	16,540,983.00
1886	21,555,900.00	753,931.50	3½	21,540,900.00
		753,931.50	3½	21,540,900.00
1887	21,596,900.00	754,456.50	3½	21,555,900.00
		755,891.50	3½	21,596,900.00
1888	21,610,900.00	755,891.50	3½	21,596,900.00
		540,272.50	2½	21,610,900.00

Year Ending June 30	Preferred Stock Outstanding June 30	Dividends Declared During Year	Rate (%)	Paid On
1889	21,610,900.00	432,218.00	2	21,610,900.00
1890	21,839,900.00	540,272.50	2½	21,610,900.00
		756,556.50	3½	21,615,900.00
1891	22,198,900.00	764,396.50	3½	21,839,900.00
		767,756.50	3½	21,935,900.00
1892	24,364,900.00	776,961.50	3½	22,198,900.00
		795,651.50	3½	22,732,900.00
1893	25,767,900.00	852,771.50	3½	24,364,900.00
		898,586.50	3½	25,673,900.00
1894	25,973,900.00	901,876.50	3½	25,767,900.00
		907,336.50	3½	25,923,900.00
1895	26,156,900.00	909,086.50	3½	25,973,900.00
		909,716.50	3½	25,991,900.00
1896	26,895,900.00	915,491.50	3½	26,156,900.00
		930,821.50	3½	26,594,900.00
1897	29,054,900.00	941,356.50	3½	26,895,900.00
		955,006.50	3½	27,285,900.00
1898	31,818,400.00	1,016,921.50	3½	29,054,900.00
		1,087,324.00	3½	31,066,400.00
1899	35,595,400.00	1,113,644.00	3½	31,818,400.00
		1,165,286.50	3½	33,293,900.00

Year Ending June 30	Preferred Stock Outstanding June 30	Dividends Declared During Year	Rate (%)	Paid On
1900	40,454,900.00	1,245,839.00	3½	35,595,400.00
		1,270,689.00	3½	36,305,400.00
1901	44,658,400.00	1,415,921.50	3½	40,454,900.00
		1,435,136.50	3½	41,003,900.00
1902	46,682,400.00	1,563,044.00	3½	44,658,400.00
		1,601,404.00	3½	45,754,400.00
1903	47,724,400.00	1,633,884.00	3½	46,682,400.00
		1,657,999.00	3½	47,371,400.00
1904	48,374,400.00	1,670,354.00	3½	47,724,400.00
		1,675,254.00	3½	47,864,400.00
1905	49,327,400.00	1,693,104.00	3½	48,374,400.00
		1,707,419.00	3½	48,783,400.00
1906	49,654,400.00	1,726,459.00	3½	49,327,400.00
		1,736,434.00	3½	49,612,400.00
1907	49,808,400.00	1,737,904.00	3½	49,654,400.00
		1,741,159.00	3½	49,747,400.00
1908	49,976,400.00	1,744,344.00	3½	49,838,400.00
		1,746,199.00	3½	49,891,400.00
1909	115,931,900.00	1,749,174.00	3½	49,976,400.00
		1,749,174.00	3½	49,976,400.00
1910	115,931,900.00	4,057,616.50	3½	115,931,900.00
		4,057,616.50	3½	115,931,900.00
1911	115,931,900.00	4,057,616.50	3½	115,931,900.00
		4,057,616.50	3½	115,931,900.00
1912	115,931,900.00	4,057,616.50	3½	115,931,900.00
		4,057,616.50	3½	115,931,900.00
1913	115,931,900.00	4,057,616.50	3½	115,931,900.00
		4,057,616.50	3½	115,931,900.00
1914	115,845,800.00	4,054,603.00	3½	115,845,800.00
		4,054,603.00	3½	115,845,800.00
1915	115,845,800.00	4,054,603.00	3½	115,845,800.00
		4,054,603.00	3½	115,845,800.00
1916	115,845,800.00	4,054,603.00	3½	115,845,800.00
		4,054,603.00	3½	115,845,800.00

Year Ending December 31	Preferred Stock Outstanding December 31	Dividends Declared During Year	Rate (%)	Paid On
1916	115,845,800.00	4,054,603.00	3½	115,845,800.00
1917	115,845,800.00	4,054,603.00	3½	115,845,800.00
		4,054,603.00	3½	115,845,800.00
1918	115,845,800.00			
1919	115,845,800.00			
1920	115,845,800.00			
1921	115,845,800.00			
1922	115,845,800.00			
1923	115,845,800.00			
1924	115,845,800.00			
1925	115,845,800.00			

Year Ending December 31	Preferred Stock Outstanding December 31	Dividends Declared During Year	Rate (%)	Paid On
1926	115,845,800.00			
1927	115,845,800.00			
1928	119,175,000.00			
1929	119,238,800.00			
1930	119,280,100.00			
1931	119,293,900.00			
1932	119,296,300.00			
1933	119,307,300.00			
1934	119,307,300.00			
1935	119,307,300.00			
1936	119,307,300.00			
1937	119,307,300.00			
1938	119,307,300.00			
1939	119,307,300.00			
1940	119,307,300.00			
1941	119,307,300.00			
1942	119,307,300.00			
1943	119,307,300.00			
1944	119,307,300.00			
1945	112,174,000.00			
	(par value — $100)			

CHICAGO, MILWAUKEE, ST. PAUL AND PACIFIC RAILROAD COMPANY

Finance and Accounting Department

Funded Debt 1874 to 1945

Year	Funded Debt Issued in Hands of Public	Miles of Road Owned	Funded Debt per Mile
December 31			
1874	$27,100,500.00	1,399.00	$19,371.34
1875	27,129,000.00	1,400.00	19,377.86
1876	30,010,500.00	1,400.00	21,436.07
1877	29,954,500.00	1,412.00	21,214.24
1878	32,088,500.00	1,512.00	21,222.55
1879	41,349,500.00	2,231.00	18,534.07
1880	67,172,000.00	3,775.00	17,793.91
1881	79,059,000.00	4,217.00	18,747.69
1882	89,635,500.00	4,520.00	19,830.86
1883	96,272,000.00	4,760.00	20,225.21
1884	100,254,000.00	4,804.00	20,868.86
1885	101,470,000.00	4,921.00	20,619.79
1886	111,658,000.00	5,298.00	21,075.50
1887	115,871,000.00	5,669.95	20,435.98
1888	118,221,000.00	5,678.15	20,820.34
June 30			
1889	123,027,000.00	5,678.15	21,666.74
1890	123,515,000.00	5,656.83	21,834.67

Year	Funded Debt Issued in Hands of Public	Miles of Road Owned	Funded Debt per Mile
1891	124,105,000.00	5,721.40	21,691.37
1892	123,199,000.00	5,721.40	21,533.02
1893	121,981,500.00	5,724.13	21,310.05
1894	134,810,200.00	6,147.77	21,928.31
1895	134,703,000.00	6,168.73	21,836.42
1896	134,615,000.00	6,150.75	21,885.95
1897	132,329,000.00	6,153.83	21,503.52
1898	130,001,500.00	6,153.83	21,125.30
1899	127,630,500.00	6,153.50	20,741.12
1900	122,256,000.00	6,422.67	19,035.07
1901	122,058,500.00	6,596.32	18,504.03
1902	119,785,500.00	6,603.85	18,138.74
1903	118,610,500.00	6,682.57	17,749.23
1904	117,747,500.00	6,906.48	17,048.84
1905	116,264,500.00	6,911.62	16,821.60
1906	117,772,500.00	7,043.54	16,720.64
1907	117,541,500.00	7,186.69	16,355.44
1908	117,078,500.00	7,301.32	16,035.25
1909	115,765,500.00	7,296.55	15,865.79
1910	147,809,500.00	7,296.55	20,257.45
1911	192,860,654.66	7,296.43	26,432.19
1912	227,599,154.66	7,296.40	31,193.35
1913	299,554,754.66	9,424.91	31,783.30
1914	331,227,454.66	9,681.38	34,212.83
1915	356,146,654.66	9,720.67	36,638.08
1916	356,157,254.66	9,856.77	36,133.26
December 31			
1916	356,076,254.66	9,856.77	36,125.04
1917	380,829,254.66	9,950.35	38,272.95
1918	381,961,254.66	9,917.80	38,512.70
1919	379,255,254.66	10,289.37	36,858.94
1920	409,762,087.85	10,267.63	39,908.15
1921	410,877,347.65	10,268.85	40,012.01
1922	418,548,880.40	10,263.73	40,779.41
1923	431,065,115.42	10,251.43	42,049.27
1924	440,807,115.42	10,251.38	42,999.78
1925	447,764,115.42	10,251.75	43,676.85
1926	441,367,615.42	10,237.79	43,111.61
1927	438,071,115.42	10,237.35	42,791.46
1928	459,378,289.00	10,235.35	44,881.54
1929	463,822,789.00	10,234.87	45,317.90
1930	484,399,977.27	10,284.69	47,099.13
1931	478,838,046.30	10,280.81	46,575.91
1932	482,110,199.60	10,253.22	47,020.37
1933	477,523,527.66	10,169.96	46,954.32
1934	476,443,181.97	10,135.00	47,009.69
1935	478,548,901.25	10,091.86	47,419.30
1936	480,097,718.00	10,038.44	47,825.93
1937	484,604,853.95	10,036.53	48,284.10

Year	Funded Debt Issued in Hands of Public	Miles of Road Owned	Funded Debt per Mile
1938	482,688,891.44	9,962.17	48,452.18
1939	481,576,175.86	9,909.98	48,595.07
1940	482,375,594.36	9,873.28	48,856.67
1941	479,629,024.53	9,839.72	48,744.17
1942	473,581,050.11	9,838.96	48,133.24
1943	467,177,194.86	9,773.20	47,801.87
1944	470,035,890.07	9,758.80	48,165.34
1945	191,155,833.74	9,748.72	19,608.30

CHICAGO, MILWAUKEE, ST. PAUL AND PACIFIC RAILROAD COMPANY

Finance and Accounting Department

Investment in Road and Equipment and Material and Supplies, Net Railway Operating Income and Rate of Return on Investment 1874 to 1945

Year	Road-Equipment and Material and Supplies	Net Railway Operating Income	Rate of Return on Investment (%)
December 31			
1874	$55,293,303.83	$3,081,900.73	5.57
1875	55,259,773.34	3,085,389.93	5.58
1876	56,521,947.40	3,100,847.36	5.49
1877	57,086,019.27	3,574,460.70	6.26
1878	58,888,311.22	3,659,454.24	6.21
1879	62,429,417.04	4,539,024.82	7.27
1880	99,750,398.98	5,343,692.93	5.36
1881	121,102,393.98	6,707,530.52	5.54
1882	139,127,061.94	8,200,652.65	5.89
1883	147,316,707.86	9,881,785.53	6.71
1884	150,910,099.05	9,611,369.85	6.37
1885	155,771,991.49	9,900,801.57	6.36
1886	167,947,600.90	10,158,139.07	6.05
1887	180,301,600.79	10,039,430.18	5.57
1888	182,658,923.39	7,490,377.17	4.10
June 30			
1889	185,822,362.29	8,874,173.81	4.78
1890	188,038,670.93	9,232,610.56	4.91
1891	191,937,951.21	9,137,724.42	4.76
1892	193,929,854.20	11,468,503.84	5.91
1893	197,854,899.66	11,486,946.88	5.81
1894	212,667,281.80	11,213,618.30	5.27
1895	212,911,050.48	10,291,616.10	4.83
1896	213,677,246.78	13,005,020.84	6.09
1897	214,506,001.91	11,909,228.91	5.55
1898	216,461,196.72	12,988,097.07	6.00
1899	220,974,428.70	14,347,795.67	6.49
1900	221,797,578.45	13,463,854.99	6.07
1901	227,506,123.98	14,391,509.33	6.33

Year	Road-Equipment and Material and Supplies	Net Railway Operating Income	Rate of Return on Investment (%)
1902	232,727,934.37	15,416,229.80	6.62
1903	240,164,459.98	16,064,563.34	6.69
1904	244,183,604.65	16,453,744.90	6.74
1905	245,173,732.31	17,590,072.80	7.17
1906	255,597,962.19	18,978,721.51	7.43
1907	265,138,666.12	18,862,047.64	7.11
1908	271,186,367.12	17,369,365.56	6.40
1909	280,595,864.64	17,877,672.81	6.37
1910	288,187,636.27	16,043,200.96	5.57
1911	297,193,683.78	13,189,713.72	4.44
1912	307,084,345.34	11,242,002.51	3.66
1913	529,962,973.46	26,449,302.64	4.99
1914	560,966,383.05	26,516,375.49	4.73
1915	572,998,553.84	24,159,627.11	4.22
1916	591,981,557.49	29,778,047.27	5.03
December 31			
1916	604,105,907.33	29,607,212.00	4.90
1917	619,267,420.93	20,148,334.00	3.25
1918	643,268,765.07	3,643,191.00	.57
1919	649,994,419.60	3,134,850.00	.48
1920	678,647,183.03	5,819,216.00 *	—
1921	677,291,906.35	5,117,329.40	.76
1922	685,108,176.39	13,284,244.57	1.94
1923	704,275,232.86	20,167,713.01	2.86
1924	705,725,352.20	18,972,106.19	2.69
1925	719,270,118.90	16,873,635.97	2.35
1926	718,424,518.83	18,394,932.74	2.56
1927	722,043,772.69	14,072,934.50	1.95
1928	695,420,923.92	29,119,053.52	4.19
1929	714,202,876.95	26,274,323.35	3.68
1930	732,928,539.43	15,954,547.86	2.18
1931	734,249,817.94	8,334,406.19	1.14
1932	733,040,172.67	518,115.99 *	—
1933	729,755,638.19	8,597,319.49	1.18
1934	691,100,678.90	6,539,053.99	.95
1935	689,564,752.74	4,723,982.78	.69
1936	690,616,004.45	9,461,358.38	1.37
1937	703,557,868.06	8,790,661.48	1.25
1938	706,273,392.56	5,274,538.90	.75
1939	711,125,606.43	8,124,194.40	1.14
1940	720,134,670.91	13,845,644.47	1.92
1941	729,317,638.87	28,181,975.28	3.86
1942	734,556,733.14	34,504,654.37	4.70
1943	741,977,210.88	50,668,953.82	6.83
1944	764,057,866.94	32,709,518.77	4.28
1945	820,175,306.19	26,582,330.27	3.24

* Deficit.

CHICAGO, MILWAUKEE, ST. PAUL AND PACIFIC RAILROAD COMPANY

Finance and Accounting Department

Road and Equipment Per Mile of Road Owned, and Net Railway Operating Income Per Mile of Road Owned 1874 to 1945

Year	Road and Equipment	Miles of Road Owned	Road and Equipment per Mile	Net Railway Operating Income per Mile of Road
December 31				
1874	$54,591,871.34	1,399.00	$39,022.07	$2,202.93
1875	55,022,860.15	1,400.00	39,302.04	2,203.85
1876	56,277,226.65	1,400.00	40,198.02	2,214.89
1877	56,886,833.25	1,412.00	40,288.13	2,531.49
1878	58,755,184.22	1,512.00	38,859.25	2,420.27
1879	62,043,445.61	2,231.00	27,809.70	2,034.52
1880	99,185,683.39	3,775.00	26,274.35	1,415.55
1881	120,073,629.99	4,217.00	28,473.71	1,590.59
1882	137,631,949.12	4,520.00	30,449.55	1,814.30
1883	146,093,664.69	4,760.00	30,691.95	2,076.01
1884	149,426,734.35	4,804.00	31,104.65	2,000.70
1885	154,228,774.75	4,921.00	31,340.94	2,011.95
1886	165,898,616.21	5,298.00	31,313.44	1,917.35
1887	177,374,429.79	5,669.95	31,283.24	1,770.64
1888	180,452,974.35	5,678.15	31,780.24	1,319.16
June 30				
1889	183,889,871.34	5,678.15	32,385.53	1,562.86
1890	185,631,301.37	5,656.83	32,815.43	1,632.12
1891	189,624,727.91	5,721.40	33,143.06	1,597.15
1892	191,544,852.57	5,721.40	33,478.67	2,004.49
1893	195,223,233.67	5,724.13	34,105.31	2,006.76
1894	210,440,713.45	6,147.77	34,230.41	1,824.01
1895	211,168,036.96	6,168.73	34,232.01	1,668.35
1896	211,830,735.42	6,150.75	34,439.82	2,114.38
1897	212,594,714.15	6,153.83	34,546.73	1,935.25
1898	214,195,294.69	6,153.83	34,806.83	2,110.57
1899	218,506,634.82	6,153.50	35,509.33	2,331.65
1900	218,302,680.50	6,422.67	33,989.40	2,096.30
1901	224,288,832.69	6,596.32	34,002.12	2,181.75
1902	228,731,116.31	6,603.85	34,636.03	2,334.43
1903	235,610,737.20	6,682.57	35,257.50	2,403.95
1904	240,075,053.44	6,906.48	34,760.84	2,382.36
1905	242,431,436.52	6,911.62	35,075.92	2,545.00
1906	250,654,089.84	7,043.54	35,586.38	2,694.49
1907	259,148,727.01	7,186.69	36,059.54	2,624.58
1908	264,860,733.05	7,301.32	36,275.73	2,378.93

Year	Road and Equipment	Miles of Road Owned	Road and Equipment per Mile	Net Railway Operating Income per Mile of Road
1909	274,468,163.11	7,296.55	37,616.16	2,450.15
1910	280,828,179.04	7,296.55	38,487.80	2,198.74
1911	292,211,730.30	7,296.43	40,048.59	1,807.69
1912	301,592,893.65	7,296.40	41,334.48	1,540.76
1913	518,808,393.23	9,424.91	55,046.51	2,806.32
1914	553,243,345.05	9,681.38	57,145.09	2,738.90
1915	564,740,361.95	9,720.67	58,096.86	2,485.39
1916	582,706,280.24	9,856.77	59,117.37	3,021.08

December 31

Year	Road and Equipment	Miles of Road Owned	Road and Equipment per Mile	Net Railway Operating Income per Mile of Road
1916	595,169,096.67	9,856.77	60,381.76	3,003.74
1917	604,578,835.94	9,950.35	60,759.55	2,024.89
1918	628,036,781.51	9,917.80	63,324.20	367.34
1919	636,332,073.12	10,289.37	61,843.64	304.67
1920	658,157,161.47	10,267.63	64,100.20	—
1921	661,811,512.64	10,268.85	64,448.45	498.34
1922	671,778,028.23	10,263.73	65,451.65	1,294.29
1923	689,060,550.55	10,251.43	67,216.04	1,967.31
1924	692,150,064.13	10,251.38	67,517.75	1,850.69
1925	705,282,852.67	10,251.75	68,796.34	1,645.93
1926	704,366,719.00	10,237.79	68,800.66	1,796.77
1927	708,536,467.53	10,237.35	69,210.93	1,374.67
1928	682,548,785.91	10,235.35	66,685.44	2,844.95
1929	700,277,366.42	10,234.87	68,420.74	2,567.14
1930	720,377,652.81	10,284.69	70,043.69	1,551.29
1931	723,876,983.49	10,280.81	70,410.50	810.68
1932	723,553,873.99	10,253.22	70,568.45	—
1933	721,097,511.27	10,169.96	70,904.66	845.36
1934	681,984,319.00	10,135.00	67,290.02	645.20
1935	681,100,991.05	10,091.86	67,490.13	468.10
1936	681,258,006.78	10,038.44	67,864.93	942.51
1937	691,592,842.34	10,036.53	68,907.56	875.87
1938	697,077,711.36	9,962.17	69,972.48	529.46
1939	701,219,152.46	9,909.98	70,758.89	819.80
1940	709,745,920.22	9,873.28	71,885.53	1,402.33
1941	713,239,952.99	9,839.72	72,485.80	2,864.10
1942	717,285,008.16	9,838.96	72,902.52	3,506.94
1943	724,573,209.95	9,773.20	74,138.79	5,184.48
1944	741,246,162.40	9,758.80	75,956.69	3,351.80
1945	799,137,296.12	9,748.72	81,973.56	2,726.75

Bibliography

BOOKS

Austin, H. Russell. *The Milwaukee Story.* The Journal Company, Milwaukee, Wis., 1946.

Buck, Solon Justus. *The Granger Movement.* Harvard University Press, Cambridge, Mass., 1913.

Cary, John W. *The Organization and History of The Chicago, Milwaukee and St. Paul Railroad Company.* Press of Cramer, Aikens & Cramer, Milwaukee, Wis., 1892.

Cleveland, Grover. *The Government in the Chicago Strike.* Princeton University Press, 1913.

Corey, Lewis. *The House of Morgan.* G. Howard Watt, New York, 1930.

Encyclopaedia Britannica. Library Research Service. Chicago, Ill.

Farrington, S. Kip, Jr. *Railroads at War.* Samuel Curl, Inc., New York, 1944.

——. *Railroading from the Head End.* Doubleday, Doran & Company, New York, 1943.

——. *Railroading from the Rear End.* Coward-McCann, New York, 1946.

Feick, Fred L. *The Life of Railway Men.* Shepard, Chicago, Ill., 1905.

Field, H. H. *History of the Milwaukee Road 1892–1940.* 1941.

History of Dane County. Western Historical Association, Madison, Wis., 1906.

History of LaCrosse County. Western Historical Company, Chicago, 1881.

Hovey, Carl. *The Life Story of J. Pierpont Morgan.* Sturgis & Walton Company, New York, 1911.

Hubbard, Freeman H. *Railroad Avenue.* McGraw-Hill Book Company, New York, 1945.

Josephson, Mathew. *The Robber Barons.* Harcourt, Brace & Company, New York, 1934.

Kalmbach, A. C. *Railroad Panorama.* Kalmbach Publishing Company, Milwaukee, Wis., 1944.

Kane, Joseph N. *Famous First Facts.* The H. W. Wilson Company, New York, 1933.

LaFollette, Robert Marion. *Autobiography.* Madison, Wis. 1912.

Leech, Harper, and Carroll, John Charles. *Armour and His Times.* D. Appleton-Century Company, New York, 1938.

Lowenthal, Max. *The Investor Pays*. Alfred A. Knopf, New York, 1936.

Lundberg, Ferdinand. *America's 60 Families*. The Vanguard Press, New York, 1937.

Merk, Frederick. *Economic History of Wisconsin During the Civil War Decade*. State Historical Society of Wisconsin, Madison, 1916.

Moody's Manual. Moody's Investor's Service, New York. 1900–1946.

Myers, Gustavus. *History of the Great American Fortunes*. Modern Library, New York, 1936.

Nye, Edgar W., and Riley, James W. *Nye & Riley's Railway Guide*. Chicago, 1888.

Philipp, E. L. *The Truth About Wisconsin Freight Rates*. 1904.

Poor's Manual of the Railroads of the United States, 1875–1900; 1928–1939. Poor Publishing Company, New York.

Porter, H. H. *A Short Autobiography*. 1915.

Pyle, Joseph G. *The Life of James J. Hill*. Doubleday, Page & Company, New York, 1916, 1917.

Riegel, Robert E. *The Story of the Western Railroads*. The Macmillan Company, New York, 1926.

Russell, Charles Edward. *Railroad Melons, Rates and Wages*. Charles H. Kerr & Company, Chicago, 1922.

Satterlee, Herbert L. *J. Pierpont Morgan, An Intimate Portrait*. The Macmillan Company, New York, 1939.

Spearman, Frank H. *The Strategy of Great Railroads*. Charles Scribner's Sons, New York, 1904.

Tarbell, Ida. *History of the Standard Oil Company*. The Macmillan Company, New York, 1925.

Usher, Ellis Baker. *Wisconsin, Its History and Biography 1843–1913*. The Lewis Publishing Company, Chicago and New York, 1914.

Walthers, W. K. *Handbook for Model Railroaders*. Modelmaker Corporation, Wauwatosa, Wis. 1939.

Wittemore, Henry. *History of the Sage and Slocum Families*. New York, 1908.

Who's Who in Railroading. The Simmons-Boardman Publishing Company, New York, 1930, 1946.

Wisconsin Historical Collections. Vols. I–XXI. Madison, Wis., 1903–1915.

BOOKLETS AND PAMPHLETS

Borak, Arthur. *Financial History of The Chicago, Milwaukee and St. Paul Railroad Company*. Journal of Economics and Business History, November, 1930.

Commercial Travelers Guide, 1871.

Corliss, Carlton J. *Development of Railroad Transportation in the United States*. Association of American Railroads, Washington, D. C., 1945.

Facts. The Milwaukee Road, 1944, 1945, 1946.

Henry, Robert S. *The Great American Railroad.* Kalmbach Publishing Company, Milwaukee, Wis. Reprinted from *Trains Magazine,* January, 1945.
Information for the Men and Women of the Chicago, Milwaukee, St. Paul and Pacific Railroad. The Milwaukee Road, Chicago (Public Relations Department), 1944.
Johnson, F. H. *The Milwaukee Road, 1847–1939.*
———. *The Milwaukee Road, 1847–1944.*
Kaysen, James P. *The Railroads of Wisconsin, 1827–1937.* Railway and Locomotive Historical Society, Boston, Mass., 1937.
Milwaukee Road Flashes. Public Relations Department, November, 1945; November, 1946.
Milwaukee Road Time Table. 1945.
Nichols, H. E. *The Early History of the 'Milwaukee.'* The Railway and Locomotive Historical Society, Boston, Mass. Bulletin No. 35, October, 1934
Notes Along the Olympian Trail. The Milwaukee Road, Chicago.
Olympian Hiawathas. The Milwaukee Road, Chicago. 1947.
Petersen, William J. *The Milwaukee Comes. The Palimpsest.* State Historical Society of Iowa, 1933.
Railroads At Work. Association of American Railroads, Washington, D. C., 1945.
Railroad Facts. Western Railways Public Relations Office, Chicago, 1944.
Railway Literature: A Bibliography. Compiled by Association of American Railroads, Washington, D. C., September, 1942.
Taylor, Horace. *To Regulate Railroad Traffic in Wisconsin.* Madison, 1889.
Victory Vacations. The Milwaukee Road, Chicago, Ill., 1946.
What's New? Association of American Railroads, Washington, D. C., February-March, 1947.

PERIODICALS AND NEWSPAPERS

American Weekly, The, 1924; December 4, 1943.
Boston Herald, The, December, 1882.
Bulletin No. 58. The Railway and Locomotive Historical Society, Boston, Mass., 1942.
"Butte Miner," June 20, 1926.
Capital Times, The, Madison, Wis., 1941.
Chicago *Daily News,* December, 1943.
Chicago *Daily Tribune,* June 22, 1938.
Chicago *Evening Post,* June to December, 1924.
Chicago *Herald and Examiner,* 1924.
Chicago *Sun,* February 14, 1947.
Chicago *Times,* April, 1874; August, 1875.
Crichton, Kyle. *The Railroads Fight Back.* Copyright 1946 by The Crowell-Collier Publishing Company, Ohio, for *Collier's,* December 28, 1946.

Daily Argus and Democrat, Madison, Wis., 1850; 1854–1856.
Fond du Lac *Journal*, July, 1850.
Harper's Weekly, June 12, 1858.
La Crosse *Tribune*, August, 1929.
McClure's Magazine. March, 1910.
Milwaukee *Daily News*, March 29, 1895.
Milwaukee *Evening Wisconsin*, June, 1884; May, 1894; March, 1895; October, 1913.
Milwaukee *Free Democrat*, 1858.
Milwaukee *Journal*, March 2, 1935; May 22, 1938; March, 1925; April, 1932; February, 1939; March, 1943; June, 1947.
Milwaukee Magazine, The. Chicago, Ill. April, 1913, to May, 1947.
Milwaukee Road News Bureau. Chicago, Milwaukee, St. Paul and Pacific Railroad Company, Chicago, Ill.
Milwaukee *Sentinel*, 1850–1947.
New Republic, The, February 4, 1931.
Quiz on Railroads and Railroading. Association of American Railroads, Washington, D. C., January, 1946; August, 1946.
Railroad Gazette, The. June 6, 1883.
Railroad Magazine. Popular Publications, Inc., Chicago, Ill. December, 1941, 1945; 1946; 1947.
Railroad Man's Magazine. The Frank A. Munsey Company, New York, May, 1911.
Railroads. Merrill Lynch, Pierce, Fenner & Beane, New York, December, 1946.
Railway Age. January 21, 1928; July 6, 1935; November 5, 1938.
Railway Review, August 14, 1926.
Seattle *Daily Times*, October, 1905, to March, 1906.
Seattle *Post-Intelligencer*, November, 1905, to March, 1906.
Social Justice Review. June, 1946.
Spokane *Daily Chronicle*, December, 1905; September, 1914.
Spokesman-Review, The. Spokane, Washington. December, 1905, to February, 1906; August, 1913; September, 1914; March, 1920.
Survey, New York, December 11, 1909.
Trains. Kalmbach Publishing Company, Milwaukee, Wis., September, 1945; October, 1946; November, 1946; December, 1946; February, 1947.
Warner, Paul T. *Chicago, Milwaukee, St. Paul and Pacific Railroad. Baldwin Locomotives*, October, 1930.
Waukesha *Democrat*, 1850–1851.
Wisconsin Daily State Journal, Madison, Wis. 1854; 1858; 1860–1861.
Wisconsin Express, Madison, Wis. 1850–1851.
Wisconsin Magazine of History. Publications of State Historical Society of Wisconsin, Madison. 1925–1947.
Wisconsin Mirror, Kilbourn, Wis. 1856–1859.
Wisconsin State Journal, Madison, Wis. May to September, 1874; December, 1882; March 20, 1925; November 23, 1942; June, 1947.

Wisconsin State Palladium, Madison, Wis. 1852.
Wisconsin Statesman, Madison, Wis. 1851.

MANUSCRIPTS AND DOCUMENTS

Annual Reports of The Milwaukee Road, 1849–1946.
Campbell, F. D. *Montana Earthquake,* July, 1925.
Catlin, John. Letters.
Corporate History of The Chicago, Milwaukee & St. Paul Railway Company and Subsidiary Companies (as of June 30, 1915). Prepared in compliance with valuation order No. 20 entered by the Interstate Commerce Commission at Washington, D. C., the 18th day of May, A. D. 1915. Office of Chief Engineer, Chicago, Illinois.
Cummings, Mrs. A. P. Letter.
Dodge, Joseph. Papers and Reports.
Earling, Mrs. A. J. Letters.
Federal Writers' Project of Wisconsin: Files on Biographies of Alexander Mitchell, S. S. Merrill, John W. Cary, Edward Brodhead, Hans Crocker, Moses Strong, John Plankinton, Edward Holton, Byron Kilbourn, John Catlin, Philip Armour.
Freight and Express Records, 1857–1876. McFarland, Wisconsin. William H. McFarland, Agent.
In the District Court of the United States. For the Northern District of Illinois, Eastern Division. No. 60463.
In the Supreme Court of the United States, October Term, 1892. No. 180.
Interstate Commerce Commission Docket 17021.
Legislative Documents, 1874–1875.
Linsley, Charles. Letters, 1852.
Martner, W. E. *Lady Franklin.*
Milwaukee Land Company Records.
Nystrom, K. F. *Studies and Development of High-Speed Passenger Car Trucks.* 1944.
Spettel, George. *Pontoon Bridge Controversy.*
Strong, Moses. Letters.

Index